THE REMINISCENCES OF
Rear Admiral Denys W. Knoll
U.S. Navy (Retired)

INTERVIEWED BY
Paul Stillwell

U.S. Naval Institute • Annapolis, Maryland

Copyright © 2013

Preface

The memoir that follows is detailed and thorough, which is certainly in keeping with Admiral Knoll's personality. His great strength was as a consummate staff officer. The list of individuals on whose staffs he served is impressive: Admiral Thomas C. Hart, Admiral Ernest J. King, Ambassador Averell Harriman, Admiral Richmond Kelly Turner, Rear Admiral Walter F. Boone, Vice Admiral Arthur D. Struble, Admiral Arleigh A. Burke, Vice Admiral Alfred M. Pride, Vice Admiral Stuart H. Ingersoll, Vice Admiral Wallace M. Beakley, Vice Admiral Glynn R. Donaho, and Admiral Robert L. Dennison. It was a measure of the value of his skills that Knoll was in the last group of Americans to be evacuated before Corregidor in the Philippines fell to the Japanese in World War II. His special knowledge of weather forecasting sent him to the Soviet Union later in the war. Subsequently he was involved in staff work for the creation of the United Nations and in helping develop the nation's "New Look" military strategy during the administration of President Dwight D. Eisenhower.

Denys Knoll was intelligent, inquisitive, ambitious, energetic, eager to please, and the embodiment of a workaholic. He conceded in the interviews that that his devotion to duty, including long separations, led to the collapse of his first wife's health. His tours in command at sea were remarkably brief—less than a year each—in the oiler *Severn*, the attack transport *Menard*, the cruiser *Roanoke*, and Destroyer Flotilla One. They were intended to make him eligible for promotion so that he could resume his staff work at increasingly higher ranks. Knoll was ever mindful of his service reputation and its relationship to his promotion opportunities. In the end he was not promoted to the rank of vice admiral, even though he believed that his record entitled him to it. In this memoir he blamed it on politics. As in reading the result of any oral history, the reader needs to keep in mind that memory is an imperfect tool. Admiral Knoll had a number of successes in his career, but at times he exaggerated his own role while recounting events. For those interested in additional sources on Knoll's naval service, a box of his personal papers is in the archives of the Naval War College in Newport, Rhode Island.

The pages that follow have been transformed considerably from the raw transcript of the oral interviews conducted in 1984. Symptomatic of his thoroughness, Admiral Knoll rewrote by hand virtually every page of the original transcript. I then retyped the result to incorporate his changes. During the interviews, Admiral Knoll often talked in a stream-of-consciousness fashion, leaping from one topic to another as each came to mind. The result was often out of sequence chronologically and also resulted in considerable duplication when the same stories occurred to him in different interviews. Thus in the editing process I have rearranged a good many paragraphs so that the resulting document essentially reads in the same sequence as the admiral experienced events. I have sought to eliminate a good bit of the duplication. In a few cases, in order to provide transitions in the rearranged sections, I have introduced questions that were not in the oral interviews but are in keeping with the flow of the material.

Thanks go to Ms. Janis Jorgensen of the Naval Institute staff who has coordinated the printing and binding of the finished product.

In completing this volume, the Naval Institute expresses its gratitude to the Tawani Foundation and the Pritzker Military Library of Chicago for their generous financial support of the oral history program that produced this memoir.

Paul Stillwell
U.S. Naval Institute
August 2013

REAR ADMIRAL DENYS WILLIAM KNOLL
UNITED STATES NAVY (RETIRED)

Denys William Knoll was born on 7 March 1907, in Erie, Pennsylvania, the son of Edmund A. Knoll and Ida Marie Illig Knoll.

After graduation from Cathedral Preparatory School, Erie, Pennsylvania, he entered the U.S. Naval Academy, Annapolis, Maryland, and graduated with the class of 1930. He subsequently had six years of duty afloat in the USS *Texas* (BB-35), USS *Southard* (DD-207), USS *Preble* (DD-345). In the USS *Oglala* (CM-4), he participated in the Aleutian Survey Expedition for six months in 1934. Upon completion of the expedition, he was transferred to the USS *Oklahoma* (BB-37) for gunnery duty.

In May 1936 he began an extended period of study, first at Edgewood Arsenal in Maryland, later the Postgraduate School, Annapolis, Maryland, and completed instruction at the Massachusetts Institute of Technology, Cambridge, Massachusetts, from which he received the degree of master of science in aeronautical engineering (specification, aerology) in June 1939).

Following the completion of his postgraduate work, he was assigned staff duties on Patrol Wing Five as aerological officer (1939-40) and later (1940-42) as aerological officer on the staff of the Commander in Chief U.S. Asiatic Fleet, Admiral Thomas C. Hart. During this period his staff duties were in addition to his service as assistant first lieutenant on board the USS *Augusta* (CA-31) (March 1940-November 1940) and the USS *Houston* (CA-30) (November 1940-July 1941).

In July 1941 he represented Admiral Hart and General Douglas MacArthur at special meetings held at Singapore Strait Settlements with A-B-C-D Powers (American-British-Chinese-Dutch) pertaining to the coordination of meteorological and communication matters prior to World War II.

In September 1941 he was transferred to the 16th Naval District as officer in charge of the Fleet Weather Central, located at the Cavite Navy Yard, Philippine Islands; the weather central was destroyed by Japanese bombing on 10 December 1941 and reestablished in Manila. Upon the evacuation of Manila on Christmas Day, 1941, Knoll went to Corregidor with the Commandant of the 16th Naval District, continuing to supply weather information for forces in the Philippines and Western Pacific. Knoll assisted the commanding generals of U.S. Forces in the Philippines, General Douglas MacArthur and later Lieutenant General Jonathan Wainwright, on naval operational and meteorological issues. Knoll was ordered to leave Corregidor on 3 May 1942 in the last submarine, USS *Spearfish* (SS-190), prior to the capitulation of that island.

After he returned to the United States, Lieutenant Commander Knoll was assigned to Headquarters, Commander in Chief, U.S. Fleet, and in addition served as officer in charge of the Navy Weather Central, Washington. During this period he assisted with weather advice for the planning of amphibious landings in North Africa in November 1942. He later served as an assistant secretary, Joint Chiefs of Staff.

During 1944 and 1945 he was a naval member of the U.S. Military Mission to the Union of Soviet Socialist Republics in Moscow and for six months in Vladivostok. After World War II he served as naval advisor at the organizing meetings of the United Nations in London and later as secretary, Military Staff Committee of the U.S. delegation to the United Nations in London and later in New York. He commanded the oiler *Severn* (AO-61), November 1946-October 1947; the attack transport *Menard* (APA-201), April-December 1952; and the cruiser *Roanoke* (CL-145), March-October 1955. He had two tours of duty in the Strategic Plans Division, Office of the Chief of Naval Operations: November 1947-March 1942 and January 1953-February 1955.

In November 1955 he was ordered to duty as chief of staff and aide to Commander Seventh Fleet, Vice Admiral Stuart H. Ingersoll. In April 1957 he reported to the Office of the Chief of Naval Operations as Director of the staff, Ship Characteristics Board. On 30 November 1957 he became Director, Fleet Development and Maintenance Division, with additional duty as chairman of the Ship Characteristics Board.

On 13 October 1959 he assumed command of Destroyer Flotilla Four and in June 1960 was assigned to the Office of the Chief of Naval Operations, where he served as Director of the Technical Studies Group. In June 1961 he assumed duty as Commander Service Force Atlantic Fleet and in August 1963 reported as Oceanographer of the Navy, Office of the Chief of Naval Operations, and Commander Naval Oceanographic Office, Suitland, Maryland. In September 1965 he became Deputy Commander of the Military Sea Transportation Service with headquarters in Washington, D.C., where he remained until relieved of active duty pending his retirement, effective 1 May 1967. He then returned to his native city of Erie, Pennsylvania, where he lived until his death there on 12 April 1989. He married Genevieve Parker Hawkins in 1940 and after her death married Jean Shaw in 1969.

Dates of Rank:

Midshipman: 21 August 1926
Ensign: 5 June 1930
Lieutenant (junior grade): 5 June 1933
Lieutenant: 30 June 1937
Lieutenant Commander: 30 June 1942
Commander: 1 September 1943
Captain (temporary): 10 December 1945 to 1 January 1948
Captain: 1 September 1948
Rear Admiral: 1 March 1958

Chronological Record of Commissioned Service:

Jul 1930-Dec 1930	USS *Texas* (BB-35), gunnery
Jan 1931-May 1931	Naval Air Station, Pensacola, Florida, flight training
Jun 1931-Jun 1932	USS *Texas* (BB-35), gunnery
Jul 1932-Jul 1933	USS *Southard* (DD-207), gunnery
Jul 1933-May 1934	USS *Preble* (DD-345). gunnery
May 1934-Nov 1934	USS *Oglala* (CM-4), survey officer
Nov 1934-May 1936	USS *Oklahoma* (BB-37), gunnery
May 1936-Jul 1936	Edgewood, Maryland, Arsenal, training in chemical warfare
Aug 1936-Jun 1938	Postgraduate School, Annapolis, Maryland, student
Jul 1938-Jun 1939	Massachusetts Institute of Technology, Cambridge, Massachusetts, student
June 1939-Feb 1940	Patrol Wing Five, aerological officer
Mar 1940-Jul 1941	Staff, Commander in Chief Asiatic Fleet, aerological officer
Mar 1940-Nov 1940	USS *Augusta* (CA-31), additional duty as assistant first lieutenant
Nov 1940-Jul 1941	USS *Houston* (CA-30), additional duty as assistant first lieutenant
Aug 1941-May 1942	16th Naval District, temporary duty as staff aerological officer
May 1942-Jun 1942	USS *Spearfish* (SS-190), temporary duty
Jun 1942-Jul 1942	USS *West Point* (AP-23), temporary duty
Jul 1942-Feb 1944	Headquarters, Commander in Chief U.S. Fleet, Washington, D.C., officer in charge, Weather Central, Washington, and assistant secretary, Joint Chiefs of Staff
Feb 1944-Dec 1945	U.S. military mission, Soviet Union, naval member and assistant naval attaché Vladivostok for six months
Dec 1945-Nov 1946	U.S. delegation to the United Nations, naval advisor and secretary, U.S. military delegation

Nov 1946-Oct 1947	USS *Severn* (AO-61), commanding officer
Nov 1947-Mar 1952	Office of the Chief of Naval Operations, Navy Department, head, Subsidiary Plans Section, Strategic Plans Division
Apr 1952-Dec 1952	USS *Menard* (APA-201), commanding officer
Jan 1953-Feb 1955	Office of the Chief of Naval Operations, Navy Department, head, Basic Plans Branch, Strategic Plans Division
Mar 1955-Oct 1955	USS *Roanoke* (CL-145), commanding officer
Nov 1955-Mar 1957	Staff, Commander Seventh Fleet, chief of staff and aide
Apr 1957-Sep 1959	Office of the Chief of Naval Operations, Navy Department, director, Fleet Development and Maintenance Division, and chairman, Ship Characteristics Board
Oct 1959-May 1960	Commander Destroyer Flotilla Four
Jun 1960-Jun 1961	Office of the Chief of Naval Operations, Navy Department, director, Technical Studies Group
Jun 1961-Jul 1963	Commander Service Force Atlantic Fleet
Aug 1963-Sep 1965	Oceanographer of the Navy, Office of the Chief of Naval Operations, and Commander Naval Oceanographic Office, Suitland, Maryland
Sep 1965-Apr 1967	Deputy Commander Military Sealift Command Headquarters, Washington, D.C.
1 May 1967	Transferred to the retired list of the U.S. Navy

Awards:

Legion of Merit
Army Bronze Star Medal
Letter of Commendation (SecNav) (Ribbon)
Letter of Commendation (SecNav) (Bronze Star)
Letter of Commendation (SecNav) (Bronze Star)
Army Distinguished Unit Emblem Oak Leaf Cluster
American Defense Service Medal with fleet clasp
American Campaign Medal
European-African-Middle Eastern Campaign Medal

Asiatic-Pacific Campaign Medal with star
World War II Victory Medal
Navy Occupation Service Medal with Asia clasp
China Service Medal
National Defense Service Medal with bronze star
Korean Service Medal with star
United Nations Service Medal (Korea)
Philippine Defense Ribbon with star
Philippine Republic Presidential Unit Citation Badge

Deed of Gift

The U.S. Naval Institute is hereby authorized to make available to individuals, libraries, and other repositories of its choosing the tapes and/or transcripts of four oral history interviews concerning the life and naval career of the late Rear Admiral Denys W. Knoll. The Naval Institute may also, at its discretion, use the material in electronic/digital format, including posting on the Internet. The interviews were recorded on 8 May 1984, 9 May 1984, 28 June 1984, and 29 June 1984 by Admiral Knoll in collaboration with Paul Stillwell for the U.S. Naval Institute.

The undersigned does hereby release and assign to the U.S. Naval Institute the rights and title to these interviews, with the exception that the Knoll family retains the right to use the material for its own purposes. The copyright in both the oral and transcribed versions shall be the property of the U.S. Naval Institute. The tape recordings of the interviews are and will remain the property of the U.S. Naval Institute.

Signed and sealed this __11__ day of __March__ 2013.

Mary Therese Craig
Dorothy M. Knoll
on behalf of Denys W. Knoll

*Executrix of the Estate
of Dorothy M. Knoll, Deceased*

Interview Number 1 with Rear Admiral Denys W. Knoll, U.S. Navy (Retired)
Place: U.S. Naval Institute, Annapolis, Maryland
Date: Tuesday, 8 May 1984

Paul Stillwell: Admiral, the appropriate place to begin with any life is at the beginning, so could you please tell me something of your early years and your family background?

Admiral Knoll: I am a descendant of two of the older families of the city of Erie, Pennsylvania. My father's side of the family settled in Erie in the 1830s, my mother's side in the 1840s. The interesting thing is they both came from the Palatinate of the Rhine.* My father's family, the Knolls, had migrated to the palatinate at the time of Henry VIII from Oxford, England, where at least one of his ancestors was a don at Oxford.† My mother's family, the Schultzes, had lived at the palatinate for a few generations and intermarried with English. Following the Congress of Vienna, 1814-15, freedom declined, and poverty increased. Families with resources again migrated to new areas.

My grandmothers on my mother's and father's side of the family were English. The Germans had intermarried, creating a combination called the German-English settlement on the Palatinate of the Rhine. It's rather interesting. Both my mother's grandparents and my father's great-grandparents came from the Herksheim, Landau, and my father then married a Schultz descendant from Herksheim. His great-great-grandfather came over on the SS *Equator* in about 1837, for which we have a manifest. His name was Benedict Knoll, with son Peter; they were the leading flax and linen weavers of Herksheim. Their homestead is still well preserved, one of the leading dwellings today in Herksheim, Germany.

They settled in Erie from the beginning. Both came via charter ship to Castle Garden, New York, then via the Erie Canal to Buffalo and by boat to Erie. I'm the

---

* The Palatinate of the Rhine is a region in southwestern Germany.
† Henry VIII was King of England from 21 April 1509 until his death on 28 January 1547.

second oldest of a family of 14, the first cousin of Charles and Thomas Weschler; their mother and my mother were sisters.* My mother was the youngest of 16 children.

I was in the first graduating class of Cathedral Preparatory School in Erie, founded by Bishop John M. Gannon in 1921. The bishop wanted me to study to be a priest. However, I convinced him that I did not want to be a priest. With the help of friends at Hammermill Paper Company, leading lawyers, and Congressman Milton Shreve, the bishop obtained an appointment for me to the Naval Academy.† My record at the Naval Academy was instrumental in helping Cathedral Prep become an accredited educational institution about 1927. The congressman had a lot of failures at the Naval Academy; he finally encouraged anyone who received an appointment while he was a congressman to take at least a semester of mathematics at the Cathedral Preparatory School before going to the Naval Academy because of the academic record of Weschler and myself at the Naval Academy.

Paul Stillwell: What occupation was your father in?

Admiral Knoll: My father was interested in drama for a while. He was attracted to the New York stage for a short period, but he stayed at Erie and raised a family. His father had been in the grocery business, with which he assisted. For a few years he had a very successful shoe store. He did writing, was the editor of a Catholic newspaper for a while. He wrote under different names for national periodicals and Catholic magazines. He also coached dramatics at the different churches and high schools at home and was the director of the dramatics program at the Community Place in Erie for a period of about 15 years. He died suddenly from peritonitis in 1932, at the age of 52.

Paul Stillwell: That was quite a burden for your mother to support the family in the Depression, I would think.

---

* Lieutenant Charles J. Weschler, USN, Naval Academy class of 1932, died while a prisoner of the Japanese in World War II. His younger brother, Thomas R. Weschler, class of 1939, reached the rank of vice admiral. The oral history of Thomas Weschler is in the Naval Institute collection.
† Milton W. Shreve, a Republican from Pennsylvania, served in the House of Representatives from 1913 to 1915 and from 1919 to 1933.

Admiral Knoll: Well, not completely. During the Depression, my father was there during part of it.* We all helped as errand boys, etc., but my mother did have some inheritance from her father, who had done quite well as a merchant tailor in northwestern Pennsylvania from 1865 to 1900. My mother's father was property poor, having lost his money more than once in bank failures. He invested in real estate, so during the Depression most of the real estate was occupied, but no one was paying rent. Some of the inheritance from that helped. My brothers had a paper route or a magazine route, so each of us earned enough money to take care of our own clothes. I worked as an usher in a theater, was area distributor for *Literary Digest*, worked weekends as a sales clerk in department stores, and things of that nature. Each one tried to take care of himself.

My oldest brother was successful in banking, managing short-term loans in a local bank for over 40 years. My sister was a nun in St. Joseph's Order and was comptroller of her order for many years. Another brother is still active in the Redemptorist Order. He was in Annapolis at St. Mary's off and on for some years. Another brother was manufacturing representative for a plumbing business in New York State, and another had a rubber-fabricating factory in Indiana.

Paul Stillwell: How did you get motivated to go to the Naval Academy, as opposed to the priesthood? Those are two quite different vocations.

Admiral Knoll: Well, my prime objective was to obtain a college degree in engineering or the law. I was never motivated for the priesthood. I had told the bishop, "You have to have more priests in this world if we're going to have it safe for democracy and everything else. I'm going to make my mark in the world." I had made some effort to go to Rensselaer or to Harvard and had literature from those as well as from Catholic University in Washington—all with the idea that I would get involved in some kind of engineering or higher education.

---

* Following the crash of the New York Stock Exchange in late October 1929, the United States was plunged into the Great Depression, from which it did not recover until the nation geared up for World War II at the beginning of the 1940s. The Depression was marked by high unemployment and many business failures.

Paul Stillwell: What led to that desire?

Admiral Knoll: As a youngster I had a complete tool chest. I could do anything with wood and was interested in electric circuitry. I made a Galena set radio with which I could get KDKA Pittsburgh. I borrowed a headphone from a neighbor. I wound the radio myself and did many things of that nature. I was interested in staying in the forefront of scientific development. I enjoyed working with my hands and was inquisitive about new developments. I always had the philosophy, "If someone else can do it, I can do it too."

Paul Stillwell: Did you know then the requirements necessary to get into the academy?

Admiral Knoll: Oh, yes, I had known that. My one problem was that initial classes at Cathedral Prep stressed a classical education: four years Latin, one year Greek, four years math, but no chemistry and no physics. They did not have science. In the interim after my graduation from Prep in June '25, I took a course in physics at the local high school. I did very well and became very interested in physics. I would say from the time of my seventh or eighth grade on through my education, I always had one or two books from the library that I read, and I was interested in *Popular Mechanics*. I used to visit some of the hardware stores and industries at home just to see what was new. I had a friend with the same interest. He became involved with adding machines, but we had sort of a mutual interest.

I wasn't afraid to try something to innovate. We had a pretty big lot at home, so one summer my brother and I, with some friends, built a whole tennis court with backstops and graded it so our neighbors could play tennis at our home. (This large brick home had been built by my mother's grandfather when he arrived in Erie about 1844.) We were always doing something constructive. My parents encouraged us. They were understanding and did not interfere. All neighborhood events started and ended at our home.

Paul Stillwell: Did you have to get into the political situation to get this appointment to the Naval Academy?

Admiral Knoll: No. It involved a combination of Charles English, a leading Pennsylvania corporation lawyer; Ernst Behrend, who was the founder and original owner of the Hammermill Paper Company; and the bishop, who had contacts with U.S. Steel. They were able to persuade the congressman to give an appointment to the Naval Academy or West Point. Bishop Mark Gannon, later archbishop, was a fantastic individual who helped make Erie's Gannon University what it is today. He knew how to get an appointment to help establish prestige for his new prep school.

We had to have an elimination exam among eight different students, contemporaries of mine. The head of the school gave a fantastic mathematics exam. I received the highest mark on that and satisfied the bishop that I was qualified for an appointment. Two of the people who took the exam later became priests, and one of them recently commented, "If I'd have won, I would have never become a priest."

The bishop did have the political influence when it was needed. As soon as I found there was a possibility of getting an appointment, I went to call on Congressman Shreve at his home and continued to call on him occasionally. I became good friends with his children. While at the Naval Academy, I heard that Congressman Shreve was going on a junket to Italy. I quickly got in touch with the bishop and said, "Make sure the American College in Rome meets him when he arrives in Naples or Rome and make sure he sees the right things."

I can tell you, the next time I saw the congressman, he said, "I am a 32nd-degree Mason, but I have never been so royally entertained in Rome and saw everything that I should have seen, all because the bishop and you arranged it for me." So it didn't do any harm; it helped with further appointments.

My mother and father always said they made no direct effort—they didn't have to—to bring this about. I thought out what I should do and did it, made the contacts, and said, "I'm going to the Naval Academy." I was working at the Columbia Theater as an usher at that time when I got a call from the bishop saying the congressman had a principal appointment available. He asked, "Would you like to go to West Point or

Annapolis?"*

I said, "Yes, Annapolis."

He said, "Well, come around and see me." When I met him, he said, "If you still would study for the priesthood, I'll send you to St. Bonaventure, Olean, New York, for two years. Then I'll have a reservation for you to go to Louvain University in Belgium for four years."

I said, "No, thank you. I'm going to the Naval Academy."

Paul Stillwell: Why did you pick that rather than West Point?

Admiral Knoll: One of the reasons, after all, we lived on Lake Erie. It doesn't have much salt in it, but I was oriented that way. In 1913 I observed the centennial celebration of Perry's Battle of Lake Erie.† In addition, at that time a movie with Ramon Novarro, *The Midshipman*, was a big hit.‡ This made a big impression, and, of course, I was the usher at the theater at the time they showed it in Erie. I never had any feeling for West Point. My first cousin, Jim Illig, finally went to West Point.§

My mother's side of the family was the Erie family the "stars fell on." Charles J. Weschler was lost in World War II as a POW. In the family plus myself are Vice Admiral Thomas R. Weschler and Brigadier General James M. Illig. Charles, if he had survived, had distinct flag officer potential. During my first visit with the bishop after a year at the academy, he expressed surprise about rumors that Charles Weschler might go to the Naval Academy. The bishop and others in the family all thought Charles Weschler would study for the priesthood.

---

* An individual who received a congressman's principal appointment for an opening at the Naval Academy was admitted if he met the physical and academic qualifications. Someone with an alternate appointment would get in only if the person with the principal appointment was found to be unqualified or if he decided not to accept the appointment.

† Oliver Hazard Perry (1785-1819) was an officer in the fledgling U.S. Navy. He was famed for the victory of his force in the Battle of Lake Erie on 10 September 1813. He reported the result of the action with a brief message, "We have met the enemy, and they are ours."

‡ *The Midshipman* came out in 1925. One of the other actors in the film was William Boyd; years later Boyd was the star of the 1950s television series "Hopalong Cassidy."

§ Cadet James M. Illig, USA, graduated from the Military Academy in the class of 1936. Illig was the maiden name of Knoll's mother.

Paul Stillwell: It's interesting that he probably would have lived longer had he gone into the priesthood.

Admiral Knoll: Yes, probably.

Paul Stillwell: What do you recall about the entrance exams, both physical and mental, when you got to Annapolis?

Admiral Knoll: Well, in those days the entrance exams, with my scholastic record, were surprisingly easy. I never had any real difficulties at Annapolis. Probably I should have studied harder, but I got by rather easily. My roommate, Tom Haley, studied three times as much as I did, and I still got about as good marks as he did.* I was normally in the first section. I think if I had it to do over, I would work harder. As I got older, at postgraduate school and the Massachusetts Institute of Technology, I did make extra effort. Again, as I look at it, while I was a midshipman and studied navigation, seamanship, and meteorology, I didn't seem to be too interested then.

Paul Stillwell: Why didn't you push yourself harder at the Naval Academy?

Admiral Knoll: I think it grew on me. I was the first one to leave home and be on my own. I was still maturing, I guess. And it came so easy, I said, "What the heck?" I was studying hard, but I could have stood a little higher. Admiral Rickover used to ask all candidates for nuclear training, "Why didn't you stand first?"† Well, knowing what I do now, I might have stood higher, but I couldn't today say why. I was never really homesick, but I think I was exposed to a completely different environment and becoming acclimated. I did spend a lot of time at the academy library. I was involved with company sports but never to the large degree that other people did. I did more reading than anything else on the average, and extracurricular rap sessions with friends.

---

* Midshipman Thomas B. Haley, USN, class of 1930, eventually retired in 1961 as a captain.
† Rear Hyman G. Rickover, USN, was considered the father of the nuclear Navy. He ran the U.S. Navy's nuclear-power program for many years, from 1948 until he eventually left active duty in 1982 with the rank of four-star admiral on the retired list. Rickover Hall at the Naval Academy was named in his honor, as was the nuclear-powered attack submarine *Hyman G. Rickover* (SSN-709).

Paul Stillwell: What sorts of things did you read?

Admiral Knoll: Normally biographies. I felt that real personal experiences with past events were the best history.

Paul Stillwell: Do you think the Naval Academy had an effective means of teaching leadership in the years you were there?

Admiral Knoll: Yes. My father gave me a fundamental guide to look for excellence, and to look for the right picture and historical facts. As a result, I would say the Naval Academy emphasized this: it all depends on you. The second thing is, if someone else can do it, you can do it too. I never necessarily aspired to be the Chief of Naval Operations or President or anything, but I aspired to help other people do a good job, because I knew in doing so I was helping myself. That's what I did, later in my career, with Arleigh Burke or Slim Ingersoll and others. And some of these men, Tommy Hart and Kelly Turner, are tough people to work for, and I've had pretty good arguments with them, but not with any other idea than to portray to them how I look at something and make sure we were looking at all the facts and ending up with a decision we could live with.

Paul Stillwell: You talk about acclimating yourself at the Naval Academy. What was involved in that?

Admiral Knoll: Well, you select your friends that you see regularly, go on liberty together, and take evening strolls after evening meal and before study period. I had a terrific roommate, Tom Haley, who came from Lebanon, Tennessee. A lot of people from the South told him he was foolish to room with a damn Yankee from Pennsylvania, but we ended up with an excellent relationship and were roommates for the four years. In

1931 he married a girl from my hometown, a girl that I introduced to him when we were plebes.*

The Naval Academy was a new experience. In Erie one-third of the people in the city were related and knew the family history of each other. This was a whole new environment where you didn't know anybody, so you sort of had to find your center of gravity and your lowest common denominator in people. I did develop a series of interests in different people that I would meet at the library. We'd go to liberty together; One classmate I remember was Aubrey Bourgeois, who was a bilger out of '29, but he retired as a rear admiral in the Supply Corps.† Haley was on the varsity football team for three years; our free hours seldom permitted recreation together, particularly when football practiced spring and fall and used all his free time. We went many places together.

I spoke some German the first year or two in grammar school. World War I started, and in Erie it was anathema for anybody to speak German or admit German ancestry.‡ I did have a facility with a foreign language. Then at the Naval Academy I studied Spanish for two years. I was able to use Spanish on the European cruise, particularly at Barcelona for the International Exposition. Later, German was required for going to MIT because many scientific references for aeronautical engineering and meteorology were in German.

Prior to the Naval Academy, I had the equivalent of about five years of Latin and a year of Greek at Cathedral Prep School, so I did acquire background for international communications early in life. I used some Latin in Italy in 1929 to obtain directions and to make myself understood to some Italians. My parents trained me that every time you ran into a word, look it up in the dictionary. When you heard something about history or a technical subject, you looked it up in the encyclopedia or world almanac. "Find out, be inquisitive" was my motto, I think, as a result of this. I was always intrigued by the library and happy to browse there.

---

* A midshipman in his or her first year is called a plebe; second year, youngster or third classman; third year, second classman; fourth year, first classman.
† Midshipman Aubrey J. Bourgeois, USN, started with the class of 1929, dropped out, then returned to graduate with the class of 1930. He retired as a Supply Corps rear admiral in 1963.
‡ World War I was from August 1914 to November 1918; the United States entered in April 1917.

Paul Stillwell: Did you have any trouble adapting to the naval discipline that you encountered at the academy?

Admiral Knoll: Never. I was never what you would say hazed as much as some of my classmates. We had certain senior classmen that were tougher than others. For example, you sat on the green bench and were fanned with a broom. I know with the first classmen when I was a plebe, they normally would ask you questions, and you had to have the answer for the next meal. Frequently they'd ask a question, and I would know part of the answer. Never say, "I don't know." Say, "I will find out." By the next meal I always found out. Later on, I knew a few of these people, Johnny Clark and others.[*] He said, "You know, we always were amazed at how many current events and other things you knew compared to your classmates. So there was no fun in hazing you and asking you questions."

Paul Stillwell: How did you know these things?

Admiral Knoll: Well, I don't know. For years I had read with interest the daily newspapers, editorials, and weekly periodicals such as *Time*. Today I always work the crossword puzzle in *The New York Times*. I've done that for 25 years or more. At the Naval Academy many were interested in a Rhodes scholarship. I applied. There were many applicants with only one or two selected. Having knowledge of the facts of life, current events, and general world topics is fundamental for eligibility for a Rhodes scholarship.

Paul Stillwell: What kinds of questions were these that you were asked?

Admiral Knoll: Oh, everything imaginable, frequently relating to some current studies, significant events of naval history. Many were of historical nature, location of cities, state capitals, political figures, and anything in the world almanac. They were challenging. I always tried to have available various reference books. I could always

---

[*] Midshipman John E. Clark, USN, class of 1927.

find an answer if I needed to find out, even if a visit to the library was necessary. I never had to say, "I can't find an answer."

Paul Stillwell: Was this a useful tactic, do you think?

Admiral Knoll: Yes. It did in many ways; I would say it separated the sheep from the goats, because some classmates at the table could answer more questions than the other ones. Some could never find the answer. I would know, but I couldn't help them at the table. Those of us who were in the first and second section had the advantage, I guess. We had about 10 to 12 sections, because we were one of the larger classes. The class of '27 was a large class, and then there were small classes in '28 and '29. Then '30 was a big class again, so we had more sections. We didn't have as many first classmen days as we did with the class of '27. They were a big class, but the two classes after that were not as effective. They had some good people in them but not in numbers.

I would say that was one of the challenging things of our development that we went through. I enjoyed it more or less; I didn't consider it hazing. If you could get in this kind of a dialogue, it was good training for the future. I think I've run into this sort of thing with every officer or every captain or admiral for whom I worked. If they wanted to know something, I found any answer, and if I didn't know, I could find out. It is a valuable training in itself. Even at sea I have always had available a selection of standard references. Of course, I do have all the standard references at home I can think of, whether it's a *Who's Who* or *Roget's Thesaurus*, encyclopedia, world almanac—all the rest of them; they're all there. If you work crossword puzzles, you have to go to the reference books, and you find some answers by intuitions that are confirmed ultimately.

Paul Stillwell: What about physical hazing? Did you undergo that?

Admiral Knoll: Not too much, no. I think one of the few people who did some memorable hazing with a broom was Don Griffin.*

---

* Midshipman Charles D. Griffin, USN. Griffin eventually became a four-star admiral. His oral history is in the Naval Institute collection.

Paul Stillwell: He was in '27.

Admiral Knoll: Yes, as a first classman he was hateful and mean.

Paul Stillwell: Did he work you over?

Admiral Knoll: Oh yes, a couple of times. I don't know what for. Every once in a while, every plebe at our table had to go up just because you were at the table with him. He always had a mean streak to him, and I've known him all these years and been involved with him. He was never a pleasant individual. He was a very capable officer, apparently, and I've had some work with him when I was going out to be chief of staff in Seventh Fleet with Slim Ingersoll.* I had a lot of respect for his professional ability, and he always treated me with respect. But he had a gruff nature that warned you to be on guard. He was ready to "bark" or "bite."

Paul Stillwell: Did he intimidate you in that respect.

Admiral Knoll: No, I honestly say never. I was trained with the conviction that whomever I worked for could never intimidate me.

Paul Stillwell: Maybe Griffin smoothed out some as he got senior.

Admiral Knoll: Well, of course, he matured and was A-one aviator. He always had a twang in his voice. As a midshipman, he could be pretty mean.

Paul Stillwell: What can you say about the quality of the academics at the Naval Academy when you were here?

---

* Vice Adm. Stuart H. Ingersoll, USN, served as Commander Seventh Fleet from 19 December 1955 to 28 January 1957. Rear Admiral Griffin was special assistant to the Chairman of the Joint Chiefs of Staff, 1955-56.

Admiral Knoll: In terms of how they prepared me for both postgraduate school and MIT, they were quite satisfactory.

Paul Stillwell: Did the Naval Academy give you enough practical training?

Admiral Knoll: Yes, I thought the cruise for three months every year on a ship with duty in the engine room one year and another year with the deck work, and the final year navigating was terrific. It was the practical way of getting you ready for what you were supposed to be. I think one of the big losses for present midshipmen is that they do not have the chance of really being aboard ship for three years in a row—to go aboard ship and live out of a little cruise box and seabag, and sleep in a hammock at least once. That's the lowest common denominator, but that prepares you for the future vicissitudes of the system.

Paul Stillwell: Tell me about your youngster cruise then. What ship were you in?

Admiral Knoll: I was in the battleship *Florida*.* I enjoyed that. We transited the Panama Canal and visited the West Coast. We stopped at San Diego, Los Angeles, and San Francisco. It was a thrill seeing Panama, Cristóbal on one side and Balboa on the other. You obtain some foreign experience, and then you're at sea off the coast of Mexico, the Gulf of Tehuantepec, famous for storms. Then San Diego, and you go ashore with a working party to get sand for holystoning the decks.† The boatswain says, "When you get through loading these motor launches with sand, you can take a swim." The biggest surprise in your life is when you jumped in that water near Ballast Point in San Diego, thinking you were going to take a swim. Then you come out as fast as you went in, because it's awful cold. Not like warmer water at the same latitude on the Atlantic Coast. I mean, that's education.

---

* USS *Florida* (BB-30) was commissioned in September 1911. She had a standard displacement of 21,825 tons, was 522 feet long, and 88 feet in the beam. Her top design speed was 21 knots. Her main battery comprised ten 12-inch guns.
† Holystoning refers to the practice of cleaning a ship's wooden decks by scraping them with bricks pushed back and forth across the planks by means of wooden handles. It is a laborious operation.

Paul Stillwell: Tell me about your time in engineering on board ship.

Admiral Knoll: That was on the second-class cruise. I stood the watches, but I was never intrigued in terms of wanting to be in the "black gang."

Paul Stillwell: On your second-class cruise, what ship was that in?

Admiral Knoll: The battleship *Utah* with Captain Littlefield.* We went up and down the Atlantic Coast, visiting New England, for example, Camden and Rockport, Maine, Boston, and Newport. It was, again, an ideal indoctrination. At the end of each of these cruises we would spend two weeks in Guantánamo for firing a short-range battle practice, which was always a good finale.†

Paul Stillwell: Did you enjoy going to sea?

Admiral Knoll: Oh yes, I enjoyed it. As long as the weather was good, I would take my hammock and sleep on deck, occasionally woke up to find I was being rained on. I know more than once when it got too rough, I'd go up behind the stack and lash the hammock topside amidships rather than stay below decks. I enjoyed it. I looked forward to these cruises, because it broadened your horizons and showed you the differences in short distances in the U.S.A. It was rather interesting. Within a year after I graduated from the Naval Academy, I had been in every state in the union, one way or another, cross country via auto or railroad. Going to Pensacola via auto from New York City and then returning to join the *Texas* in California.

Paul Stillwell: How was the food?

---

* USS *Utah* (BB-31) was commissioned as a *Florida*-class battleship in August 1911. She had a standard displacement of 21,825 tons, was 522 feet long, and 88 feet in the beam. Her top speed was 21 knots. Her main battery comprised ten 12-inch guns.
Captain William L. Littlefield, USN, commanded the *Utah* (BB-31), 23 January 1927 to 29 August 1928.
† Guantánamo Bay, on the south coast of Cuba, near the eastern end of the island, for many years provided a fleet anchorage and training area for U.S. Navy ships.

Admiral Knoll: I never had any complaint about the food. I was always amazed that some of the people who at home never had food that compared with what we had as midshipmen would complain the most about the food. It didn't matter where we were; I'm sure it was superior in most instances to what they ate at home. We always had good food at home, but I was impressed with the selection and quantity of food.

Paul Stillwell: What can you say about your relationships with the enlisted men in these ships?

Admiral Knoll: Well, I never had anything but a good relationship wherever I served. I tried to look at people and evaluate their capabilities and find out what made them tick, identify those you could rely on, those that you could talk to, and those that would listen to you.

Paul Stillwell: I'm just wondering how it was that you were getting exposed to some of these men of the world after you had just come from perhaps a sheltered home life.

Admiral Knoll: It was sheltered. It was a parochial thing. I am slow to accept people until I can identify the good and the bad, the can-do individual vs. the pessimist. You have cliques that try to avoid work or do only mediocre work. Every ship in which I served was a cleaner and happier ship. I never had a problem locating enough people to do the job. The challenge is to carefully tell them what is wanted, let them ask questions concerning any doubts, then go to work. It is easy to give orders; the task is to give clear, unambiguous orders.

Paul Stillwell: Do you think that some of these enlisted guys would ever try to lead midshipmen astray?

Admiral Knoll: They might, but I would say that our biggest difficulty, over a period of time, was the possibility of young, immature midshipmen being exposed, like today, more to homosexuals or the drug situation, that they're uninformed and not strong enough characters to start with. Some lack adequate training and character that should have been obtained at home.

Paul Stillwell: What do you remember about the superintendent?

Admiral Knoll: Well, Admiral Nulton was the superintendent.* As much as I can remember, I didn't think that he had the entrepreneurship of Captain Jonas Ingram, who would build up the spirit of the regiment.† They're all characters unto themselves. He was an impressive gentleman, and he was a good example for the midshipmen. That's what a naval officer should be. Admiral Nulton, on the other hand, was not dynamic. It appeared that his wife was more impressive than he was.

Paul Stillwell: Why do you say that?

Admiral Knoll: He never gave the impression of being my ideal of an admiral, you see, like Kelly Turner or Ernie King.‡

Paul Stillwell: We've talked about your first two cruises. What about your first-class cruise?

Admiral Knoll: The first-class cruise was to Europe, which included ten days in Barcelona, Spain, for the international exposition. And then from there ten days in Naples, Italy, then to Weymouth, England, for ten days. I think the experience in Barcelona was a chance to use a foreign language intelligently. Talking with natives is a fantastic incentive for finding out how much you have to learn, to pick up idioms and different customs.

---

* Rear Admiral Louis M. Nulton, USN, served as superintendent of the Naval Academy from February 1925 to June 1928.
† Captain Jonas H. Ingram, USN, was the Naval Academy's athletic director from 1925 to 1930.
‡ Admiral Ernest J. King, USN, served as Chief of Naval Operations from 26 March 1942 to 15 December 1945 and as Commander in Chief U.S. Fleet from 20 December 1941 to 2 September 1945; he was promoted to the rank of fleet admiral in December 1944.

I think average individual who learns Russian in the United States and then goes to the U.S.S.R, the first couple of months they're the most confusing people in the world because they don't know the distinction between English and Russian. Such terms like "in time" in terms of short time, long time, or time of day all have separate words in Russian. A newcomer uses them interchangeably. You order breakfast or something, and your servant looks out the window and doesn't understand and says, "That man is crazy."

The cruise to Europe gave you a feel for the foreign environment. I spent a lot of time going around Rome for about eight days. I didn't get to see Mussolini.* I visited his office and talked to his secretary. I had a letter to Mussolini from the Italian consul in Erie. It was a big office at that time in '29. It was the beginning of Mussolini's influence there. Italy was about to change. And then I had letters to the Catholic American College in Rome. As a result, I was instrumental in arranging for two midshipmen's visits to the Vatican and a special audience with Pope Pius XI.† I was authorized to stay in Rome for seven days, three days with each group. Aubrey Bourgeois and I had a private audience with the Pope at that time. I enjoyed planning for the future, doing things like this. Bourgeois was with me for many of these events. We also went to Barcelona, Spain, a different country from Italy, with a different kind of history.

I've traveled all over the world, and I've been to almost every place at least twice when I was younger, and now in the last 15 years I have revisited places to detect differences. It's amazing to see what differences have taken place and to compare what you've seen developing. So the chance that I had then to get an appreciation of the foreign environment and to use the language was challenging for the future. In England we were there for ten days and had a chance to go to London and go to the usual tourist attractions, as well as having a chance to navigate and other duties of an officer. This you wouldn't get any other way except on board ship with supervision.

Paul Stillwell: What professional training do you remember from that cruise?

---

* Benito Mussolini organized the Fascists in Italy in the 1920s and ruled as dictator in that country until he was executed in 1945.
† Pius XI was Pope from 1922 to 1939.

Admiral Knoll: Well, I think conning ship and navigation. Today the average individual wouldn't know how to sit down and work out a spherical triangle with Marcq St. Hilaire and logarithmic tables.* Positions are available today by just pushing a few electronic buttons. Imagine in battle if you lose the effect of all this electronics and you had to go back and use Dreisenstock or Ageton for navigation. They wouldn't know how to use it until they read the book. In the meantime, it would take them a day or so until they'd take an accurate star sight and know how to plot their position on the chart. And we've lost that. I think this is true of much of the computer technology today. We have to be very careful that we don't shortcut this experience level in mathematics that led to what the computer can do for you in a short time. In the old days, with a slipstick and plotting equipment, you did a lot of work to find answers.† Now it is abbreviated for you.

Paul Stillwell: How good was that cruise in teaching you to be a leader, handling men?

Admiral Knoll: Well, to put your finger on it, I don't think there was real emphasis on leadership at that time probably as much as it is now. At the Postgraduate School there was excellent emphasis on leadership. I think the old story is that you don't make leaders yourself; people make you. There were people like Admiral Burke who helped me be a leader, helped me have confidence, the idea that I wouldn't argue with people, but I wasn't afraid to express my view and defend my positions without antagonizing anyone. That's a type of leadership. It's hard, I would say, to develop automatically a leader in everybody.

I think you have to have a certain innate contribution that you've inherited before you get to that level. Some of it came from my ancestors; some of them who came from Oxford were not afraid to say, "To hell with Henry VIII. We'll go to the Palatinate of the Rhine." And when things started happening with mad King Ludwig and Bavaria, they said, "We're going to go to the United States." They had it in their blood that they weren't afraid to make a move and go someplace and say, "I'll make my livelihood and survive anything."

---

* The Marcq St. Hilaire method is a type of celestial navigation.
† "Slipstick" is a nickname for the slide rule.

Paul Stillwell: How was your social life at the Naval Academy?

Admiral Knoll: Oh, I had an occasional date with girls from Washington. I was never engaged to any of them. I dated one girl maybe more than the others; I had a few dates with Lloyd Mustin's future wife, Emily Morton.* I took her to the first class hop. She was just a cute youngster, and I knew her mother pretty well. Some of her neighbors were related to people who had lived in Erie some years ago. Her uncle was Doug Howard, and he was quite a naval character.† I could tell a story about him, very practical and to the point. He was taking this exam for lieutenant, an engineering exam. They had a question something like, "You're on watch in the fireroom. You start checking the tri-cocks, check the top cock, steam comes out. You check the next one, steam comes out. You check the lowest cock, and steam comes out. What do you do?"

On his examination paper he said, "Well, under those conditions the regulations say to haul all fires, but Doug Howard would haul ass." He told this story after the exam.

Paul Stillwell: You dated the daughters of senior officers, didn't you?

Admiral Knoll: From time to time. I went to parties with them, yes. Had occasional dates. It didn't do you any harm. I had dates with Admiral King's daughter and with Admiral Adolphus Andrews's daughter.‡ I married a girl from Norfolk from a nice family, a Virginia family.§

Paul Stillwell: Well, there wasn't anything calculated, then, on your part in going through a roster of senior officers?

Admiral Knoll: Not at all, not at all. I didn't have that ambition, and I didn't go around emphasizing that I had dated So-and-so. No, I wasn't looking to build up my promotion

---

* Midshipman Lloyd M. Mustin, USN, graduated in the class of 1932 and married Emily Morton, whose brother, Midshipman Thomas H. Morton, USN, was in the class of 1933. The oral histories of both Admiral Mustin and Admiral Morton are in the Naval Institute collection.
† Douglas L. Howard graduated from the Naval Academy in 1906. He retired as a captain in 1933.
‡ Adolphus Andrews graduated from the Naval Academy in 1901 and eventually reached the rank of vice admiral. He commanded the battleship *Texas* (BB-35) when Knoll was an ensign in that ship.
§ Knoll married Genevieve Parker Hawkins on 29 February 1940.

potential. In fact, I never did in that. I mean, I was never really worried about it. If I did my best, okay. Becoming serious with a girl and getting married was not one of my objectives.

Paul Stillwell: What extracurricular activities were you in at the Naval Academy?

Admiral Knoll: Well, not a whole lot, except company football or something like that. At that time there wasn't the emphasis on extracurricular activity. Today I'm all in favor of more of this emphasis, and more of this emphasis before they enter the academy. The period that I came in was an interesting transition period. It can't be ignored. I would say within the two years when I came to the Naval Academy, the average midshipman at the Naval Academy came from a WASP environment.[*] There were few ethnic groups involved—Polish, Italian, or even German. It was a very selective group, and you could see that. I had a few Jewish boys in my class. Up until that time, like Rickover, they were the exception.[†] Therefore, everything was very conservative. Someone once told me after graduation, "'You'll never get beyond lieutenant commander because you're Roman Catholic, and the Masons control the promotions."

I said, "Well, I'm not worried about that."

Sometimes you could see it portrayed, and you could see it portrayed in some of the people in my class. Look at the earlier classes, and they didn't have Italian and Polish names or other ethnic groups, which was wrong, because during the war they performed just like everybody else. The Congress did start appointing—and I don't know how they determined it, but there was a screening before that that made sure they got the type with the family and ethnic background they were looking for. That was true a lot in terms of political environment, in terms of our lawyers in this country until a certain period. And normally after World War I, I think it changed.

Paul Stillwell: That would make the opportunity for you, I guess.

---

[*] WASP – White Anglo-Saxon Protestant.
[†] Hyman G. Rickover graduated from the Naval Academy in the class of 1922.

Admiral Knoll: You were competing with people from all over the United States who were essentially, say, in the top 10% of their class wherever they came from. At that time, academically the people from the South in no way compared to the quality of education of those of us who came from the northern schools. You could see it in class, the questions that were asked and the dealings we had with professors. That's changed now, but you could almost tell them by the way they acted and the way they reacted to questions. They didn't have the imagination.

Mathematics is one of the most important educational fields for any youngster who wants to train himself to think on his feet, to rely on facts, to analyze those facts, and come up with answers. It's very finite and abstract, and the more you can look at problems, we had some excellent professors in prep school at home. I enjoyed getting new questions and finding the answers. I don't think we're doing enough today in our educational system with challenging questions. I think that's a loss for the technicians of the future if they don't have basic mathematics as a background. I'm sure the mathematics that we received here, the mathematics that we received with Professor Ruth and others at the Postgraduate School helped develop my conviction that nothing's impossible. You can find solutions by an orderly approach without getting excited.

Paul Stillwell: Did Tom Haley, your roommate, depend on you a good bit for academics?

Admiral Knoll: No, no. He studied a lot harder. He was every bit as smart as I was but a very practical engineer. We both were at MIT together. He was in aeronautical engineering, and I was in aeronautical engineering, specifically meteorology, but we studied theory and were in many MIT classes together.

Paul Stillwell: Then he didn't have this deficiency in background, would you say?

Admiral Knoll: Not completely, but I saw some of it, because he came from Tennessee, and he recognized the times I had an inquisitiveness in terms of history, in terms of current events, that he didn't have. I think this was inherited because my father was in the newspaper business and theatrical director and had written editorials. I had gone to the theater many times for his opening performance to critique what was good or bad about it. My father put his confidence in me, and I enjoyed making the return.

Paul Stillwell: What were the forms of recreation available in Annapolis at that time?

Admiral Knoll: Tennis. I played some tennis, and I ended up with a stone bruise that slowed me down. At that time, for recreation we did a lot of walking around the yard, going out every night after the evening meal and having discussions with some of the classmates and exploring things, discussing current events, in which I always had an interest, analyzing the big political picture rather than the parochial one.

Paul Stillwell: How did you first assignment come about when you graduated?

Admiral Knoll: My orders to the battleship *Florida* came while I was at the Naval Academy. A graduate of the academy living in Erie was a friend of Ernie King. He said, "Now, remember, get on the biggest and most important ship in the Navy." I had asked for a battleship in the Atlantic Fleet. They gave me the *Florida*. She was an old ship and was alive with bedbugs. Upon graduation, I went to pre-flight training at Norfolk Naval Air Station, where I soloed in July 1930. My orders were modified upon my arrival in *Florida*, and after one night or so I proceeded to the West Coast to join *Texas*.*

Paul Stillwell: What was involved in pre-flight training?

Admiral Knoll: As soon as we graduated we went either to Norfolk or to San Diego for elimination flight training. You flew many hours of training with an officer instructor and then soloed for about three or four days before going to the fleet. You had to do a loop and other maneuvers while soloing. They would say you'd be ordered to Naval Air Station Pensacola when there was an opening for flight training.

---

* Ensign Knoll reported to the *Texas* in July 1930. The *Florida* was removed from the active fleet to comply with the provisions of the 1930 London Naval Treaty on disarmament.

The battleship *Texas* was the fleet flagship, an ideal assignment. Admiral William Veazie Pratt was Commander in Chief U.S. Fleet.[*] Adolphus Andrews was the skipper of *Texas*.[†] My gunnery officer was Commander McClung.[‡] I immediately became assistant turret officer of turret two. I took an interest in gunnery. My orders to Pensacola came in January '31, while *Texas* was at New York Navy Yard.

I went to Pensacola and was there until May. When I didn't get my wings down there, I admit that I was depressed, because I wanted to be an aviator with the rest of them. Every ground school course that they gave us, they'd start each morning, "Remember only 20% of you are going to get your wings, because the future naval aviator is going to be an enlisted man, and we need only a few officers to be in charge of squadrons." So it sort of indicated, "Well, I want to be one of those who's going to be in charge of all this."

There was a personality conflict between my instructor and the check pilot. Why I left was never officially recorded. They said upon detachment, "You can go and come back in a year or so." I didn't go back, even when I was invited. I was lucky. I also say my mother always prayed me out of naval aviation because in those days it was not too safe an occupation flying old Yellow Perils, NY-2s.[§]

I returned to *Texas*, which by that time was back on the West Coast. I traveled to the West Coast as officer of the deck on the *Vega*. It was a supply ship, took supplies to the Marines at Corinto, giving me a chance to see Nicaragua. I joined the *Texas* at San Diego, because Admiral Pratt went there to have his teeth fixed by his favorite dentist and to play golf.[**] I got aboard ship, talked to the skipper and the exec, and they said, "What did you do on the *Vega*?"

I said, "Officer of the deck."

"How many officers of the deck?"

"Four."

---

[*] Admiral William V. Pratt, USN, served as Commander in Chief U.S. Fleet (CinCUS) from 21 May 1929 to 17 September 1930.
[†] Captain Adolphus Andrews, USN, commanded the *Texas* (BB-35) from 9 July 1929 to 13 May 1931.
[‡] Lieutenant Commander Edgar R. McClung, USN.
[§] The NY was a pontoon-equipped version of the Army's PT-1 biplane trainer. Entering service in the late 1920s, it was the first Consolidated-built aircraft to carry a Navy designation. The NY-2 model was 28 feet long, wingspan of 40 feet, gross weight of 2,627 pounds, and top speed of 98 miles per hour.
[**] Pratt had already left the *Texas* in September 1930 to become Chief of Naval Operations.

"If you've been officer of the deck on the *Vega*, you're not going to return to junior officer of the deck on *Texas* again. You start off as officer of the deck." I was officer of the deck a few months before the rest of my class on the *Texas*, and I was assigned fourth division and turret officer of turret four. Prior to that I had been with Lieutenant Flynn as assistant turret officer.* I had my own division with turret four and fired some very successful gunnery practices.

I worked with Deak Parsons.† Every time the ship was in port and other battleships were going out to fire, we'd go aboard and go to the foretop and spot fall of shot of various exercises.‡ Over a period of time, when I visited all the battleships, I had ridden and observed gunnery firings of every battleship in the fleet. I observed the good and bad features of different organizations and gunnery procedures. You learn a lot from practical experience and provide refinement for doctrine relating to gunnery exercises.

Paul Stillwell: What do you remember about Parsons?

Admiral Knoll: His high bald head and charming personality. We were compatible.

Paul Stillwell: There was something in that baldhead.

Admiral Knoll: Probably the smartest gunnery authority in the Navy. I worked with him and Pete Persons. Pete Persons was number-one range keeper in the plotting room of the *Texas*, and I had the other.§ Persons was in charge.

Deak was a character—a genius. He knew more about the electronics and instruments in the plotting room than anyone else. He could locate and correct any malfunction without hesitation.

---

* Lieutenant (junior grade) Joseph A. Flynn, USN.
† Lieutenant William S. Parsons, USN. During World War II, as a captain, Parsons was involved in the development of the atomic bomb in New Mexico. On 6 August 1945, Parsons was the weaponeer on board the B-29 *Enola Gay* that dropped the bomb on Hiroshima, Japan.
‡ The foretop was a gunfire control station atop the foremast.
§ Ensign Henry S. Persons Jr., USN.
The range keeper was an analog computer that controlled the guns in bearing and distance to hit the intended target.

Paul Stillwell: In what sense was he a character?

Admiral Knoll: I tell you, before every practice, he'd live in the plotting room, and he would check every range keeper, make replacement of parts where necessary. He would check circuitry to all guns and turrets. He'd go to the control board and check all the thyraton electronic tubes. He knew more about every instrument than any technician on the ship. He had helped to design many instruments and knew how they were supposed to work. He was very thorough, calm, cool, and collected. He was an authority on fuzing. There wasn't a better man on fuzing in the United States.

He was very methodical, as quiet as could be. He never worried that people weren't helping. The crew was always ready to carry out any order. His equipment never broke down during any battle practice. He knew what it was supposed to do, he knew how it was designed, and he made damn sure ahead of time that everything was working properly. He would spend many hours in the plotting room before getting under way for a gunnery practice. I learned a lot from him.

Paul Stillwell: Was Parsons one who inspired a good deal of loyalty as a leader?

Admiral Knoll: He was a quiet man that knew his business. We all admired what he knew and liked what he did. People would say, "That guy knows what he's doing." I could talk to him. He never scared you. He was married to Cluverius's daughter. Admiral Cluverius was chief of staff to the fleet commander in chief.[*] Her brother was in my class, but he didn't graduate from the academy.[†]

You work with an individual like Parsons and the same way, you meet many senior officers as the officer of the deck on the fleet flagship, particularly in San Diego. Side boys were given at that time for Lieutenant Colonel Arnold, U.S. Army, when he

---
[*] Rear Admiral Wat T. Cluverius Jr., USN. As a junior officer he had been on board the battleship *Maine* when she exploded and sank in Havana Harbor in 1898.
[†] Midshipman Wat T. Cluverius III, USN, resigned in 1928.

was commanding officer of an Army air base in California.* Hap Arnold of the Air Force was later a general and a member of the Joint Chiefs of Staff during World War II. Many officers would come aboard for various ceremonies and for conferences. The officer of the deck had to know them all and what they commanded. This was good experience with protocol and diplomacy that was invaluable for many future duties.

Paul Stillwell: What do you remember about Andrews as a skipper of the *Texas*?

Admiral Knoll: He had more uniforms and civilian clothes than any man I ever knew. Every time the weather was nice, they'd hang them out on the upper deck to be aired. He was effective. I would say I've had some better skippers, but he was well off financially, from Texas, and his wife was a terrific person. I know when I was promoted to admiral I got a nice note from her.† She said, "If Adolphus was still living, he'd have been thrilled because he always said from the time you were on the *Texas* in 1931 that you'd be an admiral someday."

Paul Stillwell: That's a nice touch.

Admiral Knoll: It was nice to hear from her.

Paul Stillwell: In what sense wasn't he as good as some of your other skippers?

Admiral Knoll: In the year I was with him, he was always pleasant and never had close contacts as a junior officer. He did not show friendliness that some other skippers had with whom I had a closer relationship. One of the characters in the old Navy was old Vice Admiral Pluvy Kempff.‡ He was just like a brother, whatever was going on, and he liked to meet with people. I think that Adolphus Andrews had a certain reserve he had

---

* In August 1931 Lieutenant Colonel Henry H. Arnold, U.S. Army Air Corps, became commanding officer of March Field near Riverside, California. It later became March Air Force Base.
Side boys are crew members stationed in two ranks at a ship's gangway on the arrival or departure of officers or officials for whom side honors are rendered. The number of side boys varies from two to eight, depending on the rank of the individual.
† Knoll became a rear admiral in 1958.
‡ In the mid-1930s Vice Admiral Clarence S. Kempff, USN, was Commander Battleships, Battle Force.

inherited. He was naval aide at the White House and could call his own shots.* Later he had a difficult job in New York when the *Normandie* capsized.† He was a real friend when, as Chief of Naval Personnel, he found enough money for two of us to go to MIT rather than Cal Tech.‡

Paul Stillwell: Well, his effectiveness as a commanding officer is not the same as being outgoing.

Admiral Knoll: The real challenge is having the right kind of staff around you and seeking the best. That's where Ernie King was the ideal tough boss. He had a tough job to do. He got the job done because he got the best people around to help do it, and that's the secret of the Navy. Don't do it all yourself. In that area, I think Adolphus Andrews was a good skipper, but he didn't impress me as a skipper when I was young and immature, as much as other ones that I worked with in later years.

Paul Stillwell: What about Admiral Pratt?

Admiral Knoll: He would impress you and a good example for young officers to aspire to being an admiral. He got to the top, and he and Cluverius were terrific individuals to get along with. And the same way with Admiral Jehu Valentine Chase.§ The interesting thing is Chase was so much younger in appearance when he relieved Pratt. When Chase was relieved by a capable man that lived on goat's milk more than anything else, it looked like death was relieving youth. What was his name?

Paul Stillwell: Schofield?**

---

* Captain Andrews served as naval aide to the President from 1922 to 1926.
† In 1942 the former French passenger liner *Normandie* accidentally caught fire while being converted to the Navy troop transport *Lafayette* (AP-53). Water from fireboats caused the ship to list and roll over into the mud at her berth on the west side of Manhattan. Rear Admiral Andrews was then based in New York while serving as Commandant Third Naval District.
‡ Rear Admiral Andrews served as Chief of the Bureau of Navigation from 30 June 1935 to 11 June 1938.
§ Admiral Jehu V. Chase, USN, was CinCUS from 17 September 1930 to 15 September 1931.
** Admiral Frank H. Schofield, USN, was CinCUS from 1931 to 1932.

Admiral Knoll: Yes, Schofield. Jehu Chase and his daughter Betty, with whom young officers had good relationships. Yes, Schofield was the one. He was really feeble but the smartest in the Navy. Chase was a different type. He was a jolly character, and he gave the impression he was relaxed and enjoyed that he was the boss. Young officers meet you and experience various bosses. You just try and keep them happy and do your job. In those days we had certain executive officers on battleships that really scared all hands, like Commander Clyde Robinson of the *Texas*.* If you made one mistake as officer of the deck, no matter how small it was, you were relieved and sent to your room for a couple of days.

Paul Stillwell: Mistakes like what?

Admiral Knoll: Maybe you didn't retire the side boys expeditiously or there were Irish pennants hanging from boat booms or rigging.† It was insignificant, but the fleet flag had to be a smart ship. He had that fear of God, and he never sent me to my room, maybe because I was acquainted with his wife, and she lived up here with Mrs. Grace Howard and her daughter Emily Morton. He had everybody scared to death. If anything was wrong on deck or anything was out of order, he wouldn't tell you what was wrong. He'd tell you to send for your relief, and your relief had to figure out what you had been punished for. That's good training and keeps you on your toes when you are officer of the deck on the fleet flagship.

Paul Stillwell: So obviously spit and polish was an important part of the fleet flagship routine.

Admiral Knoll: You're damn right it was. As the in-port officer of the deck in the fleet flagship, I knew every flag officer that came aboard to call on Admiral Pratt or Admiral

---

* Commander Clyde R. Robinson, USN.
† Side boys are crew members stationed in two ranks at a ship's gangway on the arrival or departure of officers or officials for whom side honors are rendered. The number of side boys varies from two to eight, depending on the rank of the individual.
"Irish Pennant" is Navy slang for a loose piece of line left adrift. It can also be used in a figurative sense to refer to something that is sloppy because it hasn't been completed properly.

Chase, by his features, and I knew his order of seniority; that was part of the training. Aviators had never had adequate experience for seagoing command of an aircraft carrier. They had to learn quickly. How do they know how to handle shipboard things if they didn't grow up in the system, as well as conning a ship in different kinds of weather, giving the right orders to the helm and reacting to emergencies and also conducting the regular inspections below decks? They never had this.

Paul Stillwell: How was the ship in rough seas?

Admiral Knoll: One of the most interesting experiences I had in going through heavy weather was in *Texas*. We hit heavy weather north of San Francisco, and in some way or other the big steel desk of Admiral Pratt in the office in his cabin let go. The first lieutenant, boatswain, and myself got in there with manila lines and tried to lasso each leg and take a turn, but every time the ship rolled, the desk would slam into another corner of the cabin. We were standing at each door to be out of the way so the desk didn't hit us. It weighed a ton or more. It was like a bull in a china closet; nothing we could do about it. The desk was finally secured with manila lines.

Paul Stillwell: What do you recall about the antiaircraft capability in the *Texas*?

Admiral Knoll: Well, with 3-inch, we would hit quite a few, but lacked fire control for rapid fire. The trainers and pointers tried hard, but installations were preventive. I would say the ammunition was erratic to that degree, and the gun mounts were not good. They vibrated and interfered with keeping guns on target. Specialists like Deak Parsons did a lot of hard work with antiaircraft fire control and ammo. That led to what we have today; there's no doubt about it. And some of that in terms of fuzes, fire control directors, and new electronic circuits. Parsons had his finger in it, no doubt about it. He was recognized as an enthusiastic leader in gunnery developments.

Paul Stillwell: Was he recognized already at the time you were serving with him?

Admiral Knoll: Yes. His assignments afloat were with gunnery and ashore with the Bureau of Ordnance and Dahlgren, Virginia. It's too bad, because he would be living if they had taken him promptly to a hospital when he had a heart attack at home.* He rode the bomb in *Enola Gay* in over Hiroshima and armed it just before it was dropped. The nation had a naval officer who was entrusted with arming the first atomic bomb.

Paul Stillwell: They had a naval officer as the weapons man on the flight that bombed Nagasaki, too. Dick Ashworth.†

Admiral Knoll: Yes.

Paul Stillwell: What can you say about being a turret officer in the *Texas*?

Admiral Knoll: Well, the main thing was to have an ample crew and regular trainers and pointers that you could rely on. There was loading drill every day. It was necessary to let the chief petty officers and boatswain's mate handle as much as possible. They were more knowledgeable than junior officers and knew how to get the performance. I learned a lot listening to more senior petty officers. In those days, gunnery scores in competition with other battleships kept us on our toes. The people in gunnery took pride in keeping the equipment up to shape and trying to put E's on the ship.‡ The biggest problem was the continual change in personnel and keeping the loading crew fully trained.

Paul Stillwell: How many men did you have in the turret crew?

Admiral Knoll: About 20 men in the gun chamber. You had two guns with the loading crew for shell and for powder. You had a man on each rammer. If you were preparing

---

* Rear Admiral William S. Parsons, USN, died on 5 December 1953 at the National Naval Medical Center in Bethesda, Maryland. He was 52 years old.
† Commander Frederick L. Ashworth, USN, was involved in the atomic bomb development. During the mission of 9 August 1945 against Nagasaki, Japan, Ashworth was the weaponeer on board the B-29 "Bocks Car." The oral history of Ashworth, who retired as a vice admiral, is in the Naval Institute collection.
‡ An "E," for excellence, is generally awarded to a ship or component of a ship as a result of top performance in competition with other ships during a given time period.

for a major exercise, you had people in the handling room down below who provided support with shell and power through chain hoists.

Paul Stillwell: So maybe 50 altogether?

Admiral Knoll: Oh, easily. Yes, if you were going to have any extended period. In the actual turret itself, you normally had about 12 people, plus two trainers and pointers at gunsights.

Paul Stillwell: What safety features were built into those turrets?

Admiral Knoll: The primary thing is that once a gun was loaded, the primer was inserted, there were interlocking devices. Normally, you shouldn't open the breech until the gun fired. The turret officer had control of the firing circuit in a separate chamber from the gun chamber. There were portholes permitting the turret officer to observe all activity in the gun chamber. Every evolution had to be followed in accord with doctrine, and the turret officer was responsible to assure that all safety precautions were observed. Flood control of all spaces and firing circuits were under the control of the turret officer. Each gun was loaded with one 14-inch shell and four powder bags, each weighing 60-90 pounds. Each powder bag of smokeless had a packet of black powder on the rear end, colored red. When the gun was fired, the primer ignited the black powder first.

Paul Stillwell: I take it there was great emphasis on safety during training.

Admiral Knoll: All the way through. I'll never forget one time on turret two in the *Texas*. We had a possible hang fire.* I was looking in there, and I saw the gun captain start to trip the safety latch to open the breech. That could have blown up the whole gun chamber if it was a hang fire. I hollered for him to stop. When I realized what I had said and done, I had each hand on the flooding valves for the turret. If it had blown up, they'd have found me in there with hands on valves. Of course, you have to give credit to the

---

* A hang fire is a delayed detonation of an explosive charge inside a gun.

man who designed the turret officer's booth. That's the thing you're going to grab. Also daily training with loading drills makes this second nature to react. The gun captain knew how to trip the safety catch, but he shouldn't have tried to do it. He never really moved the breech, so there was no danger. A bad primer was removed after a few hours' wait.

Paul Stillwell: How often did you shoot the main battery in the *Texas*?

Admiral Knoll: There were different types of gunnery exercises in battle practice. The first practice each year was the short-range practice for individual ships to get everybody oriented and trained. After firing, the targets were brought aboard to count the hits and compute score. Shells had a special color for each ship. So the edges of each target were checked for traces of paint. As observers we were alert that someone with paint on the heel of his shoe did not try to add the right color to the edge of a target and claim credit for another hit. Gunnery scores were very important in determining the battleship annual competition.

The targets came on aboard and were spread on deck. The skipper, the gunnery officer, and observer would count the number of hits. Short range was fired at 1,600 to 1,800 yards. Another exercise with three ships would be fired at 18,000 or 20,000 yards. For this the shells were loaded, and a splash of colored water near the target would help you spot your own shells. Battleship shells would be dye-loaded with yellow, white, blue, or red. The biggest exercise would be a force battle practice with many battleships firing in line of battle; and there were night practices when star shells were fired to illuminate the targets.*

Paul Stillwell: Could you describe the link-up between the spotter, the plotting room, and your target?

---

* A "star shell" is a type of gunnery projectile that detonates in the air and provides a parachute flare for night illumination.

Admiral Knoll: Well, the spotter in the foretop would say the fall of shot was over or short about 200 yards, and the amount of deflection right or left on the first three salvos. Normally after three spotting-in shots, rapid fire of six or eight salvos at one-minute intervals.

Paul Stillwell: This was by radio?

Admiral Knoll: We had no radio, only sound-powered headphones. This was before we did spotting from aircraft. You were in the foretop, and you were estimating whether it was over or short of the target. You telephoned to plot: right, left, up 200, down 200 yards. Normally with two or three salvos you would straddle the target and go to rapid fire. To improve our spotting, we went aboard other ships and observed their practice. We would be in the foretop, observe fall of shot, and hear if our estimates agreed with the spotter controlling the ship's exercise.

Paul Stillwell: Who was your gunnery officer?

Admiral Knoll: Well, let's see. McClung was one of them in the *Texas*; then Commander Simons relieved him.[*]

Paul Stillwell: What do you remember about the aviation capabilities in the *Texas*?

Admiral Knoll: One of my old friends, Wu Duncan, was the senior aviator with a Loening amphibian plane, the first type on a battleship.[†] It was on top of number-three turret. He ended up being VCNO when I was in OpNav.[‡] You frequently met the same people again and again, though he didn't necessarily remember me. I was an officer of the deck when he came aboard, and we carried the one plane always on top of number-three turret. They were strange planes. The Loening amphibian was easy to hoist from

---

[*] Commander Robert B. Simons, USN.
[†] Lieutenant Commander Donald B. Duncan, USN, who served on the staff of CinCUS.
[‡] As a four-star admiral Duncan served as Vice Chief of Naval Operations from 10 August 1951 to 1 September 1956. His oral history is in the Columbia University collection.

the water with a crane. Later on, when we got newer planes—I forget what type they were; they were a more stable plane, easier to recover. We started using them for spotting. I know I went out a few times and did some spotting with them for the *Texas*.

Paul Stillwell: Did you have a separate junior officer mess in the *Texas*?

Admiral Knoll: Oh, yes.

Paul Stillwell: Were there any names from that mess that would be familiar?

Admiral Knoll: Kemp Tolley.[*] Let's see, who else?

Paul Stillwell: What do you remember about Tolley from then?

Admiral Knoll: Kemp was a good shipmate. We were in San Francisco, and he had an attractive girl. I can't think of her name. He was supposed to be engaged to her. She was the daughter of an official of Standard Oil of California.

Paul Stillwell: Yes, he proposed to somebody.

Admiral Knoll: Sure, sure. He writes about her in the book.[†] He doesn't name her in his book, but as I recall it, he was on the fleet staff when I was a ship's officer. I knew him quite well. Kemp is a great character. He has had many unique experiences. That's why we have a great Navy.

Of a sudden, Kemp came back to the ship quite depressed. The impression was that his girlfriend was sort of delaying or canceling their engagement, and because of this

---

[*] Ensign Kemp Tolley, USN, who graduated from the Naval Academy a year before Knoll, was a communications watch officer on the U.S. Fleet staff. The oral history of Tolley, who retired as a rear admiral, is in the Naval Institute collection.
[†] Kemp Tolley, *Caviar and Commissars: the Experiences of a U.S. Naval Officer in Stalin's Russia* (Annapolis: Naval Institute Press, 1983). As did Tolley, Knoll also served as an assistant naval attaché in Russia during World War II.

disappointment he quickly volunteered for duty on China Station. That is the truth, in terms of how I recall it.

Jack Galbraith and I were roommates on the *Texas*.* Then we were roommates on the *Southard* after he was in the 1932 Olympic Games. Then we were on the *Houston* together. He was the one who swam away from the foretop of the *Houston* as it sank in Sunda Strait.† He was in charge of the antiaircraft battery when the *Houston* was sunk. He spent the whole war in a prison camp.

In fact, he married an old girlfriend of mine. When I left New York in December 1930 to go to Pensacola, I asked him to take care of Grace Munsey. When I came back later, we shared a room on the *Southard*. I went home for Christmas. When I came back from Christmas, people said, "Things happened while you were gone."

I said, "What happened?"

They said, "Jack Galbraith went to Yuma and married an old girlfriend." Have you ever debriefed him on prison camp and his experiences?

Paul Stillwell: No.

Admiral Knoll: Terrific story.

Paul Stillwell: What kind of a guy was he?

Admiral Knoll: He was awarded the Silver Medal for rope climbing in the Olympics in '32 in Los Angeles. He learned it here at the Naval Academy. A terrific guy from Tennessee, a terrific gunnery man. He finally retired as a rear admiral. He lost most of his teeth in prison camp and almost starved to death. One of the demoralizing things is when they gave seeds to last a year and said, "You have to grow these seeds. Otherwise, you're going to starve next winter." They were up on a mountain where seeds couldn't grow, and he said they kept figuring on how they were going to starve to death next winter. Fortunately, the war ended when it did. He's got some fantastic stories, just like

---

* Ensign William J. Galbraith, USN.
† The heavy cruiser *Houston* (CA-30) was lost in the Battle of Sunda Strait the night of 28 February-1 March 1942. Knoll had been on board the ship when she was Asiatic Fleet flagship in 1940-41

Tarnowski has some stories that you should have about people shot by Japs after the fall of Corregidor in May 1942.*

Paul Stillwell: What was the quality of the enlisted men in the *Texas*?

Admiral Knoll: We still had the old days with old real seagoing people. Some of the best in the Navy, but some couldn't get promoted beyond seaman first. They would be a petty officer, they'd go ashore and get stinking drunk and then be demoted back to seaman. I remember going to mast a couple of times.†

Paul Stillwell: Tell me about your flight training at Pensacola, when you were away from the *Texas*.

Admiral Knoll: It was at the beach for flight operations, and 50% of the work was very educational, including excellent ground-school work, such as overhauling a plane, removing and repainting fabric, correcting webbing in the wings or replacing needed damaged wood, glue it or nail it in place, renew plywood where damage had been done, and then reassemble the whole plane, overhauling the engine and testing it, cover wings with fabric, put the dope on, and then paint it. We worked on one of these planes, number 21, for a couple of months as part of the ground-school work. Eventually the plane was returned to the beach for operations.

Looking over plane assignments for soloing was a plane I'd been working on at ground-school class. It had been checked and tested. The first time it was on the beach ready for students, I was assigned number 21. In those days, you would only fly about a couple of hours a day. You'd frequently go out with your instructor about once a week for an hour. Then you'd fly solo two hours each day and repeat various maneuvers. We'd fly, I'd say, about 20 hours a week. Some of the first maneuvers were at NAS Norfolk and also at Pensacola would practice a loop-de-loop, things like that, put yourself

---
* Aerographer's Mate First Class Zemo C. Tarnowski, USN, had been part of the Asiatic Fleet flag allowance. He was captured on Corregidor on 6 May 1942.
† Captain's mast is a sort of court in which the commanding officer of a unit listens to requests, awards non-judicial punishment, or issues commendations. Most often captain's mast is used for punishment of lesser offenses than those that merit courts-martial

in a spin and pull it out and increase your confidence. Many landings each day, learning to identify direction of wind. Over the years, after I've looked at those days of flying, I decided that I would probably not have been as safe a flier as I should have been. Good aviators are competent, never take chances, and those I flew with convinced me they are a special breed who have my admiration and respect.

Paul Stillwell: Why did you think you would not have been safe as an aviator?

Admiral Knoll: First of all, you have to have a special sense of caution. You have to have that second sense, to be relaxed and always ready for an emergency. When I'm driving along in an automobile, I can't remain as relaxed as good pilots are, an integral part of every maneuver without excitement. It is a special temperament I have observed over the years. In terms of safe aviation, that's a necessity. When I was with the Asiatic Fleet, I flew from time to time with the PBYs as part of neutrality patrol around the Philippine Islands to investigate and determine nationality of merchant ships.* I'd go out with some of my classmates, and I would take turns as a copilot while they would sleep. So that way I understood the harder jobs like the fighter pilots or the smaller planes that required a special temperament. I wasn't the type of pilot they were looking for. I could be a big boat pilot rather than the fighter plane pilot. Tom Haley, my roommate at the Naval Academy, was in VF-1.† During the war, as engineering duty only on the staff, he did a lot of planning for operations against the Japanese homeland. His fleet staff was ready for the invasion of Japan, which never took place.

Paul Stillwell: You have to say something for the ability of the instructors at Pensacola who could spot somebody like you who wouldn't—

Admiral Knoll: It didn't necessarily start that way. I was sent back to the fleet not because I had failed to pass the tests. Rather, my instructor got involved with a shooting incident. Eddie Mulheron on one side with my instructor Chick Lee on the other had

---

* The PBY Catalina was a twin-engine flying boat that performed extensive service before and during World War II.
† VF-1 – Fighter Squadron One.

adjoining homes at the station.* One night they got drunk, and each one was trying to dare the other to come out of his house. When he'd come out, he had a shotgun and shot across. So the next day at the air station Chick Lee said to me, "Oh, my God, Eddie Mulheron is your check pilot today. We were shooting at each other last night, and he's out for my blood. I'm going to call the beach commander and see if he can have it changed for next week, because he's not going to give up an up check."

Paul Stillwell: Why you? Did you get caught in the middle?

Admiral Knoll: I was one of Lee's students, and Mulheron knew it. To remain at Pensacola I had to receive an up check from Mulheron or take two further up checks from two other check pilots.

Paul Stillwell: This was a way of getting back at him.

Admiral Knoll: Sure. He told me ahead of time. Lee said, "If you're going out with Eddie Mulheron, you're not going to get an up." Lee was a hell of a capable pilot. My instructor at NAS Norfolk when I first soloed was Dan Harrigan.† He used to fly one of the planes attached to the dirigible *Los Angeles*. Eddie Mulheron retired early. He had various problems in the Philadelphia area. During the check flight, I never touched the stick. We flew around the course once and landed. He gave me a down check on everything. This meant I had to fly two up checks the following week with two of the toughest check pilots at Pensacola. Some were sympathetic to Mulheron and were ready to protect him.

Chick Lee privately said, "You're not going to win right now. They're closing ranks. You're an ensign, and anything you say about us, you're on their list." Lieutenant Compo was there and Lieutenant Dan Gallery. Lieutenant John Crommelin.‡ All of a sudden, I was in the middle of a fight between Chick Lee and Eddie Mulheron. I

---

* Lieutenant (junior grade) Edward S. Mulheron, USN. Lieutenant (junior grade) Charles L. Lee, USN.
† Lieutenant Daniel W. Harrigan, USN.
‡ Lieutenant George L. Compo, USN. Lieutenant Daniel V. Gallery Jr., USN. Lieutenant John G. Crommelin, USN.

attended a hearing with senior aviators about what happened, and I told the truth. I never mentioned anything about the fight between Lee and Mulheron. They gave me my log of flight operations, and they never recorded in the log except the down check from Mulheron. I was detached from Pensacola and returned to the battleship *Texas* in California. Mulheron's report on the check flight was a lie, because I never flew the plane for him to observe. His friends wanted to avoid this in a senior officer's record.

Paul Stillwell: Did you get a chance to fly the two for up checks?

Admiral Knoll: Yes, I did. Lieutenant Laverents was one of the check pilots.* As an ensign, with this kind of situation, I was disturbed. I realized at that time I was at the center of controversy. I more or less realized, "I don't think I should try to win this argument, because every instructor at the beach knows what happened." The mistake was after the flight with Mulheron I said, "I never was able to demonstrate any of the things on the checklist. He gave me a down check on all items." My report actually said Eddie Mulheron was a liar. All the senior officers knew this, and I was making charges against their friend.

They said, "You never should have told people that you hadn't really touched the stick, just flew around the course." They were full lieutenants, and I was an ensign. So you can readily see where they were going to protect him at a hearing of the board.

I said, "Under the conditions and what has happened, it's better I go back to the fleet rather than try to fight city hall of senior instructors at NAS Pensacola." It was a unique experience that provided me with good background for controversy in the future.

Paul Stillwell: So did you have the opportunity to go back later when different people were there?

Admiral Knoll: About two years later, I had an inquiry from BuNav, asking if I wanted to go back, and I said no. I was happy with main battery in battleships, and that's where I

---

* Lieutenant Arthur Laverents, USNR.

stayed.* I knew my mother and father were happy about it. When I got home, they said, "We prayed you wouldn't finish down there." In those days flying was a little bit hazardous.

Paul Stillwell: Well, you might not have survived the long, rich life you've had if you had stayed in aviation.

Admiral Knoll: In addition, I obtained the feel for aviation and its potential future. I was on flight pay at different times—Patrol Wing Five in Norfolk and most of the time with the Asiatic Fleet in the Far East as aerological officer.

Paul Stillwell: You went from the *Texas* to the *Southard*.† What do you recall about that ship?

Admiral Knoll: I returned to the fleet flag in battleship *Texas* and was there until June 1932 and thence to USS *Southard*.‡ The *Southard* was a four-pipe destroyer, and at that time the nation was in an economy wave. I spent one year on the *Southard*, with Commander Bill Causey, a smart officer and a fine skipper.§ Then the *Southard*, a good destroyer that you'd put in good condition, was sent into reserve at Mare Island, and we transferred to a ship that had been in Mare Island in reserve for a year and a half or so.** This was the USS *Preble*, and it was called the rotating reserve.†† It was the worst fiasco ever conceived, because you put a ship that's in good operating condition in reserve in the Navy yard. The *Preble* had been exposed to weather, and no upkeep for 18 months. Machinery had received no lubrication. All boat falls had to be renewed, all manila lines

---

* The Bureau of Navigation made officer assignments to various duties in the years prior to World War II.
† Ensign Knoll served in the *Southard* (DD-207) in 1932-33; as a lieutenant (j.g.) he was in the *Preble* (DD-345) in 1933-34.
‡ USS *Southard* (DD-207), a *Clemson*-class destroyer, was commissioned 24 September 1919. Displacement was 1,215 tons, length 314 feet, beam of 31 feet, and maximum draft of 9 feet, 4 inches. Top speed was 35 knots. She was armed with four 4-inch guns, one 3-inch gun, and 12 21-inch torpedo tubes.
§ Lieutenant Commander William I. Causey Jr., USN.
** Mare Island Navy Yard, Vallejo, California.
†† USS *Preble* (DD-345), a *Clemson*-class destroyer, was commissioned 19 March 1920. Full-load displacement was 1,700 tons, length 314 feet, beam of 31 feet, and maximum draft of 9 feet. Top speed was 35 knots. She was armed with four 4-inch guns, one 3-inch gun, and 12 21-inch torpedo tubes.

had deteriorated in the weather and had to be renewed. The gunnery department had to be realigned. The money and time involved were exorbitant. It cost more for each ship than if all had stayed in operation. It reduced the number of ships in commission and decreased the need for personnel. In other words, economy of personnel with increased cost for ships.

At the same time, we were promoted from ensign to lieutenant (junior grade). We were getting about $95.00 a month, which was 15% off our ensign pay. We were not paid for over a year and a half the increase in pay due to the rank of lieutenant (junior grade). We were promoted to lieutenant (junior grade) and supposed to spend extra money to put on our extra half stripe. Some of my classmates had half stripes with elastic on the inside, so they put the elastic half stripe above the ensign's stripe. After World War II, Congress finally determined loss of pay for lieutenant (junior grade) was wrong. We finally got back some of that money and said 15% off the pay of lieutenant (junior grade) was the pay you were entitled to, rather than pay of an ensign, less 15%. When we received the back pays for the period 1933-34, we had to pay income tax on the back pay according to the tax rates in effect about 1948.

Paul Stillwell: No justice. Did you get interest then?

Admiral Knoll: Oh, no, but we received some money back. Some of the people had fought for it. When Congress acted on a couple of cases, precedent was set, and it was retroactively applied to all. Not only for the ensigns but for other ranks who had been promoted. More senior people had quite a bit coming. The law had specified there would be no increases in pay for anyone 1933-35; this was interpreted to mean promotions without increase in pay.

Paul Stillwell: What do you remember about promotion exams?

Admiral Knoll: I thought that they were not too difficult. They weren't out to find anything except if you knew your job. In those days they paid more attention if you kept a journal when you were a junior officer, which more or less required that you answer certain questions. They would investigate. It was really to your advantage to have participated in engineering duties, damage control, deck force, and gunnery so you could answer all questions. The more you had participated in all departments, the more it proved that you had the right aptitude and knew the duties of rank. I never had any trouble with these exams.

Paul Stillwell: Had you gotten around engineering enough to know?

Admiral Knoll: Oh, sure. Every place I'd ever been, I had known enough about engineering. I didn't just go out seeking such assignments. I think I had about four tours in engineering in the *Texas* and *Oklahoma* but never in destroyers. As duty officer on each ship a broad knowledge of engineering is acquired.

Paul Stillwell: These destroyers were fairly old by the time you got into them.

Admiral Knoll: Four-pipers that provided valuable service with convoys, etc., during World War I.*

Paul Stillwell: How capable were they?

Admiral Knoll: Everything considered, they were better for their age and good sea ships, with good speed. One thing, you had to be careful you didn't take green seas over the bow, or it would break the bulkhead from the deck near the forward cabin.† That's where the commodore or supply officer would be assigned on these ships. You'd better make sure records were not down near the deck, or they'd all be flooded.

One of my innovations involved the 3-inch/23 antiaircraft gun on the fantail. The ship also had four 4-inch guns and two torpedo mounts with three tubes. The 3-inch gun was for star shells.‡ Firing star shells was done with an elevation. All the smokeless

---

* Both the *Southard* and *Preble* were commissioned after the end of World War I.
† Green water means the ship is taking solid ocean water over the bow, not just sea spray.
‡ A "star shell" is a type of gunnery projectile that detonates in the air and provides a parachute flare for night illumination.

powder from those shells did leave the gun when firing. As the shell was fired, some of the loose powder would foul the gun. A new shell could not be loaded; the breech could not be closed, and then you couldn't fire and provide illumination. Well, I had heard about this. I made sure when I was firing night battle practice with my destroyer that I rigged an extra hose with compressed air from the torpedo compressor with a nozzle on it. An extra member was added to the loading crew, and every time the breech was opened on this 3-inch/23 the compressed air nozzle gave it a blast to blow all the loose powder from the gun. I had no failure. This was written up as an innovation and adopted by other destroyers. We used to put out ordnance bulletins of how to improve your gunnery accuracy and other procedures. I'd have something in these bulletins for improving destroyer gunnery and developed a service reputation as a gunnery officer.

Paul Stillwell: Did you stand deck watches in the destroyer?

Admiral Knoll: Oh, sure. That's where you found out those who got seasick and those who didn't. And those who didn't worked harder than those who did. Normally four hours on watch under way and four hours off. Destroyers were plane guards for *Lexington* and *Saratoga*, and you had to be ready to increase speed on short notice to stay with the carriers.

Paul Stillwell: Did you get seasick?

Admiral Knoll: No. I felt sorry for those who did, though. We had a torpedo officer, and every time we'd come around for a run with the torpedoes, he'd get sick and grab a bucket, so we'd have to go up in the torpedo director and fire the exercise. In self-defense, a lot of us smoked a pipe on the bridge, because if the captain smoked a pipe, you might as well smoke one too so you didn't get sick from his pipe. Under way with lots of fresh air, things weren't too bad. Normally on the bridge relations between the captain, executive officer, and officer of the deck were friendly and cooperative. The esprit de corps on the bridge of a small ship develops a mutual understanding of seamanship and ship handling.

Paul Stillwell: Were the living accommodations fairly cramped?

Admiral Knoll: Not too bad. After all, we had good officers on there, the skipper and the exec and chief engineer like Marty Lawrence and some of those.* They all knew their job and enjoyed being together. The biggest problem came from the wives. They complained if you were a bachelor. Wives thought bachelors should take the duty so their husbands could go home. We were independent and went ashore without worrying about these complaints.

Paul Stillwell: That was their problem, not yours.

Admiral Knoll: I lived through this a long time. It's amazing how these things build up. The same way, even though I had a designation as an aerological officer, not necessarily a line officer in the chain of command, the only time I more or less had nothing but aerological duties was Patrol Wing Five at Naval Air Station Norfolk, where I didn't have any direct line duties.

Paul Stillwell: How were the destroyers in ship handling?

Admiral Knoll: They were not bad. I think they provided a lot of good experience in ship handling. We steamed from San Diego to San Francisco for four days with foghorns sounding day and night. We were in a fleet formation when the cruiser *Chicago* was hit off Point Sur by a diesel-powered cargo ship.† We heard the collision.‡ Under way in ships and with towing spars to keep station and seldom seeing the ship ahead for three or four days was good training for handling a ship with confidence.

    Operating as a plane guard is tedious as the carrier makes quick changes of course and speed, and the carrier never tells you when they're going to increase speed or decrease speed. All of a sudden, more steam is needed, and you haven't had enough time

---

* Lieutenant (junior grade) Martin J. Lawrence, USN, in the *Preble*.
† On 25 October 1933, the heavy cruiser *Chicago* (CA-29) was rammed by the 6,000-ton British commercial oil tanker *Silver Palm* in a heavy fog off Point Sur, California. The collision killed three of the cruiser's officers and left a large gash in the port side of the cruiser's hull, forward of number-one turret.
‡ Knoll was then serving in the *Preble*.

to put more boilers on the line, and the carrier wonders why you're not on station. As officer of the deck you had to be on your toes. As a destroyer, you were supposed to be like an automobile. Whatever they did, you were supposed to be ready to follow. And, as a result, we had different ideas about various skippers on the carriers, who seldom kept you informed as to future moves. Of course, that was before the days that you could talk to each other by phone.* Complete dependence was on flag hoists and flashing lights. We spent a whole summer off San Diego proving or trying to prove that we could talk by telephone to an adjacent ship. For the first test each ship had to have four antennas on each quadrant of the mainmast. Then it was possible to talk to each other by phone from the one bridge to the other at no more than a mile distant. Now we can talk around the world.

Paul Stillwell: You're talking about the *Lexington* and *Saratoga*?

Admiral Knoll: Yes. The carriers seldom even gave us visual signals. They were supposed to, but they were quick to ask, "Why aren't you closing up?" They had no appreciation that we didn't have all the reserve steam or had to light off more boilers on the line. Cruising along at 15 knots, they might tell you, "Be prepared for flight operations." All of a sudden, without further word, the carrier would increase speed, and you had to stay on the quarter, one on each side. It was the worst rat race you've ever seen. It never improved, regardless of the complaints by destroyers. We worked the whole summer trying to speak by voice to each other between two destroyers with RCA engineers, the Bureau of Standards, and Office of Naval Research. We have come a long way since the days in 1933 with limited abilities to talk between ships under way.

Paul Stillwell: Do you have anything else to add on your destroyer service?

Admiral Knoll: Old Gus Wellings was the gunnery officer of the destroyer squadron I was with.† He came aboard while I was the gunnery officer of the *Southard* and later on

---

* This is a reference to voice radio, also known as radiotelephone.
† Lieutenant Augustus J. Wellings, USN, was gunnery officer of Destroyer Squadron One.

in the *Preble*. People who would come aboard to observe you during a gunnery exercise. They were diabolical in my eyes. They weren't interested necessarily in helping you make a good score. They wanted to test your organization and how you reacted to emergencies they created. I'd check over all my directors and make sure everything was working correctly. Then the day of the practice I'd assign a couple of extra gunner's mates to watch these visitors. They guarded the various control boards for my fire control system and put padlocks on important cabinets and stood ready with the key. The gunnery exercise did not have a casualty, and nothing broke down; we made a good score. Gus Wellings said, "How are you going to repair a fuse if it goes out during your practice with all your control panels locked?"

I said, "The gunner's mate was there with the key to make sure that one of your staff didn't take the fuse out and create an emergency during the exercise. I know your tricks."

Gus Wellings was a good friend and able gunnery specialist. He smiled and said nothing more.

In my free time during my destroyer days, I started taking a correspondence course in law. I was a bachelor. When everybody went ashore and at night, I'd spend a couple of hours working assignments for the law course. All of a sudden, one my skippers gave me an unsat fitness report, because during normal liberty for others I was spending my spare time studying law.

Paul Stillwell: Who was the skipper?

Admiral Knoll: Commander Theo Westfall.* I didn't consider it an unsatisfactory fitness report. I was improving my knowledge and everything else. I had a chance to write a statement. Nothing ever happened to it. Instead of other people going home to their families, I was using my spare time to improve myself, and I didn't think I deserved an unsat fitness report. I was always interested in the law to some degree. Another skipper was in the same destroyer division, and he said, "One of my good petty officers is getting a general court-martial. Would you defend him?"

---

* Lieutenant Commander Theo D. Westfall, USN, skipper of the *Preble*.

I said, "I'd be happy to. Tell him to come over and see me."

So he came over to see me, and I talked to him. It was about some scandalous conduct or something at night in a field. He told me of an affair, and it was so vague and inexact that I was sure nothing could be proved. I sent word to Captain Brown in the destroyer tender there; he was president of the general court-martial.[*] I said, "I'll be the counsel for the defense for this case." So I went in and defended the petty officer and got the man acquitted. I defended a couple of more cases just like that in the San Diego destroyer force and obtained acquittals.

Paul Stillwell: How did you manage that?

Admiral Knoll: How did I manage it? For the simple reason that the evidence against him was questionable. I'd say to the witness, "How dark was this night? How far away were you? Where were you?"

"I was on the corner of a building."

"Did you have a flashlight?"

"No."

"This man was doing so-and-so?"

"Yes."

"What did you see?" Well, he tried to say he saw a penis, and I said, "Could you tell at a distance of more than 100 feet in the dark if that was his uniform handkerchief or his penis or something else?" And he'd stop. I said, "Can you?"

He said, "No." And time and again the evidence broke down as soon as you cross-examined the accuser or his witnesses. The evidence wasn't worth a lead cent. I got three different acquittals like that.

Paul Stillwell: Why had they brought the case in the first place?

Admiral Knoll: The people who wrote out the charges never did their job to start with and lacked experience with respect to evidence and truth. I still think the accused—I

---

[*] Captain Alfred W. Brown, USN, was commanding officer of the destroyer tender *Whitney* (AD-4).

don't know, I would think he was a little drunk or had an argument with the accuser. Some shore patrols would go around in those days and try to get someone in trouble. They would see something suspicious, try to make it look bad, and write it up bad or worse than the facts, not realizing they were going to be called up as witnesses and convince intelligent officers what they saw or what happened. They couldn't substantiate their charges. That's the third acquittal.

They weren't all moral turpitude. One of them was desertion, and that's hard to prove. In other words, you'd prove that he tried to get back, and that was nothing to prove he got rid of his uniforms and made no attempt so they couldn't find him. It is hard to prove that a man made up his mind that he was never going to return to the Navy. Drunkenness or a fight with a favorite girlfriend starts the desertion. Then, upon second thought, they find their way back.

Paul Stillwell: Did you ever consider going to law school?

Admiral Knoll: Yes, when I was on the midshipmen's cruise in New England, I went up and talked to the people at Harvard Law and had obtained data from Harvard before going to the academy. The interesting thing, after I got these three acquittals, I got a letter from Captain Brown, president of the court-martial, advising me that I was designated as judge advocate of his court.* So I couldn't take any more cases as defense counsel.

Paul Stillwell: He was tired of getting beat.

Admiral Knoll: He was very pleasant and was most understanding. After all, he said, "You brought out the facts." Things like this I enjoyed doing. They were extracurricular, but after all, I liked helping different people out of difficulty. It didn't do any harm either to my service reputation. Your promotion is based upon your service reputation and doing things for others.

---

* The judge advocate in this case would be the prosecutor.

Interview Number 2 with Rear Admiral Denys W. Knoll, U.S. Navy (Retired)
Place: U.S. Naval Institute, Annapolis, Maryland
Date: Wednesday, 9 May 1984

Paul Stillwell: Admiral, when we finished up yesterday, you were talking about your service in destroyers yesterday. Can you now cover your tour with the Aleutian survey expedition?

Admiral Knoll: Well, yes. I was the gunnery officer on the *Preble* with Commander Westfall.[*] When I had the duty over this weekend, the message came out from Washington asking for officers that were interested in going out on a survey expedition for three or four months in the Aleutians, and it asked for volunteers. Being young and looking for diversity and new experience, as duty officer I proceeded to initiate a message and volunteer. Of course, when the captain came aboard on Monday and found out I had volunteered without talking to him about it, he became a little annoyed. Well, I was his gunnery officer, and we had a good gunnery record. I thought this would give me good experience in a new area. It wouldn't hurt my record and would give me another part of the world that I probably wouldn't see otherwise.

So, sure enough, I was ordered. He tried to get it cancelled, but he didn't. I went to the Aleutian Islands and was senior boat officer of all small surveying boats. I think at that time I sort of opened my eyes to how much we didn't know about weather forecasting, also how much we needed to know about the Aleutians for the future. The commander of the expedition was Rear Admiral Sinclair Gannon. Captain Mallison commanded the flagship, the *Oglala*, a minelayer that was half wood and half steel and loaded with vermin.[†] We were there and surveyed from about the first of May until October 1934. Some work had been done the year before but not much surveying. We

---

[*] Lieutenant Commander Theo D. Westfall, USN.
[†] USS *Oglala* (CM-4) was a former commercial steamer commissioned in the Navy in 1917, renamed *Shawmut* in 1918. She was involved in the North Sea Mine Barrage of World War I. Later she was converted to an aviation tender. The ship was renamed *Oglala* in 1928. The ship was 386 feet long and displaced 3,746 tons. Her top speed was 14 knots. Commander William T. Mallison, USN, was skipper.

took about eight small sounding boats housed in the *Oglala*. They were 40-foot motor launches all rigged with canopy and bridge structure. They were ideally equipped for surveying, the use of sextants for taking your angles as soundings were recorded. I was the senior one.

The interesting incident was up to that time the water between all of the major Aleutian Islands with the change of tide looked like a tidal wave in shoal water. There was the wildest tide change going through these passes. It looked like there was no safe navigable water through straits. The only charts we had to refer to were the ones that were given the U.S.A. when Seward bought Alaska from the Russians.[*] Their locations were within a mile or so of their true geodetic positions. There had been nothing done to survey that area since the purchase of Alaska.

Again, if we got in a war with Japan, we had to know these islands and be able to use them. At that time Kulak Bay and Adak was just another piece of land and water. So early in the affair I started surveying the coastline of Adak and down around Kagalaska, and the straits between Adak and Tanaga, and Adak and Kagalaska. As I went up and down these straits, to my amazement, I found out the water in the center of the strait between these islands was 20 to 30 fathoms deep, and no shallow water near shoreline. The impression with the change of tide between the Bering Sea and the Pacific Ocean never gave any indication there was anything but rocks and shoals between islands. I remember I took soundings up and down, and when I returned to *Oglala* I talked to Lieutenant Kelly, the senior survey officer aboard.[†]

I talked to Captain Mallison and showed him my chart, and then I went up and talked to Admiral Sinclair Gannon and showed him. I said, "There's good water between these islands. We haven't wire-dragged it, but there are no pinnacles in the middle here." I outlined the shoreline, and I showed them the soundings. In fact, today I have a photograph at home of the original boat chart that was used when the soundings were entered. And on the side of it I have a copy of the current chart that was given to me. I

---

[*] In 1867 Secretary of State William H. Seward engineered the U.S. purchase of the territory of Alaska from Russia for $7.2 million. At the time it was labeled as "Seward's Folly." History has since given Seward credit for an intelligent move. Alaska became a state in 1959.
[†] Lieutenant Thomas E. Kelly, USN.

did the first sounding, and all these soundings are reproduced on the charts being used today.

Well, when Admiral Gannon heard that, he said, "Go tell Captain Mallison that we're getting under way the next morning. We'll do a little reconnaissance."

I said, "Okay."

He said, "You have no doubt about the water?"

I said, "No, fine."

So we got under way from Kulak Bay in Adak with the *Oglala*, and some of the other boats were along the shoreline taking soundings. I was up on the bridge to more or less see, and as soon as we started heading for the strait between Adak and Kagalaska, Admiral Gannon said, "Admiral Knoll will take us through." And so, of course, we were watching the Fathometer to make sure it checked against my soundings made with the sounding boat. We just had regular old sounding leads with the wax loading at the end and had to crank it up and down by hand. People always cranked them; others did plotting. The weather was lousy all the time. You always had foggy weather and windy weather. We did a good job. Anyway, I went down through the strait to the Pacific and reversed course and brought it to Kulak. The trip checked out the soundings on my chart. Again, as I say, I was damn sure I had enough knowledge to know how safe it was, that the ship would not go aground.

Later on we had a critique at the Naval Air Station San Diego the following summer. Admiral Gannon gave the surveying officers special recognition for the work done in preparation for future operations. The fleet was invited to be there, and we had a presentation, and Gannon talked about what we had encountered up there and the foul operating conditions. I was with him, and then he told some of these stories about how we found navigable water that everybody, even the fishermen around there, wouldn't navigate because of the recurring tidal waves passing between the Bering Sea and the North Pacific.

Paul Stillwell: Did you tie these soundings in with celestial so you'd know the exact position?

Admiral Knoll: There were other people that established geodetic positions in the Aleutians. It required the whole season to get a good geodetic position. Dutch Harbor was the first geodetic position. You set up a tent with a man on watch all night to take 24 time angles on a third-order star. The trouble was time and again one was able to sight that star only three or four times due to the fog. So kept working and working every night to get enough clearance of fog in order to establish a new accurate geodetic position. A marker was then embedded in concrete for reference.

Paul Stillwell: In 1929 there had been an aerial survey that Admiral Radford was involved in.*

Admiral Knoll: The aerial part, but we did the hydrographic survey, together with some shoreline work, and established a series of geodetic positions.

Paul Stillwell: I was going to ask, was there any aviation tied in with your work?

Admiral Knoll: No. It was interesting. Cat Brown had command of a seagoing tug, and Bill Kanakanui had command of another.† These tugs augmented the sounding boats and ran different sounding lines, using targets that we built on the shoreline. Instead of building signals on the beach made of wood, we selected prominent rock formations and painted targets on the rocks. The locations of these targets were cut in so sounding boats and tugs could use them for running sounding lines. Such positions had to be selected so they would not give "revolving" positions when used to plot the soundings. It was good experience, and accurate charts were achieved.

Paul Stillwell: Did you enjoy the work?

---

* Lieutenant Commander Arthur W. Radford, USN, later a four-star admiral.
† Lieutenant Charles R. Brown, USN, a naval aviator, commanded the USS *Gannet* (AM-41), a minesweeper designated for duty with aircraft. Lieutenant (junior grade) William A. Kanakanui, USN, commanded the USS *Tanager* (AM-5), a minesweeper.

Admiral Knoll: Oh, yes. The worst experience I ever had was on a 40-foot motor launch. They're very safe, thank God, and the length of the boat was covered with a canopy. For lunch we'd go to the mouth of a stream and catch salmon to fry, together with canned baked beans or something, and then continue with sounding. This one day we left the *Oglala* and headed for one of the narrow straits to do some soundings. We had about eight people in the boat. The plotting was done for each sounding, which I supervised, and bearings were taken with sextants. Another man acted as recorder.

We were in a dense fog when, without warning, the launch hit a tide rip, a wall of water three or four feet high. The boat rolled over on beam's end practically. We all hung on. We all wore different layers of waterproof clothing. When we'd come back at night, we could erect stiff clothing on the deck beside our bunk. They would stand right up due to the heavy moisture in them. A good deal of equipment was lost overboard while the launch was on beam's end. We had been away from the ship less than an hour and a half. We had to re-equip. Forty-footers were excellent seaworthy boats, or it would have capsized. These boats could take a lot of punishment; they had many watertight compartments built into the hull.

Paul Stillwell: Did you live in the ship/?

Admiral Knoll: Yes, we lived in the *Oglala*. We had bunks in the old mine storage area. It was a minelayer with a big storage area, which was an ideal place. It was divided into office space for plotting work, bunkrooms, and other administrative stores. Some of the skippers, like Cat Brown, would come aboard from the *Gannet* and talk to us about the articles he was writing for the Naval Institute and reminded us as lieutenants (junior grade) that none of us would ever achieve promotion beyond lieutenant commander.[*]

Paul Stillwell: He's a very colorful character. What was his purpose as an aviator in being along on this survey in the Aleutians?

---

[*] Lieutenant Charles R. Brown, USN.

Admiral Knoll: This was the early idea, for a year or so, that aviators should have some handling of ships. The *Gannet* was configured as a small seaplane tender at that time, but planes were not on there. Seaplane tenders had aviators as commanding officers.

Paul Stillwell: Did he have a part in the survey?

Admiral Knoll: Yes, the *Gannet* did some of the surveying with their Fathometer and helped transport heavy cargo. They all could go out and run different sounding lines in the open area. As a result, we developed quite a bit of Aleutian area that season, from Atka westward to Tanaga. From this data some very good charts were published and used during World War II.

Paul Stillwell: Did you have a drafting capability on board the ship to make the charts?

Admiral Knoll: No, we collected and recorded all basic data, boat charts, the rough charts, geographical info, photos that were needed by the Hydrographic Office to produce smooth charts.

Paul Stillwell: I'm interested in just how you did this. Did you take old charts and make corrections there on board the *Oglala*?

Admiral Knoll: There were no former charts for this area. We did make rough charts on special paper. The paper was backed so when you'd get out there in all that fog and rain, it still didn't absorb moisture. Boats recorded all these bearings in special books, and the geodetic location of each target was recorded so they could be reproduced in Washington. The trouble is, when you tried shoreline with a plane table, it was fantastically inaccurate.

Paul Stillwell: What do you remember about Gannon from that period? Did he have a special qualification for this type of work?

Admiral Knoll: No, not really, but I always like to tell the story of his giving commands. Sinclair Gannon had been the commandant of midshipmen when I was a midshipman.* I had dated his daughter Jane from time to time. He'd call an individual in and discuss something with the idea of giving him some kind of a task to do that couldn't necessarily be done right away: "I want something like this, so-and-so." About two days later, he'd send for you. He would say, "Knoll, the other day I talked to you about so and so. I'm not worrying about having an answer yet. What did I tell you to do?"

I said, "Well, Captain, you told me thus and so, and this is what I'm doing about it." Then he'd start smiling and say, "Don't be on the defensive. This was only reassuring me, but over the years I've developed this habit. When I want an important job done, I assign it to somebody. Then, after a day or so when this individual has had a chance to evaluate what he is going to do, I like to get him in and find out if he actually is doing what I wanted him to do. I found that 50% of the time that when someone doesn't do what I wanted him to do, it is because I didn't give him the correct instructions." This is an interesting exercise for someone who's going to give commands or ask to have a task done. He said, "This is part of being a leader. You have to train yourself that you're giving proper clear instructions when you want someone to do the right thing."

I enjoyed being up there on that expedition. It was a real experience. On the way up we stopped at Ketchikan and Juneau and stopped again there on return. I've been up there again in the last five or seven yeas to see the development there, cruise in Glacier Bay. It takes you an hour to go in and find the glacier. When I passed there in '33, it was practically out of the straits near Cape Spenser. When you see how the Taku Glacier and the Mendenhall Glacier near Juneau have receded in 50 years, you are stunned. You could walk out there in 1934 from downtown. Now you have to take a bus. You have a sense of history and geographical change.

Paul Stillwell: Why did you need a flag officer for an expedition like that?

---

* Captain Sinclair Gannon, USN, served from 1925 to 1928 as the Naval Academy's commandant of midshipmen.

Admiral Knoll: The importance of the expedition and the number of ships involved, I think, gave it emphasis. In 1932, they had a small group, and Captain Lockhart had gone at that the time as the weather officer.* Tim Rafferty was the weather officer on this one in 1934.† It was an exciting experience to be anchored close to a bluff, deep water, and have winds of 60 miles an hour coming from the side of the hill and other phenomena. We would take turns as officer of the deck on the *Oglala*. We put one anchor out at 90 fathoms and another one underfoot. The ship would yaw back and forth with nothing but rock on the bottom. There were a lot of experiences that you'd never get any other place. You were in the wilderness, in a primitive area. There aren't many places left. During any weather with high winds, the ship would have watches the same as under way with steam to the throttle. If the ship started to drag anchor, we were ready to get under way or take the strain off the anchor chain by using the engine.

Paul Stillwell: How can you anchor on a rock bottom?

Admiral Knoll: Well, if there's enough rocks, you get an anchor caught in crevasses. That's why you lay out about 90 fathom on your bow anchor and then the other anchor underfoot, so you're going to drag a little bit. Once in a while, we'd just get under way and drop it again. You'd just keep steam to the throttle if you did start dragging. By using the pelorus for bearings, you checked your position and knew where to move for a safe mooring.‡

Paul Stillwell: Did you have williwaws during that?

Admiral Knoll: Yes, almost once a week—you never saw anything so unusual as williwaws. In those days we didn't have radar, and when you went up through the Inland Passage in the fog, you had to rely on soundings and the echo from sounding boards

---

* At the time he was Lieutenant Commander Wilber Lockhart, USN, attached to the 13th Naval District.
† Lieutenant Thomas J. Rafferty, USN.
‡ A pelorus is a combination of a compass repeater and stand, usually mounted on the wing of a ship's bridge in a place that has a wide arc of vision. The compass is usually about chest high to facilitate the use of a bearing circle or alidade top take azimuth bearings on other ships or on objects ashore.

when using the whistle. Navigating without radar in narrow passes in a fog was excellent training and made competent seamen for the future.

Paul Stillwell: But you didn't know what you were missing, though, by not having radar.

Admiral Knoll: No one thought something like radar was a possibility. We developed a type of caution and were always alert for every emergency. Seamen today never acquired that attribute.

Paul Stillwell: What do you remember about Mallison?

Admiral Knoll: Not too much. He was a good skipper, and I always had a good relationship with him. It was an excellent experience. It excited my interest in meteorology, seamanship, and the opportunities for adventure for a naval officer. From there I returned to battleships and gunnery.

Paul Stillwell: *Oklahoma.*[*]

Admiral Knoll: *Oklahoma*, yes. Prior to reporting, I had temporary duty in the Canal Zone. Captain Wilbur Rice Van Auken was in command.[†] The ship had been in the Atlantic for a fleet exercise with other battleships. I joined the *Oklahoma* after it transited the Panama Canal into the Pacific to return to California. I had temporary duty on the staff of Commander Ainsworth at the naval communications station.[‡] We were a security group. This was part of a test that would evaluate how long it would take to send the whole fleet from the Atlantic with the canal closed to all commercial traffic. The one thing for which they were warned was the Communist threat in Panama and the Panama Canal Zone.

---

[*] USS *Oklahoma* (BB-37) was commissioned 2 May 1916. She had a standard displacement of 27,500 tons, was 583 feet long, and 95 feet in the beam. Her top speed was 20.5 knots. Her main battery comprised ten 14-inch guns. She later capsized at her berth during the Japanese attack on Pearl Harbor in December 1941.

[†] Captain Wilbur Rice Van Auken, USN, commanded the battleship *Oklahoma* (BB-37) from 1 May 1934 to 1 November 1935.

[‡] Commander Walden L. Ainsworth, USN, stationed at Balboa, Panama, later a World War II flag officer.

The first ships that transited the canal before the fleet could go through were four minesweepers, two abreast in both sides of each set of locks and often stretches of the canal to make sure there was no sabotage, such as mines or foreign objects. The biggest problem was getting enough pilots returned from the West Coast to the Atlantic entrance so other ships could transit without delay. The entire fleet went through the canal in about 32 to 36 hours—fantastic.[*] There was no liberty on the Atlantic side prior to transit.

Mame Kelly and many of her girls were annoyed because many did not arrive in Panama from New York in time to entertain the fleet. Mame Kelly had to concentrate all girls on the Pacific side, because the time that the fleet was due in Panama was closely held. The fact that it would quickly transit without a stop on the Atlantic side was also closely held. As a result, the ships with girls did not arrive until the fleet had started the transit. Mame Kelly and her sister used to have some of the big brothels around New Orleans. She had a beautiful cane studded with diamonds. She was a character, a madam of the old school. When she heard the fleet might be due soon in Panama, she called us every day at the Balboa YMCA, where three or four of us were housed. We had daily meetings over security incident to our reply to Mame Kelly about the surprise transit. We said, "We don't know what you're talking about."

She was suspicious and pestered us. When the ships came through and fouled up all her planning to take care of sailors on both coasts, she was really mad. It was strange that she knew who to call and try to find out classified info. Perhaps a special group on temporary orders attracted attention.

Paul Stillwell: The fleet visited New York in 1934.[†] Was the canal transit after that visit?

Admiral Knoll: Yes.

---

[*] News reports of the period indicated that 79 warships of the U.S. Fleet completed the Atlantic-to-Pacific canal transit on 25 October 1934 following an elapsed time of 42 hours. The fleet's transit of the canal from Pacific to Atlantic on 23-24 April 1934 had involved 110 ships and took 47 hours.

[†] On 31 May 1934, President Franklin D. Roosevelt was on board the heavy cruiser *Indianapolis* (CA-35) when he reviewed the ships of the U.S. Fleet as they steamed into New York City.

Paul Stillwell: Had you requested orders to battleship duty?

Admiral Knoll: No. I thought that I might return to destroyers. But my old friend Charlie Fischer, class of 1899, would say, "Always stay on the big ships.[*] You might meet the right people and get exposed to the big Navy. Your small boat work was with the destroyer; you're ideal to go back." So I ended up having turret four on *Oklahoma* and doing a lot of work with damage control.

Commander Schrader was the gunnery officer in the *Oklahoma*.[†] Individuals normally had the job about two years. You just couldn't assemble a good group quickly and get good scores. On the *Oklahoma* with me there was Frank Tibbitts as the plotting room officer, and we worked very closely.[‡] We generally would go to the other battleships to spot. Each foretop was different; some of those foretops bounced back and forth quite a bit while the guns were going off.

I had three guns in turret four. You only had two hoists; the center gun was loaded by passing shell and powder over from side trays to the center gun. The crew really worked as a team. They finally did finish one exercise without any remnants, proving the powder and shell were loaded in record time. The only time in history that turret four in *Oklahoma* completed a major gunnery exercise without remnants. I couldn't do anything about the loading as a turret officer; it proved the daily drills had developed the teamwork to load the guns with two hoists. Guns have to be loaded in a few minutes, then fired, and then quickly reloaded once "Commence firing" is ordered. The loading crew works as a team without verbal orders.

Paul Stillwell: But you had something do to about it training, though.

Admiral Knoll: In training them, I emphasized that it could be done. I said, "We're going to do it so we can prove it will work as designed. Don't worry about how fast you're doing it. Keep working as a team to get it over there." The emphasis was on getting each loading in a minimum time. Turret four had to be loaded and ready to fire

---

[*] Lieutenant Commander Charles H. Fischer, USN (Ret.), lived in Erie, Pennsylvania, Knoll's hometown.
[†] Lieutenant Commander Albert E. Schrader, USN.
[‡] Lieutenant Frank P. Tibbitts, USN.

with the other three turrets; if not on time, the other turrets would be fired, and turret four would have remnants. Actual firing was done by the ship's gunnery department in the conning tower near the bridge.

Paul Stillwell: Was there a separate projectile device for the center gun?

Admiral Knoll: Yes, there was a rammer for loading the projectile in the center gun, but the powder bags had to be passed from a side tray to the center tray for loading.

Paul Stillwell: I see.

Admiral Knoll: You had to have a ram to load each projectile, because the ram is at the after end of the tray.

Captain Van Wilbur Auken, commanding officer of the *Oklahoma* at that time, said, "Well, we made a record."[*] I took an interest in things of that nature, as well as helping develop esprit de corps in the whole turret crew.

Now, Captain Van Auken could be one of the meanest commanding officers in the world, and he would haze you to the nth degree. You would be the officer of the deck, and he wouldn't come into the pilothouse. He's say, "Are we in position? Where is the ship ahead?"

My reply, "It's right up there, Captain."

"I can't see it."

My reply, "We are right in position; there's the towing buoy." It was foggy, but I'd never let him get me excited. I enjoyed just seeing him getting all excited and me not get excited. This happened a couple of times, and then he selected three officers who wanted to be officers of the deck in bad weather. Every time the weather got bad and *Oklahoma* was in a fleet formation, he'd say, "Put on the first team." The first team was Joe Martin, who ranked with the class of '20; Frank Tibbitts, the class of '25; and myself.[†] I was a lieutenant (j.g.); Tibbitts and Martin were full lieutenants. We would be officers of the deck every eight hours until the weather got better. Well, that didn't do

---

[*] Captain Wilbur Rice Van Auken, USN, commanded the battleship *Oklahoma* (BB-37) from 1 May 1934 to 1 November 1935.
[†] Lieutenant Stanley E. Martin, USN.

our record any harm. There were 27 other officers whom he did not trust, and some of them had to be junior officer of the deck, even though they were senior to me. All because the captain did not get me excited. Fortunately, sometimes I wasn't too sure the *Texas* was still exactly ahead as guide, but I wasn't going to give him the satisfaction of a doubt.

There are the things you realize at times. I always have tried to be realistic. You're never going to find something perfect. And I've seen how different commanding officers have handled delinquents. Captain Van Auken would scare the hell out of people. You can correct this. Without getting people excited and creating a dangerous reaction, you can get more performance.

This one individual was a good man, excellent in the fire control division of the gunnery department. His brother was also in the fire control, and they did terrific jobs and were very reliable. The older man had been in the Navy a lot longer, probably 10 or 12 years older than the other. He had been in Panama, and he got stinking drunk, and they had to bring him back to the ship. He'd been to mast more than once before, so Wilbur Rice Van Auken—he just had a bad stomach, and he was mean all the time. Everybody knew it, and he knew it. So he got them up to mast. His brother came there with him, and the chaplain was up there, the division officer, and executive officer. The skipper said, "You've been up here now at different times for the same offense. The last time you were up here, I told you that if you came up here again with this offense, since you can't behave yourself ashore, we'll have to get you out of the Navy, even though you're a good man and you've got good experience, you've been in for a couple of tours. We're happy to have you, but we can't tolerate this. What happened this time?"

"I went ashore with my brother, and he didn't take care of me."

Everybody sort of held their breath and didn't know which way Van Auken was going to jump. He said, "Well, I told you the next time you came up here, I was going to lower the boom on you. I'm not going to tolerate this any longer. So what do you think I ought to do about that?"

This older fellow looked at him, looked as meek as he could be, and said, "Well, Captain, I didn't keep my promise. I don't know why you want to keep yours."

You never saw a group of people smother their laughing and hold their breath. The captain let him off with a warning, with no overt reaction to the remark.

Paul Stillwell: That's a good story.

Admiral Knoll: No one present would have had the nerve to say a word.

I'll tell you another one about Captain Van Auken. When I had left the destroyers in 1934, Commodore Willson, a very nice, capable officer, was the squadron commander.* I said, "Commodore, I'm from Erie, Pennsylvania. The Navy is going to build a gunboat named *Erie*. How do I go about it so I can get my mother to christen the *Erie*?"

He said, "I don't know. You have to be a pretty good politician or have influence."

I said, "Well, I have Erie friends I can line up to help. Whom do I work with in the Navy Department?"

He said, "That's hard to say, but my father is on the General Board. I'll mention it to him. You'll have to do the real work."†

I said, "All right, I'll work on it."

He said, "Let me know if I can help you."

I got in touch with certain individuals in Erie who wrote to the Navy Department, gave my mother's background as descendant of one of the older families and her work with social programs and different developments in Erie—a logical candidate. I wrote to the congressman and other people with political influence. I thought it would be correct to go tell Wilbur Rice Van Auken was I was doing, that I was getting involved with politics for this purpose. I went in and told him what I was planning to do. He almost read me the riot act. He said, "Wait a second. You're way over your head. You're no politician. You don't want to get involved with this stuff. Just forget all about it. You can't do anything about this. Just forget about it."

"Thank you very much."

---

* Captain James D. Willson, USN, Commander Destroyer Squadron One.
† The roster for the General Board at that time did not contain an officer named Willson.

So about three months later, I went in, and I said, "Captain, I've been invited to be in New York for the christening of the gunboat *Erie*. My mother's going to christen it."

He said, "Why didn't you come and tell me so I could have helped you?" He did not remember having told me to cease and desist. I received the leave for the occasion.*

Paul Stillwell: Earlier you mentioned damage control in the *Oklahoma*.

Admiral Knoll: The *Oklahoma* at one time was in the forefront of improved damage control. Air tests had been made of all compartments, and drills were held to correct simulated battle damage, which was not an easy job. We had a good first lieutenant and a good assistant, and I had the fourth division.† We did a lot of work, because the older ships were like a sieve and could not pass air tests. The older ships had been remodeled a couple of times and modernized with slight attention to watertight integrity. They removed the cage masts and installed better masts.‡ The yard never gave a damn whether a watertight compartment resulted after its work. So we had a progressive affair that improved watertight spaces considerably.

When we talk about underway replenishment today, the *Oklahoma* was probably the most sensitive battleship we had in terms of ship handling. It had temperamental characteristics. It was finally changed after I left, but if you used more than five degrees of rudder for a turn, it would begin to spin, unless it was countered with a reverse of 15 degrees. I remember I had the deck going through the canal in 1936. As we approached Gatun Locks, the pilot said, "Right standard rudder," and I quickly said, "Rudder amidships."

I told the pilot, "For God's sake, this ship will spin out of control in close quarters." The captain was there, and he knew. I said, "Don't give any more than five degrees. When you get it to turn, you have to meet it with 15 degrees to prevent spinning." It had a dangerous characteristic around the skeg forward of the rudder. If

---

* The gunboat *Erie* (PG-50) was launched 29 January 1936 at the New York Navy Yard, sponsored and christened by Mrs. Ida May Illig Knoll. The ship was commissioned 1 July 1936.
† In those days the first lieutenant was a department head, responsible for the physical upkeep of the ship and for damage control.
‡ The major modernization and rebuilding of the *Oklahoma* took place at the Philadelphia Navy Yard from 1927 to 1929.

you gave it too much rudder, she couldn't meet it and steady on a new course. Something like this made the *Oklahoma* undesirable for underway replenishment, where you steam at 12 knots and maintain your course with very little rudder. If you've got an inexperienced officer at the conn, you could have a collision.* Having handled various ships enough, I knew this characteristic of *Oklahoma*. I knew it better than Van Auken did, and I believe he realized it.

Paul Stillwell: Why do you say that?

Admiral Knoll: Well, he never entered the pilothouse and took the conn. As officer of the deck, I handled her a lot more than he ever did. He would stand on the wing of the bridge and harass the officer of the deck. The executive officer normally brought us to anchor. The captain trusted the few of us who knew the ship's handling characteristics. We proved that we could handle it. Joe Martin, Frank Tibbitts, and myself were officers of the deck that he trusted in fleet maneuvers.

Paul Stillwell: Are you saying that you actually did underway replenishment, or this would have been—

Admiral Knoll: No, we did not. I said this would be one of the hazards if we ever tried underway replenishment with the *Oklahoma* or other older ships with poor ship handling and rudder. Underway replenishment required a lot of refinements and new operating doctrine until it became safe and reliable.

Paul Stillwell: But you didn't during that time.

Admiral Knoll: No, no. The Navy did some testing. The *Oklahoma* did not participate the time we operated near Midway. A tanker came along, and the flagship queried her captain: "What are you doing?"

    He said, "Just peddling oil."

---

* The individual with the conn—normally an officer—directs the ship's movements in course and speed.

The fleet commander recognized the opportunity and announced, "We're going to have some practice. Come alongside." Everybody came topside to witness whether the ships would bump. The weather was ideal, seas calm. A fleet tanker was in formation. It was probably the first time the battleships approached a tanker to see how close they could steam and have control for replenishment.* Battleships under way went alongside a tanker and did some refueling. The older skippers were alarmed when ships under way at 12 knots and at a distance of 150-200 feet passed hoses for refueling.

Paul Stillwell: Describe that.

Admiral Knoll: There was little advance word that such an evolution was planned. Up to that time, big ships under way never got that close to another ship and still had good control. We just approached slowly to see if the tanker could pass a hose to the battleship. This was the beginning of a fleet operation that added greatly to readiness. Today it is standard practice and was an asset for World War II.

Paul Stillwell: Did you work on that quite a bit?

Admiral Knoll: Not much at the time. The idea was practical, and doctrine was developed and equipment provided for future operations.

Paul Stillwell: I can understand the reluctance that your people had back in the '30s, because it just hadn't been done.

Admiral Knoll: It was never thought to be possible. For old hands it was dangerous.

Paul Stillwell: What can you recall about formation steaming with the battleships?

---

* Beginning in 1924, the battleship *Arizona* (BB-39) did some refueling at sea experiments in which the tanker towed the battleship astern and sent oil through a hose that trailed from one ship to the other. See Paul Stillwell, *Battleship Arizona: An Illustrated History* (Annapolis: Naval Institute Press, 1991), page 82.

Admiral Knoll: Everything was without radar. We had to rely on special towing spars to keep position in low visibility. We generally had to stay about 700 yards from the ship ahead, and you relied on everybody not changing speed or course without giving the signal and receiving acknowledgement before executing.

Paul Stillwell: When the *Oklahoma* got around to the Pacific, were you home-ported then at San Pedro?

Admiral Knoll: Yes, yes.

Paul Stillwell: What do you remember about that as a fleet base?

Admiral Knoll: In those days, it was a good fleet base, lots of activity. I would say as a whole, the most realistic thing that ever happened was the fact that a maximum part of the Battle Force of the U.S. Fleet was based at Southern California. We went out regularly and carried out a quarterly schedule without having missed any real days on account of bad weather, which you could never do in the Atlantic. So we had good weather, and we got in all our gunnery practices. Occasionally all ships had to get under way on short notice and go to sea, frequently without the skipper and senor officers aboard. Admiral Reeves liked such surprise maneuvers, and we had good skippers.[*]

We tried to have all kinds of realistic practices. We were tough on each other about observing, and on night battle you'd go out and see how well you could do. I went to the *West Virginia* one night to observe. A star shell was fired at the wrong angle and hit the end of one of the guns of *West Virginia*'s 16-inch turret number two. The *West Virginia* had to go to Bremerton to have the gun replaced.[†]

Paul Stillwell: When was this?

Admiral Knoll: I was observing there on a visit from the *Oklahoma* in 1935 or '36. You never saw so many sparks. No injuries. Someone had trained the turret to observe with

---

[*] Admiral Joseph M. Reeves, USN, served as Commander in Chief U.S. Fleet from 15 June 1934 to 24 June 1936.
[†] Puget Sound Navy Yard, Bremerton, Washington.

guns raised in the air, and at the same time a 5-inch gun in the upper deck fired the star shell. It was a night battle practice. If all safety precautions for firing arcs had been observed, it would not have happened. It hit about two feet from the muzzle of the right gun of number-two turret. It made a big dent and displaced the liner of the gun. If the turret had been fired, it could have been a serious accident.

The families could normally get home for weekends. Then we'd go to sea for the five days of operations in that whole area. I think it did a great deal to have the fleet ready for World War II. An ideal operating area was near San Clemente or the Channel Islands. The smaller ships were based in San Diego, and the battleships were in Long Beach and San Pedro. They finally developed an extensive breakwater for the battleships and the aircraft carriers near Long Beach. We received a lot of good experience getting under way in formation and attempting amphibious landings from motor launches. The weather and the relatively calm Pacific were really great assets for the training of the fleet in Southern California during the 1930s.

Paul Stillwell: Who were some of your shipmates that you remember from the *Oklahoma*?

Admiral Knoll: Well, I mentioned Joe Martin and Frank Tibbitts. Tommy Booth was one of the aviators, and Greer was another.* After Van Auken we had an excellent captain, Hall, and at that time we had Vice Admiral Pluvy Kempff, who was Commander Battleships Battle Force.† He was in command of the battleship *Nevada*, in which I made a midshipman cruise in 1927.‡

Paul Stillwell: What do you recall about Kempff?

---

* Ensign Charles T. Booth II, USN, later a flag officer. Lieutenant (junior grade) Julian D. Greer, USN.
† Captain William Alden Hall, USN, commanded the battleship *Oklahoma* (BB-37) from 1 November 1935 to 25 June 1937. Vice Admiral Clarence S. Kempff, USN.
‡ Captain Clarence S. Kempff, USN, commanded the battleship *Nevada* (BB-36) from 11 June 1926 to 20 September 1927. In the previous interview Knoll said his 1927 cruise was on board the battleship *Florida* (BB-30).

Admiral Knoll: Well, he was the most practical officer you ever met. He could put on a clean white uniform, and within a half hour he'd be so messed up with his smoking. I remember later on, when he was a vice admiral, we went to some kind of a party. I guess it was at his house, and his wife made the jesting remark, "The admiral is all cleaned up and looking nice. Take a good look. I don't know how long it'll be, and he'll be messed up."

We discussed with him when he was selecting his staff.* He said, "I've got the most realistic and the most capable bunch of officers in the fleet." He did. Everybody on his staff were pros and practical officers, and he relied on them. He was that kind of an officer. He knew what had to be done. He knew how to select the right people, and he let them advise him what to do, and they wrote the right kind of orders. He was always approachable and a jolly fellow. The whole operation showed it was a well-organized thing. You can't do these things alone. When you have the right staff to help you, you can conquer the world. Nothing is impossible.

Paul Stillwell: He had a good sense of humor, didn't he?

Admiral Knoll: Oh, terrific.

Paul Stillwell: Do you recall any examples of that?

Admiral Knoll: He had a parrot, I think, in 1927, and we were in bad weather. This was the midshipmen's cruise, and he was more concerned about how the parrot in his cabin was taking it than whether the crew were getting seasick. The mess attendant brought the parrot on the bridge.

He was a realist, he knew his business, and he wasn't pompous. He was an officer you knew you'd go through hell with. He had that temperament. For midshipmen on watch under way he had a mess attendant who brought huge plates of butter-cinnamon

---

* Kempff was promoted to vice admiral in early 1936 when he moved up from command of Battleship Division One to become Commander Battleships Battle Force. His flagship as type commander was the *West Virginia* (BB-48).

toast from the pantry to the bridge, so each midshipman on the morning watch could eat morning toast with him.

Paul Stillwell: What qualities were considered in an officer of the deck in the mid-1930s?

Admiral Knoll: Well, I think I've mentioned before that if you were the officer of the deck on a battleship, and if you were the junior officer of the deck on the forward gangway, your reputation was how you handled all the official calls on the admiral and the commanding officer, such as the right number of side boys, the right honors, calling the correct barge or gig alongside for the departure of guests. As officer of the deck of a smart ship, you kept everything in order. No Irish pennants, boats clean, flags two-blocked.* The officer of the deck made sure there was no loitering or skylarking near cabins. The orderlies were in uniform, and they were alert. You didn't have to be tough about it, but you had to be effective, such as handling the liberty parties, maintaining boat schedules, not getting excited, making sure you got results.

Paul Stillwell: I was thinking more in terms of under way.

Admiral Knoll: Under way, as officer of the deck, you were the boss. The main thing was that you had to be sure everyone knew his responsibilities, that you gave the right orders to the helm, knew how to keep the correct distance with the stadimeter, they knew when to post the lookouts, particularly in low visibility, when a lookout was stationed in the bow. In general, the main thing was keeping the signal bridge alive to any kind of signaling area and making sure you're in position. You had to keep the captain informed of any change of course, and all ships sighted, and when land was sighted, and anything unusual.

Paul Stillwell: How responsive was the engineering plant?

---

* "Irish Pennant" is Navy slang for a loose piece of line left adrift. It can also be used in a figurative sense to refer to something that is sloppy because it hasn't been completed properly. Two-blocked means hoisted all the way up.

Admiral Knoll: The relationship with the duty officer in the engine room was always good. If you knew a change was coming up, you alerted them when you were to increase power or some important event. Of course, the *Oklahoma* had one advantage. She had reciprocating engines, which could respond to a quick increase in speed. I had the deck, and Commander T. J. Doyle was the navigator.* We were off the Monterey area when we heard the dirigible *Macon* send an SOS and might crash.† Commander Doyle picked it up on our direction finder, and we left the battle line and outdistanced all battleships heading toward the *Macon*'s site. All craft ultimately appeared, and *Oklahoma* resumed position in the battle line.

The officer in tactical command had released the ships to stand by for rescues. I promptly called the engine room, and this proved the advantage of the reciprocating engine over the steam turbine. I turned and headed in the direction indicated by the direction finder, and we told other ships the last bearing we had when we received the SOS. Within five minutes we were 1,000 yards ahead of all the other battleships heading for *Macon*, because the navigator was on the bridge, it was a beautiful day, and I had the deck. We each did what was expected. I just went up to flank speed and headed for *Macon*. We never quite got over there, because we found out other ships got there, but we were heading for it about ten miles distant before it went down off the coast of California.

Paul Stillwell: Now, in your turret office role, what were your casualty procedures?

Admiral Knoll: Many drills were conducted daily, and you knew all the safety precautions. You always had to be watching the crews during their drills, as well as when the guns were being fired. This one time, one gun captain of the starboard gun, number-two turret, there was some kind of a misfire in practice, and he proceeded to try

---

* Commander Thomas J. Doyle Jr., USN.
† On 12 February 1935, while participating in fleet maneuvers, the dirigible *Macon* (ZRS-5) encountered a sudden updraft. Structural members failed, gas escaped, and she crashed and sank at sea off Point Sur, California. This disaster ended the use of rigid airships in the U.S. Navy. For an account by one of the *Macon* survivors, see the Naval Institute oral history of Rear Admiral Harold B. Miller, USN (Ret.). The *Macon* was based at Moffett Field, Sunnyvale, California, near San Francisco.

to trip the safety lock to open up the breech.* I screamed for him to cease and desist. If he had opened that breech, a hangfire could have been a disaster.† In the turret officer booth, I jumped and reacted to training. My two hands grabbed each flooding valve without a second thought. It showed with good training that you automatically reacted to do the right thing. In your booth you had a porthole of reinforced glass through which you could observe what they were doing in the gun chamber. Just below the portholes were these two flooding valves. The flooding would quickly fill the whole gun chamber.

Paul Stillwell: Would that flood the booth itself?

Admiral Knoll: There was nothing in the booth to be flooded. Exit from the booth was through a hatch in the bottom of the turret, with access to the main weather deck of the ship.

Paul Stillwell: Was he just absentminded?

Admiral Knoll: No, he knew he could open the breech that way during drills, but it was a violation during actual gunfire. If you attempt to fire a primary fuze, you might obtain a reaction. If not, you treat it as a misfire. You wait a couple of hours before opening the breech after a misfire. This is how things happen. I have said time and again that safety precautions in engineering and gunnery for the Navy have all been written in blood. Mistakes require new regulations to prevent a repetition.

Paul Stillwell: Could you flood the magazines from the turret?

Admiral Knoll: No, not with the valve in the turret officer's booth.

Paul Stillwell: What do you remember about night operations?

---

* A misfire involves a propellant charge that fails to ignite when the trigger is pulled.
† A hang fire is the delayed detonation of an explosive charge in a gun.

Admiral Knoll: For night operations we lacked radar and modern communications, so we relied a whole lot on the Mark Number 1 Eyeball, and basic seamanship. Modern electronics have radically changed the safety for night operations.

Paul Stillwell: What about searchlight practice?

Admiral Knoll: Well, searchlights were never too practical. Star shells were better. For main battery exercises the searchlights were inactivated, lest the large mirror reflectors would shatter by concussion. You can illuminate with star shells. Every time for a main battery practice, you'd dismount all the reflectors and stow them between life jackets so they wouldn't be shattered when you're firing the main battery, so why plan to use searchlights for gunnery? They were more for night navigation work in peacetime, for illuminating aids to navigation, or to pick up something such as recovering boats. I don't think we could use them to pick up a target at distances of a mile or more.

Paul Stillwell: Wouldn't you also have the disadvantage of showing the enemy exactly where you were?

Admiral Knoll: Certainly. With a star shell, you could illuminate a target. They were never too effective. They did not last long enough, but they were there if you had to illuminate and an enemy would not have a steady target at which to aim.

Paul Stillwell: What can you say about medical facilities on board ship at that time?

Admiral Knoll: We had good doctors, at least on the battleships. For a time one of our Navy doctors who had been a surgeon was always on loan to the Mayo Clinic.[*] A surgeon in the Navy had experience with a wide variety of surgery, more than anybody would ever get in civilian life. They would be at the Mayo Clinic in charge of the surgery department.

---

[*] The Mayo Clinic in Rochester, Minnesota, is highly regarded for its medical excellence.

Paul Stillwell: Why more varied experience in the Navy?

Admiral Knoll: All the different kinds of operations that you might run into, such as hernia, appendicitis, fractures, brain, etc., across the board, where the average civilian doctor was limited to tonsils and appendicitis. A Navy surgeon had been exposed to everything imaginable, and different types of injuries and casualties that required surgery. I do not know it's still done, but at that time it was an accepted policy.

Paul Stillwell: Did you find that you had a very capable enlisted force because the Depression made the job market selective?

Admiral Knoll: I don't think that was too apparent in those days, no. I think the chief petty officers and the petty officers had great aptitude; they wanted to be a part of the Navy, and they enjoyed being there and wanted to stay 20 or 30 years. They weren't separated from their families, particularly in California; they got home for weekends. A large percentage were not married. As a whole, it was a happy life, and it wasn't too expensive living in those days. Today, I don't know how they're going to get people to make it a Navy career when they're reducing your allowance for transfer of station, and it costs money out of your own pocket to move.

Paul Stillwell: Was there a lesser proportion of the enlisted force married and had families then?

Admiral Knoll: Yes, to a degree. It started after World War II. I was a bachelor for a good bit of the time until I went to the Far East. There were more bachelors as officers. Those that were married always wanted us to take their duty so they could go home to Momma. A lot more people stayed aboard. Petty officers were professional and really knew their stuff. Chief petty officers and senior petty officers that made the Navy a career were very good, and you could rely on them. I think we made a real effort with new people coming aboard to teach them and make them understand their job and like the Navy. With the liberty boats each ship was able to give them good liberty. I think we did more visiting to various ports like San Francisco, Seattle, and others. "Join the Navy and see the world" was a reality. Too many foreign operations today have almost eliminated planned liberties to foreign ports.

There was Fleet Week in Seattle, and we went to San Francisco once or twice a year. Many ships were involved with four or six days in port. We went to Honolulu every other year and an occasional cruise to the Atlantic. The way you'd get people around, and they saw many U.S. and foreign ports. In addition to that, where they went, they were well received and entertained by the populace ashore. There was good entertaining—dances and good parties for them. A lot of them met their future wives that way. So all that was an advantage. Wives often came to San Francisco and Seattle to join their husbands for entertainment.

Paul Stillwell: What was the social status of naval officers in that era?

Admiral Knoll: For example, when you arrived at the fleet base in Long Beach, you immediately received an honorary membership at the Pacific Coast Club, which included the club at Long Beach, the Uplifters Club at Will Rogers's place, and some of the golf clubs in and near Los Angeles.* You didn't have to pay dues. You were welcome to come there and use their dining facilities for a nominal fee. Food in those days was rather inexpensive. I used to attend polo games to see Bob Montgomery and Hal Roach play polo at the Uplifters Club.† We were welcome there as naval officers. In other words, you had real status in the community because you were naval officers. You didn't wear the uniform ashore, but you had a membership card to show. You received it automatically when you joined any ship in the fleet. Nothing like this has been done since the end of World War II.

Paul Stillwell: What do you recall about the visits to Hawaii?

---

* The Uplifters was a men's social club at the Los Angeles Athletic Club. Humorist Will Rogers was a member.
† Robert Montgomery, who later served as a Naval Reserve actor in World War II, was a movie actor; Hal Roach was a movie producer.

Admiral Knoll: Upon completion, we tested out the battleship moorings that were the scene of the disaster in Pearl Harbor on the seventh of December 1941.* We were amazed with these moorings—the fact that you'd have two battleships alongside each other, knowing full well that if you had to get under way in a hurry, the inside one couldn't move until the outer one had cleared the mooring. In those days you could not spin a battleship with a spring line or anchor underfoot. There weren't enough tugs to pull the ship clear. The other one probably was that ships were too close to maneuver safely and get clear. It was an ideal way to get all the battleships moored in Pearl Harbor, but under an emergency situation you couldn't get under way and deploy rapidly. It was not a realistic concept for mooring ships of war in times of strained conditions.

Paul Stillwell: Especially since everybody had to thread through one narrow channel.

Admiral Knoll: When we went to Pearl Harbor the first time, the channel had just been made deep enough for battleships to get in and out. The clustering of ships, in addition to the narrow channel, was contrary to the need for quick emergency departure.

Paul Stillwell: There was a bar across the mouth.

Admiral Knoll: Yes, on either side of the narrow channel.

Paul Stillwell: Wasn't the whole area, though, very primitive at that point?

Admiral Knoll: Well, I wouldn't say too primitive, but it had ideal climate with many attractions for recreation of ships' personnel. The airplane hadn't been developed, so it was more a Pacific paradise for ship visits, and the Royal Hawaiian was really plush.† It wasn't until the Navy took over the Royal Hawaiian as a submarine headquarters that it started losing its opulent nature around Waikiki. It was a great place to visit. You'd spend more time downtown at some of the excellent restaurants than on the beach at

---
* On Sunday, 7 December 1941, Japanese carrier planes attacked and heavily damaged American warships at the naval base at Pearl Harbor, Hawaii. The U.S. Congress declared war on Japan the following day.
† The Royal Hawaiian is a luxury hotel, still in business on Honolulu's Waikiki Beach all these years later.

Waikiki. On the whole, when the Navy went there, the officers got more out of the visits to Honolulu. Enlisted men did not have as many places to go, but they had a good time. There were never too many problems for shore patrol.

Paul Stillwell: Were the enlisted men just not welcome?

Admiral Knoll: Everyone was always welcome. There was never a complaint from officers or enlisted men about Honolulu for a recreation visit.

Paul Stillwell: Was it just that they couldn't afford very much?

Admiral Knoll: There wasn't much recreation ashore like the USO in World War II and today.[*]

Paul Stillwell: How much rivalry was there between the fleet units back in your *Oklahoma* time?

Admiral Knoll: Well, I think there was a certain amount between what was called the Scouting Fleet in the Atlantic, which didn't amount to too much, and the Pacific Fleet, which was really all the good battleships oriented to fighting a war. As a result, we won most of the various type competitions. I think we had a better caliber of people and newer ships. We probably had better types of ships, and we had some of the new cruisers. We had many fleet exercises, including battleships, carriers, cruisers, destroyers, etc., operating in wartime formations.

Paul Stillwell: Was there rivalry among the ships within a division?

Admiral Knoll: To a degree, yes, because I was generally on older ships, but at one time or another I had observed firing as a spotter for gunnery practices, both daytime and

---

[*] USO – United Services Organization is a group of U.S. civilians who put on entertainment programs for service personnel and provide hospitality for them in many parts of the world.

nighttime firing, on every battleship in the Pacific Fleet. As a turret officer, I also was a spotter. I had worked in plotting rooms. I was always a member of visiting groups to these different ships. That's the reason you'd meet the skipper, the gunnery officer, and the exec, and then you got to know a lot of the people who were on their way up. I had met Admiral Taussig when he had the *Maryland*.* Later on Taussig was one of the more capable individuals in the Navy. Once he had met a person or a member of the crew, he would make sure to call their name and could recall them by name when they met again. He was just like Jim Farley on names.† When he was around Norfolk as Com 5, I met him different times, and he remembered me.‡ I said, "Admiral, I can't figure out how you can always remember all these people's names."

He said, "Well, you always have to associate them with something. When you meet people, you try to observe them and more or less ask them how to spell it or something like that. Once in a while, you hear a name, and they say, 'How do you spell that?' and they said, 'Smith.'" Because you didn't quite get the name to start with. He had a hobby of knowing people by name if they had ever served with him. I have sat with Jim Farley at a Circus Saints and Sinners dinner in New York when I was there with the United Nations, and I asked him the same thing. He said you develop this association. It's a terrific asset for a politician. Once you meet someone, you must be able to call him by name when you meet again. And Taussig did that better than anyone.

Taussig supported the idea that to keep the Japanese in 1941 from moving south into the South China Sea and Indochina, he wanted the U.S.A. to deploy a division of cruisers to establish a blockade between Hong Kong and Manila.§ It was never accepted, but at that time before the Japs consolidated the occupation of Indochina and the base at Camranh Bay, it would have changed the situation. The other side of it is that Washington sometimes made policies but never recognized the time required to implement the policy, and that got us in trouble in World War II.

---

* Captain Joseph K. Taussig, USN, commanded the battleship *Maryland* (BB-46) from 16 May 1930 to 3 February 1931.
† James A. Farley was U.S. Postmaster General from 1933 to 1940.
‡ Rear Admiral Joseph K. Taussig, USN, served as Commandant of the Fifth Naval District, 1938-41.
§ Taussig was forced to retire from active duty in 1941 for testifying to Congress on the likelihood of war in the Pacific against Japan.

Paul Stillwell: What can you say about the handling capabilities of the *Oklahoma* in rough weather?

Admiral Knoll: In rough weather I would say that of all the ships I ever handled, it was always very temperamental. Those of that did handle it made a lot of different recommendations which led to the final modification that was made in Bremerton to build up around the skeg forward of the rudder to give better control. I think this was improved before she went to the bottom at Pearl Harbor. Being a reciprocating engine, it didn't have the fine engine control that you have with a diesel because you had a different type of prop and different types of RPMs. I think it had a slow number of RPMs for the same speed, but it didn't have that same effect on the rudder.

The average battleship, with its bow, very straight and very close to the water, which was changed when they built the *Iowa* class with a clipper bow; they were a very wet ship in any kind of a heavy sea.* When you did start plowing into heavy seas, then you start burying your nose. You slowed down because it damaged ventilator and topside gear and made a very wet ship and bad ship.

In a battleship, you never plan to fire your guns directly ahead or directly astern, because the concussion may do major damage to everything internally. Hulls were held together with rivets that occasionally failed. We didn't have the welded seams like you have today. You had rivets, and they let go. So you ended up with a lot of leakage at times that you should avoid. That's the one advantage of the welded hull.

Paul Stillwell: Did those old battleships in the '30s roll very much?

Admiral Knoll: Not as bad as the carriers. They were the worst rolling ships at that time, probably because of the height of the flight decks above the waterline. When the battleships were modernized, extra blisters were added on the outside of armor belts, which gave them better stability, and they had a pretty good draft. I never felt a battleship with a snap roll like a destroyer or cruiser. That's why the battleships buried

---

* USS *Iowa* (BB-61), the lead ship of her class, was commissioned 22 February 1943. She had a standard displacement of 45,000 tons and full-load displacement of 57,600 tons.

their bows in green seas. It was an earthquake shock, and you could sense that such a type of shock could do real damage, maybe not to the hull but to stores and sensitive gear within the hull.

Paul Stillwell: What about personnel injuries from that kind of pounding?

Admiral Knoll: No, I never encountered any on a battleship. Occasionally on a cruiser or a destroyer you might, if someone was careless. But, on the whole, I think that the more you go to sea, the more you're prepared for the unexpected and can brace yourself in heavy weather.

Paul Stillwell: What do you remember about the annual fleet battle problems when you were in the *Oklahoma*?

Admiral Knoll: I think the most challenging one was the force battle practice when ships in battle line of three or six ships fired at targets 10,000-12,000 yards distant. The *Oklahoma* always had a record as a good-shooting ship. Another one that had a good record, I think, was the *West Virginia*, a newer ship, of course, and the *Maryland*. The *Arizona* I don't remember. Some of those, like the *West Virginia*, the *Maryland*, the *California*, were not mediocre. All of them had good gunnery departments. We had good stability in most of the crews. I would say that 60% or 70% of the gun crews had been around for a couple of years, and there was not too much change of key personnel in those divisions. You got a good gun captain, turret captain, and plotting room officer, some good spotters, and a good gunnery officer—everybody working together—it showed what could be done when the equipment had been checked and ready.

That proved itself as we got more technology and more computer control than with the selsyn director system, which couldn't get any closer than a couple of degrees when matching up; you never had the accuracy we achieve today.* You could stay on one bearing, but when you were following a selsyn director, which went in degree increments, not all the guns would be exactly lined up, because there was some error in

---

* Selsyn was short for self-synchronous.

the system. Those things you had to accept during rehearsals and checking out your system. The officers, the petty officers, and yourself worked closely as it was checked out. You spent enough time to know the system. A lot of us inherited that careful check from people like Deak Parsons, because they were perfectionists, and you would inherit it if you grew up in that system. The competition within ship and between ships was keen; it paid dividends with good gunnery scores.

Paul Stillwell: How much antiaircraft gunnery did you do?

Admiral Knoll: I never got involved with antiaircraft. I was always acquainted with those in it, like Duke Chandler and some others.* They knew their business, and they had to work at it. They achieved terrific scores with essentially mediocre 3-inch mounts. Antiaircraft gunnery was slow in achieving the accuracy of other guns. World War II made major breakthroughs that were needed.

Admiral Knoll: The *Oklahoma* left for Spain in 1936, when I was detached to go to the Postgraduate School.

Paul Stillwell: You had a preliminary tour at Edgewood Arsenal, didn't you?†

Admiral Knoll: Yes.

Paul Stillwell: What did that cover?

Admiral Knoll: At the time it happened, I had some extra time before going to the Postgraduate School. For me it was a really illuminating indoctrination in the pluses and minuses of chemical warfare. It was well done. The Army had a terrific realistic course. You became acquainted with every type of chemical warfare agent that had been used during World War I, what was being done today, what possibilities for the future, the

---

* Lieutenant Alvin D. Chandler, USN.
† Edgewood Arsenal was part of the Army's Aberdeen Proving Ground in Harford County, Maryland.

countermeasures. For your graduation exercise, you divided up into two enemy forces and then went out in the woods and did evasive moves through the woods to see if you could catch the other one with a gas attack before the enemy could get their masks on. The biggest surprise was boarding an old Ford Eagle boat designed for training how to protect from gas through a ship.[*] There was gas in different compartments, nothing serious but enough gas that you could open up your mask and take a smell and try to identify what it was. The final thing, just before you came to the last ladder to go up to the main-deck hatch, someone was there to pull your gas mask off from behind, and you had to clear the mask, put it back on, and go up the steps. It was very realistic and a good fresh-air course.

Paul Stillwell: How sophisticated were the countermeasures during that period?

Admiral Knoll: They were effective; masks and protective clothing were excellent. All you needed was a good gas mask, except if exposed to smoke or less of oxygen more than the gas masks are needed, such as the rescue breathing apparatus. A gas mask will not help with carbon monoxide. For carbon monoxide the canister of the gas mask will make oxygen in a carbon monoxide atmosphere.

Paul Stillwell: Did your course cover the morality of this at all?

Admiral Knoll: No, not at that time. It was emphasized to know what the capabilities were and how it was used in World War I, and, of course, at the time it hadn't been outlawed.[†] Enough of us had been exposed to various gases to know how to react and the approved countermeasures. It was an ideal experience going to Postgraduate School. There were not too many in the class. It was an ideal sequel to the many tasks for

---
[*] During World War I, the Ford Motor Company built dozens of steel-hulled antisubmarine patrol craft known as Eagle boats. Each was 200 feet long and displaced 615 tons. None was in combat during the war.
[†] Poison gas was among the weapons used in World War I, with the result that some soldiers wound up with damaged lungs. In the Geneva Gas Protocol, signed in 1925, a number of nations pledged not to use poison as in the future.

improving the watertight integrity of the *Oklahoma* that preceded duty at Postgraduate School.

Paul Stillwell: Were any of the instructors men who had been gassed in Europe?

Admiral Knoll: They had been involved with chemical warfare in Europe but not gassed to my knowledge. Some of the mustard gas effects were really extreme; the injuries for some were permanent and ultimately fatal. In an atmosphere of high humidity, it's a lot worse than in a dry-air situation. The Army had assembled an up-to-date knowledge of all aspects.

Paul Stillwell: Did the Navy not have a course at that time in chemical warfare?

Paul Stillwell: The only exposure we had was what the Army gave us. There was one naval officer there as a liaison with the Army group. At the time the threat was only to ships in port; on the high seas the gas cloud would quickly disperse.

Paul Stillwell: That was a rare early instance of inter-service cooperation.

Admiral Knoll: It wasn't unusual. There were a few other things like that, but it was an enjoyable course, and it was just up here at Edgewood Arsenal. It gave me something different. Having been in gunnery, I think it gave me some ideas for the future if chemical warfare had not been made illegal. Some chemical shells were available for possible use.

Paul Stillwell: Please tell me about the Postgraduate School.

Admiral Knoll: I was in the first group from the 1930 class because of the small classes of '28 and '29. The upper third of my class went to Postgraduate School after six years of sea duty instead of the previous seven. Up until that time, you had to be at sea seven years. So I started to Postgraduate School a year ahead of time, not the normal pattern.

And most of those in that group were individuals who stood higher in the class at graduation.

Paul Stillwell: Had you applied for any specific area in PG training?

Admiral Knoll: Ordnance. Deak Parsons was in charge of gunnery at Postgraduate School.[*] He was the one that said, "You've got a terrific record in gunnery. We need someone to improve the ballistic wind and knowledge of the upper air for future gunnery. We're going to fire at greater ranges, and we have to improve our knowledge of ballistics. We want you to become an authority on the ballistics of naval gunnery of the future." Of course, at that time it made a lot of sense, so he said, "I think with your background you can make a contribution. You will be in the Bureau of Ordnance when you finish your course."

Paul Stillwell: Please cover your training there.

Admiral Knoll: I was impressed with the caliber of the professors at PG School and the dedication of all students in the different groups.[†] We had students that were interested in improving their knowledge; we had excellent professors in meteorology and mathematics. We started plotting weather charts and received excellent practical experience. Rafferty had the Norwegian course and gave us a good idea about meteorology and weather charts, based upon air-mass theory. Also in terms of physics, aerodynamics, and the theory of airflow, whether you're designing an airplane or looking at the continuum flow of air around the earth. When you get into the laws of hydrodynamics or aerodynamics, the stream-flow functions are different only in terms of the coefficient for aerodynamics or hydrodynamics; the basic functions are the same. We studied quite a bit about hydrodynamics and those, of course, were the fundamental

---

[*] In the summer of 1936, when Knoll reported to the Postgraduate School, Lieutenant William S. Parsons, USN, was executive officer of the destroyer *Aylwin* (DD-355). He had not been assigned to the PG school since he was a student there in the late 1920s.

[†] The Navy's Postgraduate School was then at Annapolis, Maryland.

theories we had at Postgraduate School. There was a lot of math and quite a bit of homework too.

One of the better courses there, which was taught by Commander George Fort, emphasized executive leadership by giving a cross section of the great leaders of past history.* Each student would be allocated a specific leader to research and discuss in class. We would have two about two weeks to research; then on a specific day you gave your presentation. Normally you'd have four of them in one period, about 15 minutes each. I had Otto von Bismarck one time, I remember.† The presentation would say what history and problems influenced Bismarck's decisions. I discussed his strengths and weaknesses, why was he different from someone else, how did he operate, how he was recognized as a world leader, not whether he was a world leader for good or evil like a Hitler or Stalin or vice versa. Others such as Genghis Khan and many different leaders were analyzed over a semester.

As we found out what made them leaders, we compared the variety of leadership characteristics as demonstrated in terms of crisis, and knowing why each leader was quite different. Time and again, people don't realize that it's only by seeing how other people took advantage of situations, faced disaster, and overcame difficulties that you realize that you have to keep making an effort to have confidence in your own ability to survive. Keep an optimistic point of view and pray.

It was rather interesting as we approached some of the leaders of the Civil War. Commander Fort, professor and instructor, proceeded to assign General W. T. Sherman to Lieutenant Rags Parish, who was born and raised in Atlanta.‡ The class showed some excitement. Commander Fort said, "What is the problem?"

We advised him, "Rags Parish was born and raised in Atlanta."

He said, "I assure you, Lieutenant Parish, I'm not trying embarrass you. I didn't know that. But if you do not want to do Sherman, I have no objection. But if you want

---

* Commander George H. Fort, USN.
† Prince Otto Eduard Leopold von Bismarck-Schoenhausen was first Chancellor of the German Empire, 1877-90.
‡ Union General William Tecumseh Sherman, USA, is widely known for the quotation "War is hell." He demonstrated that during the Georgia campaign of 1864. Hostilities began in Atlanta on 6 May, and then he and his men marched toward the Atlantic. They captured Savannah two days before Christmas and essentially split the Confederacy in two, leading to the war's end in April 1865.
Lieutenant Elliott W. Parish Jr., USN.

to take a couple of days and look at it and come back and tell me whether you want to do it or not, all right. We can always give it to someone else. Are you willing to look into it and see if you want to tell us how a native from Atlanta looks at Sherman?" We all knew about Sherman's operations to the sea and the overall strategy that was designed to win the war.

He came back a couple of days later and said, "Commander, I looked into this. I heard all the stories I ever want to hear about Sherman from my grandparents, but I think I should be the one to tell the class about Sherman." He gave the most impressive talk. He started out, "Sherman was a northerner, and when the war started, he was teaching school in New Orleans." He reviewed the whole operation, the purpose, discussed some of the atrocities and many events that were news to all. He was very honest. He ended up by saying, "Thank you, Commander and the class, for allowing me to tell an unslanted story about Sherman." When you go through something like that, you get a whole new appreciation of past history. Let's not be led astray by the propaganda of history; let's find out what really did happen.

Paul Stillwell: Where did you live when you were here at Annapolis for Postgraduate School?

Admiral Knoll: I lived on Church Circle in one of the apartment houses near the State House, about three or four of us. I lived alone up there for the first year, and the second year I lived out in Flood family apartment near Spa Creek and the new high school.

When I was in school there, I frequented the library because I found all the different textbooks that had been used for mathematics at the Naval Academy. I would get them out and use them when we were going through quadratic equations, calculus, etc. Our math professor extracted problems for exams from these books. I had acquaintance with exam problems, because I had seen them and worked them at the library. For a long time, I had a set of math books. Some of them I bought to have my own copies. I was always checking through the library to find out how one author explained or looked at things and to get the other point of view on some topics. I was inquisitive, and my marks were good. It broadened my view, impressed upon me the volume of knowledge that I didn't know.

Paul Stillwell: Was there a social life among the PG students?

Admiral Knoll: Oh, very much so. Most of them were married, so I was always being invited out to parties to meet some girl. We really studied every night. We didn't do partying except on Saturday night. Any time there was a new road show or play at a Baltimore theater or Washington theater, I always had tickets for them and did studying before going to the theater. I had dates with Admiral Adolphus Andrews's daughter for Washington shows.* Frequently I'd receive a call, "You're having dinner with us" at their home before we'd go to the theater. They lived on Kalorama Road, and it was very convenient. My father having been involved in the theater, I always had an interest in the theater—melodramas, musicals, and comedies. I seldom missed a good show in Washington or Baltimore. I would order tickets by mail as soon as I knew a show was due.

Paul Stillwell: Had your undergraduate education prepared you for this kind of course?

Paul Stillwell: Oh, yes. I think part of it was your standing in the class in terms of mathematics and the sciences. I mean, that is part and parcel. If you didn't have that, of course, they wouldn't even select you, and the right kind of marks and aptitude. Everybody didn't go to Postgraduate School. It was those that were being groomed for broader fields. That was well done. You had to have really demonstrated a proficiency in the field you asked for. Some of them, of course, were in the engineering side. I was in aeronautical engineering, specializing in meteorology. Some of my classmates, like Andy Jackson and Tom Haley and others were in aeronautical plane design and aeronautical engines.† Those of us who were in general aerodynamics were in the same

---

* Rear Admiral Adolphus Andrews, USN. As a captain he commanded the battleship *Texas* (BB-35) when Knoll was an ensign in that ship.
† Lieutenant Andrew M. Jackson Jr., USN. The oral history of Jackson, who retired as a vice admiral, is in the Naval Institute collection. Lieutenant Thomas B. Haley, USN.

class, because we were going to Caltech or MIT for continuation.* At MIT some of the people in aeronautical design or engine design were in the same theory classes with me; I was taking aerology because we were at the Guggenheim School of Aeronautics under the supervision of Captain Hunsaker, U.S. Navy (Retired).†

Paul Stillwell: Why were you in aeronautical engineering? That usually was a specialty for aviators.

Admiral Knoll: Aerology or meteorology is an earth science. Oceanography is also an earth science. Theory of steam flow and fluid mechanics are equally applicable to water and air. For air a special constant exponent is included to make each theoretical equation for water flow; otherwise, all variables for water and air are the same. Aviators and aerologists attended the same classes on theory, including mathematical functions.

Paul Stillwell: Were there that many students in weather study?

Admiral Knoll: In 1936 my class had the largest number that ever assembled at Postgraduate School. Previously there were only two or three.

Paul Stillwell: How many in your class?

Admiral Knoll: We started with eight. Two went to MIT because of Adolphus Andrews's effort, and the other six went to Caltech.‡ The other Navy officer with me at MIT was Sam Denham, plus a Coast Guard officer and others.§

---

* Caltech – California Institute of Technology, Pasadena. MIT – Massachusetts Institute of Technology, Cambridge, Massachusetts.
† Jerome C. Hunsaker graduated from the Naval Academy in 1908 and stood first in his class. He resigned his regular commission in 1926 and subsequently taught engineering for many years at the Massachusetts Institute of Technology. He retired as a Naval Reserve captain in 1947.
‡ Rear Admiral Adolphus Andrews, USN, served as Chief of the Bureau of Navigation from 30 June 1935 to 11 June 1938. The Bureau of Navigation made officer assignments to various duties in the years prior to World War II.
§ Lieutenant Walter Sam Denham, USN.

Paul Stillwell: Tell me how that worked out.

Admiral Knoll: I had been dating Adolphus Andrews's daughter Frances from the time of the Christmas party with President Roosevelt and family at the White House.* We went to the theater about once a month. One time I was having dinner with the Andrewses at their home before going to the theater, and the admiral asked, "Where are you going after Postgraduate School?"

I said, "It's rather indefinite, but I guess we're all going to Caltech."

He said, "Why do you say that?"

I said, "The Navy convinced the Massachusetts Institute of Technology to start a graduate course in meteorology as a result of Reichelderfer's experience in Norway.† The Navy should continue to use MIT with a few students and not send all students to Caltech because the tuition is less."

He said, "That makes a lot of sense. Why isn't the Navy going to send someone to the Massachusetts Institute of Technology?"

I said, "I understand that the Chief of Naval Personnel does not have enough money. The MIT course is going to cost $600.00 a student while the Caltech course is going to cost $250.00. There are eight of us to go."

He sort of smiled and said, "Well, where do you want to go?"

I said, "I want to go to MIT."

He said, "Is that course that much better?"

I said, "I'm not in a position to evaluate, but I think if I had a choice in the matter, I'd like to say I got my postgraduate degree from MIT rather than Caltech because it's a prestigious institution, and it's on the East Coast. I have a preference to be on the East Coast, and it's closer to home."

He said, "I probably can find $600.00 to send you there."

I said, "That would be wrong."

"What do you mean?"

---

* Franklin D. Roosevelt served as President of the United States from 4 March 1933 until his death on 12 April 1945.
† Francis W. Reichelderfer (1895-1983) served in the U.S. Navy in World War I. He was in the first class of military personnel to study meteorology at Massachusetts Institute of Technology. He later headed the National Weather Service from 1938 to 1963.

I said, "You can't send one officer to one institution. There should be at least two for competition and impartiality. Secondly, there should be some criteria as to who would go."

"What do you mean?"

"Well, if the choice comes out for who should go to MIT, individuals standing highest in the class should be recognized and rewarded. The Caltech course up to this time has not really been used much by the Navy, and we don't know the quality of the course. We know people like Tony Danis and others who have completed the courses at MIT. They have been a credit to the Navy and have made an excellent contribution to improvement in weather forecasting."[*]

So he said, "Well, we should send two there. Will you be in the two?"

I said, "Well, I stand first in the group right now. I think I will be one of the two."

He sort of smiled. A couple of days later, Commander Lockhart in OpNav (Aerology) called me at Postgraduate School.[†] He said, "Have you been talking to Adolphus Andrews?"

"Yes, I've been dating his daughter."

"Oh," he said. "Well, I received word from the Chief of Naval Personnel that two of the eight people in your group would be going to MIT. With your standing in the group, you'll be one of the two."

I saw Admiral Andrews a couple of weeks later, and he said, "Did you hear anything?"

I said, "Yes, Commander Lockhart called me in and said I'll be going to MIT."

"Fine."

I didn't go out of my way to tell him, but I was asked the question, and I volunteered the answer.

Paul Stillwell: What was the purpose of the two-step PG course, part in Annapolis and part somewhere else?

---

[*] Lieutenant Commander Anthony L. Danis, USN.
[†] Lieutenant Commander Wilber M. Lockhart, USN, Bureau of Aeronautics.

Admiral Knoll: From what I observed, the first year of PG was to bring you back to speed academically after being away from the Naval Academy six years. Review and refreshment in mathematics and physics was good for graduate work. Secondly, the Navy wanted to be sure that officers at civilian institutions had a broader education and good foundation for scientific work. As a result, with operational experience we were able to excel above the class average. Navy officers were in the upper half of the class and had a good reputation.

The Navy wanted the benefit from personnel who had graduate degrees in various areas. Association developed with civilian scientists, and as you grew up, you would go to meetings as naval officers, and you would run into your contemporaries, either as professors or important officials who had been in school with you. It's a cross-fertilization.

Later on, I renewed acquaintances with Jerry Weisner when he was scientific advisor to Jack Kennedy and later on when he was president of MIT I had meetings with him about the school of meteorology and oceanography.* I was persona grata because I was an alumnus of MIT and he was head of MIT. In the same way, Stark Draper, who developed inertial navigation, graduated with me in 1939.† Dr. Hurd C. Willett was an A-1 instructor.‡ Jerome Namias, later an outstanding long-range forecaster, was a classmate of mine at MIT.§ These individuals had stature worldwide. Later, as an alumnus of MIT and a rear admiral, U.S. Navy, I could meet with them with greater success than a Naval Academy graduate. We proved it over the years with people like Deak Parsons. They were more than naval officers. They grew up in the scientific and technical environment. They were accepted for many conferences not limited to the specialty at the Massachusetts Institute of Technology. Graduate training has paid big dividends for future work with civilian scientists.

---

* Dr. Jerome Weisner was a scientific advisor to Presidents Dwight Eisenhower, John Kennedy, and Lyndon Johnson. He was an advocate for exploration of space with unmanned satellites. He was president of the Massachusetts Institute of Technology from 1971 to 1980.
† Dr. Charles Stark Draper of the Massachusetts Institute of Technology had an important role in the development of the inertial navigation systems used in Polaris missiles and later in the space missions sent to the moon.
‡ Dr. Hurd C. Willett was a meteorologist who was known for his five-day weather forecasting.
§ Jerome "Jerry" Namias did not have an undergraduate degree. He arrived at MIT in 1936 as a student and research assistant. He received his master's degree from MIT in 1941. Later in life he was involved in researching the El Niño phenomenon in the Pacific Ocean.

Paul Stillwell: Was there some weeding-out at the Annapolis level of who would go on to these secondary places?

Admiral Knoll: Normally if you were only at PG School for one year, you didn't go to a civilian school for graduate work. There were some that came just to give them further background in engineering or naval communications. If you stayed for a second year of Postgraduate School, you were pretty well identified as going to Columbia, Michigan, MIT, the University of California, or Caltech for specific graduate work. Some of the people in ordnance went to the University of Michigan. The Navy tried to have a few alumni at each institution to stay in the know on technical developments and new theories.

Caltech was logical for all the people going into aircraft manufacture, particularly in airframes, because the industry was concentrated in Southern California. Those of us who went to MIT were in aeronautical engineering and meteorology. The logical place for engines was in the East, where United Aircraft, General Electric, and General Motors were located. These institutions fulfilled a need for research and development. Some professors were part-time at educational institutions and familiar with production. Educational institutions had been keeping themselves on the forefront of technology, and had R&D contracts with the Navy. As a result, being associated with them was a part of being up to date on new developments.

When I was secretary of the Joint Meteorological Committee in 1941 and 1942, my background at MIT was valuable. I had meetings with officials from the weather service of Canada, British Empire, or the Air Force or the Army or the Coast Guard. They knew as the secretary of the Meteorological Committee of the Joint Chiefs of Staff or the U.S. secretary with the British secretary of the combined British-U.S. Meteorological Committee, I was not just another naval officer. They knew I had a specialty with a degree.

The Navy has a fantastic aviation museum at Pensacola. I've been down there recently to check and remind the curator that, "The status of modern weather forecasting in the weather bureau in this country today is directly to related to what the Navy did to bring the weather service into the modern ages. One, by getting Commander

Reichelderfer and sending him to Norway to learn the new air-mass theory and bringing him back here. We needed better forecasting for lighter than air, and we trained other people initially for lighter than air. When the airplane came into its own, we really needed it for all air operations."

Admiral Hart told me, when he was chairman of the General Board before going out to be commander in chief of the Asiatic Fleet, about 1938, the General Board sent a strong recommendation to President Roosevelt that the U.S. Weather Bureau was archaic and had to be brought into the modern age. They recommended that the President immediately reorganize the U.S. Weather Bureau and assign as its head a man qualified in the modern Norwegian system of weather forecasting, and that individual was Commander Reichelderfer. As a result, Admiral Hart said, "We will be in readiness for war, since this would be a great weakness if we didn't have a modern weather system." Admiral Hart told me this personally.

Paul Stillwell: Back to PG School, you said before that you had a concern about the practical. How was that brought into your meteorology course?

Admiral Knoll: It was particularly at the Massachusetts Institute of Technology. We had too little practical laboratory work. Drawing weather maps, plotting data, analyzing and preparing forecasts received little attention. Some of this work we had performed during the second year at Postgraduate School. I wanted more of this training under supervision of professors at MIT. There were many lectures on theory, which were useful.

At MIT we had too much theory, and it wasn't bad. We had excellent professors, like Dr. Rossby, an outstanding authority on mathematics, aerodynamics, and hydrodynamics.[*] Without seeing a satellite view of the earth in terms of air-flow continuum in the Northern and Southern hemispheres, the distribution of air masses, in 1938 he determined empirically that there should never be more than seven nor less than five major low-pressure areas in the Northern Hemisphere or Southern Hemisphere at one time. More or less would interfere with the stream-flow functions in the hemisphere.

---

[*] Dr. Carl Gustav Rossby, a Swedish meteorologist at MIT until 1939, when he joined the U.S. Weather Bureau.

With a satellite at 22,000 miles, when a picture of the Northern Hemisphere is taken you will see there are never less than five or more than seven low-pressure areas. He proved this theoretically in 1938. We were able to look at the big picture, consider the continuity. Estimate how soon a molecule of air is going to require to travel completely around the earth and return to the same position and the route it will probably take.

Paul Stillwell: Did you ever have a homework assignment to see what the weather was going to be on a given day?

Admiral Knoll: We had to write a thesis on specific phenomena. We did some of the long-range forecasting. We would take today's weather map and locate each low pressure and each high pressure, do mathematical computations as where they would be each day for four days. This was an early application of stream-flow functions that computers today resolve in a few minutes. We did not do too well, but we were anticipating some of the advances that were certain to develop.

Paul Stillwell: Did you do any work with civilian weather stations at all as part of your course?

Admiral Knoll: No, we didn't.

The practice work at MIT, such as drawing a weather map under the supervision of people such as Dr. Rossby, the head of the course, did occur. He was interested in theory. Hurd Willett and some of the assistants did not draw weather maps. He did observe and make suggestions. My complaint was not against too much theory. We were drawing enough maps and having these people give professional guidance, such as, "You're not giving too much attention to the isobars here," or "The force and direction of the wind suggests the front should be located differently. This accuracy does affect your forecast." Locations of isotherms and wind shifts are phenomena that help you to learn over a period. Ultimately it becomes second nature when looking at a weather map. Having such advice from pros coming around and watching you draw is indispensable for experience. Such work you could never get out of a book or from a lecture. I wasn't getting enough of it, so I told Dr. Rossby we were not getting our money's worth for the course.

I talked to Jerry Hunsaker, a former naval officer who was head of the Guggenheim Laboratory in Aeronautics at MIT. I told him and Rossby, "When we leave here and go back to the Navy, we must tell an admiral what the weather is going to be. I can't start talking to an admiral about a theory of what's going to happen. I have to make a realistic forecast, and he wants to know enough upon which to make plans. He doesn't give a care how it got that way. That's my responsibility, upon which I base my forecast. I'm not getting enough practical work. When I leave here and report for duty on a ship, the admiral, whoever I work for, is going to want a forecast, and I want to be able to give the best forecast, based on what I learned at MIT." They did not argue. I said, "That's what the Navy's paying for and that's why the Navy asked you to initiate this course a few years ago."

As a result, Tony Danis came to MIT for a visit. He had taken over from Lieutenant Commander Lockhart. He spent only 24 hours at MIT, but he called me and asked, "What are you doing up there? I understand you're raising hell."

I said, "Well, we're not getting our money's worth."

"I'll be up there tomorrow." I talked with him. Tony Danis did not argue. Rossby was agreeable. The rest of them said, "We'll adjust the course," and they did. They did mention that I might not receive a master's degree, to which I replied that, "Giving an admiral what he wants is more important than a degree." I received an MS degree.

Paul Stillwell: What do you remember about Hunsaker? He had been involved in the NC-4.[*]

Admiral Knoll: Yes. Not too much. He was smart and was essentially emeritus at the time of this discussion in spring 1939.

---

[*] In May 1919 three Navy/Curtiss flying boats—the NC-1, NC-3, and NC-4—set out on a transatlantic flight from Trepassy, Newfoundland, to the Azores. Two of the aircraft dropped out, but the NC-4, whose crew was headed by Lieutenant Commander Albert C. Read, USN, became the first plane to fly nonstop across the Atlantic. For details, see Richard K. Smith, *First Across* (Annapolis: Naval Institute Press, 1973).

Paul Stillwell: Very highly regarded.

Admiral Knoll: Oh, very capable. When he got in on it, he wasn't about to argue. He said, "Sure, we want the naval officers to leave here properly trained at MIT."

Paul Stillwell: Let's cover the PatWing 5 tour, which came after you finished at MIT.

Admiral Knoll: The PatWing 5 commander was a senior great aviator by the name of Squash Griffin.[*] He was from the old school that weather wasn't too important, and modern planes could fly through any kind of weather. The main thing, all he wanted to know, was whether he had enough visibility to land. He had a good staff around him. We had Warren Berner, Buster Isbell, and Frank Bridget, all good squadron commanders.[†] I had a good relationship with them. For the short time I was there, I had good exposure to patrolling operations. A couple of months after I reported for duty, the war started in Europe.[‡] The commander of the wing, Griffin, proceeded to do reconnaissance visits to Charleston, Newport, Rhode Island, and other places up and down the East Coast as possible anchorages or places to develop stations for patrol wing operations with less of them being concentrated at Norfolk.

We visited Charleston, which hadn't been used as a Navy yard for almost a generation.[§] Silting from the Cooper River had fouled up the waterfront near the former Navy yard. They did have a small ramp used by the Coast Guard, which was attractive as a base for a few PBYs that we wanted to operate in and out of Charleston.[**] We looked at places in Puerto Rico and Narragansett Bay and started equipping them. We had four

---

[*] Commander Virgil C. Griffin Jr., USN, Commander Patrol Wing Five.
[†] Lieutenant Commander Warren K. Berner, USN; Lieutenant Commander Arnold J. Isbell, USN; Lieutenant Commander Francis J. Bridget, USN. As a captain, Isbell was killed on board the aircraft carrier *Franklin* (CV-13) on 19 March 1945 while in transit to take command of the carrier *Yorktown* (CV-10). The destroyer *Arnold J. Isbell* (DD-869) was named for him.
[‡] World War II began on 1 September 1939, when German ground forces invaded Poland. Two days later Great Britain and France declared war on Germany.
[§] Admiral Knoll's claim here is an exaggeration. The Charleston Navy Yard did dwindle in work force and service in the 1920s but experienced a resurgence of activity in both shipbuilding and repair in the 1930s.
[**] The PBY Catalina was a twin-engine flying boat that performed extensive service before and during World War II. Built by Consolidated, it first entered fleet squadrons in 1936. The PBY-2 model had a wingspan of 104 feet, length of 65 feet, gross weight of 28,400 pounds, and top speed of 178 miles per hour. Cruising speed was 103 mph.

patrol squadrons ready to fly to these advance bases. As the planes went out to these areas, they would load key members' stuff aboard so operations could proceed away from Norfolk.

When a PBY is heavily loaded with its extra gear and people, you start throwing a lot of rivets from the hull during takeoff. Once airborne, the water will drip out while you fly to the next destination. PatWing 5 was actually involved with Neutrality Patrol, which was essentially an intelligence service for the British.* All merchant ships in the Western Atlantic were located and reported by code in Navy broadcasts. The code was held by the British as well as ourselves. The British ships received our regular broadcast and knew every ship that was sighted on the Neutrality Patrol. I would fly about once a week, particularly when the weather got cold. The fall of 1939 was a cold, severe winter. Within an hour after being airborne, everything in the plane—your coffee and other liquids—was frozen solid. We wore electrically heated flight suits and spent six or eight hours in the air, up and down the coast, looking for ships and determining nationality. It was about this time that our eyes were opened vividly as naval officers. We found out how Allies operate and how neutrality was evaded.

There were some German ships; for example, the *Columbus* had loaded a lot of strategic and leather material in Veracruz, Mexico. The *Columbus* attempted to make a dash at high speed up the East Coast and ultimately to Germany until detection by the British.† Initially a couple of U.S. Navy destroyers tried to tail it, but it was beyond the speed of the four-pipers in bad weather. Captain Daehne on the *Columbus* maintained high speed and arrived off Norfolk and Cape Hatteras.‡ We observed it and kept giving its position. Captain Badt was patrolling in the cruiser *Tuscaloosa* on the fringes of the Neutrality Zone, which was many miles eastward.§ Messages were exchanged with Washington: "Trailing the *Columbus*, German cargo ship. Request instruction. *Columbus* about to leave the east boundary of the Neutrality Zone."

---

* In the period from 1939 to 1941—when the United States was not yet an active combatant in World War II—the American republics maintained what was euphemistically called a Neutrality Patrol of a zone in the western Atlantic. Ostensibly neutral, it in fact aided Britain in its war against Germany.
† The *Columbus* departed Veracruz on 16 December 1939.
‡ Captain Wilhelm Daehne was master of the *Columbus*.
§ Captain Harry A. Badt, USN, was commanding officer of the heavy cruiser *Tuscaloosa* (CA-37), which rescued 567 men and nine women from the scuttled *Columbus* on 18 December 1939 and delivered them to Ellis Island in New York Harbor.

An encoded message came back from Washington, "Continue for one more hour." Within five minutes after receipt of that message, the British destroyer HMS *Hyperion* came over the horizon heading for the *Columbus*. As the *Hyperion* closed the *Columbus*, the German crew came topside and began setting drums of oil on fire. *Columbus* sent a message to *Tuscaloosa*: "Stand by for survivors." So the *Hyperion*, which knew that the *Columbus* carried valuable strategic contraband, was ready to intercept, except the *Tuscaloosa* was closer. *Tuscaloosa* picked up Captain Daehne of the *Columbus* and crew while the ship burned and sank.

During debriefing, Captain Daehne knew that the U.S. was not neutral with regards to combatants, that the U.S. Navy was overtly providing intelligence to the British Navy. The Germans were not about to complain, because ultimately they hoped the U.S.A. would remain neutral or even be on their side. So Hitler was not about to antagonize anybody. The final disposition of Captain Daehne and his German crew never became known to us at Norfolk.*

Paul Stillwell: Did you have any qualms about helping the British when you were supposed to be neutral?

Admiral Knoll: My father-in-law in Norfolk had already attended meetings with the Army Transportation Corps. He was president of the Norfolk Southern Railroad. At these meetings about future transportation requirements various assumptions were made. He'd explain some of the topics discussed and was surprised about how the U.S.A. was observing neutrality. He said, "I didn't know wars went this way, but I can really see it's not what you see in the newspaper or what you think. It's what the U.S. Government decides today." From then on, I became a very conformed realist.

A good intelligence capability is indispensable The U.S. intelligence capability was greatly weakened just when we needed it in Iran to let us know what was happening

---

* The *Tuscaloosa* rescued 575 survivors from the *Columbus* and delivered them to Ellis Island, the immigration portal in New York Harbor. They proceeded from there to internment camp at Fort Stanton, New Mexico.

internally with respect to the Shah.[*] The only two things you need before you resort to military action are reliable intelligence and deception/surprise. If you can't have them, principally the element of surprise, you can't win. You must avoid wishful thinking. You have to seek the facts, and you have to know whom you can trust. Many intelligence assets in the Middle East were destroyed, and we lost the confidence of the Norwegians, the British, the French. They couldn't afford to tell us what they knew because there was no guarantee we could keep it secret. It was a sad period that should never have happened.

Paul Stillwell: Having a father-in-law means you had a wife. When had you met her?

Admiral Knoll: I didn't meet her until I was with PatWing 5 at Naval Air Station Norfolk and treasurer of the officer mess at the BOQ.[†] I didn't know her very long.[‡] I met her, and we started playing bridge. Her home was near NOB.[§] She dated various Navy people, and her mother was determined that her daughter, her only child, would never marry in the Navy because she inherited the unfortunate idea then prevalent. On the front lawn of her mother's home in Portsmouth, they had a sign warning sailors going back and forth to the naval hospital, "Sailors and dogs keep off our grass." So I wasn't too popular.

Paul Stillwell: When you were flying over the *Columbus*—

Admiral Knoll: I wasn't flying over *Columbus*. At the end of each patrol we had a critique and determined any clarifying report that should be sent to Washington.

Paul Stillwell: How many of these patrols did you make, would you say?

---

[*] When the Shah left Iran in January 1979, the Ayatollah Ruhollah Khomeini seized power and declared the nation to be an Islamic republic. On 4 November 1979 Iranian militants seized the U.S. embassy in Teheran and took the staff members there as hostages. The hostages were ultimately released on 20 January 1981.
[†] BOQ – bachelor officers' quarters.
[‡] Knoll married Genevieve Parker Hawkins on 29 February 1940.
[§] NOB – naval operating base.

Admiral Knoll: At least once a week from October 1939 to February 1940. I would normally fly with Buster Isbell. We would leave in the afternoon and spend overnight in barracks on Goat Island at Narragansett Bay. Take off early the next day and fly along the Maine coast and cover shipping lanes, checking each ship as to nationality. The most important concern was keeping warm. All inland bays and swamps were frozen over. Landing on Narragansett Bay and near Norfolk required care to avoid ice. Willoughby Bay at Norfolk froze over solid for a short period in January.

Paul Stillwell: What was the purpose of having an aerologist along on these flights?

Admiral Knoll: The more you fly and encounter the weather phenomena, the better your forecasts for patrol planes. You make the forecast and then go out to find how it could be better. At Lakehurst during our summer training in 1937 I made the morning flight as passenger in a fighter plane to an altitude of 35,000 feet.[*] I had some difficulty when we got above 30,000 and the pilot put the stick over and started a quick return to Lakehurst. I had to level off once in a while because of a quick increase in air pressure. It felt like two hot pokers were coming in my ears. I kept trying to relieve the pain. Some of these pilots developed a technique they could go through a quick dive without having any effect on their ears.

On these flights we recorded all data—temperatures, cloud layer—and obtained an appreciation of cloud stratification and other phenomena necessary for a good forecast. Similarly, we flew in blimps at Lakehurst for the summer with Tex Settle, Charlie Roland, and others.[†] Blimps are temperamental with regard to winds. The location of where the sea breeze would change to the land breeze and the exact direction of wind are very important when come in for a landing. You had to be careful when you came in that a wind shift or turbulent area did not make landing impossible. With the blimp you had to make sure you didn't make any radical increase or decrease in altitude or you'd lose the formation cone on the front, and the helium gas might at be the wrong end of the balloon. Exact attention is mandatory for blimps or dirigibles. An aerologist

---

[*] Lakehurst Naval Air Station, New Jersey. In 1937 Knoll was a student in the Postgraduate School.
[†] Lakehurst was the Atlantic Fleet base for lighter-than-air craft. Commander Thomas G. W. Settle, USN; Lieutenant Commander Charles W. Roland, USN.

must have experienced these problems so that a meaningful forecast is given to operations. It's practical work.

The beauty of it today is knowing how we tried to forecast, and now that you can fly from the East Coast to the West Coast over the mountains and be able to avoid the mountaintops. As soon as you're up to 25,000-30,000, you know there are going to be few clouds, and you can fly around high thunderheads. In the old days, I'm telling you, the forecasting was hard work, because you had to make a whole chart giving a cross section of different types of cloud masses and their altitude—the freezing levels, visibility, and cold front to encounter on the way. It was no easy job to make up a flight plan together with what kind of weather to expect along the flight path. It had to be pretty accurate, based on teletype data normally available to give you hourly information. The flight plan today is generally flying over surface weather. Satellites provide the locations continually of each high and low pressure and the nature and extent of all cold and warm fronts.

Paul Stillwell: Had there been any development of Argentia as a patrol plane base yet?*

Admiral Knoll: It happened after I left in February 1940. It was discussed as to where they would go. The Navy's contribution to improved weather service, including asking the President in 1938 to modernize the U.S. weather service, has not been adequately documented—what the Navy did in this area in terms of lighter-than-air work, as well as forecasts for military aviation. It should be a matter of history, because the Navy also made a contribution to aviation medicine. An effort is being made to include some of this in the Naval Aviation Museum at Pensacola. The Navy developed some of the aerial radio sounds for upper air data with the Bureau of Standards and the Office of Naval Research. Upper-air soundings with balloons and radio sounders were by the Navy about 1940.

Paul Stillwell: Have you finished up the PatWing 5 tour? Are there any loose ends there?

---

* Argentia, Newfoundland, Canada.

Admiral Knoll: It was a surprise to everybody when I was quickly detached. I left fast. The detail officer for aerological officers had no choice in the matter. When I got my orders to the Asiatic Fleet, I was the only officer with weather training who hadn't had Asiatic station duty. There was no way of getting out of it. Admiral Hart was determined he wanted a good weather forecaster, so they said there was nothing to do but go out.* I thought I'd be going out as a bachelor. I was surprised when my future wife told her parents I wasn't going out alone; she was going with me. So we had a quick wedding and went to the Asiatic station on our honeymoon. She was there for less than six months when they ordered all the wives home, and I didn't see her until two years later. That was the beginning of a very unhealthy and frustrating separation.

Admiral Hart was just great. If an officer came out there and Hart looked at the cut of his jib and didn't think the officer could do the job—and it happened more than once—he said, "You don't have to unpack. I'm sending word to the Bureau of Navigation that you're unacceptable. I'm sending you back home. I'll ask for someone else." Admiral Hart, with his seniority, was determined to have only the best-qualified officers on his staff. He knew that a possible war with the Japanese was during his tenure.

Paul Stillwell: What did he base these judgments on?

Admiral Knoll: He wanted BuNav to send qualified officers. He would interview each new officer and find out if his qualifications were in keeping with his request. An officer recently selected to rear admiral came out to relieve Admiral Smeallie, who tried to commit suicide because they had spent $125 million to build tunnels at Corregidor and Mariveles, and it was not from appropriated money.† Admiral Smeallie was sure he was

---

* Admiral Thomas C. Hart, USN, served as Commander in Chief U.S. Asiatic Fleet from 25 July 1939 to 4 February 1942. James R. Leutze's biography of Hart is *A Different Kind of Victory* (Annapolis: Naval Institute Press, 1981).
† Corregidor was a heavily fortified island at the entrance to Manila Bay. Mariveles is an area at the southern tip of the Bataan Peninsula on the island of Luzon.
On 16 January 1941, Rear Admiral Harold M. Bemis, USN, relieved Captain Eugene T. Oates, USN, as Commandant of the 16th Naval District and Commandant of the Cavite Navy Yard. Oates had been acting commandant following the incapacitation of Rear Admiral John M. Smeallie, USN, in December 1940. On 5 November 1941, Rear Admiral Francis W. Rockwell, USN, became Com 16.

going to get court-martialed for spending money that had never been appropriated. The new admiral lasted about two to three months, and he was sent home. He was never promoted back to admiral after his return to the States. During his short tour he had no idea that the Philippines had more than 1,600 islands. He didn't try to find out.

Admiral Hart sent him home, and he just sent back a personal message to Admiral Stark, such as, "What are you trying to do to me, Admiral? I'm out here on the front lines. Don't send me out these incompetents. I'll send them back, and please send me someone else right away."* In those days you couldn't get back and forth that fast. The Pan American plane only arrived once a week. The Navy had priority. I knew hundreds of people who had reservations to leave on the last Pan American plane in the event of war with Japan, and not one of them got out by plane after December 7, 1941. The last PanAm planes were found by the Japs in Hong Kong or at Guam. There were many people around that Manila Hotel for days, hoping a plane might materialize.

Paul Stillwell: You say that you were the only one who was qualified. How many qualified aerologists were there at that time?

Admiral Knoll: Probably not more than 10 or 12.

Paul Stillwell: And out of that number, all the rest had previously had Asiatic Fleet duty?

Admiral Knoll: All the 12 had. In other words, in that number, we just had about enough for every carrier, because the carriers were added to the fleet. So I would have gone to a carrier if I hadn't gone to the Asiatic station. I probably was lucky to have gone to the Asiatic station, based on subsequent events.

Paul Stillwell: Why do you say that?

---

* Admiral Harold R. Stark, USN, served as Chief of Naval Operations from 1 August 1939 to 26 March 1942.

Admiral Knoll: The carriers were more vulnerable than where I was. I was lucky to have had combat exposure on Corregidor, then be ordered to leave Corregidor on the last submarine and avoid capture by the Japs.

I think in terms of experience a carrier would have been ideal; I like shipboard duty, but as aerologist on a carrier I would have been more or less predestined to be in engineering duty only status, rather than maintain my status as a line officer.

Paul Stillwell: Several of the carriers were sunk in the first year of the war.

Admiral Knoll: If not sunk, they went through hell. Many new aerologists had little prior experience and were not first-rate weather forecasters. A new group were selected and trained, like George Kosco and others who received an abbreviated course and went to sea.* They didn't have the advantage of three years of postgraduate training. With less than two years of study, they never could be expected to be ready for operational forecasting. Someone like Admiral Hart would just send them back home. In my assignment they said, "We're sorry. You're the only one that's fully qualified who hasn't had Asiatic duty."

Paul Stillwell: Could you describe the atmosphere on board Admiral Hart's flagship, the *Augusta*, when you reported?†

Admiral Knoll: I couldn't have asked for a more congenial and pleasant crowd. Commander Frank Beatty was the exec, and Captain Magruder was the skipper.‡ Magruder's father had the large Magruder grocery store on Connecticut Avenue, a very fine gent, and Beatty was a very good officer. The staff had Commander Robinson for

---

* Lieutenant George F. Kosco, USN, was assigned to the aircraft carrier *Ranger* (CV-4) before the start of World War II. In 1944-45 he was Admiral William F. Halsey's staff meteorologist when the Third Fleet was hit by devastating typhoons.
† USS *Augusta* (CA-31) was commissioned 30 January 1931. She had a standard displacement of 9,050 tons, was 600 feet long, 66 feet in the beam, and had a draft of 16 feet. Her top speed was 33 knots. She was armed with nine 8-inch guns and eight 5-inch guns. Because she was configured as a flagship, she frequently performed that function, both before and during World War II. She was eventually decommissioned on 16 July 1946.
‡ Commander Frank E. Beatty, USN; Captain John H. Magruder Jr., USN, commanded the *Augusta* from 7 March 1939 to 31 May 1941.

gunnery and Rosie Mason for intelligence, a top Japanese language student.* Practically everyone on the staff was ultimately selected to rear admiral.

Paul Stillwell: Please tell me about your weather work on the staff.

Admiral Knoll: My weather forecasts always emphasized the facts, rather than worrying about a mathematical score. My policy was to state if I thought it was going to rain tomorrow at 3:00 o'clock. I didn't try to say drizzle, a hedge to make a better score on the accuracy of my forecasting for the record. I attempted to give the admiral the best available.

I think there were unique areas in the Far East that required attention, such as the typhoon season. Another concern was the fog along the China coast, particularly around Shantung Peninsula in northern China. The fog would be dense for days, and you could scarcely see your hand in front of your face. It would stay there for days at a time. It was a wonderful place to spend the summer, a nice beach, a nice place for the Navy, ideal for gunnery operations in the northern East China Sea and return to port every night. The families enjoyed it, and so did I. I lived at the German consulate with other Navy families. We had rickshaws that took us back and forth. Fog would come in, and I knew it concerned the admiral and his staff.

Assisted by my aerographer's mate, we determined, "The fog is going to lift if we get a good north wind. How are we going to find out when the north wind is due unless I have some reliable observations from the northern side of Shantung Peninsula?" So we had a good relationship with some of the British in Chefoo on the other side, the Gulf of Pechili, and we arranged regular weather reports. Every time there was fog around Tsingtao, I would wait for the wind to shift into the north with some reliability and continuity at Chefoo. When a fresh northwest wind appeared at Chefoo within three to four hours, I would forecast the fog would be lifting in Tsingtao Bay in 12 hours. Particularly one time there was a bad week of fog. The flagship *Augusta* was waiting to go out for a short-range gunnery exercise. I always would go in morning and evening and take a small piece of the weather map to show the admiral where the typhoons were

---

* Lieutenant Commander James M. Robinson, USN; Lieutenant Commander Redfield Mason, USN.

located, where various ships were located, and what the forecast was. I went in one morning, and he asked, "How soon can we go out to fire?"

I said, "We'll be able to go out today."

He said, "Yes, but look at the dense fog out there.'

I said, "It'll clear around 10:00 o'clock. Then we can get under way"

He said, "Okay, tell the captain to get under way at 10:00 A.M. We'll go out and fire this afternoon."

I went to the captain. The admiral told me to tell you that we're getting under today at 10:00 A.M. and firing this afternoon."

"Are you crazy?"

I said, "No, it'll be clearing around 10:00 o'clock."

He said, "All right."

The ship had quarters about 9:00 o'clock, and all hands fell in for muster. The exec said, "The fog doctor says the fog will be clearing about 10:00 o'clock. We'll get under way, and we'll fire this afternoon."

The fog was still dense. Everybody looked around at me: "You dumb So-and-so."

Sure enough, we got ready to get under way about 10:00 o'clock. At five minutes to 10:00 you could start seeing the lighthouse that we hadn't seen for a week. By the time we got out to the mouth of the channel, there wasn't a cloud in the sky. Of course, the north wind had come in and just blown in the dryer air. It cleared the fog, and we fired the exercise. My training and experience made me unafraid to commit myself, since I had something to base it on. I wasn't guessing. Admiral Hart knew I was trying to give him my best advice, and he trusted me. We never had any ship get in trouble due to weather the whole time I was with him for those two years, with many typhoons all over the place. I would suggest that some ship better delay or change course, and we avoided every typhoon during the height of the season in the Far East. There were one or two typhoons each month from July through December. At the time the number of weather reports upon which to draw a map were few and widely scattered. We emphasized single station forecasts and maintaining maps every 12 hours for continuity and occasional revision.

Paul Stillwell: In the flagship was there a big plot that showed where all the ships were?

Admiral Knoll: Oh yes, in the operations. I also knew just about where every ship was and its destination. We would move them out of the area if there was going to be a chance of encountering a storm. The tracks of typhoons I have in my book on Asiatic weather.* I indicated different tracks for each month of the year and how many could be expected. This had never been developed in this way before. It came in rather handy for the people who were interested. In July through December we could locate a typhoon, find the percentage that recurve, and the percentage that go due west. The average knots of advance, how fast they move, initially about five knots and increase to 12 knots and even 18 knots farther north. You locate a typhoon for a month of the year; for example, in August, there's a good chance most of them will recur. September, they recur about the same, but you have more going west into China and after crossing northern Luzon. This was developed for each month of the year. It was a good empirical guide once you knew a typhoon was moving.

Paul Stillwell: What was Dennison's job on the staff?

Admiral Knoll: He had command of a destroyer and then came to the staff a few months before the war started.† With Admiral Hart's staff he was involved with plans, and he also did some special work with Admiral Purnell, the chief of staff.‡ He did not join us until July 1941, when the staff moved from the *Houston* to the Marsman Building in Manila.§

Admiral Hart had decided that only the ships in Cavite would stay in the northern part of the Philippines, and the fleet as a whole would concentrate in the Sulu Sea and the

---

* This publication was HO number 219, *Climatology for the Asiatic Station*, published by the Navy Department Hydrographic Office in 1941. The title page says, "Prepared for the use of the United States Navy by Denys W. Knoll, USN, Asiatic Fleet aerological unit."
† Lieutenant Commander Robert L. Dennison, USN, commanded the *John D. Ford* (DD-228) in 1940-41.
‡ Rear Admiral William R. Purnell, USN.
§ The heavy cruiser *Houston* (CA-30) relieved her sister ship *Augusta* (CA-31) as Asiatic Fleet flagship on 22 November 1940 at Manila.

southern Philippines.* Admiral Hart suggested, "You continue to be attached to the *Houston* but move your weather activity to a building in the Cavite Navy Yard."

It took quite a while for me, a lieutenant, to get Admiral Hart's approval for the weather central at Cavite and an Asiatic weather service by exchanging weather with many natives before the war stated in the Far East. Time and again, I would meet with him, and Hart would say, "We can't do this. There are too many Jap sympathizers in the Philippines, and they'll know what we're trying to do."

I said, "Admiral, first, I'm going to set up a system so I can continue to draw weather maps in peace or war and tell what's happening in this part of the world, and I have to do it with these other nations involved. The people I'm working with are reliable. The Japs are not going to pay too much attention to what I'm doing. We have to get this started. The Jesuits in charge of the Philippine Weather Service are all on our side." And we knew that Aquino's father and grandfather were then in charge of the department the controlled the weather bureau in the Philippines with Vice President Osmeña and President Quezón.† I said, "I don't think we should worry about them. The real solution is we have to have this when the war starts."

We would discuss this about an hour, and I would leave. Bob Dennison had a desk next to me as part of Hart's staff. When I came out, he queried, "Did you win or change anything?"

I said, "No, but I didn't lose yet. We talked for a while."

Eventually the admiral started getting excited. I said, "This is going to work. We'll be the first setup like this, the first weather service for the U.S. Government that'll provide something that everybody needs. I've been writing this book, I've been talking to the director of the observatory in Shanghai, the director in Hong Kong, and I've collected information from Indochina, the Dutch East Indies, and Australia." I went through all kinds of books, climatic records, and Asiatic scientific data, translating Dutch

---

* Cavite, on a peninsula about a dozen miles south of Manila, was the site of the U.S. Navy Yard serving ships in the area.
† Manuel L. Quezón served as president of the Commonwealth of the Philippines from 1935 until his death in 1944. As the Japanese advanced in 1942, Quezón was evacuated and spent his remaining years in exile in the United States. Sergio Osmeña was Vice President of the Commonwealth of the Philippines from 1935 to 1944. He subsequently served as President, 1944-46, following Quezón's death. Benigno Aquino Jr. was a Filipino senator who was assassinated in 1983. His widow Corazon later became President of the Philippines.

into English, etc. It's amazing, the tradition of the Jesuits over the years. Wherever they were, if there was any local scientific document that came out, they obtained 15 copies and sent one to each one of their technical observatories around the world, particularly those dealing with microseisms or anything relating to earthquakes, typhoons, weather, and seismographs.

A visit to each library, like the one in Manila or Shanghai, the Royal Observatory, and the Jesuit observatory at Hong Kong, or the Jesuits at Ateneo College in their observatory, which also was the Philippine Weather Bureau, of which Father Selga was the chief.[*] I had a close relationship with him. Copies of the same documents in a special area were available for study. Each Jesuit library had all the records of weather and scientific information from the Dutch East Indies, Australia, China. They had all the records from Japan and from Indochina. I had to go through them; some were in different languages, but I extracted all that I needed to write a record of Asiatic climatology. I had a couple of good aerographer's mates, and this gave me and them something to do.

I obtained a weather numerical code from Shorty Orville in BuAer in Washington, so I could with code collect the weather in the Western Pacific.[†] Finally, after more meetings with Admiral Hart, he said, "Well, I see that I'm not going to change your mind. Okay, try it, but I hope we don't get involved in a lot of Japanese reactions when they learn what we're trying to do."

I've been told by people who were in the know that in my fitness reports at the time, 1940 through the start of the war, 1941-42, Admiral Hart is supposed to have written, "This is the only officer on my staff who was in a wartime operating condition when the war started."

It's because of the foregoing that Hart and MacArthur sent me to Singapore in July 1941.[‡] I flew down with the Royal Air Force taking deliveries of PBYs out of Manila loaded with U.S. Navy coding machines that they were going to need. The whole

---

[*] Ateneo de Manila University. Father Miguel, Society of Jesus.
[†] Lieutenant Commander Howard T. Orville, USN, was a weather specialist stationed in the Bureau of Aeronautics in Washington.
[‡] Douglas MacArthur, who had been Chief of Staff of the U.S. Army in the early 1930s, commanded the Philippine Army later in the decade. On 26 July 1941 President Franklin Roosevelt nationalized the armed forces of the Philippine Commonwealth. He appointed MacArthur field marshal of the Philippine Army and Commanding General U.S. Army Forces Far East with the rank of lieutenant general.

bomb bay was full of about eight coding machines. When we left Manila, I knew there was a typhoon between us and the southern islands of the Philippines. It was raining but not too much. I told them, "We're going to come pretty close. We're probably going to fly through a typhoon as we head south southwest."

The RAF officers said, "We're still going. We'll fly around it." It really was a wild flight. They had planned to fly from Manila to Singapore nonstop, but we spent an hour and a half going through the center of the typhoon. Rain was leaking through all parts of the hull. I never saw a plane leak that much rain in flight. The pilot asked, "Where's the best place to fly?"

I said, "Let's fly as close to the water as we can. That way we can see where we're going and encounter less wind." We knew we were out over water of the South China Sea, and we wouldn't have as strong winds as if we were up aloft. We finally were able to get down near the water off Borneo. All of a sudden, because of headwinds, we didn't have enough fuel to get to Singapore. It started clearing, and we landed at Kuching, Sarawak, which was an interesting visit. The white sultan of Sarawak was at Kuching in the southern part of Borneo. We spent the night there.

During my visit to Singapore, I had an excellent reception. I had a chance to visit with Sir Brooke-Popham, General Percival, and Admiral Layton, who was the senior British naval officer in the Far East.[*] I worked with the senior staff, particularly Lieutenant Colonel Blackwood, who was the senior intelligence officer and security officer for the staff of General Percival. I had some interesting discussions with Percival. At that time the British said, "Well, you should go out and see our naval base at Singapore," about which there had been a great deal of publicity. "It could be an ideal fallback position for us and the U.S. Asiatic Fleet."

Paul Stillwell: That was considered impregnable, according to the common folklore.

Admiral Knoll: It might have been impregnable from the sea, yes, except the amazing thing was that it could do no repair work when I got out there. A British cruiser was in

---

[*] Vice Admiral Sir Geoffrey Layton, Royal Navy, Commander in Chief China; Air Chief Marshal Sir Robert Brooke-Popham, Royal Air Force, Commander in Chief Far East; Lieutenant General Arthur E. Percival, British Army, General Officer Commanding Malaya.

dry dock. It had been hit in the Mediterranean with a torpedo in the skeg, and that after deck had a blister, and around the admiral's cabin you could walk on a ledge amidships was open water like a swimming pool. Below waterline the torpedo had blown off the whole stern. The ship slowly came to Singapore for repair at the dockyard, coming from the Mediterranean. It was no easy job.

They showed me the various shops around the dry dock. Each one of these shops was spacious and new. The locations were ready for the machinery, and not one piece of machinery had arrived to make it a Navy yard. The work they were doing on the cruiser was ship to shop. All work was done in civil yards in Singapore and brought to the dockyard for the ship. The Navy yard had no mechanical capability to do any kind of major repair work. It was beautifully built, buildings new and spacious, and ready to work when the actual machinery arrived to make it a good repair yard. It was a Navy yard only in name, with a dry dock.

At the same time, I ran into Bill Rice, a Naval Academy graduate who was the Pan American representative in Singapore.[*] The Navy always had good relations with the Pan American people near Sangley Point. That was where the Pan American planes used to land on weekly flights across the Pacific, occasionally twice a week. They were negotiating with the British to set up the Pan American operations from the new airport at Singapore. The Pan American rep requested, "When you talk to your British friends, see what you can do to expedite their approval for Pan American to operate a regular service from Singapore to Manila." Fortunately, I did mention it to Colonel Blackwood, and before I left Pan American received approval to start operations at Singapore.

As a result of that visit, I had a new appreciation of many problems to be resolved between the British and the United States. We talked along the lines that attack on any one of us was an attack on all of us. It appeared to be U.S. policy. Whether it was formally approved in Washington or not never came to my attention. We never doubted for a minute that an attack on the French or the British or the Dutch singly or collectively would be an isolated attack.

Afterward, I reported to Admiral Hart and Admiral Purnell, "With all the excess machine equipment that we have at the Cavite Navy Yard, I think it would be ideal for us

---

[*] Lieutenant (junior grade) Tolbert A. Rice, USNR.

to select and ship key machines to the Navy yard at Singapore. We could quickly give them repair capabilities in the empty shops at Singapore." It made quite an impression, and to my understanding, after this discussion an appeal was made to Washington to do something like this. A reply quickly came back, "Absolutely not." The explanation: anything done to lessen the capability in Manila at that particular time would lessen the confidence of President Quezón and Vice President Osmeña that the United States was not prepared to stay and hold the Philippines. In other words, we were all talking realistically and knew we had to get ready to fight a war.

I can say that when I went to the China station in February 1940, I was warned in Washington that we'd be at war with Japan before I came back. During 1941 we talked about when war with Japan was going to start and how we could improve our readiness. As I mentioned, in July 1941, we set up the Navy Weather Central at Cavite Navy Yard. It was actually the first weather central established by the United States. All weather equipment, records, and people were moved from the *Houston*, and operations commenced at weather central in Cavite Navy Yard. The amount of data we could collect improved, and communications were superior. We organized and printed codes for collection of data and sent them to all the weather observing stations in the Philippines, in Hong Kong, Shanghai, and the Dutch East Indies.

I think it was about September 1941 that the Japanese, who had been exchanging weather reports in clear international code from the Mandated Islands—without warning they started coding their weather reports. We arranged with Pan American and the people in Guam and Yap, and Jesuit observatories, to receive a copy of our code and to encode their data. So when the Japs started exchanging weather in code, we and Pan American exchanged our weather in our own code so the Japs couldn't use it. We conditioned the people to use a code for collecting our weather. It was a numerical code and worked quite well.

Paul Stillwell: Could you explain how you used numbers to encode a map?

Admiral Knoll: There's an international numerical code for sending the weather observations for pressure, temperature, wind direction, wind velocity, clouds, precipitation. With this data a weather map is made showing the high and low pressure. Wind direction is another group, rain, clouds, visibility, with four to five groups of four numerals in proper sequence will give you encoded weather. The start gives that station symbol, followed by time and date of observation. With these reports, you develop a weather map. During training we made all this work. Aerographers entered that information for every station on a map. I drew the map, found out where the highs and lows were, where the fronts were, and then when that map was finished, we proceeded to use another code that has been prepared that was not in numbers. You would proceed to send an encoded message, locating where the centers were, their intensity, and the locations of different warm fronts and cold fronts, highs and lows. Occasionally direction of certain winds and the location of a typhoon were included. When this was received in Pearl Harbor or elsewhere, they could plot and reproduce the highlights of your map. From September 1941 on, we maintained a file of all maps so we could always check back to previous maps to ensure continuity and make corrections. Lacking station observations, we moved the fronts and the highs and lows in keeping with empirical formulae and tried to keep the map up to date and make estimates in specific instances.

When the Japs finally landed on Corregidor, they found all of my maps, which someone was supposed to have destroyed. They found out I had been drawing weather maps twice a day for the Western Pacific from September 1941 until they got there in May 1942. Japs saw the reports and said I had better weather maps than they were able to collect. We sent this information particularly to Washington and Pearl Harbor, who had no other weather forecasts from the Western Pacific.

Just writing the book kept me occupied, as did creating these maps. When I look at it today, I don't know how I did it. I had to change temperatures from centigrade to Fahrenheit and pressure from millimeters to inches. Reports from different stations, for writing this book on climatology, were in different languages. The amazing thing, all the important places in the Philippines for which I collected data, as well as the Dutch East Indies, were the scenes of important battles in 1941 or 1942. There are two reasons for that. One, the economic, social and other importance of each locality made it a logical weather observing station over the years. I have never seen anybody who used my technique for trying to help people find out where the hurricanes were going to go and frequency of occurrence each month. You knew a percentage were going to continue west for the different months of the year, and the percentage that would recur.

Paul Stillwell: Did you pioneer that technique then?

Admiral Knoll: I never saw it used before. I developed all these charts, based on the information of all previous typhoons that had been recorded in the Far East. I've never seen it used in the Atlantic or elsewhere.

Paul Stillwell: Where did you get the idea to do that?

Admiral Knoll: I don't know. I wanted a technique and had to innovate. The interesting thing is that I used to go to Admiral Hart once a day or even twice a day if there was a typhoon in the Far East. I would select a piece of the chart without taking the whole big chart of the Western Pacific, and my section would never be bigger than this 8 by 11 piece of paper. I'd say, "Admiral Hart, we're here. The different units of the fleet are here. The typhoon is here. Right now there's no unit of the fleet that's going to be in trouble. It will move here in the next 24 hours."

The next time I'd go in with the previous one, a new one, and so in a couple of minutes, he'd get a whole view of the picture. I went out of my way to avoid using anything but normal weather terms familiar to him. I didn't try to get in all kinds of technical words or anything to confuse him. As a result, in two and a half years, we never had one of our ships get in trouble in a hurricane or a storm.

Paul Stillwell: What else do you remember about Mason, the intelligence officer?

Admiral Knoll: He was a terrific friend, probably the most capable Japanese language student the Navy ever had. His Japanese was perfect. I met the wife of the poet laureate of Japan after the war. She ran a restaurant on top of the mountain near Admiral Togo's place in Sasebo.* Every time we were in Sasebo with the Seventh Fleet, particularly when I was the chief of staff, I maintained a liquor basket with my name, "Yama-san," on it. She was a good friend of Rosie Mason. She met him when he was a Japanese language student. She said he was one of the smartest, nicest American officers she ever knew. He was just terrific and admired by Admiral Hart. The Japanese had the utmost respect for him. There were many problems we had in which he could arrange a visit. Admiral Hart had complete faith in him, and the Japanese admired his knowledge of their language.

My wife was a good friend of Isabella Hart, the admiral's daughter, and they used to play golf together. In the summer months, when you were in China, you had to have a fresh cholera shot every week or carry a ticket to prove that you had had it. If you failed to produce a ticket for the Jap police, a Japanese would come up in a white coat with a long syringe and inoculate you on the spot. The rickshaw drivers always had a couple of extra slips with them to help so the Japs would not inoculate you. More than one rickshaw driver died because he took too many shots to have these extra tickets. My wife and Isabella Hart were out playing golf in Tsingtao, and my wife didn't take her cholera slip with her. This Jap came down the fairway in his white coat, and Isabella asked, "Do you have your slip?"

My wife said, "No, I left it at the hotel." So Isabella showed her cholera shot, and the Japanese turned to my wife. She said, "I don't have it." He pulled up her sleeve to give her a shot. She took out a golf club, and she said to the Jap, "Do you want this around your neck if you give me that shot?"

All of a sudden, when I returned to the ship, I was advised, "Your wife and Isabella Hart have caused an international incident. Your wife had an argument with a Japanese medic." She didn't hit him with the golf club, but they got off the golf course and came back to their hotel.

Rosie Mason collected all the facts and said, "Just go ashore, and don't worry. Don't worry." We always wondered what would have happened if she had hit him. Rosie arranged a prompt meeting with the Japs, and nothing ever happened.

---

* In the 27 May 1905 Battle of Tsushima Strait (which connects the Sea of Japan with the East China Sea), Japanese forces under Admiral Heihachiro Togo overwhelmed the Russian Baltic Fleet led by Admiral Zinovy Rozhdestvensky, during the Russo-Japanese War. Togo's flagship was the battleship *Mikasa*.

Isabella said, "He knew she would wrap that club around his neck." That was one of many incidents.

Rosie and I had a good relationship later, because he was ComServPac when I was ComServLant for over two years.* We had regular annual meetings. We always arranged to have the annual meeting when the weather was good in San Diego around the first of February. There were lots of fleet problems, and we made sure we were working together in procedures for underway replenishment, highline transfer, and the characteristics of the new logistic support ships. Having worked with him so many years, he was a great friend and superb naval officer. We've never had a more capable man to study the Japanese language with such thoroughness. The Japs respected him. They had no doubt they were talking with a man who knew their language, and some Japs said he spoke more accurate Japanese than many Jap officials.

An interesting thing—this is really of note—before the war started, when I was working in Admiral Hart's office in the Marsman Building, I became involved with the Army Air Forces and the movement of the B-17s from the U.S.A. to the Philippines.† I had meetings with General Clagett and General Brereton and their staff to arrange for the weather forecasts and advisories for the B-17s coming out from the States to Clark Field.‡ I said, "I'll provide them."

They said, "That's fine." The Army Air Forces in the Philippines did not have weather service. Their liaison with me was Captain Colin Kelly, who was lost in the first days of the war after bombing a Jap battleship.§ His code name was "Boy." He lived with me each time a group of B-17s was en route. I would provide the forecasts to Wake and to Darwin and to planes en route from Darwin. The first group came from Darwin,

---

* Rear Admiral Knoll served as Commander Service Force Atlantic Fleet from June 1961 to July 1963.
† In September 1941 a flight of nine B-17 Flying Fortress bombers made a series of long over-water flights while being transferred to the Philippines. The planes were part of the 19th Bombardment Group (H), 14th Squadron, under Major Emmett O'Donnell Jr., USAAF. They departed Hickam Field in Hawaii on 5 September, going via Midway, Wake, Port Moresby, and Darwin before arriving a week later. Clark Field was about 50 miles north of Manila, on the island of Luzon in the Philippines.
‡ On 4 November 1941, after the initial flight of the B-17s, Major General Lewis H. Brereton, USAAF, arrived in the Philippines and on 16 November became commanding general of the newly activated Far East Air Force with headquarters at Clark Field. Brigadier General Henry B. Clagett, USAAC, had arrived in the Philippines in May 1941.
§ Captain Colin P. Kelly, Jr., USAAF, was pilot of a B-17 Flying Fortress on a mission out of Clark Field in the Philippines on 10 December 1941. He was killed when his plane exploded after he made an attack on a Japanese transport, erroneously believed to be the battleship *Haruna*. He was one of the first individuals to be recognized publicly as an American hero after war started.

even though we alerted them that a typhoon was moving over Luzon. They came in spite of the typhoon and landed at Clark Field. The Army Air Forces sent Lieutenant Whitaker, who had just finished a course in meteorology to be a weather forecaster. He was a nice chap. I had some meetings with various people of General Clagett's staff at the air offices at Nichols Field. They told me about the number of fighter planes that were en route on merchant ships and how they were going to base them in the different islands. I asked about the weather service. They planned to use many teletypes, which were en route.

I asked, "Are they radio teletypes?"

They replied, "Don't know."

I asked, "What do you mean they're teletypes? How are you going to use them?"

They replied, "We'll connect them onto cables between the islands."

I asked, "You're going to connect them by what cable?"

They said, "You mean there's no cable between these different islands?"

"No." The equipment they were sending out on merchant ships was intended to build Little America in the Philippines, without ever analyzing the actual infrastructure that existed in the Philippines. This equipment never got beyond Darwin, Australia, where it may have been used.

Paul Stillwell: Before we get to that, you had worked into the shipboard organization in the *Augusta*, hadn't you?

Admiral Knoll: I was the assistant first lieutenant, including damage control.

Paul Stillwell: Why did you take a shipboard job in addition to the staff job?

Admiral Knoll: To maintain my status as a line officer with my contemporaries in the chain of command. I never wanted to be EDO.[*]

Paul Stillwell: Was there a risk that you would become one?

---

[*] EDO – an officer designated for engineering duty only.

Admiral Knoll: Yes, if I didn't maintain my status with my contemporaries. I'd have been buried as, "Oh, he's just another 'fog doctor' weather officer. What ship handling does he know?" Shorty Orville never liked the fact that I was more than just an aerological officer. My objective: "I'm a naval officer, but I'll do weather forecasting in addition." My predecessor rode around as a staff officer, not as a line officer.

Paul Stillwell: What did your duties entail there in the *Augusta*?

Admiral Knoll: I wrote this book *Climatology for the Asiatic Station* using the fighting top aft as an office.[*] I set up an office with four aerographer's mates and worked on this book. When we were in port in Shanghai, Tsingtao, and Manila, I spent at least half of my time ashore at the Jesuit libraries, weather observatory, and other libraries collecting material from different languages and translating them into English and taking it back. The book was in manuscript form when I sent it to Washington for Orville. He surprised me; I didn't know he was going to publish it so promptly. The first I knew was when copies came to the Asiatic Fleet before the war started. In the first year of the war military action occurred near every city that was included in the book.

Paul Stillwell: What about your damage control duties and first lieutenant?

Admiral Knoll: I was able to do that to the satisfaction of the captain and the damage control officer. I stood officer of the deck watches under way as well as in port. Of course, in China I was one of the senior watch officers, so I was one of the three duty officers who were senior shore patrol officers, every third night with a motorcycle driver and a sidecar. Every third night, with Dave Wooster Todd, we would be shore patrol officers in Shanghai, and that's an experience you ought to go through.[†] At my hotel the motorcycle and driver waited to take me anyplace there was a crisis. There were murders, rapes, and other human disagreements. It's amazing the things sailors got

---

[*] The publication was HO number 219, published by the Navy Department Hydrographic Office in 1941. The title page said, "Prepared for the use of the United States Navy by Denys W. Knoll, USN, Asiatic Fleet aerological unit."
[†] Lieutenant David Wooster Todd Jr., USN.

involved with. Gals got raped so easy. And there were murders, particularly in Shanghai. Anything can happen over there. It was a foregone conclusion that the three senior duty officers on the flagship would be the senior shore patrol officers. For serious problems with the Japs, we quickly sought the assistance of Rosie Mason.

Paul Stillwell: Were American sailors told to keep a low profile in that situation?

Admiral Knoll: Oh, no. There was no necessity for this. We had advance word that Italy was going to war with the Axis. An Italian gunboat was still in the Whangpoo River near us and a British gunboat at another anchorage.* They still had Italian Marines at their small compound up near the U.S. Fourth Marines on Bubbling Well Road. The British troops and sailors of other nations went to various dance halls on Bubbling Well Road. There was always competition for girls and the usual commotion. We had to go to these places once in a while to make sure there wasn't too much roughhouse, particularly sailors on Blood Alley. We would check these different places with intelligence that Italy was going to war. I contacted a senior officer of the Italian Marines, and I arranged to have trucks to move Italian Marines and sailors to their compound before the announcement.

I asked, "Where do most of your men go for liberty and dancing?"

The Italian said, "Down at the dance hall very close to my hotel, across from the golf course there on Bubbling Well Road."

I said, "Well, be there about 9:00 o'clock at night, and we'll ask all Italian Marines and sailors to leave the dance hall." And we had trucks ready. They all got in the truck and were back at the base before word came that Italy had declared war against the British. The British and Italians might have fought their first battle on the dance floor in Shanghai. In those days, the Japanese kept all foreigners out of Hongkew.† From the top floor of our hotel, we could look across Suchow Creek and see different kinds of massacres and shooting taking place in the Hongkew areas. There was nothing we could do about it. Every once in a while, one of our sailors would start roughing up a Japanese

---

* On 10 June 1940, Italy's dictator Benito Mussolini declared war on Britain and France. German forces occupied Paris four days later.
† Hongkew was essentially a ghetto in Shanghai.

sentry at the guardhouse on the Suchow Creek Bridge just beyond the Cathay Hotel. One night I responded there on an emergency. A drunken sailor from the *Augusta* had pushed the Japanese sentry inside the sentry box and had used a gun with bayonet to wedge him into in the sentry box corner, so the Jap couldn't move. That's when Rosie Mason quickly responded early the next morning to placate the Japanese. We knew there was going to be something every once in a while, and it could be serious if we did not take prompt action.

I ran into a former shipmate when I was out there, Kemp Tolley.[*] The amazing thing is, I hadn't seen him for quite a long time after he left the *Texas* in 1932 and went to China. I joined the Asiatic Fleet in 1940. The first or second day in Shanghai, I was going up Bubbling Well Road to Park Hotel, across the racecourse. I saw Kemp Tolley walking down Bubbling Well road with his mustache and his goatee and other disguise. I was riding in a rickshaw and called him by name. He kept right on walking. It wasn't until I read his book in detail that I realized he went around incognito and didn't want to be recognized by a U.S. naval officer. He never told me.

One time I saw him in the lobby of the Palace Hotel, the Metropole, or something. He came over and said, "Don't you ever recognize me or call me by name on the street." He wouldn't tell me more and disappeared.

Paul Stillwell: How good was the damage control capability in those cruisers then?

Admiral Knoll: Well, the *Augusta* had been on the China station, away from major overhaul for five or six years.[†] It was no longer up to standard in anything. It didn't have a good antiaircraft battery, no radar. When the *Houston* came out, it did have the new 1.1-inch quadruple rapid-firing antiaircraft gun, which jammed half the time. At last it was removed from *Houston* and put topside on Corregidor. It was finally hit and destroyed by a Japanese bomb. When it worked, it was terrific. Half the time it wouldn't work. In fact, we ran out ammunition very fast.

---

[*] Tolley by this time was a lieutenant.
[†] The *Augusta* served as Asiatic Fleet flagship from 9 November 1933 until 22 November 1940.

The *Houston* came out after a fresh overhaul to relieve *Augusta*. It was refreshing to get aboard a ship that seemed so much newer. Considering the short time she'd been out there, she was in good shape when the war started. She couldn't complain about it, because you could hire Chinese by giving them the scraps out of your galley to paint the ship for you and keep it clean, and even clean up your galley and the main deck area where the garbage cans and trash were. Sampans came alongside to take all the refuse of the galley. At that time, all our mess attendants were Chinese, which was a plus—excellent, clean service, and their mess bill was minor because of their diet of fish and rice.

They enjoyed being on a Navy ships and were quiet workers. With a Filipino mess boy, you'd ask him for something, and he'd say, "I'm sorry, I'm not the watch boy." With a Chinese mess boy, you'd ask him anything, and he'd say, "Sure, sure, sure."

When I was with the Asiatic Fleet, we visited many different cities in the Philippines. We went to Zamboanga and many other places with different groups of the Asiatic Fleet or with the *Augusta* or the *Houston* to the Sulu Archipelago, places like Tawitawi, where we went ashore and explored. The interesting thing was, we all enjoyed having a chance to see as many places as possible in the Philippines. We saw the Moorish influence in the south compared to the Spanish attitude in Luzon and the Visayan area around Cebu. You found that they weren't a homogeneous bunch of people, neither in language nor ethnic heritage.

Paul Stillwell: What did you do on liberty when you were in China?

Admiral Knoll: There were ideal places to eat, like the French Club and places like Fiakre restaurant and others in the French concession on Avenue Jacques. The French Club in Shanghai was superb. You could go in and check your clothes, and the man in charge at the cloakroom wouldn't give you anything like a check or number. When you were ready to go, he correctly gave you your clothes. No matter the size of the crowd, he remembered: "Yes, sir, okay." We'd give him a good tip.

Most of these places, you only paid your bill once a month, using a Hong Kong basket to carry bundles of paper money. The exchange rate was about 1,200 yuan to one U.S. dollar. It was worthless paper. The monthly bill was based on chits you had signed. I was in charge of a group to pay all chits signed by naval personnel, in anticipation of our final departure from Shanghai. We were amazed to see the crazy names that had been signed to chits. Some naval personnel had taken an encyclopedia and adopted the signature of noted individuals, like Warren G. Harding, Abe Lincoln, and others, rather than their real names.

Many bars were operated by Americans. O'Riley was one of the outstanding characters who was born in the United States and ran various nightclubs and gambling casinos on Bubbling Well Road and Blood Alley (Rue de Paisan). We collected bundles of chits and bartered: "How much do you want to settle the pack?" We would pay what they asked. Most drinks were cheap, never more than a dollar. George Washington, Alexander Graham Bell, and others had been forged. The Chinamen trusted every American without question. Most Americans would promptly pay up on all chits the first of each month or the day before departure from Shanghai or Tsingtao. The Asiatic Fleet paid up all outstanding chits without the crew knowing that we were about to leave for a long absence.

Paul Stillwell: So the sailors were actually being subsidized by the ship, is that it?

Admiral Knoll: No, this was only when we departed the last time. Sailors would willingly pay their bills, because everything was so very cheap. A fifth of gin cost 90 cents, and a fifth of the best Scotch a dollar and a quarter. The rooms weren't expensive if you wanted to stay at a hotel. I forget what we paid by the month for our room at the New Park Hotel, perhaps about $150.00. We had a nice suite on the sixth floor, and we could sit near the living room window and watch the horse races across Bubbling Well Road. We couldn't bet from there; it was too far to go down and cross the street.

A wonderful friendly Hungarian managed the hotel, with a fine dining room on the top floor. We had a Chinese amah who did all our laundry in the anteroom, adjacent to the bath. Sinclair was her name, and she'd been educated at a convent school in

Shanghai and spoke some English. I tried to learn Chinese from her, but whenever I asked for cracked ice she'd think I was losing my mind. I had to be careful what I said in Chinese, because my dialect was poor, and the same Chinese characters had confusing pronunciations.

The hardest thing in the world in this nation of 200 years of history is that many Americans think the U.S.A. has all the answers and all foreigners have the same likes and dislikes they do. We are the foreigners when we go aboard, and the quicker we try to know how to say, "I thank you," and "Good morning," or "I don't know," we start making friends. We must try to start using their language; then you start making a friend. Some Americans think unless they can talk to us in English that they are inferior. Look at the Chinese, who have 6,000 years of history.

Interview Number 3 with Rear Admiral Denys W. Knoll, U.S. Navy (Retired)
Place: Bel-Aire Hotel, Erie, Pennsylvania
Date: Thursday, 28 June 1984

Paul Stillwell: Admiral, it's about a month and a half since we had our last sessions in Annapolis. It's a pleasure to see you again, this time in your hometown. Last time you covered some of your service on board the *Augusta*, and I would appreciate it if you could compare her with the *Houston*, which relieved her as the Asiatic Fleet flagship.[*]

Admiral Knoll: I think one area that was noticeable was the whole new freshness of the officers and crew when the *Houston* arrived on Asiatic Station. There were quite a few old friends. We had to indoctrinate them in the peculiarities of the Orient, which was not easy to do in a short time. Nevertheless, they were an excellent crew of officers and men. It was a pleasure to work with them and get acquainted with them. At the time that we changed over, we didn't spend too much time in the Manila area, because Admiral Hart had determined that we had to start getting out and become acquainted with the various potential anchorages, particularly in the southern Philippine Islands.

We went down and checked out various anchorages in Sulu Archipelago and the Mindanao area. We'd anchor at Tawitawi or similar places more than once. Occasionally I would ride in one of the planes and drop smoke bombs to guide the ship through a narrow channel. We were not too sure of the accuracy of the charts. In that way, we found different anchorages that were quite good and safe. *Houston* would visit them and provide guidance to these places for future use of other ships of the fleet. It was to Admiral Hart's advantage to obtain a good appreciation of this area.

---

[*] The heavy cruiser *Houston* (CA-30) relieved her sister ship *Augusta* (CA-31) as Asiatic Fleet flagship on 22 November 1940 at Manila in the Philippines.
The month before, on 10 October 1940, at the direction of the Navy Department in Washington, Hart issued an unpopular order sending home dependents of active naval personnel in the Far East. The result was that Mrs. Knoll returned to the States around seven or so months after she had gone overseas as a bride in March 1940. A long separation ensued for the Knolls.

Finally, about July 1941, a decision had to be made as to where the fleet command should locate. Admiral Hart moved to the Marsman Building on the Manila waterfront and set up headquarters of the Asiatic Fleet ashore. He couldn't handle all the problems between Washington and the other ships of the fleet by cruising around in a flagship. When that happened, initially I had a desk ashore as well as spent some time aboard ship. Finally it came to a point, Admiral Hart determined, that the best place for me was with the rest of the staff ashore. In that way I more or less lost the opportunity of continuing to be a seagoing naval officer. I moved to a house at Sangley Point near the naval air station.[*] I had to commute back and forth to Manila since I had a desk with the staff in the Marsman Building and also had an office at the weather central at Cavite.

Paul Stillwell: To go back to your time in the *Houston*, what did you do in the shipboard organization there?

Admiral Knoll: I had exactly the same job as I did on the *Augusta*. On the *Houston* was Captain Rooks.[†] The antiaircraft officer, I remember was Jack Galbraith, with whom I had served on three other ships.[‡] He's still living. He spent the whole war in a prison camp after he swam ashore from the *Houston* as it sunk in Sunda Strait. Lieutenant Commander Gingras was chief engineer with an excellent crew.[§] We did a lot of training with gunnery and damage control. *Houston* had a more modern sound-powered telephone communications, which the *Augusta* hadn't received, even though they were sister ships. It was amazing to see the difference. The *Augusta* had been used by President Roosevelt before it went to the Orient. The *Houston* came out after it had been equipped for President Roosevelt's cruises.[**] *Augusta* and *Houston* were both among the best cruisers the Navy had at that time. One good cruiser with the U.S. Asiatic Fleet had limited effectiveness in Asia alone.

---

[*] Sangley Point Naval Station, eight miles southwest of Manila on a peninsula that extended into Manila Bay.
[†] Captain Albert H. Rooks, USN, was commanding officer of the heavy cruiser *Houston* (CA-30) up to the time of her loss in the Battle of Sunda Strait the night of 28 February-1 March 1942. Captain Rooks was awarded the Medal of Honor for his actions during the battle.
[‡] Lieutenant William J. Galbraith, USN.
[§] Lieutenant Commander Richard H. Gingras, USN.
[**] Roosevelt was paralyzed from the waist down and used a wheelchair.

Paul Stillwell: What do you remember about Captain Rooks?

Admiral Knoll: I didn't encounter him too much. Captain Oldendorf brought the *Houston* to Asia, and he was relieved by Rooks about the time I moved ashore.*

Paul Stillwell: What about Oldendorf then?

Admiral Knoll: I had a good relationship. He was a jolly individual. He was the ideal skipper on the bridge. You didn't have to worry about him, like some of the older ones in battleships. They enjoyed being pretty tough on the officer of the deck. Of course, I was getting more senior then. I knew something about ship handling and kept the bridge watch on their toes. I enjoyed working with him. I had heard from him from time to time after I left *Houston*. He finally was in charge of the battleships during the decisive Battle of Leyte Gulf and gained special recognition.†

Paul Stillwell: Surigao Strait.

Admiral Knoll: Yes. I had lost track of him. I would say it was a happy ship. I don't think there's enough recognition been given to what *Houston* did do in the early days of World War II. Some books have been written recently about the Asiatic Fleet. It was the Asiatic Fleet in name but not in composition. It was there to show the flag and to show that we had military presence in Asia. The Army criticized us because they felt a "fleet" should give even more support, even though there was only one new cruiser plus the old cruiser *Marblehead*, about 12 destroyers and six submarines, which were augmented with the P-type submarines later on. It was not a modern fleet; it had very limited combat potential. If we had had a more balanced fleet, we would have been able to provide the military support that the Army had expected.

---

* Captain Jesse B. Oldendorf, USN, commanded the *Houston* from 16 October 1939 until relieved by Captain Rooks at Cavite Navy Yard on 30 August 1941.
† Rear Admiral Oldendorf was the officer in tactical command during the Battle of Surigao Strait on 24 October 1944 when U.S. surface combatants were victorious over a force of Japanese warships attempting to interfere with U.S. amphibious landings on the island of Leyte in the Philippines.

There had been a lot of preliminary work done in putting caches of gasoline near the different harbors and on different strategic islands such as Cebu and Panay and the coastline of Mindanao. The Sulu Archipelago had many caches of gasoline ready for seaplane or PT boats. Lieutenant Morell took a motor launch all the way from Corregidor to Australia. He knew where these caches of gasoline were located, with Filipinos available to help. The entire staff of Admiral Hart was very realistic and competent in preparing for war. I know during '41 the civil engineers, working both for Admiral Hart as well as the Cavite Navy Yard, had searched the Philippine Islands to locate portable motor generators and diesel engines that might be commandeered for use in an emergency.

The first week of the war, the Army complained there were no surplus diesel generators since the Navy had control of all of them. This is an example of the realistic planning that was made. The unfortunate thing was that too many new kinds of problems arose. I keep using "we." I don't mean myself but I'm talking about the various people I worked with. I wasn't the manager or supervisor, but I was knowledgeable of the team effort being made at all levels.

When mines were planted in the channels around Corregidor, the first mines were dropped in the water and detonated before they anchored to the bottom. They would blow up and almost blow the crew off the stern of the mine-laying tug. There were many complaints to Washington. Admiral Hart sent some tough messages to BuOrd about these mines.* Finally, after an analysis was made, they realized the mines had been stored in Manila too long in a very humid atmosphere. Soluble washers were supposed to dissolve in seawater after anchoring. Storage for too long in high humidity had deteriorated these soluble washers. Once Admiral Hart rode in the *Pigeon* to personally observe that the mines were being launched exactly as BuOrd advised, new mines arrived, but they were not reliable either. It took a long time for BuOrd to recognize that mines for tropical use had to be different than those designed for a temperate zone. Correspondence frequently conveyed the impression that the Philippines were near the Hawaiian Islands rather than the Far East.

---

* BuOrd – Bureau of Ordnance.

After the war started, I was on Corregidor, and messages would arrive from Washington asking about the status of mines and how soon they would be placed. There was no idea that the Navy had evacuated Manila. One message was prepared saying the mines, the last time observed, were on the beach near Cañacao Hospital. If more accurate info was needed, someone from Washington better come out to observe for themselves. Many crazy questions from Washington had no appreciation of the battle conditions under which we were existing immediately after the war started.

From July 1941 on, more antiaircraft guns were requested to protect Cavite. The only guns were 3-inch/23½ caliber that could not shoot more than about 6,000 feet. Such small shells could not harm or hit a modern airplane. There were no real modern antiaircraft guns for protection of the Navy shore establishments. The Army had some fighter planes; however, most of the fighter planes intended for the Philippines were on cargo ships en route to Manila when the war started.

While I was with the Asiatic Fleet and getting ready for collection of wartime weather information in the Far East, I asked the Bureau of Aeronautics, Shorty Orville, to develop meteorological buoys that we might put in the South China Sea off Manila and let them drift with the Japanese current past Taiwan, toward Japan, and give us an idea of where typhoons or low-pressure areas existed. He sent word because BuAer was developing three of them at the Bureau of Standards.

Paul Stillwell: When was that proposed?

Admiral Knoll: In the fall of 1940.

Paul Stillwell: Why had they never been provided to you in the Asiatic Fleet?

Admiral Knoll: They were never completed prior to December 1941. There were more than 35 shiploads of material on the way from the U.S.A. to the Philippines when the war started. The lag between when the decision is made in Washington and the delivery at the useful point is ignored by planners. The people made the decision in Washington in the spring of 1941. Material to improve defense of the Philippines was to include food, ammunition, guns, mines, and airplanes. The ships were gradually loaded. They could have been in Manila in the seventh of December 1941. They started for Manila with the fighter planes needed for Clark Field and Nichols Field and the antiaircraft guns needed for Cavite and Subic Bay—the ammunition and mines and the food, together with personnel to operate new equipment.* The people arrived, such as pilots for the Army Air Forces planes, but the aircraft never got there.

The decision had been made in Washington to improve combat capabilities of the Philippines. Many shiploads were en route but never arrived. The amazing thing, they might have arrived before the seventh of December 1941 if they had not been diverted. About once a month, one cruiser visited the Far East. The *Boise* was joined by a Japanese cruiser. The Japanese ship trained out their guns toward *Boise*, and the *Boise* trained out her guns.† They steamed alongside like this for a time. They were a couple of miles apart at first. They were in the Guam area. After a time, the Jap cruiser left *Boise* and departed over the horizon. This caused a lot of concern, so all those cargoes were diverted to Darwin, Australia, to avoid the Japanese Mandated Islands. This doubled the time it would take for all the extra ammunition, the airplanes, and combat material that was supposed to arrive to augment the capabilities of the Philippines, particularly of Bataan and the Manila Bay area. To my knowledge, additional antiaircraft guns were en route, but the emphasis was to acquire more fighter planes. The crews for these fighter planes for the Army had already arrived and were waiting. They came earlier on merchant ships before the *Boise* incident. The war started as these ships—I forget how many there were, a considerable number—with combat supplies were in Darwin, Australia, ready to come to Manila.

After the war started, many efforts were made to move some of these ships with air support. Smaller ships might convoy some cargo to Corregidor from Cebu. We knew that help was on the way. Not having control of the air that was needed meant that ammo, etc., never arrived. Read the book *At Dawn We Slept* and observe the lack of

---

* Clark Field and Nichols Field were Army Air Forces bases on Luzon in the Philippines. Cavite, on a peninsula about a dozen miles south of Manila, was the site of the U.S. Navy Yard serving ships in the area. Subic Bay is a protected anchorage on the island of Luzon. It borders the Bataan province and is about 35 miles north of the entrance to Manila Bay.

† This account is probably exaggerated, since U.S. Navy units had been directed to keep a low profile and not be confrontational. The convoy escorted by the light cruiser *Boise* (CL-57) reached Manila on 4 December 1941.

realism first in people in Washington who did not realize the great distances to Manila.[*] Supplies were promised, and we knew they were coming. One of the most unfortunate events occurred about July 1941. The United States embargoed oil and scrap iron going to Japan. With that decision, Japan had to act; Japan had 18 months' reserve of fuel to operate as a viable nation and operate their Navy and merchant marine.

Their first reaction was, "Where is the oil that we must obtain to stay in operation?" There was only one place, the Dutch East Indies. Japan must have made a decision concerning Pearl Harbor and war. Towards the month of November, about a week before Thanksgiving, there was a complete blackout every night around Manila. Navy ships, except a couple in the Cavite Navy Yard, were absent from Manila Harbor. All remained south from July 1941 on, after this embargo had been announced. PBY planes on Neutrality Patrol observed an increase in the number of Japanese ships combat loaded for Camranh Bay, Indochina. Washington was kept informed. The Japanese, when told "You're not going to get any more oil," had to make an effort to control the Dutch East Indies and have access to the oil they needed.

Some reaction expressed in intelligence analyses envisioned, "Well, the Japs are probably going to invade Indochina or Malaya, but they're not going to involve the United States right away." And there was a continual emphasis, even in *At Dawn We Slept*, that the officials in Pearl Harbor did not know the U.S. forces in the Philippines were working with the understanding that a Jap attack on any one of us—British, Dutch, U.S.A.—was an attack on all of us. They avoided realism with the argument the Japanese wouldn't initially involve the Philippines because it was the United States.

They were supposed to be afraid of the U.S.A. Any military man knows full well the Japs were not going 1,000 or 1,500 miles to get oil from the Dutch East Indies with the United States on their flank in a peaceful condition. There again was a lack of realism, a lack too frequently observed during a crisis by officials in high position. Wishful thinking creates dangerous delusions. Washington didn't realize that once they'd approved to rearm the U.S., how long it would take to deliver. If they had

---

[*] Gordon Prange, in conjunction with Donald Goldstein and Katherine V. Dillon, *At Dawn We Slept: the Untold Story of Pearl Harbor* (New York: McGraw-Hill, 1981).

checked how soon it could be delivered, they should have delayed the embargo for six months. A violent reaction by the Japs on the embargo of oil had to be assumed.

According to Admiral Hart's records, the first remark by the President, when Hart saw him at the White House after he was relieved and arrived in March of '42, was reported to have been, "I was assured by MacArthur and Marshall you were ready out there. If I had known that the conditions were not as good as we thought, I could have held off the embargo for another six months." He's absolutely right. If he had held it off for another six months, the Japanese might have delayed the war.

Paul Stillwell: Why do you say that? If he had held off for six months, the Japanese still would have had only a year and a half's supply at that point.

Admiral Knoll: I'm thinking of the political situation in Japan itself. There were a lot of officials in Japan, particularly in their Foreign Service and the Navy, who did not support the idea that war with the U.S.A. ultimately would be needed. So the embargo ultimatum gave the power to militant leaders to say, "Now we have to fight." If we hadn't announced an embargo, they probably wouldn't have attacked that soon.

In July 1941, there was a discussion that the U.S. should maintain a couple more cruisers in Asia when there was an indication the Japs were moving to Camranh Bay and Indochina. Additional cruisers would maintain a blockade between Hong Kong and Manila, and the U.S.A. would state, "Now, don't cross that line." Who knows what might have happened?

At this time a decision was made to build tunnels at Mariveles.[*] As tunnels were developed for the Army on Corregidor, principally the Malinta Tunnel, the Navy added smaller tunnels more or less independent of Manila, with safe access to Malinta without getting outside. They were never finished, such as back-filling with sand. The concrete interior was solid. They were ideal bomb shelters and were wonderfully stocked with a lot of food. Food in the Navy was better than what the Army stocked. It showed there was more realistic planning by the supply people and the engineers. All communication equipment, our NPO radio station, was inside one of these tunnels. NPO never went off

---

[*] Mariveles is an area at the southern tip of the Bataan Peninsula on the island of Luzon in the Philippines.

the air during all the Jap bombing. Antennas were rigged outside and inside the tunnels, so if one antenna was knocked down, a different one was ready for use.

Occasionally, the Japanese raiders would complain that NPO was still on the air as planes departed from bombing us. It showed that Admiral Hart and his staff had done some realistic planning. There was a lack of good coordination between MacArthur and Hart.

Paul Stillwell: How was that time spent between when you moved ashore in July and when the war started? What was your routine in the Marsman Building?

Admiral Knoll: Almost daily short meetings with Admiral Hart and the staff operations officer. Everybody had specific tasks at that time. My primary task was maintaining accurate weather broadcasts to the fleet and Pearl Harbor, assisting the Army with weather forecasts to the Army Air movement of B-17s to Manila, meetings with Father Selga, director of the Philippine Weather Service, working at the weather central at Cavite part-time, and other times at the Marsman Building. Bob Dennison had the desk next to me.

Paul Stillwell: What do you remember about him?

Admiral Knoll: Well, he's been a good friend for years. He made commander the same time I made lieutenant commander in 1941. He was from Warren, Pennsylvania, and we had mutual good friends in Warren. He was a very steady and capable officer. After he retired, I used to have lunch with him about once a week when he was a Washington representative of Copley Press in San Diego.

Paul Stillwell: He was Hart's emissary to MacArthur, wasn't he?

Admiral Knoll: Well, I wouldn't say emissary; rather, he was one of a few of us who had regular liaison with members of the Army staff. I had good access to MacArthur's staff via Lieutenant Sid Huff, who had been my division officer the first year in the first division of the *Texas*.* Huff was personal aide to General MacArthur. When the Navy refused to recall him to active duty, MacArthur made him a lieutenant colonel in the Army Reserve. He was a 90-day wonder who retired and went to the Far East and became involved with the British in setting up a Thornycroft assembly plant for PT boats on the waterfront in Manila. At one time the Philippines talked about building 60 PT boats for the defense of the islands. MacArthur, as field marshal of the Philippine Army, was interested and was a close friend of Sid Huff. In that way, he and the girl he was going with and finally married were close friends of General MacArthur and Jean MacArthur. They frequently were together at important parties.

As field marshal, MacArthur lived in superb quarters provided by the Filipino Government on top of the Manila Hotel. In 1941 he was called back to active duty as a U.S. lieutenant general. So he and Sid Huff and their wives were very close for the entire war. When the war started, Sid Huff wore the uniform as a lieutenant in the U.S. Navy. MacArthur immediately asked Admiral Hart to have Washington promote Sid Huff to commander or captain so he could be his protocol officer.† Admiral Hart refused. At that time, spot promotions were not in vogue. Finally I met Sid, and he was a lieutenant colonel in the U.S. Army. I said, "What happened?"

"Well," he said, "the Navy wouldn't promote me, so MacArthur got me an Army commission." He was a lieutenant colonel and handled all the protocol for Jean MacArthur and the general. He was a savoir faire guy. He would get involved with anything the MacArthurs wanted. He was pleasant, and I always had good relations with him. He got in a couple of incidents when I was with him in *Texas*. He went ashore in Panama City and was robbed of the ship's service funds to buy perfume and stores. He encountered an old girlfriend who robbed him of the money. Anyway, I saw Sid when I moved to Corregidor on Christmas day in 1941. Before Sid left on the PT boats to go to Australia with the MacArthurs in March 1942, I asked Sid, "Who's paying your salary?"

He said, "That's a good point."

I said, "You still getting your retired pay from the Navy?"

---

* Lieutenant Sidney L. Huff, USN (Ret.), was with the military advisor's office in Manila.
† Huff eventually became a colonel in the Army and in 1964 collaborated with Joe Alex Morris on a book titled *My Fifteen Years with General MacArthur*, published by Paperback Library. It was a compilation of a series of articles Huff wrote about MacArthur for *The Saturday Evening Post*, beginning with the issue of 8 September 1951. His relationship with MacArthur began in 1936.

He said, "Yes."

I said, "You also getting active duty pay from the Army?" He said that he was getting Navy pay and also Army pay.

I said, "Sid, to protect yourself from a court-martial, you ought to tell Washington." We prepared a message to send to the Navy Bureau of Supplies and Accounts and explained this unusual situation. A stop payment on retired Navy pay was recommended since he was receiving active duty pay as a lieutenant colonel in the Army. The amount of overpayment could be determined later. The message was sent, and acknowledgement was received.

Later on, when I saw Huff in Tokyo after the war, MacArthur tried to have me join his staff. Huff was then a full colonel, and he said, "We have quarters reserved for you at the Imperial Hotel when you join the staff. Your wife can join you here and stay at the Imperial Hotel if the Navy will order you to MacArthur's staff." BuPers determined that I required some sea duty, and the request was refused.* I had good access to MacArthur through Sid. Dennison and I were the few members of the staff who had regular meetings with MacArthur's staff. We kept Admiral Hart informed of everything we did.

Paul Stillwell: How did Admiral Hart spend that time in the last months before the war?

Admiral Knoll: He was a man of very few words. He was a realist, and he wanted to deal with the facts. Whenever I gave him the weather forecast, I knew that I had to keep it simple but be sure he understood the situation. If he asked questions, I gave him short, direct answers. Every night before he turned in, he kept a meticulous diary, probably the most complete diary that anybody at that time maintained. A copy of that diary went by airmail to Admiral Stark, the CNO. That's a matter of record someplace. I don't know if you people have it or not.

---

* BuPers – Bureau of Naval Personnel.

Paul Stillwell: Hart's biographer had access to the diary.*

Admiral Knoll: I know that, but I believe one of the diaries is with his daughter Isabella.

The final month Hart worked long hours and showed the strain. The morning after Pearl Harbor I saw him for a few minutes. I greeted him, "Admiral, you look ten years younger now that the situation is clear and real." He nodded and smiled.

He was meticulous and a man of few words, exact with facts and details, with many an admonishment to keep it simple. I didn't attend all the staff meetings, but quite a few. Of course Admiral Purnell, the chief of staff, handled the meetings, calling on each in order of seniority, to report developments in area of responsibility. You made sure to say as little as possible but to be ready to answer questions. It was at some of these meetings that I was able to sell my idea of a weather central after giving a briefing on my Singapore experiences. You made sure to say as little as possible but to be ready to answer questions. Admiral Purnell was an ideal chief of staff for Hart.

Some people were afraid of Tommy Hart. It was not to your advantage if you showed timidity. He was a Napoleon type. Any time I went to talk to him, I had to sit down, and he would stand up so he didn't have to look up to me, since he was short, and I was six feet tall. We got in some pretty good discussions from time to time about the weather central and dealing with the Philippine Weather Bureau, which might have some officials friendly to Japan. He would only talk so long. Then he'd say, "Okay, leave."

Normally, the next day he would send for me and say, "Let's continue that discussion." I had a great deal of admiration for him. He was a capable, effective leader. He knew what he was doing, and everybody in the Navy knew he was a smart individual.

Paul Stillwell: What were some of the effects when the war started.

Paul Stillwell: For one thing, the fleet intelligence officer, Rosie Mason, left Manila a few days after December 7. As a result, I gradually got involved in setting up support of the underground and guerrilla movements in Manila and near Baguio. Once a week we

---

* James R. Leutze's biography of Hart is *A Different Kind of Victory* (Annapolis: Naval Institute Press, 1981). Hart's oral history is in the Columbia University collection.

would land an agent on the south shore of Manila Bay, and he would work his way along the coastline to find out what the Japs were doing and where they were located and find out the status of Americans near Manila. Some of my friends, like the RCA representative, British-American Tobacco, and his wife hid out at different farms and barrios. They spent the entire war hiding and never met a Jap. The Japs normally did not bother the farmland.

The Filipinos went to town and set up charge accounts with Compradors at grocery stores on Dewey Boulevard and the vicinity of Manila. Charge accounts were set up so merchants did not accept worthless Jap scrip. At the end of the war the merchants received full payment in U.S. currency with a bonus. Merchants gave what Filipinos ordered, did not reveal the Americans would pay at the end of the war. With the Chinese merchants, they read between the lines because they didn't want to accept worthless Japanese scrip.

In addition to that, some of the people who were on active duty with us on Corregidor, like Wilson, who was a printer, went to Australia as fast as he could and joined MacArthur's staff. Wilson forfeited unlimited amounts of each new Japanese currency sent to the Philippines. Each time the Japanese came out with a new issue of paper currency, copies were rushed to Australia, where millions of copies were printed. This was sent north by sub to flood the islands with counterfeit. Every merchant thus avoided Jap scrip because they knew it was worthless. The Japanese never did counteract it, because it was sent in by submarine and put ashore at night to be distributed.

At one time we set up with a couple of people who were very good to blow up pier seven on the Manila waterfront, which was a monolith structure. The Japanese had stored an awful lot of ammunition or gasoline there. The plan was to take some drums of gasoline, pour gas on the dock at night around the various doors. As it flowed in underneath the doors, it would set afire and blow up the pier shed. Before the plan was implemented, we checked with MacArthur's staff, and the orders came back, "We do not want pier seven damaged during this part of the war, because we need it when we come back." This was a specific guideline.

Our biggest trouble was sending people out on ferret jobs with boats. We had a couple of speedboats manned by good reliable people. The hardest thing was to send them on night observation up the coast of Bataan. They would see something slightly tempting as a good target. They wouldn't refrain from opening up with machineguns and expend a lot of lead and thus reveal themselves. Time and again, we wanted to collect the information clandestinely and return with the Japanese never knowing we had been there. Every time we sent out a mission we had to send out another man as a buddy system. Both of them had to guarantee they would keep the other guy from using machineguns. These American troops were fearless; they'd do anything that was wanted, but the hardest thing was to prevent from giving themselves away with dangerous results.

We knew that most Filipinos never had a real rifle in their hands until they ended up on Bataan. They had trained at different universities with wooden guns. They'd never fired live ammo before. We found out morale was bad. Most untrained Filipinos were on the East Corps area near Manila Bay, with General Wainwright's original corps was on the left side with well-trained Filipino scouts near the South China Sea.* The scouts were a terrific outfit. There was no overall fighting capability, and the Japanese would quickly exploit weaknesses when Bataan started to fall.

I'll never forget, when I was on Corregidor, having gone there on Christmas 1941 after the evacuation of Manila on Christmas Day. There were some Japanese planes around, and they did some bombing but never got too close to any of the ships en route to Corregidor. It took us a couple of hours to cross Manila Bay. After the Japs bombed Cavite Navy Yard on December 10, 1941, I moved to the Army-Navy Club since it was convenient to the Marsman Building. The Philippine Weather Bureau was at Jesuit Ateneo College with Father Selga, so my duties could be carried out. The building I was in at Cavite was one of the first ones to burn down. All personnel had been evacuated before fire swept through the yard. The Cavite Navy Yard burned for more than two days. You could read a newspaper at night in Manila, illuminated by the fire at Cavite Navy Yard a mile away.

I arrived on Corregidor Christmas Day about 4:00 or 5:00 P.M. Leaving Manila we were limited to one handbag, and that's all we had to live with on Corregidor. A lot of us hoped to be back soon. I left all my trunks and possessions in a room at the

---

* Lieutenant General Jonathan M. Wainwright, USA, who was the senior Army officer in the Philippines after the evacuation of General MacArthur.

Army-Navy Club. About 9:00 P.M. Christmas night, word came through the Navy tunnel, "Where is Commander Knoll? Where is Commander Knoll? Admiral Hart wants to see you on the forecastle of the *Shark* at bottomside, north dock."

So I went down to the north dock of Corregidor, and the *Shark* was alongside. In those days, if a submarine came in, it stayed on the bottom during daylight and came to the surface at night to take on torpedoes or supplies. They did this until Bataan surrendered.* Admiral Hart was walking up and down the first deck of the *Shark* when I arrived. "Admiral, do you want to see me?"

Hart said, "Yes, I'm going to leave you here with Colonel Clement.† You're going to have some tough days ahead, but I'll get you out eventually. You continue to work with Generals MacArthur and Wainwright, Admiral Rockwell, and others. I know when you make up your mind, no one is going to change it. I couldn't." I started laughing, and he said, "No, I'm not going to worry. I'll be thinking of you, and I'll take care of you. Don't worry."‡

Well, the interesting thing, finally, everybody on his staff had left, and the only two staff people left were Colonel Clement and myself. As intelligence officer of the 16th Naval District, I knew a couple of days in advance that General MacArthur was getting ready to leave with Admiral Rockwell and Captain Ray, his chief of staff.§ I was alerted that I was to be the principal advisor to Captain Hoeffel, the senior naval officer present.** I was essentially his chief of staff. I had a better appreciation of Admiral Hart's policies and of the Philippines. Other more senior officers lacked experience, and some had only been there less than a year. You have something like 6,000 islands, including 1,600 bigger ones. They don't have any idea where they are and the strategic areas on the Asiatic station.

Paul Stillwell: Why do you say that Admiral Purnell was well suited to be Admiral Hart's chief of staff?

---

* On 9 April 1942, on the Bataan peninsula, U.S. forces under Major General Edward P. King Jr., USA, surrendered to the Japanese.
† Lieutenant Colonel William T. Clement, USMC.
‡ The submarine *Shark* (SS-174) evacuated Admiral Hart from Corregidor at 0200 on 26 December 1941.
§ Captain Herbert J. Ray, USN.
** Captain Kenneth M. Hoeffel, USN, became 16th Naval District Commandant when Rockwell departed on 18 March 1942. Rockwell had been Com 16 since November 1941.

Admiral Knoll: Admiral Hart could be tough on you. But Purnell would be so pleasant. Purnell was quiet and approachable. He understood Admiral Hart and was ready to counsel each staff member how to handle responsibilities and how to make appropriate suggestions to Admiral Hart. He was never too busy for a visit. He was a good balance wheel.

Paul Stillwell: Did you sometimes go through Purnell to get things to Hart because he was easier to approach?

Admiral Knoll: Oh, no. The chief of staff has to be the alter ego of the admiral. As his weather officer, I knew what Hart wanted, and I'd go directly to the admiral's aide for appointment. And if I did have some other problem that Admiral Hart did not need to act on, I could go in to the chief of staff. Purnell knew Hart expected to see me without involving the chief of staff. As chief of staff later for Vice Admiral Ingersoll and others, I operated the same way. If someone went over my head on staff work without me knowing about it, I'd get mad and correct it. The staff knew Admiral Hart wanted to see me normally right after his breakfast in the morning. He wanted to see the latest weather map. If the weather was unusual, he'd frequently tell me to brief the skipper and for typhoon alerts, the chief of staff as well.

Paul Stillwell: Could you describe the period of time that you spent on Corregidor?

Admiral Knoll: The accommodations were better than we expected. We had double-decker bunks, lined along the walls of the Navy tunnels. At each end of one tunnel was a torpedo shop, with a door through which we could exit and look south toward fortified islands. Most of the three Navy tunnels were large enough, from which there were short wings. I used one wing as my weather central and district intelligence office.

In this space we did the coding for operational traffic for the submarines and messages to Pearl Harbor. I had charge in this area, and accordingly I saw all the traffic between submarines in the Far East area. We saw the operational problems they were having with faulty-firing torpedoes. The crews were becoming demoralized, because they could hear the torpedoes hit the side of an enemy ship and not explode. You could sense the morale frustrations of captains and crews.

Frequently we received traffic reviewing communications between President Roosevelt and General MacArthur, between Roosevelt and General Wavell and Churchill.[*] It was good background for intelligence analyses. We had an overview of the political problems back home and were kept up to date. I developed a big chart of the whole Pacific, showing distances between different places. Frequent releases said help was on the way. I'd ask, "Now, where's it coming from? If you have so many Navy ships in the Pacific, when are you going to use them to escort cargoes to Manila?" There were regular briefings for senior Navy and Army officers. It was interesting how quickly certain individuals became adamant, lost interest, and were just waiting to be captured. I kept busy doing something all the time—morning, noon, and night.

I had people working for me. One was an aerographer who spoke Japanese. He would go over on the north side of Corregidor with a small radio. He intercepted traffic from Haneda airfield at Tokyo, picking up weather reports which we would add to our weather in making forecasts sent to Pearl Harbor, saying, "Today the weather in Haneda is so-and-so." Normally in Haneda they were broadcasting in clear Japanese language. Finally a couple of messages came through before the departure of Admiral Rockwell, and he asked, "Does this message make any sense to you?"

I said, "Yes, it says our weather advisories are invaluable for current operations. Keep it up."

He said, "What have you been doing?"

Here was the naval district commandant, arriving about the time the war started. He said, "I didn't realize you were still doing useful work here."

I told him, "I'm sending out two weather maps and forecasts a day and drawing a weather map, and I'm also sending naval intelligence to Washington." He just looked at me and seemed a bit shell shocked. He was amazed that any naval personnel were contributing to the war effort, rather than relax and await capture.

---

[*] Field Marshal Sir Archibald Wavell, British Army. He was Commander ABDACom, which included Australian, British, Dutch, and American forces.

From March 1942 to May 1942, after General MacArthur's departure, I gave a regular intelligence briefing to General Wainwright before he retired each night.[*]

Later on, Commander Dennison was with Rockwell in the Aleutian Islands operations. I talked to Rockwell a couple of times about the Philippine Islands, how many there were and their locations. He had no concept of where Cebu or Mindanao or other places were, and he didn't seem to be interested. He never would come to look at my chart and try to orient himself as to where the Philippine Islands were and where Singapore was. That's the part that always amazed me.

The same way we picked up how many planes were taking off in Taiwan to come down and bomb us. They departed near Takao in Taiwan, and we knew they would arrive over us at about 12:30. We arranged to have breakfast about 7:00 or 8:00 in the morning, and then we delayed the evening meal preparations after the raid was over, around 3:00 or 4:00 o'clock. We had only two meals per day; food was scarce.

The first raid was the worst one. That was when the 54 planes that came over Cavite Navy Yard about noon on the tenth of December. After the first pass they broke up into groups of then and then groups of three, made about eight different passes. Lacking antiaircraft guns, we just lay on the beach and carved out small foxholes. One oil line sprayed some oil on us when it was hit. When you see 54 planes come over at above 30,000 feet in a beautiful, cloudless sky, and then they just started dropping bombs at will, with no interference from fighter planes or antiaircraft guns, it was a very frustrating and demoralizing experience.

Paul Stillwell: Was it generally known in advance who would be evacuated from Corregidor and who would be left to be captured?

Admiral Knoll: No. There was no local decision on that. After General MacArthur left, I received briefings from the people at Monkey Point, including traffic from Pearl Harbor. I had a good appreciation of the world picture, and I would brief Captain Hoeffel

---

[*] On 11 March 1942, General Douglas MacArthur, whom President Roosevelt had personally ordered to leave the Philippines, escaped from Corregidor with his family and selected staff members on board four PT boats of Lieutenant John D. Bulkeley's Motor Torpedo Boat Squadron Three. MacArthur reached Mindanao on 14 March, then continued his journey to Darwin, Australia, by airplane on 17 March.

accordingly. I told him what I was hearing and kept him informed. The same lieutenant would always brief me on all the intercepts and what they were receiving. They knew I had been breaking the Japanese weather code to help make my daily map. We had started to break the Japanese weather code for the Marianas Islands before Pearl Harbor, which helped make an accurate map. Whether the Japanese broke ours, I don't know. I doubt it, because the decide procedures had been carefully distributed in the Philippines, British, and Dutch with assurance that the Japanese would not have access to them.

Paul Stillwell: Were you completely indoctrinated on the general U.S. code-breaking ability?

Admiral Knoll: No—in no way. I had taken a correspondence course for about six months, but I never got involved. I had an idea of the work being done, even before leaving Washington. It was highly classified, and I never revealed what I knew or suspected.

Paul Stillwell: I'm just wondering how much awareness you had of their capability.

Admiral Knoll: From the beginning, I knew of the location of different units that were doing this. I don't remember how I knew it. I knew what they were doing at Monkey Point and who was working there. I never talked to anyone about it. The amazing thing to me is that we had the complete capability for that at Monkey Point, and they had only a limited capability at Pearl Harbor. Why? There again, that shows the prestige and capability of Admiral Tommy Hart. He, I'm sure, was able to obtain that capability for the Asiatic Fleet before he left Washington.

Paul Stillwell: More to it, the codebreakers hadn't been supplied the machine in Pearl Harbor, which made a great difference.

Admiral Knoll: They may have had some of the machines, but they didn't have Japanese language students and cryptographers.* They were lacking in intelligence people at times.† Some of the material we were sending them, they didn't seem to realize how accurate it was compared to their work. I think the advance planning in Washington was wrong. With the same capability at Pearl and Monkey Point, it could have been a different story. The number of qualified people was scarce.

Paul Stillwell: When you were in Corregidor, was there in some people very much of a defeatist attitude, would you say?

Admiral Knoll: Oh, very much so. I've heard a senior officer say, "Well, there's no use in fighting here. What can we do with Hitler and Tojo?"‡

A couple of other ones said, "Oh, the Japanese. I knew some Japs, and they know I'm here. They're going to search for me and really punish me and torture me," and this kind of talk. I know there was a certain group I avoided because every time a discussion started with them, they were defeatist all the way through.

In addition to that, I've never seen this operation reported. We had an officer working party to burn all the U.S. paper money that was in the Manila clearinghouse. They brought it over from the Manila clearinghouse, and there were tons of silver money that they didn't try to move. They assembled all this paper money. Officer working parties took packs of $100.00 bills and tossed them in a big cauldron to personally check the serial numbers off and burn them under the supervision of the supply officer. We burned money every day like that for more than ten days.

Paul Stillwell: Why?

---

* Commander Joseph J. Rochefort, USN, a Japanese language specialist, was in charge of the radio intelligence unit at Pearl Harbor. For details see Rochefort's Naval Institute oral history and his biography, Elliot Carlson, *Joe Rochefort's War: the Odyssey of the Codebreaker who Outwitted Yamamoto at Midway* (Annapolis: Naval Institute Press, 2011).
† The Pacific Fleet intelligence officer, Lieutenant Commander Edwin T. Layton, USN, had, like Rochefort, taken the Japanese language course. The two conferred frequently.
‡ Hideki Tojo was a general in the Imperial Japanese Army and served as Prime Minister of Japan during much of World War II, from 18 October 1941 to 22 July 1944.

Admiral Knoll: So it couldn't be captured. This was January 1942. There was no use keeping it in Corregidor. They never paid any attention to the silver. I know one officer that saved all the U.S. paper money when Cavite was being bombed and burned, and for hazarding himself to save the paper money, he received the Navy Cross before leaving Corregidor. The interesting thing was, later on, they found out that most of the silver money never had been moved. I guess when the Japs arrived they were surprised to find many American silver dollars.

The interesting thing, when Admiral Tommy Hart saw me one time at the Navy Department after I got back in July 1942. He was on the General Board, and he told me, "You're getting the Navy Cross for what you've done."

General Wainwright told me when I left, "You'll be getting a decoration from the Army. You've been invaluable to me."

I was waiting to be called to come to the office of the Secretary of the Navy, Frank Knox. I think Admiral Hart was there, and Lieutenant Ann Bernatitus, Navy nurse, was there.* I went with the expectation I was going to get the Navy Cross. There was a discussion about a new decoration that was going to be the equivalent of the Navy Cross. I was the first member of the U.S. Armed Forces to receive a Legion of Merit. Admiral Hart wasn't very happy about it. Somebody at BuPers had overruled him. Subject to that, Bob Dennison told me that the Army's recommendation for me for a Distinguished Service Medal was returned to the Army. BuPers said I had enough recognition for Corregidor. They didn't want the Army to give it to me. Later on, you can observe how the Legion of Merit lost prestige. It was awarded indiscriminately, particularly by the Air Force.

Paul Stillwell: Would you put Admiral Rockwell in that group of defeatists?

Admiral Knoll: No. He had been in a close bombing, and he was slightly shell-shocked for a while. I understand after he got back for rehabilitation he was a different person.

---

* Ann A. Bernatitus served in the siege of Bataan and Corregidor. Navy nurses at that time did not have actual rank; she had a relative rank of lieutenant (junior grade). She was evacuated on 3 May from Corregidor on board the submarine *Spearfish* (SS-190) just before the Japanese captured the island. She was the only nurse there who was not captured. Bernatitus received the Legion of Merit in October 1942. Sources credit her with being the first American to receive the Legion of Merit.

General MacArthur was almost killed at being "topside" on Corregidor. His aide had to pull him into a bomb shelter. People do not realize what an individual like General MacArthur can do for morale, whether they're defeatist or not. I'll never forget his attitude. He was a fearless individual. He never wore a trench hat or took precautions. He lived out in the only house between Malinta Tunnel and Monkey Point. An air-raid alarm would sound, and his wife Jean and son, young Arthur MacArthur, would come running into Malinta Tunnel. Maybe 10 or 15 minutes later, the general would walk slowly to Malinta Tunnel with his swagger stick, wearing his embroidered hat. He walked along like nothing was happening, even though bombs had started to fall. You can imagine the effect.

I mentioned the topside incident. There were three levels. There was a bottom side, middle side, and topside on Corregidor. Troop barracks and parade ground were on topside. Coastal defense guns were on the middle side. Bottom side were docks and a Filipino village. He was walking along near the old parade ground and officers' club when a Japanese plane dropped bombs. His aide grabbed him and pulled him into a shelter. They said if he hadn't been sheltered, he certainly would have been injured from the shrapnel-loaded bombs. He didn't want to admit his aide really pulled him out of harm's way.

Paul Stillwell: Did Rockwell seem really interested in carrying on the fight?

Admiral Knoll: Oh, no doubt about that. This is an interesting story. I had a complete hydro portfolio of all the charts for the Philippine Islands. I knew the PT boats were getting ready to leave. I knew better than to mention a word to Lieutenant Bulkeley about it.* He should have obtained charts from me for the Sulu Sea and Mindanao. I knew Lieutenant Kelly and some of the other PT boat officers were getting ready to leave.

I knew General MacArthur was about to leave. I had seen the dispatches pertaining to his move. The thing that convinced him to leave was President Roosevelt's

---

* Lieutenant John D. Bulkeley, USN, received the Medal of Honor for his operations in command of a PT boat squadron around the Philippines in the early part of World War II.

appeal that if he did not go to Australia and take command, there would be an adverse reaction of the Aussie and the New Zealand people. Due to their losses in Egypt and their losses in Singapore, they threatened to withdraw from the war. The prime argument to MacArthur was that only he, with his reputation, could go and keep Australia and New Zealand in the war. Until this appeal he was determined he was going to stay on Corregidor to the end. In this way he was not ordered to leave, but he was convinced to leave by the dispatches that went back and forth. Accordingly, I knew he was going to be leaving.

I had gone in a couple of times with dispatches to Colonel Diller, his public relations officer.[*] We prepared intelligence dispatches for him to release. I would sit outside waiting while he had worked on them. The tonnages of various Jap naval ships that were in Olongapo or Subic Bay were estimated and ready for his release. He read each message, and he'd say, "Now, wait a second." He'd take his pencil and add a zero after each tonnage estimate. If we put a 1,500-ton ship, he'd put another zero, and it would be 15,000. He said, "The American people are looking for a victory, which we have to assure them, give Hearst material to write about."[†]

In addition to that, an effort was made to obtain recognition for what the Marines did to help the retreat into Bataan. The Army withdrew the First Corps and the Second Corps, while the Marines who had been at the junction point, remained about a mile and a half ahead of the new main line of resistance. No one told the Marines the Army Corps was withdrawing during the night. Colonel Sam Howard was at a joint meeting in Manila as withdrawal into Bataan was proceeding.[‡] He quickly left the meeting to order his Marines to withdraw. Later the Fourth Marines did a superb job on Corregidor. There was no beach defense on the shoreline of Corregidor until the Fourth Marines arrived. They organized a beach defense on the shoreline of Corregidor, and they lived right on that beach from then on. Until that time, the Japanese could have landed on Corregidor without opposition.

---

[*] Lieutenant Colonel LeGrande A. Diller, USA. As soon as MacArthur was evacuated to Australia in March 1942 he promoted Diller to temporary colonel.
[†] Hearst was one of the prominent U.S. newspaper chains.
[‡] Colonel Samuel L. Howard, USMC, of the Fourth Marines, who had been stationed in Shanghai, China.

There was an occasional suggestion regarding getting recognition for what the Marines had accomplished. MacArthur said, "The Marines and the Navy got too much recognition in World War I, and I'm going to take care of the Army in World War II." But as General Wainwright took over, he gave special recognition to the Navy and Marines. I used to see Wainwright every day from then on, and I would always brief him on the intelligence I was receiving.

A lieutenant would bring it to me. He asked, "Now, Commander, you're not telling anybody about this but Captain Hoeffel, are you?"

I said, "What do you mean?"

He said, "Well, you've got to be officially cleared to do this." I never signed anything for getting this information, even though I'd been working with them. Normally you had to sign all kind of control over what you can and what you can't say about it, and I never signed anything to this day.

So I said, "Yes, I'm briefing General Wainwright."

"You are?"

I said, "Yes. After all, he's the senior commanding officer of the U.S. Armed Forces here. If he doesn't have the right to know what I know, then I've never been raised right."

He said, "Well, we'll have to report you to Admiral King."

I said, "I hope you will. You can report me to anyone you want. Don't tell me this and think I'm not going to tell General Wainwright. He's our boss."

About a week later, he came in to brief me. He finished, and he said, ""We've reported you to Admiral King."

"You did?"

"Yes, Admiral King said you were right."

Paul Stillwell: What can you tell me about the role of the nurses there during the Corregidor period?

Admiral Knoll: There were two kinds of nurses, those who were experienced nurses who worked hard taking care of the infirm, and those who were quite young and trying to impress the boys and get dates. It was amazing. I think most of the nurses who did really pass the test as nurses were those who had been in the Philippines a few months before the war started. The young new arrivals never had the real training as Army nurses. They joined the Army to see the world. You'd see them during working hours in their nurses' uniforms. About 4:00 or 5:00 in the afternoon, about the time they were getting ready for the evening meal, they'd come out dressed in glamour clothes to attract the boys. Some way or another, they had civilian dresses, and they'd have their hair fixed up. Some of them were smart-looking gals. They'd look for a date and go walking off with them, have a little dance, and find a niche to do a little necking in the dark. That was the one kind.

The other nurses were really dedicated. I knew a couple that I had met before the war started. They frequented jai alai and the Army-Navy Club. When you saw the real nurses on Corregidor at night, they were still dressed as nurses, and they were dedicated and ready for an emergency. Some of them ended up on Bataan, the good ones, and they were indispensable over there, particularly towards the end. We were concerned after Bataan had fallen. We went down to the beach watching, and any time we saw one of them near the shoreline, we sent a boat over to rescue her. We knew a lot of people over there who would try to avoid Jap capture and get to Corregidor. We kept a lookout, and we saw a couple of nurses at an isolated point, and we sent a boat over.

Among them was one girl I used to have dates with from time to time. She had blood on her uniform and had not slept for 48 hours. She'd been at the last field hospital taking care of injured till the Japs appeared. How the Japanese missed her, you never know. Some way or another she got to the beach. I think part of this was written up, giving the many thousands they cared for in those field hospitals in Bataan. Most of them came over to Corregidor and were not captured. She went into the nurses' quarters at the hospital in Malinta Tunnel. We met occasionally for a movie in the tunnel when things were quiet.

It started getting tough after Bataan fell. There were about 12,000 people on Corregidor, including a lot of Filipinos as well as Navy people. General Wainwright didn't like it very much. The Navy brought over additional personnel from Mariveles, and he couldn't bring any more Army personnel to Corregidor. We had enough food to feed Navy personnel, and he finally gave in. All the tunnels were crowded. Religious services were held every morning in the Malinta tunnel. After Bataan fell, every day there would be many more in attendance. Towards the end, when I left there, it seemed everybody was crowded in for Catholic Mass in the tunnel, even those who were very despondent.

Early in the war, there was an initial surge, and the Japanese made a major attack on the U.S. forces in Bataan, supported by air raids. A lull ensued, and the Jap first-line troops were pulled out and went to Burma. For a while, you could walk practically back to Manila and not encounter Japanese troops on Bataan. They had hoped we'd try to go back, so they'd catch us the next time, trying to get into Bataan. It was the time to improve our lines of resistance, which is what Wainwright did, consistent with the limited resources available. The Japanese troops that returned to Bataan were not well trained, and many were recovering from injuries of prior actions.

About this time President Quezón and Vice President Osmeña were walking around on Corregidor. They stopped to visit us, and we had an unusual conversation. This conversation really took place. It showed President Quezón didn't share the seriousness of war. Quezón, in front of Osmeña, said, "The quicker General MacArthur and the United States make a deal with the Japanese and declare a 48-hour armistice, the Filipinos can get out of the way, and then the Japanese should fight it out with the American on the Cabanatuan Plain north of Manila. The Filipinos should be left alone, because we are not a part of this war." He went on like this, deadly serious. The President of the Philippines and his Vice President, Osmeña, deplored all the damage to the Philippines and his people. He said, "Battles on Corregidor and Bataan is a war between the United States and Japan." I relayed this comment to General MacArthur and his staff. Efforts were made for Quezón to return. Special arrangements were made to send them to the United States and keep them from talking to the troops.[*] This was in January 1942. It was startling to hear the President of the country state that he was not a loyal ally in our war with Japan.

---

[*] Manuel L. Quezón served as president of the Commonwealth of the Philippines from 1935 until his death in 1944. As the Japanese advanced in 1942, Quezón was evacuated and spent his remaining years in exile in the United States.

Paul Stillwell: There was also that report a few years ago that he took out a good deal of money, both for himself and for MacArthur.

Admiral Knoll: He probably sent it out ahead of time. There were different deals rumored. I have some silver dollars that were dropped off the dock at Corregidor, and people dove down and got them. I obtained one when I went back in the *Severn*. Some friends said, "Here are some of the silver dollars, and they're still green from the salt water, picked up with shallow-water diving gear." During the war bombing sank the liquor barge from the Army-Navy Club. Shallow-water diving recovered some liquor while we were still there. General MacArthur received a significant salary from Quezón as field marshal of the Filipino Army that he was training before the war.

Paul Stillwell: How was it determined who would go on the evacuation from Corregidor?

Admiral Knoll: The word "evacuation" never came up. One day we realized the bombing was really getting severe, after Bataan fell. Japs bombed us more, and they started shelling from Bataan. They had clusters of guns they spotted in on different key targets on Corregidor for the final assault. They were spotting in for the ultimate operation, the invasion. It was only a question of time, with the buildup of boats in Manila and at Cavite. Some of them had been attacked and damaged, but nevertheless they were making the effort to get anything afloat to bring their crews to Corregidor.

One evening, when I was sitting with General Wainwright, he said, "We have to make a list." We knew patrol planes were coming from Australia, two PBYs, and we knew the submarine *Spearfish* was due. We couldn't tell anybody about this. It was just between Wainwright and Captain Hoeffel and myself. Wainwright said, "I've about six dispatches here from Washington, Pearl Harbor, and Melbourne, et al, listing who shouldn't be captured. You're there. Your name is on every list. Your first cousin, Charlie Weschler, is on three lists. Do you want to go out on a PBY or the submarine?"

I said, "I'll wait for the submarine."

He said, "It may never get here."

I said, "That's my chance. I want to get the maximum number of people out in PBYs. My first cousin, Weschler, has had black malaria, and he's not too well. He wouldn't necessarily survive on a submarine, but if we could get him to Australia he will be better off."

He said, "All right." So he made the list of Army people. Captain Hoeffel apparently had talked to Wainwright, and that's how Tip Parker, Captain Wilson, and three other naval officers were designated. I was the junior one of the six naval officers who were designated to leave on the submarine. Ann Bernatitus, a Navy Nurse, was added, and also about six Army officers and about 12 Army nurses went out on the submarine.*

General Wainwright called Colonel Nesbit, who was the head Army nurse on Corregidor, and the 12 Army nurses were selected.† I didn't have much say in the matter, but I observed the procedure for determining who was going to be evacuated. It went along this way: "Well, this is going to be a long war. We've got a lot of people that are injured and should be taken care of. It's sad, but those who are the best nurses are the ones we need to stay here to take care of the injured. These play girls must be allowed to leave. Some of them are mamas' babies, they haven't been in the Army very long, they'll be a liability." Actually, it was finally decided that those who were the best nurses, that had done the best battlefield job, were designated to remain. A group of them were sent out on the PBYs. The ones by sub with us, practically every one of them did not act completely sane at times. They were all youngsters—not mature enough for the demands of war. You'd hate to have them come in dressed as a nurse and think they could take care of you.

---

* On 3 May 1942, the submarine *Spearfish* (SS-190) took aboard at Corregidor six Army officers, six Navy officers, 11 Army nurses, one Navy nurse, one civilian woman, and two stowaways for evacuation to Fremantle, Australia. She was the last U.S. submarine that visited Corregidor before the Japanese captured the island. Navy personnel evacuated by the *Spearfish* were Commander Raymond G. Deewall, USN, who had been captain of the yard at Cavite; Commander Earl L. Sackett, USN, commanding officer of the submarine tender *Canopus* (AS-9); Commander James D. Wilson, CEC, USN, from the 16th Naval District staff; Lieutenant Commander Thurlow W. Davison, USN, commanding officer of the minesweeper *Finch* (AM-9), which had been sunk on 10 April; Lieutenant Commander Thomas C. Parker, USN, who had been on the staff of the High Commissioner of the Philippines; Nurse Ann A. Bernatitus, Nurse Corps, USN; and Lieutenant Commander Knoll.

† First Lieutenant Josephine Nesbit, USA, was acting chief nurse at Sternberg General Hospital in Manila when the war started. She was captured on Corregidor and interned along with fellow nurses at Santo Tomas in Manila until liberated in February 1945. See Elizabeth M. Norman, *We Band of Angels: The Untold Story of American Nurses Trapped on Bataan* (New York: Random House, 1999).

There was an interesting sequel to this, and this you'll appreciate. I met some of these nurses after they spent the whole war in Santo Tomas, which is the university in Manila that they made into an internment compound for U.S. civilians as well as military, such as the wives of military people and others who had been interned, like American citizens in Manila. I knew some of the families there.

Paul Stillwell: You met some of them afterwards?

Admiral Knoll: I met some of them afterwards, and they had spent the whole war in Santo Tomas. So I talked to them about what happened after I left. Of course, the Japs started landing before the *Spearfish* was out of sight. They made their first attempted landing at Corregidor just east of the Malinta Tunnel. *Spearfish* submerged and sat on the bottom. After a little bit, we'd go to the surface and charge the battery. We were about ten miles seaward of Corregidor when radio station NPO went off the air. The Japanese destroyers knew *Spearfish* was in the area, because some navigational lights on Corregidor had been turned on for the submarine's approach. They never dropped a depth charge on us, but we could hear them.

The Japs quickly took control of Corregidor. The first thing they ordered was that all the females, and particularly the nurses, go into the hospital laterals of Malinta Tunnel. Then they put an American officer as guard on the hospital areas. The nurses took care of the patients there for a few days. It was almost a week until transportation was available to take them to Manila. The ship was manned by Americans, with the only Japanese on the bridge. This nurse, who was a retired lieutenant colonel in the Air Force, told me a few years ago that she never talked to a Jap during the entire war, on Corregidor or at Santo Tomas.

The Japs moved them under U.S. troop guard when they got ashore in Manila, took them to Santo Tomas University, and they would never be permitted to approach the gate where the Jap sentries were stationed. All this was to make sure there were no atrocities. She couldn't believe it. And I've heard this from other families. The Japs went out of their way to make sure there were no atrocities among the internees. There had been some early in the war. How many of that were true, how many of that were rumored is open to question. As soon as this one nurse had been rehabilitated in the States, she volunteered a year later to go to Japan; she was with the Air Force Hospital at Tachikawa outside Tokyo. When I was in Yokosuka with the *Severn* shortly after the war, we met her in Tokyo, and that's when I was told these stories. This is interesting background for one phase of the war.

In addition to the above, my aerographer's mate, Zemo Tarnowski, ultimately retired as a commander.* He was an aerographer's mate first class at the start of the war and helped me write the climatology book. When the Japs came into the Navy tunnel, they located the coding room in the middle lateral, including the place where I drew the weather maps and prepared coded material for Pearl Harbor. They found a large roll of daily weather maps that I had prepared. Tarnowski was the senior aerographer's mate they took and questioned on the south shore of Corregidor, near a former handball court. A Japanese general and his staff witnessed the grilling, with their swords lying on a table. Tarnowski said there were six or eight assistants. The Japs had the weather maps and wanted to know where I obtained the large amount of data. Tarnowski said he didn't know. I had given it to him, and he had plotted it, and I drew the maps.

The Japs complained that the maps were better than what they had. There were reports from Korea and China and the Dutch East Indies, and they wanted to know how I obtained them. Occasionally one of the Americans being questioned would be taken aside and shot by the Japs to intimidate the others being questioned. They took Tarnowski up three times and cross-examined him to find out where I was. The Japs told him they were trying to bring the submarine back with me aboard. Finally, Tarnowski said in desperation, the final time the Japs brought him up for questioning, "I have to tell him something different. I'm going to be one of those they pick out for shooting." The Japs were giving him a bad time, not beating him but just grilling and grilling and grilling him. He said finally he was just so fed up, and they said, "Where did this weather data come from?"

He said, "I don't know. Knoll had frequent communications with the head of the weather observatory in Osaka, Japan." The Japs told him to leave, and he never saw them again for questioning.

---

* Tarnowski later received the Navy Cross for his heroism and leadership while a prisoner of war.

Paul Stillwell: Could you relate, please, the fate of the PBY your cousin was in?

Admiral Knoll: Well, that's rather sad. Now, I have to go back a bit for the events leading up to this. Charlie's daughter was born at Cañacao hospital.* Her mother had stayed after the Navy wives were sent home. Mother and daughter returned to the States in early 1941. Weschler and family lived at Olongapo, and he was in charge of the floating dry dock *Dewey*.†

When Manila was declared an open city on Christmas Day 1941, all naval activities were moved to Corregidor, and all naval activities at Olongapo were moved to Mariveles on Bataan, across the channel from Corregidor. *Dewey* dry dock was busy around the clock, repairing PT boats and other craft. The submarine tender *Canopus*, commanded by Commander Earl Sackett, was also at Mariveles, working closely with the dry dock. During daylight, the dry dock was flooded down to reduce the danger of damage from daily bombings. More than once some bombs were dropped on Mariveles in an attempt to hit the *Canopus* or *Dewey* dry dock.

When word was received that Bataan was about to surrender, Captain Hoeffel directed me to call Earl Sackett and tell him to scuttle *Canopus* and the *Dewey* dry dock. With great reluctance, General Wainwright agreed that Navy personnel from Mariveles could join the Navy group on Corregidor. He wished that he could do the same for select Army troops, particularly the very reliable Philippine Scouts.

As the evacuation of Navy personnel started from Mariveles around midnight, the entire area was shaken with a short, violent earthquake. Early the next morning I was at the dock to meet Commander Sackett, Charles Weschler, and others as they came ashore from Mariveles. I had saved the bunk under mine in the Navy Tunnel for Weschler. For the next two weeks, he had a bad case of black malaria and was very sick. Captain Hoeffel and I were the only two Navy persons who knew that some few Army and Navy personnel would be ordered to leave via PBY and submarine. A tentative list of Navy personnel was prepared with assistance of General Wainwright.

---

* Cañacao Naval Hospital was on the Cañacao Peninsula, which juts into Manila Bay.
† USS *Dewey* (YFD-1) was a floating dry dock built for the U.S. Navy in 1905 and named in honor of Admiral George Dewey, USN, hero of the Spanish-American War. On 8 April 1942 Lieutenant Charles J. Weschler, USN, to docking officer, scuttled the *Dewey* at Mariveles, Bataan, to keep her from being used by the Japanese. The *Canopus* (AS-9) was scuttled by her crew on 10 April.

As I said, I explained to Wainwright that Weschler, my cousin would be well enough to travel by plane, but three to four weeks in a submarine would not help his recovery. I discussed with Weschler that some evacuation might be available, and he should assure the doctor he felt well enough to travel. He was assigned to one of two PBYs that landed in moonlight south of Corregidor about 11:00 P.M., April 29, 1942. The PBYs brought scarce antiair ammo, and 25 Army and Navy officers were evacuated in each plane. Commander Frank Bridget was the senior aviator in the plane with Weschler.[*]

The 29th of April was the Emperor's birthday.[†] From first light to darkness, it was the worst day for bombing and shelling of the whole war. The sun looked like a huge orange in the sky, obscured by smoke and dust. There wasn't any shrub or green item left on any part of the island. After dark, as the moon was coming up, everything had finally quieted down. Corregidor was in a shambles. We had time to notify individuals to get ready to leave. The word had been passed very carefully so other people didn't know anyone was leaving. They were told where to assemble, not knowing whether they would leave by plane, boat, or sub. As the planes were coming in, we loaded the boats at the south side dock, and all went off very well. The two planes departed in less than an hour and went to Lake Lanao, in Mindanao.

A PBY with a heavy load will blow a few rivets during takeoff and landing. Hulls are rather easy to patch. Both planes landed on Lake Lanao. While one PBY was taxiing over to fuel, the one with Charlie Weschler hit something underwater and knocked a small hole in the hull. Greasy Neale was the pilot, and he quickly taxied it over to a beach area and brought it partially out of water.[‡] The plane crew started to repair the damage. The passengers viewed the situation, and Frank Bridget said, "Well, this plane probably won't take off." He had been with PatWing 5 before he came out to the Far East. Bridget suggested, "We better go over to the Army field about ten miles

---

[*] Commander Francis J. Bridget, USN, was on the staff of Commander Patrol Wing Ten.
[†] Hirohito became Emperor of Japan in 1926 and was given the status of a descendent of the ancient sun goddess. He was above politics but wielded influence nonetheless. When Japan surrendered in 1945, the Allies forced him to renounce his divinity, but he remained Emperor and continued as the symbolic head of state until his death in 1989. Hirohito was born 29 April 1901.
[‡] Lieutenant Commander Edgar T. Neale, USN, was commanding officer of Patrol Squadron 102 (VP-102), which was part of Patrol Wing Ten.

away, because there are Army planes coming in and out of there from Australia." They hitchhiked over to the Army base to obtain a ride to Australia.

Captain McGuigan, who had been a construction officer at Cavite, helped Greasy Neale put a soft patch on the plane that had been damaged.[*] They looked around for Frank Bridget and his passengers and learned they went over to the Army field. No Army being available, they turned around and started to come back to Lake Lanao. Japanese patrols had interdicted the path between the Army and Navy base at Lake Lanao. The two PBY planes were ready to take off, and Neale couldn't find the passengers who were supposed to be with them. Captain McGuigan and some other five or six other naval personnel loaded Neale's plane and flew to Australia.

I left Corregidor the third or fourth of May, and there was no information about the PBY plane not getting out of Mindanao or being delayed. When I arrived at Fremantle about 1 June 1942, one of the first things I asked Captain Grosskopf or Captain John Wilkes, "Where is Charlie Weschler?"[†]

They said, "Well, his plane had problems on Mindanao, and he didn't get here, but a few people did. McGuigan did." So I visited the PBY plane he was on. I had given them mail for my mother and my wife to mail in Australia. I checked the documents in the engineer's compartment, and on one of the manuals were the letters I had given Charlie to mail. So the letters I gave Weschler I brought home with me. He didn't make it.

Paul Stillwell: So he was captured by patrols on that road.

Admiral Knoll: The Japs probably witnessed the landings of the PBYs and closed the road between bases. They were captured and taken to prison camp at Davao. About that time, Mel McCoy, lieutenant commander, class of '27, a clever individual and a communicator, escaped from the prison camp at Davao.[‡] Word was received that McCoy was free, and finally the Navy was able to send a submarine to the rendezvous to pick

---

[*] Captain Joseph L. McGuigan, USN.
[†] Captain Homer L. Grosskopf, USN, who had been slated to command the *Houston*. Captain John Wilkes, USN, Commander Submarine Squadron 20.
[‡] Lieutenant Commander Melvyn H. McCoy, USN, who had been stationed at the Cavite Navy Yard. His escape was on 4 April 1943—nearly a year after the evacuations from Corregidor.

him up. He had complete knowledge of naval communications to make contact and knew the call signs and procedures to arrange to be picked up before the Japanese could recapture him. The Japanese increased security at Davao after he got out, but he was the type of guy who could do it. Through him I found out Charlie Weschler was all right, and there were other communications from time to time concerning conditions at Davao.

I think it must have been when the Japanese realized they were not going to win the war that they moved these prisoners from Davao by Japanese ship with a stop at Subic Bay. Some prisoners were in miserable condition. A lot of them weren't well, and apparently Charlie Weschler was one of the more healthy ones. While they were in Olongapo, our aircraft bombed this prison ship, and Charlie Weschler and some others in better physical condition were able to swim ashore and were apparently free of the Japanese for a couple of days in Luzon, only to be recaptured. They were put on another ship going north. Weschler and others were in a Japanese ship not marked as carrying prisoners of war. He was injured seriously by shrapnel in the abdomen, I think, in January of '45 near Taiwan and was buried at sea.

It so happens that the prison ship sunk at Olongapo created a bad situation. It fouled the main dock there. When I was chief of staff to Seventh Fleet, with Admiral Pride and Admiral Ingersoll in the 1950s, it was interfering with the use of that dock. A couple of divers went down to investigate. They reported that many prisoners had perished when it was sunk. Without publication it was time to remove the wreckage of this ship. With Washington's approval, we gradually arranged to get this ship out of the way. It was completely invisible from the surface. There was no way of going in and trying to identify bodies after more than ten years of deterioration. A sad situation.

Paul Stillwell: It sounds like it was a menace to navigation.

Admiral Knoll: It was, yes. Out of respect to the many lost in the sinking, official circles were reluctant to remove it too soon.

Paul Stillwell: Could you describe your time on board the submarine?

Admiral Knoll: The one thing, the skipper, of course, was a good friend of mine, Jimmy Dempsey, a year junior to me.* When we came out with the boat, Lieutenant Morell took us out in this 40-foot launch over the minefield on the south side of Corregidor. We tried to drag some of the mines clear so we wouldn't hit a mine going out, because we didn't want to go out the main channel. We knew we had to get out of there before the submarine would show up as a silhouette in the rising moon. As soon as it was dark, we got aboard the launch and went out to wait. One boatload was everybody. I had my pistol, small valise, and my trench hat. I sent the trench hat back, but I still have the pistol I brought out. We held our breath until *Spearfish* started to surface less than a mile away. It was our first assurance that *Spearfish* had received the order and had not been delayed.

We had no word of any kind that he was going to be there. We knew his orders were he'd be there at such and such a time, but this is the way it always happened. We had no idea until they showed up, because they didn't want to show any communications to compromise them. So it was Wainwright and Hoeffel who said, "He's supposed to be here. We'll have to go out and wait for him." That was true. In January and February 1942, we sent out people from time to time to meet subs, but one hadn't been in for a couple of months. And so he broke the surface about one mile just west of Corregidor, and Dempsey was on the bridge. He said, "Are you friend or foe?" because he saw a fire behind where the Japanese had started shelling, trying to land. Navigation lights had been turned on on Corregidor to help him make landfall.

I said, "It's all right, Jimmy."

He said, "Who is it?"

"Denny Knoll."

He said, "Okay, come alongside. We went alongside, and we had prepared for a couple of days in getting all the health records and service records for the Marine and Navy personnel and packing them in boxes. We checked with the submarine people on Corregidor as to the size of the forward hatch through which the boxes would be loaded. We made boxes accordingly. We passed the 13 nurses aboard like cords of wood. They didn't know if they were going in headfirst or feet first and down through the hatch into

---

* Lieutenant Commander James C. Dempsey, USN, commanded the USS *Spearfish* (SS-190) in 1942-43.

the wardroom. They were stunned. On the deck were six or eight boxes. Jimmy asked, "What's all this?"

"They're service records for Navy and Marine personnel on Corregidor."

We tried to pass them down through the hatch, but they were too large. On the open deck we had to open the boxes with axes to get these records down below, because the dimensions we had of the hatches were not correct. These were the health records and service records of the people on Corregidor. Captain Hoeffel thought it would be good if these were sent to Washington. The first day we practically did not move beyond the Jap destroyers ten miles off Corregidor. We stayed on the surface charging batteries. When the moon was up, you couldn't charge the battery very long, or the Japs would see the silhouette in the moonlight. We charged batteries, moved a few miles, and settled on the bottom.

The Japanese destroyers based in Subic, every time they knew from navigation lights on Corregidor that something was coming in or out, they'd cruise back and forth. We could hear their screws overhead, with ping, ping, ping from sonar trying to find us, but they didn't. Everyone moved barefoot and made no noise. The second night we gradually moved out, and we went out submerged. The third night we came to the surface to charge the batteries completely out beyond the patrols by the Jap destroyers. There were rumors they had mined between Luzon and Lubang, but there was no indication of mines. In those days, cruising submerged at about four knots in that time of year, the days were pretty long, so at night you'd didn't have too much time to make a lot of speed, but you'd get on the surface and go as fast as you could to charge the batteries as fast as you could.

Previously, a couple of subs took more than 25 people from Corregidor. At least one of them had more than 25 people, and they were depth-charged and unable to charge batteries as necessary. So the second day they practically had to make everybody lie still and use no oxygen until nightfall came when they could charge batteries while on the surface. We had to make sure we didn't send more than 25 people, plus the regular crew, because there were only so many bunks. For the men, we had the hot-bunk system. They were the four bunks in the forward torpedo room. Each bunk slept three men n rotation. You slept for eight hours, and then another slept eight hours, and a third eight hours. The bunk became hot with the perspiration and was pretty lousy with high humidity in the torpedo room. But there were no complaints, because we were en route to freedom.

Paul Stillwell: It was a lot better than Corregidor.

Admiral Knoll: Much better. I weighed 142 pounds upon arrival in Fremantle, and I weighed 199 when the war started.

Paul Stillwell: Was that because there was not much food available on Corregidor?

Admiral Knoll: There was enough to survive with a daily breakfast and an evening meal. We had a lot of rice, Vienna sausage, canned salmon, coffee, and tea. There wasn't that much. The bakery ran pretty well. The Army provided that. All our Navy food was pre-stowed in the Navy tunnels. After the lull in February, we obtained some caribou meat from Bataan because U.S. troops were able to round up a couple hundred caribou when the Japanese replaced their first line with troops of lesser caliber. The caribou from the Bataan area and northward were easily corralled such that we feared they might have been poisoned by the Japs. Slaughtering was delayed for a while; then they were finally slaughtered. The problem on Bataan was the distribution of food. The truck drivers, mainly Filipinos, took care of their family and friends before delivering to the troops. When they reached the front line, there was little food left. At night the Japanese would force Filipino civilians through the front lines until there were 60,000 civilians added to the troops, and that increased the depletion of the available food. The Japs realized that as the food decreased, the morale of the troops decreased.

Paul Stillwell: Other than that dramatic weight loss, what was the state of your health at that point?

Admiral Knoll: My health was good, except for one problem that developed just before the war. I'd been in the Far East and tropics for almost two years. I developed a lot of Guam blisters under my armpits and in my crotch. They were like boils. I went to the dermatologist at Cañacao, and he said, "You've been in the tropics too long. Your fair complexion with perspiration causes this. You'll have to get in colder weather for a change."

I said, "Good requirement." So for two or three days just before the war started, I occupied a special gazebo in the Cañacao hospital, about two rooms, all screened in and open in four directions. I slept there and lived there without clothes. I washed off with an alcohol mixture every three hours, and in a few days that cured it. I had been there less than a week. On Corregidor I kept a bottle of alcohol, and after a salt-water shower I would always sponge off with alcohol, and it did not recur on Corregidor.

My health was better than most. We did take quinine daily to ward off malaria. We were not exposed to malaria. The water was always brackish from the wells in bottom side. We always had enough water from the well to take care of cooking and general use. It was amazing that such water was available in sufficient quantity. It was called Barrio San Jose, on the road between the north dock and the south dock on Corregidor.

When we boarded the submarine, we were warned to take is easy, not eat too much, and regain weight slowly.

The 13 nurses were assigned the CPO quarters with four bunks—hot bunk sleeping. It was arranged that one of them would take turns sleeping on the deck. The biggest problem was to train the women to use the head. After each use the lid had to be dogged down, and compressed air forced the wastewater overboard. More than once a nurse would use compressed air without securing the lid. The result was a scream, and one of us would rush to help.

Paul Stillwell: You say you were told to go slow on eating. Was that because there wasn't enough food?

Admiral Knoll: No, there was more than adequate good food. They didn't want us to eat too much right away. Upon arrival in Fremantle, Australia, they billeted us at the Adelphi Hotel in Perth. The hotel provided every kind of food and great amounts of lamb, as long as we wanted to eat. Some ate about three different portions. I never wanted to eat that fast, because I was afraid of gaining weight too fast. When I got back to the States about July, I was still about 150. Then in six months I went over 200 and never have been able to get under 200 pounds.

On that submarine, normally any time that Jimmy Dempsey went to the bridge at night, I would join him as we cruised on the surface charging batteries. One night in the Sulu Sea we had a target close aboard, and we made three crash dives in a matter of about two hours. We could never find out who was there. It appeared to be a sailing vessel without navigation lights. It might have been a Jap scout.

Paul Stillwell: Did you get to stand any watches?

Admiral Knoll: Not as a submarine, no. I'm not qualified. In a submarine there's only one man in charge; that's the skipper.

Generally, all I wore was a pair of shorts and a linen towel around my shoulders. It was hot in the sub and hot in the tropics on the bridge. I knew the different routes that subs had taken south, and I'd read the original dispatch warning about going submerged through Lombok Strait, which is between Bali Island and Lombok Island. The tidal rips and current when tide changes between the Java Sea and the Indian Ocean are wild. Most subs decided as a general policy not to try to go through that strait submerged, because one sub went through there, and he was rolled over on his side and tossed about by the currents. The last thing you want to do is seek another strait.

Dempsey arranged to arrive there at dark, then surfaced, and as we got closer to the narrow strait—it's about six miles across—he said, "We can go through zigzagging at top speed. As we entered the strait on the surface, shellfire and searchlights indicated that Japs had detected us. They knew something was out there, but there was no splash from shellfire that came near us. We continued on the surface at about 12 knots. No submarines got in trouble at Lombok, but Japs were listening, which gave a psychological alert as we cruised.

Paul Stillwell: Did Dempsey attack any Japanese ships during this trip?

Admiral Knoll: No. He tried to close a couple of targets in the Sulu Sea, but he just couldn't get in range. He would have if the target had been close enough. He was completing a regular war patrol, and picked us up on the way back to Fremantle. He'd had a successful patrol after he relieved Monty Pryce.[*] Monty Pryce had *Spearfish* when the faulty torpedoes caused the problems that demoralized the crew, even when the torpedo would hit Jap ships and fail to explode. Some targets were close aboard. The skipper and the crew could hear the torpedo hit the ship and fail to detonate.

Paul Stillwell: He could hit them, but he couldn't blow them up.

Admiral Knoll: I talked to Monty Pryce later on about the cruise and read many dispatches on the subject. I tell you, the one real thrill was entering the Indian Ocean and getting a day's cruising from the Dutch East Indies south of Java while en route to Australia. We knew the Australians were a little bit anxious, and at least once dropped depth charges on U.S. subs headed for Fremantle. The first day of cruising on the surface, I was on the bridge with Jimmy Dempsey. We didn't have radar. We saw a plane coming toward us. He asked, "Is that a U.S., or is that a Jap??"

I said, "It looks like a PBY."

We stood by for a crash dive, and as it got closer, it gave us a dip and circled. At last we were in friendly waters, and the crew was alerted with cheers. At that time the *Isabel* was the station ship that would come out and meet each sub some distance from Fremantle and take you in. The *Isabel* was the former yacht for Admiral Hart in the Asiatic Fleet. She did a good job shepherding subs around Fremantle.

Paul Stillwell: How long did you stay in Australia?

Admiral Knoll: It was about a week at Perth, which is the city about 10 miles from Fremantle. I saw friends on the cruiser *Phoenix* and many individuals who had been evacuated from Corregidor. One thing, we had nothing to wear, so in a matter of 48

---

[*] Lieutenant Commander Roland Fremont Pryce, USN, commanded the *Spearfish* for a few months in late 1941 and early 1942 before turning the boat over to Lieutenant Dempsey.

hours the tailors from Perth went all out providing us underwear, shirts, etc., and made us uniforms with wavy stripes for Australians and Australian buttons. We each had a new blue serge uniform to wear as we departed by train from Perth en route to Melbourne. On the sleeping car were springs, but they'd taken all the mattresses off. All we had were white Navy wool blankets. It was cool down there in June when it was warm up north. It did not get too cold.

It took us about three and a half days to reach Melbourne because each state has a different gauge tracks on the railroad. There were no through trains, so we kept changing, and our blue serge uniforms were covered with lint from white wool blankets. I did have an old uniform cap that I was wearing. I still have that. A torpedoman on Corregidor had made my lieutenant commander's insignia out of copper from the fuse boxes and polished them up. I have these memorabilia at home. When we arrived at Melbourne, they said that the *West Point* was due after unloading troops at Singapore and was bringing some troops to Melbourne. We were among 90 passengers who boarded the *West Point* for the return to the U.S.A. We remained in Melbourne about five or six days, during which time I visited General MacArthur's headquarters. I had meetings with Group Captain Warren, the head of the Australian Meteorological Service, whom I had met at meetings in Singapore.[*]

I had an interesting meeting with MacArthur's chief of staff, Dick Sutherland.[†] He was a lieutenant colonel who lived next door to me in the Bay View when I arrived in Manila. He had just relieved Lieutenant Colonel Eisenhower in March 1940.[‡]

Group Captain Warren was depressed. He said, "The U.S. Army and Air Force are coming in here, and they won't use any of my equipment; they won't work with me. They're going to set up their own weather service. They're going to develop their own communications facility and run their own weather service. I've got a good service here. I don't know why they're going to duplicate it when I'm prepared to work with them."

I said, "I'll take care of it. I told Dick Sutherland, MacArthur's chief of staff, about Warren's concern, and I said, "This is ridiculous. The army is bringing all this

---

[*] Group Captain Herbert Norman Warren, Royal Australian Air Force Meteorological Service.
[†] Richard K. Sutherland was promoted rapidly, passing through colonel and brigadier general to major general in 1941.
[‡] Lieutenant Colonel Dwight D. Eisenhower, USA, future general and future President.

equipment in to set up their new weather service and be completely independent of Australia. Group Captain Warren wants to work with them." Sutherland stopped that pretty quick. I got a letter from him later on.

I left Australia on the *West Point*, previously *America*, on June 6 and went directly to New York without stopping, including transit of the Panama Canal.* The trip from Melbourne to New York City was by record the fastest trip ever made by a U.S. ship between Melbourne and New York City. Captain Kelley was the skipper of the *West Point*.† The first stop overnight was to pick up a few troops and deliver some troops was at Wellington, New Zealand. We had a chance to go ashore. The Marines were building up for the Guadalcanal campaign.‡ I've been back there since, and it's expanded a lot since I was in there in June 1942. From there we did a great circle course to the Panama Canal. We went south to 40-some degrees latitude, where we had some snow squalls in the South Pacific. We passed the Galapagos and the coast of South America en route to the Panama Canal. We transited the canal as soon as we reached Balboa.

When we arrived on the Atlantic side, two four-piper destroyers were standing by to escort up the East Coast. Within 24 hours, we were going about 26½ knots, and the old destroyers couldn't keep up with us. The skipper told the destroyers, "Thank you very much, but I'm going on ahead. My safety is speed." We went up through the Windward Passage, and there was concern as we neared El Salvador. There had been reports that German submarines were lurking around El Salvador. I think Lieutenant Commander Miller was the navigator. It was a dark night, and the skipper sent Miller to the foretop. When he picked up the loom of the lighthouse at San Salvador, the skipper cruised a circle with a radius of the distance for the loom from the light. The skipper left San Salvador on a direct course to New York. This maneuver made sure any German sub could not see the silhouette of the *West Point* as it changed course around San Salvador.

He got all the way around until we could take the right heading to New York. There were some reports that at least one sub had sighted us near San Salvador and was

---

* USS *West Point* (AP-23) was the former passenger liner *America*, which had entered service on 22 August 1940 as the flagship of the United States Lines. The Navy acquired the ship on 1 June 1941 for conversion to a troop transport. She was commissioned as the USS *West Point* on 15 June.
† Captain Frank H. Kelley Jr., USN.
‡ On 7 August 1942, U.S. Marines invaded the islands of Guadalcanal and Tulagi in the Solomons chain as part of the first U.S. counteroffensive in the Pacific War.

supposed to have launched some torpedoes. The Germans completely underestimated our speed, because we were at 26-27 knots, and any torpedoes went astern. At least there was one report. How accurate it was, I don't know. The amazing thing was, as we got closer to New York, we expected some kind of inshore patrol vessel or escort. It was not really foggy, but the visibility was low. We were in sight of the Ambrose Lightship and exchanged recognition signals without ever being met by any surface ship or destroyers. We thought, "My God, this country's at war, and we steamed into New York without a challenge."

After I landed in New York, either the second or third of July, I went to the Burlington Hotel in Washington. I wasn't in the hotel more than about an hour or so when Admiral Hart called. I hadn't seen my wife for about two and a half years. She had just arrived when the telephone rang, and the voice at the other end said, "Knoll, this is Admiral Hart."

"Yes, sir."

He said, "You're having dinner with Admiral Yarnell and myself in my apartment on Connecticut Avenue. We want to know what happened out there."[*]

I met with them about 6:30, and I was there until about 2:00 o'clock the next morning, which was the Fourth of July. I told them all the things that happened from the time Admiral Hart left just after Christmas. As a result of that, Admiral Hart said, "I want you to put as much of that in writing as you can, and make sure it gets to the right people. He was then chairman of the General Board.

Paul Stillwell: Well, the United States was far different when you got back than when you had left. What were your impressions?

Admiral Knoll: My first impression was that the country had not yet realized they were at war in many serious ways. They had been seeing some pictures in the media. I did make a broadcast from Australia that was recorded and is someplace on record about what we'd gone through on Bataan and Corregidor. We were given excellent recognition

---

[*] Admiral Harry E. Yarnell, USN, served as Commander in Chief U.S. Asiatic Fleet from 30 October 1936 to 25 July 1939. He was Hart's immediate predecessor.

when we arrived in Australia from Corregidor. My mother and my wife, from the beginning of the war and until I sent them a message from Perth, had no idea where I was. My wife and mother had received two different messages that I was missing in action, one when the *Houston* was sunk in Sunda Strait, because in Washington my name had not been removed from the roster of the *Houston*. And secondly when Corregidor fell. They had received a few letters that I was able to release from Corregidor, through friends in Cebu. They had a letter saying I was on Corregidor. In fact, on my birthday on the seventh of March, my wife's father, being the president of Norfolk-Southern Railroad, knew how to send a message through channels that RCA would never reveal. Nevertheless, from RCA Cebu I received a message on Corregidor from my wife with birthday greetings.

The interesting thing, when we arrived in Perth, we were advised to send a message to our family who had been told we were missing in action. We went to the GPO Perth and sent messages without revealing our location. I told my wife, "Order a white uniform and cap from Carr Mears Dawson, who have my measurements, and hold." This immediately indicated to her that I'd be coming home. I sent the same message to my mother, that I arrived back in the world the way she delivered me, or words to that effect. Forty-eight hours later, through GPO Perth, I received an answer from my wife. Her father, being a railroad official said, "I don't care where this came from. I want this message sent back to where the message came from." Communications were exchanged without revealing my location. They knew that I had not been captured by the Japs when Corregidor surrendered.

Paul Stillwell: Did you get reimbursed by the government or all the personal gear you had lost?

Admiral Knoll: No. I applied for it two different times, and they said there was no provision in the law to pay for it. I said, "This would be pretty tough if you were attached to more than one ship that was sunk in battle." But no, I never got reimbursed. One of the people that came out with us—I prefer not to mention his name—lived near us on Sangley Point. At the end of the war he submitted claims to the government on what he had lost, namely, household effects, clothing, and automobile, having lived there for two or three years. He listed me as a witness to say that his losses had been destroyed during the Japanese occupation; therefore, he wanted full reimbursement. It came to me for corroboration. His lawyer was a personal friend of Lyndon Johnson, a pretty influential political man in Washington.* I called the lawyer, and I said, "Listen, it's very sad. You don't want me to certify a lie, but the last I saw the home before I left Corregidor, through a long glass I could still see that it was intact near the beach at Sangley Point. It wasn't destroyed by enemy action."

The lawyer said, "Well, just forget about it."

A lot of things like this came through, for me to corroborate. I refused to do it, because I knew certain details of what had happened in the final days. I still have a copy of all my losses, which I submitted twice. Each time it came back with no legal provision for reimbursement of such losses. One time it was routed via Admiral King's office, to no avail.†

Paul Stillwell: So you had to buy all these new uniforms out of your own pocket?

Admiral Knoll: Yes, yes. Civilian clothes as well.

Paul Stillwell: You had gone from a command that disappeared. Why don't you summarize what happened when you got back to this country.

After spending time with Admiral Yarnell and Admiral Hart, I talked with ONI, and many other officials, because I was the first to return with info on the final days on Corregidor.‡ There were a lot of letters prepared in answer to different people who had relatives out there and knew I had come back with the latest info. I guess I had about ten days' leave with my family in Erie and my wife's family in Norfolk.

---

* Lyndon B. Johnson, a Democrat from Texas, served in the House of Representatives from 10 April 1937 to 3 January 1949 and in the Senate from 3 January 1949 to 3 January 1961. He was Senate majority leader from 1955 to 1961. He was later Vice President from 1961 to 1963 and President from 1963 to 1969.
† Admiral Ernest J. King, USN, served as Chief of Naval Operations from 26 March 1942 to 15 December 1945 and as Commander in Chief U.S. Fleet from 20 December 1941 to 2 September 1945.
‡ ONI – Office of Naval Intelligence.

During that period, I think there was a debate as to whether I should return to China with Mary Miles.* A decision was made for me when Chiang Kai-shek would not accept anyone returning to China who had been there during the previous 24 months.† Accordingly, I was persona non grata, which allowed me to remain in Washington. I got orders that I was going to be officer in charge of the Fleet Weather Central Washington at the U.S. Weather Bureau, which was also connected to the Office of the Chief of Naval Operations.

Paul Stillwell: Where was this weather central located?

Admiral Knoll: In the U.S. Weather Bureau at 22nd and M in Washington. Commander Reichelderfer was chief of the U.S. Weather Bureau.

My first assignment was to prepare a long-range forecast for the invasion of Northwest Africa in the fall of 1942. This was a real challenge. Admiral King's staff came over a couple of time with his operations officer, to see what my forecasts were based on. At one point Admiral Davis asked, "What are you doing in Labrador and Greenland? We're going to invade Northwest Africa, and we want to know what the weather, sea, and swell are going to be."

I said, "I know it."

He said, "Why are you worried about the weather in Davis Strait, Labrador, and Greenland?"

I said, "Well, the low pressures that develop here ultimately cause the sea and swell off Casablanca." He looked at me in surprise. I said, "We have developed good correlation in this area and have coast watchers in Greenland and in Labrador. Also there are coast watchers on the Azores whose observations provide a correlation between the winds and low pressure and in the northwest Davis Strait with future weather near

---

* Lieutenant Commander Milton E. Miles, USN, later became a rear admiral and served as deputy commander of the Sino-American Cooperative Association (SACO), which was headed by a Chinese officer named Tai Li. Miles's posthumous memoir was *A Different Kind of War: the Little-Known Story of the Combined Guerrilla Forces Created in China by the U.S. Navy and the Chinese During World War II*, as prepared by Hawthorne Daniel from the original manuscript. (Garden City, N.Y.: Doubleday, 1967). One of the organization's responsibilities was to send weather reports from China.
† Generalissimo Chiang Kai-shek served as President of Nationalist China on the mainland from 1943 to 1949 and as President of the Republic of China on Taiwan from 1950 until his death in 1975.

Casablanca. The strength of the wind and the height of the waves that reach the Azores initiated in Davis Strait. They arrive at the Azores, and we can determine when they reach Casablanca." They finally were convinced. There was a submarine sent to lie on the bottom off Casablanca to measure the height of the waves hydrostatically. We ended up with a correlation of about 83%. An interesting additional aid became available when I queried, "The French built a fantastic breakwater at Casablanca. Let's find out the engineer who designed it and the engineering guidelines that he used." I had an officer called to active duty from the University of Chicago. I asked, "Are you French?"

"Yes, I speak French."

"Go to the Congressional Library and find out everything they have about Casablanca and who built the breakwater."

He spent a few weeks of research at the Congressional Library. All of a sudden, he returned and said, "I've located the design criteria by Professor Roux, who built the breakwater. He talks about the intensity of the wind in Davis Strait and the height of the waves there." The French text was translated as necessary. Close liaison with Dick Steere, who was the aerologist with Patton and Admiral Hewitt in Norfolk was maintained.* Later on, when Dick Steere finally reached Casablanca after the landing, he actually met Professor Roux, who had retired and was still living in Casablanca. MIT and graduate school encouraged you to look for new information, to look for related work that other people did with the same problem. We must avoid any attempt to re-invent the wheel or the wheelbarrow. Rather, always build upon previous success.

Paul Stillwell: It seems to me, though, that something like a Casablanca breakwater would be awfully obscure to locate in the Library of Congress.

Admiral Knoll: They had the records of Casablanca, and this was unique. It was a structure built on the weather coast, exposed to the open sea, and it provided a harbor the average person would not have developed there. I recently became involved with, after I retired, building a new breakwater at Sines on seacoast, south of Lisbon in Portugal. I

---

* Lieutenant Commander Richard C. Steere, USN. For the invasion of Casablanca in November 1942 Rear Admiral H. Kent Hewitt, USN, was Commander Western Naval Task Force. Major General George S. Patton Jr., USA, was Commander Western Task Force, U.S. Army.

was a consultant with a group in California with Rear Admiral Elliott Strauss.[*] The Portuguese recently built it, using armor stones and modern techniques in water 90 feet deep. It was based on some of our experience with armor stone, building a breakwater at Rota, Spain. A couple of years after giving this advice to the Portuguese Government on how to build this breakwater, a call was received. They arrived for a meeting and did not complain. Rather, pictures were available showing the new breakwater. They were adding dock facilities for handling bulk cargo. A contract with the Japanese would operate the port. The Portuguese wanted additional advice as to where bulk handling of iron ore, coal, grain, etc., should be located.

Paul Stillwell: Admiral Beshany, in his oral history, talks about the problems the swells caused the submarine tender at Rota until they did get the breakwater in.[†]

Admiral Knoll: I was involved with a small part of that. The first segment was effective and finally a second breakwater was built, and the successful use of armor stones was demonstrated. The patent rights were held by the French until recently. Present use of armor stone is now worldwide and much cheaper.

Paul Stillwell: What is armor stone? I'm not familiar with that term.

Admiral Knoll: Tetrahedrons that marry into each other but allow the water to flush through and hold the sand. They can take great pressure from waves and become homogeneous with age. They require little maintenance. They are built up from the sea bottom into a pyramid. In Majorca Island and the Black Sea ports, these are being used to enlarge and improve their harbors with armor stones of various sizes, depending upon the type of waves and the energy they must absorb. See *Design and Construction of Ports and Marine Structures* by Alonzo DeF. Quinn. Dr. Quinn was a consultant with us on the design of Sines Harbor.

---

[*] Rear Admiral Elliott B. Strauss, USN (Ret.), whose oral history is in the Naval Institute collection.
[†] Vice Admiral Philip A. Beshany, USN, was Deputy Chief of Naval Operations (Submarine Warfare), OP-02, from 15 March 1971 to 11 August 1972. His oral history is in the Naval Institute collection.

It so happened that plans for the invasion proceeded. Early on a Sunday morning, Admiral King's aide called me, Commander Kirkpatrick.* He said, "Admiral King asked me to call you and tell you that your forecasts were correct, and we're safely on the beach. You'll be getting an appropriate decoration."

I received a letter of commendation from the Navy. The Air Forces forecaster, whose forecasts were of less value, received the Legion of Merit. They had never used Air Forces forecasts. Within the month—this is a sequel—we had a message from British planners in London, who were aware of U.S. Navy forecasts. A couple of Royal Navy aerologists and scientists came over to spend a week with us to find out how we developed our forecasts. They were called the Isis Group in London and ultimately helped with forecasts in preparation for Normandy and other Allied operations. There were many activities that contributed valuable data. We were particularly lucky to locate the original studies of Professor Roux, who used the same factors. The British said, "Your forecasts were the only accurate ones we received."

Paul Stillwell: Were you in charge of this group?

Admiral Knoll: I was in charge of the weather central segment. As to the sea and swell, I did some analysis. We had feed-in from the Office of Naval Research and other observations. Commander Orville coordinated for Admiral King's office. I sent the forecasts to addressees in messages to Dick Steere or Admiral Hewitt. There was tight security, and very few knew that an invasion was planned. Many thought we were developing a new theory for forecasts of sea and swell. I was the only person decorated by Admiral King for my forecasts.

Paul Stillwell: I would think that the tabulations of these correlations would be very easy in the age of the computer. How did you do it?

---

* Allied forces invaded Casablanca in French Morocco on 8 November 1942. Lieutenant Commander Charles C. Kirkpatrick, USN.

Admiral Knoll: Computers would have expedited. However, when the war started, we had to identify the data to put in a computer. An analog method was quickly developed for weather forecasts. A warehouse with 40 years of weather maps was in Raleigh, North Carolina. These maps were refined and put into a coded form for each day in 40 years. The first thing we had to do was redraw all the maps and make sure they were all drawn more or less by the same individuals with the same Norwegian air-mass technique we had shown the fronts, since fronts had never appeared on older weather maps of the U.S. Weather Bureau. We checked the locations of the highs and lows. We would select a map for the 27th of June of some year, locate highs and lows, their intensity, and locate the major fronts. With this data we'd see what the weather was today, and if we wanted to know what the weather was going to be a week from today, we'd go through the 40 years of weather for the 27th of June and find each day with a map similar to today in the last 40 years. With this we could not how weather developed in each subsequent week in the specific area of interest. With this background we had an empirical guide to what the ten-day forecast might be for the current year.

Paul Stillwell: Sounds like a very laborious process.

Admiral Knoll: It was tedious. The wartime needs, together with qualified people, provided new background on which new technology could capitalize. Data was ready to put in computers as they came on line.

Paul Stillwell: How many people were involved?

Admiral Knoll: I don't know how many, probably less than 20 people to prepare cards with the analog method. In about six weeks' time, data became available, and special people did the coding of data. It was similar to the first method of IBM for sorting data with pegs.

Paul Stillwell: Did you have any tabulating machines?

Admiral Knoll: No, not at that time. Today you can obtain answers in milliseconds. When I was oceanographer, I gave a couple of talks showing how MIT had developed a computer to show the gradual change of daily weather. Today's weather map was put in the computer, based on formulas for movement of the weather front, force of wind behind the front, and other data. The computers showed sequentially what each daily map was going to look like for the next ten days. MIT had a movie showing development. At the beginning of the war we used a single-station forecast, and today four or five times a day we can obtain a picture of the whole earth from 22,000 miles above and readily locate every high and low pressure.

Paul Stillwell: What happened after the invasion down in North Africa?

Admiral Knoll: Shortly after the invasion, I was transferred to the secretariat of the Joint Chiefs of Staff as the secretary of the Joint Meteorological Committee and additional duty from time to time as one of the assistant secretaries of the Joint Chiefs in the Combined Chiefs meetings. My office was just inside the ground-floor door where all the rank arrived for the Joint Chiefs meetings two or three times a week.

Paul Stillwell: What building?

Admiral Knoll: The Public Health Building, which had been taken over by the Joint Chiefs of Staff. I worked there on the average of six and a half days a week from about 7:00 o'clock in the morning to about 6:00 at night. I was carried as a member of Admiral King's staff as one of the secretaries for the JCS.

Part of the job was challenging. When Churchill was in town, each morning we received many notes from the White House containing questions requiring reply for the next evening's meeting between Roosevelt and Churchill.[*] The stack was about two inches thick, all different notes, investigate so-and-so, investigate so-and-so. The secretary would assign them, depending upon subject matter, such as planning,

---

[*] Winston S. Churchill was Prime Minister of the United Kingdom from 1940 to 1945.

meteorology, research, and a lot of special requests. For example, "Madame Chiang has run out of cigarettes. She'd like to have three or four cartons of British cigarettes."

I think it was Colonel Doyle, who was liaison with the Joint Chiefs, who sent for me. He asked, "How would the Navy get Sweet Caporal cigarettes?"

I said, "Call Cunard Ship Line and find out the next time the *Queen Mary* or *Queen Elizabeth* is due in, and send a plane to pick up cartons from Cunard." He did it. Madame Chiang had her Sweet Caporal British cigarettes by early afternoon.

Paul Stillwell: This was for Chiang Kai-shek's wife?

Admiral Knoll: Yes, she was visiting at the White House with Mrs. Eleanor Roosevelt. Churchill requested a special study, how many ice machines would it take and how much power to develop an iceberg between the cliffs of Dover and the beach at Normandy for 48 hours? We had to assemble specialists for this study. Another request said, "How many ships would it take to build breakwaters off the coast of Normandy? How many merchant ships? What kind have we got?"

I volunteered, "This is a problem for a lot of people. Dr. O'Brien at the University of California should come to Washington for meetings with representatives of the U.S. Army Corps of Engineers from Vicksburg." In a matter of less than 48 hours, we had Professor O'Brien and other engineers and scientists for a special conference. Preliminary comments were sent to the White House for Roosevelt and Churchill, with the assurance that special study would be made. Before Churchill returned to London, arrangements were made to test a mock-up of the Mulberry artificial moorings at Vicksburg, Mississippi. Based on this, merchant ships were sunk and used at Normandy on D-Day. Various ideas from Roosevelt and Churchill were incorporated in the war plans.

Priority for planners was given to operations for the defeat of Germany, and then the plans for defeat of Japan. As Americans, nothing is impossible when available talent, devoid of politics, is assigned to specific tasks. The Munitions Board of specialists was given requirements for tanks, airplanes, ammo, and fuel for each operation and its D-day. In each instance American industry provided needs on time. The Munitions Board, consisting of leading American industrialists, such as the shipbuilding program, headed up Admiral Land, delivered on time.* For each operation, more than enough was available when needed. It was most impressive to observe how U.S. industry could perform in an emergency.

Paul Stillwell: Admiral Land performed some real miracles during that war.

Admiral Knoll: He was a good friend of mine. He was on Admiral Pratt's staff with us in *Texas*. Emory S. Land was terrific; he maintained close liaison with Lord Leathers, the British opposite for transportation problems. It's amazing what the United States can do if we put our minds to it, such as building airplanes, tanks, providing ammunition, fuel oil, and aviation gasoline. The entrepreneurship and ability to innovate is fantastic in this country. A competent Cabinet and the President could address domestic programs and produce long-range results in peacetime if there was less politics, and the greed of human individuals did not exist. I've seen it work with the urgency due to war and its demands.

Paul Stillwell: Did you see Admiral King at firsthand?

Admiral Knoll: Yes, to a degree I had known him when he was a captain in *Lexington*.† I'd see him very briefly. He was sort of a loner in many ways. Nevertheless, he knew who I was. I became involved more and more with the secretary of the Joint Chiefs of Staff. I was secretary for all the joint meteorological work, but I had some extra time, and I was always happy to do these other tasks. I could not just sit idle. I had two good secretaries. One of them was an Army WAC.‡ She could do the most fantastic paperwork, filed everything in order, prepared agendas for regular meetings.

There is an interesting story. For the first couple of months as secretary of the Joint Meteorology Committee, at every meeting the Army Air Forces rep could present a proposal for the Army Air Forces to take over all the airport communications and the

---

* Rear Admiral Emory S. Land, USN (Ret.), was chairman of the U.S. Maritime Commission February 1938 to January 1946. See his book *Winning the War with Ships* (New York: R. M. McBride Co., 1958).
† Captain Ernest J. King, USN, commanded the USS *Lexington* (CV-2) from 1930 to 1932.
‡ WAC – Women's Army Corps.

U.S. Weather Service and weather communications in the United States and put it in code. They would waste about 25% of every meeting saying that for the security of the country in the war, we can't let the enemy know about our weather, etc. Commander Orville was against it, and Commander Pete Hale was against it.[*] He was a representative for the Navy. The chief of the Weather Bureau, Reichelderfer was against it. We all said, "This won't work. We're not about to develop a military dictatorship." We argued up and down, and they kept returning with these different alternatives, even at subcommittee meetings that I attended, as well as plenary meetings of the Meteorological Committee.

We met with the Canadians and the British once a month. Dr. McTaggart Cowen, currently president of British Columbia University at Vancouver, with Mr. Thompson, were two people who came down from Canada as heads of their weather service. We had many meetings, and they were also against the Army Air proposal. Lots of time was wasted. Having a good friend like Reichelderfer, I called him and said, "Reich, I'd like to come over and see you. I think we have to get word to the President that the Army Air Corps is wasting our time. They're trying to take over the U.S. Weather Bureau at the airports and encode weather and airport communications."

He asked, "What do you mean?"

I said, "No one's going to stop this except the President when he knows about it. If the President knows about it, he will take some action."

He said, "Okay, I'll do it."

About a week later, he called and said, "The word reached the President." Within the week, it was never mentioned again. What happened? We heard this through channels from the White House.

The President sent for General Hap Arnold. He said, "General Arnold, I understand some of your Army Air staff are wasting a lot of time in the Joint Chiefs with the idea they're trying to take over the U.S. Weather Service and wanting to encode all U.S. airway communications. The next time anybody on your staff raises that in any meeting of the Meteorological Committee of the Joint Chiefs of Staff, you have turned in your fourth star. Now go back and win the war."

---

[*] Commander Peter G. Hale, USN.

Paul Stillwell: Whom did you hear that from? Was anybody in on this meeting between Arnold and the President?

Admiral Knoll: I don't know. Records will show that this subject was never again mentioned by anyone at Meteorological Committee meetings.

Paul Stillwell: I wonder if it got embellished in the telling.

Admiral Knoll: It could have, of course. We achieved our objective.

Another story is worth telling. This was known by a lot of people on Admiral King's staff.

Secretary of the Navy Frank Knox was a good newspaperman. Admiral Ernie King went to the White House two or three times a week for meetings with the President. He returned and visited Frank Knox. Secretary Knox wanted to know, "What did you and the President talk about?" Admiral King told him very little. Knox emphasized, "I'm the Secretary of the Navy." Secretary Knox is supposed to have said to Admiral King, "I'm going to discuss this with the President."

Reports came back in different ways. Secretary Knox went to the White House and saw the President. They were good friends. The President provided ideal leadership, had the best Cabinet made up of a balance between the best Democrats and best Republicans available. Secretary Knox didn't get very far with President Roosevelt, but when Knox started mentioning, "Admiral King is up here talking to you frequently, but he won't tell me what you've talked about. I'm the Secretary of the Navy."

The President said, "Listen, Frank. You're the Secretary of the Navy. Admiral King is the Chief of Naval Operations. This is wartime. Any time he goes back and starts telling you about what he's talked with me about, you're both going to get fired."

General Beetle Smith was the first secretary of the Joint Chiefs.[*] Then General Russ Deane took over, and his deputy was Captain Forrest Royal.[†] The first time I met

---

[*] Brigadier General Walter Bedell Smith, USA, served as secretary of the Combined Chiefs of Staff from February to September 1942.
[†] Major General John Russell Deane, USA; Captain Forrest B. Royal, USN.

them, either General Deane or Forrest Royal said, "Oh, you made quite a name for yourself."

I asked, "What do you mean?"

They said, "Well, you sent a message from Corregidor just before Bataan fell to the Chief of Naval Operations and naval intelligence, saying Bataan was about to fall. Admiral King brought it to a Joint Chiefs meeting and read it out, giving the deteriorating situation on Bataan." This was about a week before Bataan fell, a week or ten days. After Admiral King read it out, General Marshall was annoyed, saying, "The Army doesn't know anything about it. You shouldn't believe this kind of stuff; it's a rumor."[*]

Admiral King asked, "What do you think?"

Marshall asked, "Who wrote that?"

He said, "It says prepared by Lieutenant Commander Denys W. Knoll, the district intelligence officer." Admiral King added that he knew me.

Well, it so happened that when I wanted to send this, and Hoeffel didn't want me to send it, I said, "If I send it over in my own name?"

Hoeffel said, "If you put your own name," which I did.

Admiral King read this out at the meeting, and Bataan fell the following week. Admiral King reminded, "I told you."

The secretaries had told me on arrival they had heard about me before, because I was the first officer with the Joint Chiefs organization who had a combat citation, a Legion of Merit, and a letter of commendation.

Paul Stillwell: Did this association with General Deane lead to your assignment in Russia?

Admiral Knoll: Yes, yes, plus a combination of other projects.

Paul Stillwell: Why don't you cover that?

---

[*] General of the Army George C. Marshall, USA, served as Army Chief of Staff from 1 September 1939 to 18 November 1945. He was promoted to five-star rank in December 1944.

Admiral Knoll: I want to get into that a little bit further. Before Captain Forrest Royal and General Deane arrived, there were frequent meetings preparing for the invasion of Europe and Normandy. A lot of time was spent planning enough hospital and medical supplies and survival equipment in schools in southern England. Frequently this was at the Combined Chiefs meeting with Sir John Dill and British present.[*] It was very educational to sit there as assistant secretary and listen to their discussions.

General Eisenhower felt everything was in pretty good shape, but the British still were not happy with the adequacy of hospitals and medical assistance ready for a Normandy invasion, at least six or nine months before the invasion.[†] During a discussion, I think it was General Marshall who said to Sir John Dill, "You're awful concerned over there in England about not having enough hospital supplies."

Sir John Dill said, "Well, you have to realize since the British fiasco at Sevastopol, the Charge of the Light Brigade, and the Crimean War, the British Army can never be caught again without adequate doctors and nurses."[‡]

After these discussions, all of a sudden, I was called in by General Deane and Captain Royal, who said, "In addition to your other duties, we want you to coordinate for the Joint Chiefs preparation for a conference of the President, the Joint Chiefs, and Churchill to meet with Marshal Stalin in Tehran.[§] Only about 14 people in Washington know about this. You have to start setting up a liaison with Captain John McCrea on the battleship *Iowa*, with the White House, and Secret Service.[**] Call different officials, such as Lew Douglas and others that are scheduled to accompany the President for a conference.[††] No one can know where they are going or who they will meet."

I had previously arranged meetings like this, but nothing as complicated as this. We had to divide up the planning groups, one in each plane, so if you lost a plane you

---

[*] Field Marshal Sir John G. Dill, British Army, was senior British representative on the Combined Chiefs of Staff, that is, the combination of British and American Chiefs of Staff.
[†] In February 1944, four months before D-Day at Normandy, General Dwight D. Eisenhower, USA, was designated Supreme Commander Allied Expeditionary Force for the invasion.
[‡] The Crimean War took place from 1853 to 1856.
[§] Allied leaders Roosevelt, Churchill, and Stalin met at Tehran, Iran, from 28 November to 1 December 1943 to discuss war aims and strategy.
[**] Captain John L. McCrea, USN, commanded the battleship *Iowa* (BB-61) from her commissioning in February 1943 to August 1944. The oral history of McCrea, who retired as a vice admiral, is in the Naval Institute collection.
[††] Lewis W. Douglas was deputy administrator of the War Shipping Administration.

didn't lose a whole planning group. I also worked up with Dennison Label Company to get various new colored labels to identify each group and plane. Colored labels with different stripes on their labels helped sorting out luggage, when you landed, and moving to specific billets. The different people in Navy supply and Joint Chiefs helped out with these different things. It was amazing how a variety of labels simplified the movement of 60 to 80 between Washington and Tehran, with transportation on ship and various planes.

Paul Stillwell: What do you recall about John McCrea?

Admiral Knoll: I've known him different times before, when he was younger. He'd been a naval aide at the White House.[*] I was very fond of him. I went to Norfolk the first time to see him. He said, "I know why you're here."

I laughed. I said, "I don't know why you should."

He said, "No, I know the President wants to use the *Iowa*."

I said, "I know, but you don't know where you're going."

He said, "No."

I told him what he needed to know, and he wasn't surprised. He had to quietly get all these special extra ladders and handrails, presidential gear, aboard without publication or excitement of his crew. We had to have meetings with the escort destroyers, with the destroyer squadron commander, and jeep carriers ready to give air cover to the *Iowa* on the ocean. All units had to have adequate fuel for the task. I had to keep checking many deadline things. All of a sudden, I got a call to come on a special plane to Norfolk and meet John McCrea and Captain Lewis, the destroyer squadron commander.[†] No one ever argued when he requested special transportation as representative of the Joint Chiefs of Staff.

Paul Stillwell: This was out of Anacostia?[‡]

---

[*] In 1942-43 Captain McCrea served as President Roosevelt's naval aide.
[†] Commander Thomas L. Lewis, USN, Commander Destroyer Squadron Ten.
[‡] Anacostia is a section of the District of Columbia. It is across the Anacostia River from Washington. It was the site of a naval air station.

Admiral Knoll: Yes. At different places around the Navy Department, no one really knew what was going to take place or where they were going. I would clear all lists and projects with General Deane or Captain Royal. At the meeting with John McCrea and the destroyer squadron commander, Commodore Lewis, Captain McCrea said, "Wait a second. We can leave Piney Point in the Chesapeake on the *Iowa* no later than noon November 11 and still get to Oran, Algeria, in time to meet with Churchill so they can fly on to meet Chiang Kai-shek and Madame Chiang in Cairo en route to Tehran. If we leave later than noon, November 11, we can't make these important rendezvouses."

Commodore Lewis said, "Then if I start getting my destroyers on station and *Iowa* doesn't arrive on time, I'm going to have to have another group of destroyers and another jeep carrier ready when the original ships need fuel. That's another problem." The limit on leaving Piney Point was about 6:00 o'clock on the morning of November 11, 1943.

So I mentioned it to General Deane. I said, "We've got a problem here."

General Deane talked to Admiral Horne, deputy to Admiral King, and he said, "That's Knoll's responsibility."[*]

So I met with Admiral Leahy's aide at the White House, and he said I had to have a meeting with Admiral Leahy.

I never had any trouble going to the White House, going in an official car and walking into Admiral Leahy's office, which was adjacent to Roosevelt's office. Larry Freeman was his aide.[†] I told him the problem. Of course, he knew about this because he was getting things ready with the President and Admiral Leahy to go to the meeting, so we weren't compromising anything. I said, "Commodore McCrea's got a problem, and so does Commodore Lewis."

When the agreement was made to pick up at Piney Point, made by McCrea in talking to the White House, and the time and date appeared feasible. I went in to Freeman and said, "The President has to leave Washington in time to get to Piney Point no later than noon November 11." We didn't have the air transport and helicopters we do today. The President had said he would not be leaving Washington until after he spoke in Arlington at noon. "If he gets involved with that, it will be 2:00 or 3:00 in the afternoon

---

[*] Admiral Frederick J. Horne, USN, served as Vice Chief of Naval Operations from 26 March 1942 to 10 October 1945.
[†] Commander Charles L. Freeman, USN.

before he leaves, and he'll never get down to Piney Point in time." There was also a tide factor.

I had to tell this story to Admiral Leahy. He looked at me and said, "Knoll, I'd rather do any unpleasant thing I've ever done in my life than to go in and try to change the President's mind. But, okay, I see the problem. You wait here, and I'll go in and see the President."

So I waited there; it must have been a half hour until he came out. He was perspiring and tired. He looked at me and shook his head and said, "It wasn't easy, but you can plan accordingly for the time and date you've given me. If I have further trouble, you may have to come in and help me." That's how close it came. There were a lot of things that worked that way. It kept me busy. Everyone wanted to know where they were going and how long they would be gone.*

Another time Roosevelt was difficult because he didn't want to leave for a certain place till he had talked to Secretary of State Cordell Hull. Secretary Hull had landed early at Anacostia, and since Roosevelt couldn't be out at Anacostia to meet Hull on time, the air station had to park the plane with Hull at the end of the runway for about three to four hours. He could sleep aboard until Roosevelt was ready to go down and meet him. These are some of the problems of working with the White House.

I didn't hear about the fiasco when Roosevelt and Churchill got to Cairo. I hadn't been charged with that episode. The White House had failed to alert the American official at the Cairo airport that Madame Chiang and the generalissimo were due to arrive. Chiang came in unannounced on a plane. As they taxied to the terminal, they were stopped and asked to present their credentials, as to who they were and whom they were supposed to see. There was some delay. The generalissimo was ready to fly back to Chunking. The official word got through, and they were escorted to the Mena House near the pyramids. By the time Churchill and Roosevelt arrived, they complained about not being properly treated when they first landed. Security was so tight that in Washington I was not aware that they would meet the Chiangs prior to going to Tehran.

---

* The account in Admiral McCrea's oral history differs somewhat from Admiral Knoll's. McCrea recalled that the President went south from Washington on board the presidential yacht *Potomac* and boarded the *Iowa* early on the morning of 12 November in the lower Potomac River, off Point Lookout.

Cairo airport, even today, is a lousy place to visit and obtain land transportation. I went through there on my way to Moscow.

While the Joint Chiefs were at Tehran, Captain Forrest Royal was the acting secretary of the Joint Chiefs. We had our own organization for formal occasions. I had the duty to go out and meet VIP airplanes. It was my lucky duty to go out and meet Admiral King and his plane when he returned from Tehran. He had come back via Forta Leza, Brazil, and then up the Atlantic Coast, arriving at Anacostia about 6:00 in the evening. When he landed at Anacostia, his aide, Commander Kirkpatrick, came over to greet me. Sir John Dill flew back with Admiral King. Dill was a terrific individual. They don't come any better. He's buried in Arlington Cemetery, pursuant to his request. He was one of the great British officials during World War II. He really did a lot of good for the whole Allied cause. Commander Kirkpatrick said, "Admiral King asked me to tell you that your orders as operation officer to Mountbatten are being cancelled.[*] You're going with Ambassador Averell Harriman to carry out U.S.A.-U.S.S.R. agreements of the Tehran conference."[†]

Captain Forrest Royal said, "You have to be either a captain or a rear admiral to go to U.S.S.R. and work with those Russians. Don't worry. I'll take care of it." It didn't take very long for that news to get around as soon as Captain Royal heard about it. I had been a commander only a couple of months, having been a lieutenant commander on Corregidor. I have a copy someplace of the memo Royal sent to Admiral King, pointing out that I had already had combat experience and had been working with the Joint Chiefs, and with such background more rank was desirable to deal with the Russians. It was to my advantage to be at least a captain. I was in the class of '30, and the class of '24 hadn't made captain. Royal sent a memo to Admiral King, and it came back in 24 hours. All it said was, "Okay. EJK."

Captain Royal sent it to the Chief of Personnel. Many people over there were senior to me. I had to go to BuPers to get my orders and obtain permission to be frocked while my uniforms were changed in preparation for U.S.S.R. duty. I was entitled to wear captain's rank while I was getting ready to leave. The commanders who prepared my

---
[*] Admiral Louis Mountbatten, RN, Supreme Allied Commander Southeast Asia, 1943-46.
[†] W. Averell Harriman was U.S. ambassador to the Soviet Union, 23 October 1943 to 24 January 1946.

orders to be a captain were unhappy. A couple of them were mean. I said, "I've seen a lot of combat. How much have you seen?" All it took was that memo that Admiral King initialed. No one in BuPers argued because they had other memos from Admiral King telling them what to do.

My service record and reputation were known, but Admiral King didn't give a damn who you knew, if you did a good job. He was called the "thin man." He was pretty tough, however; he knew what the Navy needed and was the leading advocate to maintain a realistic level of combat operations in the Pacific while the primary objective was the defeat of Germany.

Paul Stillwell: Were there no more senior weather specialists that he might have considered if he had to have a captain?

Admiral Knoll: No, not at that time. Shorty Orville was a commander, class of 1925, when I went to see him and received instructions before I left. I wore my Navy raincoat so he wouldn't see my four stripes, because he was in charge of the Navy aerological service. Most Navy aerologists were 100% Navy forecasters, with no political, military, or diplomatic experience. My past experience qualified me for the job. My selection by Admiral King was made in Tehran, without reference to Orville or anyone in Washington. I was fairly fluent in about three different foreign languages. I picked up the Russian language in Moscow in less than six months. Whenever I'm getting ready to go to a country, I spend about a month's time with a tape recording so that I become fluent enough to get around.

I received my orders and got ready to go. To reach Moscow from Washington via air in early 1944 was very complicated. I started off priority two from Washington to Miami; from Miami to an Army airfield outside of San Juan, Puerto Rico; from there to Georgetown, British Guyana; and from British Guyana to Natal, Brazil. There was a delay at Natal. A C-54 to Ascension had been lost.* I was delayed for two days, and I was priority one going from Brazil to Ascension Island, then to Accra, British West

---

* R5D Skymaster was the Navy designation for the Douglas-built DC-4 commercial airliner. The four-engine propeller plane had a top speed of 281 miles an hour. It was 118 feet long, wingspan of 94 feet, and gross weight of 65,000 pounds. It first went into Navy service in 1941. The Army designation was C-54.

Africa. Ascension Island in the South Atlantic looked like a postage stamp from the air, and half of it is a high hill with a sole high tree. The other half of the island is the landing field. If the weather's bad, it would be hard to find. You can't imagine the number of large planes moving through there at that time. The first C-54s were assigned to this route. They were completely loaded and carried many passengers. Upon landing, planes immediately refueled while passengers had breakfast on the hilltop of Ascension Island. An officers' club was up there, and the latrine vented down the far side of the hill. It was a weird and wild place.

From there we went to Accra, British West Africa, and that's where all entries have double-barrier doors for mosquitoes. Entry to every building had two screen doors, one outside and one going in. In between you walked through a puddle about a half-inch thick of disinfectant so any larva did not enter the building, not even on your shoes. All the glasses were cut-off beer bottles, not necessary to bring tumblers from the house. The C-54 went no farther than Accra.

From Accra we flew in an RAF C-47 across Central Africa, landing at different RAF fields about 200 miles apart, such as walls of Kano and Lake Chad, and on to Khartoum, Sudan.[*] At Khartoum there was a foul-up. The crew that was supposed to be gassing the plane was teasing around some girls in uniform. After we took off, the pilot found out that the plane had insufficient gas. We were about halfway to Cairo and then returned to Khartoum to spend the night. Upon arrival in Cairo, we tried to find a place to stay until there was a flight from Cairo to Abadan or Basra, Iran, via Habbaniya, near, Babylon.

Colonel Valentine and myself went downtown in Cairo and were told, "There's no place to stay here. All the different hotels are filled. You'll be lucky." We started checking around since there was no place to stay at the airport, and we didn't know how soon we were going to get out. Finally we went in the Metropolitan Hotel. There was a Hungarian clerk behind the desk. He said, "I can't take care of you."

So we walked around and checked alcoves in the lobby and went back to him and said, "What's the matter with this part of the lobby?"

---

[*] The Douglas DC-3 went into service in the mid-1930s as perhaps the first really successful commercial airliner. Designated C-47 by the Army and R4D by the Navy, the plane was a much-used transport and cargo plane during and after World War II.

He said, "That's not a room."

We said, "Well, you've got these drapes that can enclose part of the lobby. Put up a line and place a couple of mattresses on the floor, and we'll sleep there."

He said, "Well, there's no lavatory."

We said, "The men's room is very convenient."

He looked at us and said, "Okay." So we slept for a few days in the lobby on mattresses in the Metropolitan Hotel in Cairo.

One day I met the naval attaché at the U.S. embassy in Cairo, and we visited the pyramids and the Tomb of the Bulls and other sites. He had been an archeologist prior to being called to active duty.

We flew from there to Habbaniya, in Iraq, and from there to Basra, Abadan, and then to Tehran, Iran. In Tehran we stayed in barracks at the airfield, which is near U.S. Army Camp Amirabad. Every day the Shah and his wife—they were young at that time—would come driving around, waving to everybody.* I checked in as a captain. I didn't pay too much attention. I was tired, and I went to sleep. The next day I noticed everyone around me were U.S. Army senior lieutenants. I went in to eat, and some officers saw I was a captain in the Navy. They asked me, "Where did you sleep?" I said so-and-so. The response was, "You're not supposed to be in there."

So after breakfast I went to the desk clerk and said, "You know, I'm a captain in the Navy. I rank with a colonel in the U.S. Army."

I had to check with the officer in charge to obtain better accommodations. Within an hour, they moved me, and then they found out I was priority two to go into U.S.S.R. There were about 50 people all waiting to go into the Soviet Union for various reasons. I only stayed, I think, about 48 hours, no more than three days, while other people had been there for weeks. When the Russians were checking, giving me my visa to enter U.S.S.R., I was carried as a personal representative of President Roosevelt. This came up more than once in Moscow at various meetings: "You are listed as staff of Ambassador Harriman."

---

* Mohammad Reza Pahlavi (1919-1980) became Shah of Iran (or Persia, as it was then known) in 1941 and held office until his regime was ousted in 1979 by the Ayatollah Khomeini.

We flew in a Russian C-47 from Tehran into the Soviet Union. We flew through the El Burz mountain passes because some of the mountain peaks were higher than the service ceiling of the C-47, and this was an American-built, Russian-piloted C-47, loaded with Russians. There were all kinds of extra cargo in the aisles, which could be hazardous. We entered a mountain pass en route to the Caspian Sea about three different times. It was very cloudy—low visibility. On the third try the pilot went ahead, and all of a sudden the Caspian Sea appeared. We landed at Baku on the shore of the Caspian and only spent one night there.

As soon as we reached the Soviet Union, it has a distinctive smell of sour cabbage and a heavy odor of fuel oil such as I've never smelled in any other part of the world. In Baku there were oil wells on shore and in the Caspian Sea, with leaking oil everywhere on the surface. The city smelled of oil, the hotel smelled of oil. It was not very pleasant, and we were glad to be en route to Moscow. On the Iranian shore of the Caspian is the best caviar harvested in the world. By contrast, caviar is canned by Russian people in Iran. It is the best caviar in the world, small pinhead gray caviar. It's delicious.

From Baku we flew to Stalingrad, and for 100 miles around Stalingrad there were tons of wreckage that immediately illustrated that the most wasteful thing known to man is war. Vast amounts of military equipment; it didn't matter if it was German or Russian. It was used in the Battle of Stalingrad. At the airport in Stalingrad there were 25 or 30 Fokker airplanes that had landed with invasion gear for retrenchment, the sides hanging down, filled with all the spades and all the extra fighting gear that had never been used. All was there, deteriorating in the weather. The trucks and the dead horses, the guns, the wagons, and the tanks were abandoned everywhere. It was the most ungodly waste of man's resources you can imagine. No people were in sight anywhere. We were warned not to step off two 10-by-2 planks over the gumbo mud. The planks were between the airplane and the waiting room.

The waiting room was a former station without a roof. If you stepped off in this gumbo mud, you might break your ankle trying to pull your leg out of it. More than one person did this because they didn't believe the warning. We stayed there only long enough to fuel. We began to realize that the U.S.S.R. didn't have good airways or established airway communications. Once we took off from Stalingrad and headed for

Moscow, the pilot followed railroad tracks at an altitude of only a couple hundred feet. There was a little snowstorm. It was necessary to follow the railroad tracks because there were no regular airway beacons. The pilot identified Moscow at night by picking up the towers around the Kremlin and then follow Gorky Street to land at the airport. There were no modern airways in Moscow in January 1944.

We were sent to the U.S.S.R. to carry out the agreements of Tehran. Essentially, they agreed to exchange twice a day 40 to 60 weather reports for the Soviet Union, and we would send them the equivalent number of the United States and the Western Hemisphere reports. Both of us could improve each other's ability to draw weather maps and make more accurate forecasts.

The interesting thing is that we ran into the fantastic democratic centralism, monolithic control by a police state. No one can appreciate this unless one works there. We were anxious to carry out the agreements made at Tehran. For months no official would talk about anything relating to the agreements made at Tehran until Stalin provided guidance and different controls on each level of authority down to the people with whom we hoped to talk. We were anxious to get started with the weather exchange. Fortunately, we had established a small preliminary exchange before I left Washington. Two Russian weather officials had come to the U.S.A. and initiated an exchange as a prelude to a major exchange. At least we were exchanging a small amount of data, and the Russians were getting a few reports in return.

I had an opportunity to talk to General Federov, their chief of weather bureau and discuss the preliminary exchange that was rather reliable within specific guidelines, and this earlier relationship proved to be very good.[*] I had a chance to visit various research centers of the Academy of Sciences, who were involved in hydrology, oceanography, and other earth sciences. Their bureau was called the Hydrometeorological Service, which is semantically right. I received a lot of briefing on their future plans for hydrologic dams in the Soviet Union. I participated in hydrological seminars in Leningrad. I had a chance to meet officials. They were not allowed to know or discuss any agreement made in Tehran.

---

[*] Dr. Yevgeny K. Federov was head of the Soviet Hydrometeorological Service from 1939 to 1947 and from 1962 to 1974.

I had an advantage over many other U.S. military people in U.S.S.R. The primary thing we wanted was to develop the two Air Forces bases in the Ukraine. They were needed for shuttle bombing between Europe and the U.S.S.R. We couldn't talk about this; no one could; and this went on for four to six months. Finally, when they did talk, they had assembled equipment and railroad cars, landing matting, and airport communications for quick transportation from Murmansk directly to Poltava in Ukraine. Until each one had authority as to what he could talk about and what he could do, no one at any level could innovate or anticipate. Every time we went to an important meeting on weather subjects, there was always a political observer to record everything that was said. No one may in any way criticize or embarrass the Soviet Union and its motives. You couldn't write a letter expressing frustration or complain that they were slow in carrying out the Tehran agreement. Any unfavorable comment was recorded and forward by political auditor to their superiors. It was wise to avoid incriminating anyone with whom you dealt, because you might never meet with him again.

Paul Stillwell: So how did you get around that?

Admiral Knoll: There were different ways. My relationship was good. General Federov had been made famous with Papanin living on an ice floe for months, circulating the North Pole and floating with the ice field until return to the North Atlantic.* For this exploit General Federov was made a "Hero of the Soviet Union" was a respected official of the Soviet Academy of Sciences. Most of our meetings were without the presence of a political commissar. In addition, a few times I had to put a written record that Washington was very unhappy with exchanges. The U.S.A. was not getting the right number of daily reports that had been promised. I could see his face get red and uncomfortable. I said, "General, these are the facts." I added, "Please, General, give me that letter, and here is a revised letter for your file." Both of them had been signed by Ambassador Harriman. The second letter made sure we did not criticize his inability to

---

* Ivan Papanin was a leading explorer of the Arctic. He and a team of scientists spent 274 days in 1937-38 on a drifting block of ice.

carry out the exchange. Political commissars frequently searched his files to find anything incriminating. We needed his understanding, so we had to protect him.

We used the same procedure later on in the United Nations when I was U.S. military secretary. You have to know the pressure and the suspicion that surround them. If they are caught doing anything wrong, they're finished. It's hard to convince a Free World individual that this is the system in the U.S.S.R. I kept Ambassador Harriman and Admiral Olsen advised of my work.* Admiral Olsen was the naval member of the U.S. military mission to the U.S.S.R. We had good relationships with Averell Harriman and George Kennan and had regular meetings with them and General Deane, and other officials with the military mission.†

Paul Stillwell: What are your impressions of those two individuals, Harriman and Kennan?

Paul Stillwell: I've had many important meetings with Ambassador Harriman, particularly when he was working on an urgent problem involving Roosevelt, Churchill, and Stalin at times. He wouldn't sleep for a couple of nights, and he would remain in his bunk with a desk attached for working out a solution. He wouldn't shave for a couple of days. He'd sit there and obtain news from mission officers. He'd call me in, and we'd talk about specific problems, seeking my experience in dealing with the Russians. From time to time I'd check further with different people. I had an excellent relationship with him. I'll tell you, when he's got a job to do, he's not afraid to work his tail off to get a sound, correct solution. He had the confidence of Churchill and Stalin. He understands the Russian system better than anybody else, particularly their likes and dislikes, their strengths and weaknesses.

Paul Stillwell: This is Harriman?

---

* Rear Admiral Clarence E. Olsen, USN, provided his memories of World War II service in the Soviet Union to the Naval Institute oral history collection.
† George F. Kennan was U.S. Deputy Chief of Mission in the Soviet Union from 1944 to 1946. Major General John R. Deane, USA, was head of the U.S. military mission to the Soviet Union during the second half of World War II.

Admiral Knoll: Harriman and Kennan as well. Harriman had learned the hard way. He went there with his father while his father was still planning to extend the Union Pacific Railroad with a shipping service between San Francisco and Vladivostok and finally via a continuation of the Trans-Siberian Railroad to Europe. He was planning a worldwide transportation service run by the Union Pacific, whose owner was Edward H. Harriman. Averell went there as a youngster with his father when he was about 14 or 16 years old and saw Russia in the 1920s. At that time the Russians were probably a little bit more flexible than they are today, because they were not a world power and looking for improvements in economy and world recognition. Later on, when he became a little older, he tried to set up, with the Soviet Government, his own shipping service between the Black Sea and the U.S.A. He found out it wouldn't work, so he learned how difficult it was to get any agreement with the U.S.S.R.

In addition, having been a classmate of Roosevelt at Groton School, he enjoyed the confidence and personal relationship with the President. All communications from Moscow to Washington went direct to Roosevelt, via Navy communications, and all encoding was done by the Navy. The real representative of the State Department was George Kennan, and he worked closely with Harriman and the Secretary of State in Washington. He saw only what the President wanted him to know of his communications with Harriman. Harriman was Roosevelt's man and was sent there to overcome the unhappiness of Admiral Standley, who tried to be more than an ambassador.[*] He criticized the Soviets because they were not giving their people adequate recognition of U.S. Lend-Lease and the support the U.S.A. was giving them.[†]

Harriman had to be very careful to keep himself persona grata, and he had had the advance good chance to work in London with Churchill, who was a difficult man to please. Churchill liked the way Harriman did business, and as a result, that was a plus for this work with Roosevelt. Here you had three powerful people that tended to understand each other. We finally found out that any new issue that was sent to the Soviet Union

---

[*] Admiral William H. Standley, USN, served as Chief of Naval Operations from 1 July 1933 to 1 January 1937. After being recalled to active service, he served as U.S. ambassador to the Soviet Union from 14 April 1942 to 19 September 1943. See William H. Standley and Arthur Ageton, *Admiral Ambassador to Russia* Chicago: H. Regnery Company, 1955).

[†] The Lend-Lease Act, passed by the U.S. Congress on 11 March 1941, was a device that enabled the United States to provide military aid to Great Britain without intervening directly in the European war then in progress. The program was later expanded to include aid to other Allied nations as well.

must first receive the attention of Stalin to be acted upon.* Any new idea given to Molotov, Foreign Minister, before it got to Stalin was the kiss of death.†

A new idea could only start in the U.S.S.R. from the man at the top. When an idea started with the top, Stalin initiated discussion with the Politburo and expressed his views. Stalin made no commitment one way or the other as to what should be done about it. Frequently each member tried to outguess how Stalin felt about it. They wanted to support it if he was going to support it or oppose it if they thought he was going to oppose. Few people understand how the Politburo may operate. When a project is approved, it is then studied on different levels of the Department of Defense and Foreign Ministry as to how it's going to be implemented.

It's because of this that Andrei Gromyko, whom I personally knew at the United Nations, could be a successful Foreign Minister of the Soviet Union for 27 years.‡ He knows more about all the long-range policy of the Soviet Union concerning any nation or event that can take place in the world. At times in the U.S.A. we don't know from week to week what the foreign policy is going to be in Washington. It is hard for our allies to understand this, and they don't like to believe it. Foreign policy is tailored by each administration with little regard for a consistent long-range policy that a Republican or Democratic administration can support. We keep announcing in the paper what we're going to propose at foreign conferences. As a superpower, the United States must stop grandstanding and get down to serious confidential dialogue with the U.S.S.R.

You mean to tell me General Motors and Ford Motor in competition, announce in advance in the newspaper before a policy meeting what they're going to discuss or what they're going to propose? The Soviets are the most secret, confidential-conscious people and the most realistic people in the world. Every time we publicize in the press we practically prove to them we don't seek an agreement. Soviet don't like this. They prepare with utmost secrecy in their diplomacy. We can't convince the average

---

* Joseph Stalin ran the Soviet Union essentially as a dictatorship from the late 1920s to his death on 5 March 1953. Nikita S. Khrushchev served as First Secretary of the Communist Party, 1953-64, and Premier of the Soviet Union, 1958-64.
† Vyacheslav Mikhailovich Molotov (1890-1986) was a Soviet politician and diplomat from the 1920s onward. He served as Minister of Foreign Affairs from 3 May 1939 to 4 March 1949.
‡ Andrei A. Gromyko was a long-time Soviet diplomat. Among his posts were ambassador to the United States, 1943-46; Ambassador to the United Nations, 1946-48; Deputy Foreign Minister, 1949-57; Foreign Minister, 1957-85; and Chairman of the Presidium of the Supreme Soviet, 1985-88.

American how dumb we are when we have the strength of a great power. We're a superpower. The Soviets are not a superpower. In every category practically they're not a real superpower.

They can't even grow enough food to feed their own people. They are not a homogenous people. They could not live together in freedom if it weren't for their police state. Is that a superpower? The sent a cruiser to the coronation of Queen Elizabeth of England.* The crew members were all the officers, because they could not trust regular enlisted men for such an event. That's a superpower? We have at times oversold to their advantage how big Soviets are. That's what scares me. That's what scared Harriman; that's what scared George Kennan. Soviets don't want a war, they don't want to use nuclear weapons, and they don't want us to use nuclear weapons on them.

Paul Stillwell: You said that the Soviet people or officers that you dealt with always had this fear that somebody was looking over their shoulders.

Admiral Knoll: They would. The political commissar is at all levels to keep everyone in line.

Paul Stillwell: Did you have that fear yourself?

Admiral Knoll: I would not say that I feared this. I knew about the system, because Soviet people told me about it. You cannot trust anyone, even a member of your own family, in the U.S.S.R. During war everyone seemed to have a relative who was at labor camp for unpatriotic comments.

Paul Stillwell: Were you tailed, for example?

Admiral Knoll: Definitely—for my final six months in U.S.S.R. I had a pretty good reputation in the Soviet Union except finally Senator Karl Mundt and Mrs. Bolton from

---

* Princess Elizabeth of Great Britain became Queen Elizabeth II on 6 February 1952 upon the death of her father, King George VI. Her coronation was on 2 June 1953. She has been Britain's monarch ever since. The Soviet representative was the light cruiser *Sverdlov*.

Cleveland came for a congressional visit.* Karl Mundt used to call me "commissar." Mundt, Mrs. Bolton, and Congressman Richards arrived after the end of the war in Europe.† The Soviets gave them a royal tour. I had a pretty good idea of the royal tour. They showed them certain apartment houses, took them to a railroad station, and showed them the subway. The Soviets let them talk to a couple of people and translated for them. We had a reception at Harriman's residence, Spasso House, with Ambassador Harriman, Karl Mundt, and Mrs. Bolton. I asked, "What did they show you today?"

Mundt said, "It was rather interesting."

I asked, "What are you doing tomorrow?"

They said, "What do you mean?"

I said, "I'll take you and show you part of what they showed you, and I know the Soviets didn't show you—the part you should see.

They said, "Okay."

I had a chauffeur's license for U.S.S.R. I got a license without having to take the engine apart and put it back together, which is what you have to do in U.S.S.R. if you're going to have a chauffeur's license. I did drive an embassy automobile. I drove myself around, and I knew the Soviet police would follow me wherever I went in most cases. So I took Mundt and Bolton, and I showed them a new apartment house. I said, "They showed you the front of this yesterday. Let's go back and see the rear." No windows with windowpanes in the rear, and the inner court was filthy and smelly. The Soviets showed them only the sights that had been fixed up for foreigners. I took them to one railroad station, walked in, and said, "Let's talk to a couple of these soldiers here." They asked certain questions, and I translated for them.

They said, "This is different; it is a new impression."

I said, "Yes. You must realize there is no chance to come to the Soviet Union and really talk to a Russian in a free and unsupervised manner. Each Russian has been

---

* Karl E. Mundt, a Republican from South Dakota, served in the House of Representatives from 3 January 1939 to 30 December 1948. He was in the Senate from 31 December 1948 to 3 January 1973. Frances P. Bolton, a Republican from Ohio, served in the House of Representatives from 27 February 1940 to 3 January 1969.

† James P. Richards, a Democrat from South Carolina, served in the House of Representatives from 4 March 1933 to 3 January 1957. V-E Day – Victory in Europe Day, 8 May 1945, when the German surrender was ratified in Berlin.

trained and conditioned to answer officials of your stature and say the things Soviets want you to believe." Some youngsters were visiting the Soviet Union and talked to students at Lermonosov University in Lenin Hills. They were happy about the Soviet Union. I said, "You can't talk in English directly with the Soviets over there without police control knowing about it. They're trained ahead of time. They're trained at the Foreign Language Institute." This is part of their training.

I've been in Leningrad more than once when Russians with their families returned from abroad through Helsinki after being in the United States or Great Britain or France. I was staying at the Astoria Hotel across from St. Isaac's Cathedral in Leningrad. Some Russian officials came through the lobby, some of whom I'd known in Washington. One of them was a former U.S.S.R. naval attaché in Washington and his wife. I talked with them. They went into special rooms to be debriefed by political commissars. When they came out of that room, they were pale. They were scared. They avoided me from then on. When I passed them the next time in the lobby of the Bolshoi Theater in Moscow at a ballet performance, I could pass, and they wouldn't admit that they ever saw me. They couldn't afford to, because they had been warned to give evidence of knowing any foreigners. "Never discuss what they had seen abroad. You haven't seen anything over there," I've been told about this from Russians in confidence. Secret police in U.S.S.R. maintain loyalty with intimidation. U.S.S.R. couldn't exist without a police state. In the Free World citizens are frightened that freedom-loving people will willingly become Communists.

Paul Stillwell: Did you have fears for your personal safety?

Admiral Knoll: I was about to say "No." Rather, I will say I didn't. During most of the time, I kept four $100.00 bills in my breast pocket. I think many others did the same. I always had some Russian-type clothing like a fur hat when world events looked like they were getting bad. U.S.-Soviet relations worsened towards the end of the war, when a U.S. Army Air Forces plane shot up and killed a Soviet general with Soviet troops in a valley of Yugoslavia. Soviet troops were not to be there. Stalin told Roosevelt that U.S. secret agents were in the Army Air Forces. Unfavorable relations were a preliminary to

Roosevelt's death.[*] At times it looked pretty bad, and things could go bad awful fast. We were ready to buy our way out with chocolate bars and vodka while heading towards Tashkent in Central Asia. The farther away one moves from Moscow, the better your chance you can bribe your way out. That was a possibility. Never go west toward Leningrad; it was too well controlled.

After the Karl Mundt and Mrs. Bolton trip, and for the remainder of my time in Moscow, I never went anyplace without a Soviet jeep following me, driven by two secret police. At least once, I started to drive at night. I stopped, took out my flashlight and recorded the numbers on their badges and the license number of the jeep. We had a couple good liaison officers like Mike Kostrinsky, a friend of Kemp Tolley's, who tried to reassure me, "You're not being followed."[†]

One time I said to Mike, "Mike, if I'm not being followed, then what are these police in jeep number so-and-so and these men NKVD number so-and-so who have been following me that last two nights and you say I'm not being followed?"[‡] He just looked at me and didn't say a word.

The Soviets didn't like that I showed Karl Mundt and Mrs. Bolton the true conditions of living quarters. I had also been stationed in Vladivostok for six months, and I was followed there. It had certain advantages, because if you were there as a foreigner, you were in a marked car with a diplomatic plate, and each foreigner had a code name. The gates to every Russian apartment house had an inner court to pass through for entry. So they had a block control and a house control of who was coming in, who was coming out, and that was a routine record of your movements. There were no open houses with open yards coming in. With such control, once in a while you wanted to locate someone who had gone out on an errand or a Sunday picnic on the Moscow River. You wanted to get hold of them. All you did was tell the policeman, "You know where So-and-so is?" In five minutes the individual would call you, because the secret police knew where he was.

---

[*] President Franklin D. Roosevelt died at Warm Springs, Georgia, on 12 April 1945.
[†] Commander Kemp Tolley, USN; Captain Third Rank Mikhail Ilyich Kostrinsky, Soviet Navy, Deputy Chief of Foreign Relations (Liaison).
[‡] NKVD – an abbreviation for the title that translates as People's Commissariat for Internal Affairs.

In the same way, they kept making checks of the hidden microphones in all the rooms of foreign embassies. They evidently did a lot of special wiring. The British military mission had taken over a very fine building when Soviets moved foreigners from Moscow when the Germans threatened within ten miles of Moscow. All the embassies were in Kuybyshev. At that time the Soviets were given an opportunity to further wire the rooms of the different missions attached to foreign embassies. They particularly added to the secret wiring of the U.S. and British military missions.

The U.S. Navy had one man who would go around with sensors to test for hidden microphones, wires, or speakers in a wall or ceiling. Somebody was working in the basement of the British military mission and detected some plastic wood coming from a beam in the basement. A small wire was uncovered. The British sent for our security individual. He put a ringer on those wires while we went around to different rooms. When his ringer was turned on, we could tell where each mike was located. In each meeting room a microphone was found, also in the ceiling over the general's desk. We found a total of 30 mikes, one of them buried in the plaster decoration around his chandelier.

We removed all that could be pulled out without doing too much damage. We left the mission carrying mikes by their wires like 29 dead rats. We checked their quality and date of manufacture. It was confirmed very quickly that half of them had been installed about 20-25 years before, and the other mikes were newer, less than a couple of years old. This indicated Soviets had placed a lot more while the foreigners were away in Kuybshev. Don't ever fool yourself that you're not being recorded in U.S.S.R. Today, with neon tubes and fluorescent lights, they can eavesdrop. The Turks and some other foreigners confuse any recorder here with a Maria Therese silver dollar striking a piece of glass. The silver on glass will kill the transmission. More than once I had meetings and at random clicked the glass with a silver coin to nullify any recordings.

The Soviets have the hysteria and suspicion from tsarist days, and they are a formidable people. A police state is imperative. Fifty-two percent of them are not ethnic Russians, can't even speak Russian. If it wasn't for a police state, as a non-homogeneous people they are unreliable.

I had a real scare when I was in Vladivostok. I went there for one idea, to find out why they couldn't provide the number of weather reports they had promised. Admiral Olsen and myself and General Federov had flown in Federov's private plane, and were not accompanied by any political commissars. We went for a weekend from Friday to Monday at his dacha on the Oka River, a short distance from Gorky, on the Volga. We had a friendly visit and talked about many things. We determined that I should go to the Far East, particularly Vladivostok, and take a look around. Federov said, "That's fine. I'll have my director of the Khabrovsk observatory call on you, and my people in Vladivostok will assist you."

It worked out nicely, because Commander Roullard had been in Vladivostok for two years and was due to come for a little holiday in U.S.A.[*] It was during the war, from October 1944 to March 1945. I provided some forecasting for early B-29 raids on Japan. Admiral Olsen and myself visited the U.S.S.R. Chief of Naval Operations, Soviet Navy, Alafuzov, and told him what I planned to do.[†] Before this visit, we visited Harriman and said, "They're going to try to tell me I have to leave all my military uniforms in Moscow." The U.S.S.R. was at peace with Japan.

I said, "About the time Alafuzov starts making up his mind that I can't go unless I agree not to be identified as a member of the U.S. armed forces, he will want me to leave my uniforms in Moscow. I'm not going out there and have the Soviets get involved in a war with Japan. I can be shot as a U.S. spy because I will not have a uniform to wear. So I won't make an issue of it, but at the right time I'll comment." All sort of smiled.

We went to Alafuzov, and he was interesting, a very big, jolly fellow. He was close to Marshal Voroshilov, who was a friend of Stalin.[‡] We had a very pleasant meeting. I told him I wanted his permission for me to go to Vladivostok for six months and relieve Commander Roullard so he could go home. I sensed Alafuzov was about to provide qualifications. I said, "Of course, Admiral, when you're in the United States you go places such as San Francisco or New York, and your officers always take their uniforms along, even though they don't wear them, because they may need them. So in my trunks that I take, I'll have a uniform, but I don't plan to wear it. I'll have it with me

---
[*] Commander George D. Roullard, USN, assistant naval attaché to the Soviet Union.
[†] Admiral Vladimir Antonovich Alafuzov, Soviet Navy.
[‡] Marshal Kliment Y. Voroshilov.

in the event U.S.S.R. should get involved with the war with Japan. I can dress like a military man and not be shot as a spy."

He looked at me, and he said something like, "Sly individual." He was about to tell me, "You can go out, but you can't take any uniforms with you." I worked there with Edmund Clubb, the U.S. consul general, and his wife was with him.* I lived at the consulate and had an office there as assistant U.S. consul. I helped as the coordinator for Lend-Lease cargo that was coming in great quantities. I had meetings with the U.S.S.R. diplomatic agents, Dukerov and other officials, in regards to Lend-Lease, as well as weather exchanges.

En route to Vladivostok via Trans-Siberian Railroad for 14 days, I had a shorthand pad, and every kilometer post I recorded whatever I saw. I put the kilometer number down and phenomena observed. All bridges crossing the river were guarded with dogs and sentries. Many loads of aluminum were en route to Novosibirsk, where concentration camps were sited. Some unit trains were taking Soviet troops to the east and returning back empty. This gave me something to do. The trains headed east had troops who had been injured in Europe. They were going to the Far East as reinforcements for ultimate action. At the different railroad stations, the train would stop for 30 or 40 minutes. Old Russian women would come up and kiss my hand and say, "Thank you for your food products. We're not starving to death."

I asked, "How do you know?"

"We know it's coming from U.S.A. as Lend-Lease." The Siberian people are more friendly. It's amazing. The farther east I went, near Irkutsk, Novosibirsk, Chia, and Khabarovsk, there was less evidence of secret police. The Soviets weren't telling their people they were getting Lend-Lease. However, people in the east knew. Going east, the scenery changes from the time cross the Volga, and all of a sudden you're in wide-open space. If President Reagan could visit the Soviet Union and find out how he's often flattering them for what they are, he will revise his idea of the U.S.S.R. as a nation.† He should have a chance to see what they do not have compared to the United States. He

---

* O. Edmund Clubb was U.S. consul general in Vladivostok from 1944 to 1946. His oral history is in the Harry S. Truman Presidential Library.
† Ronald W. Reagan served as President of the United States from 20 January 1981 to 20 January 1989, including the time of this interview.

hasn't the faintest idea of the U.S.S.R. environment, U.S.S.R people, and their likes and dislikes.

When I arrived in Vladivostok, I made my calls on the diplomatic agent, and then I had a liaison officer, a captain in the U.S.S.R. Navy, assigned by Admiral Yumashev.[*] U.S.S.R. officials took me down a couple of times to show me the volume of Lend-Lease stacked up on docks. I can tell you, you never saw such a mess with the Lend-Lease carelessly stacked up on the dock. They had many boxes showing which side should be kept up, with the wine glass. Crates were in every shape and form, many crushed and doubtful of further use. Large vacuum tubes in containers were broken. There seemed to be no concern about anything. Cargo was stacked some 20-30 feet high on these different piers, and nothing was really being moved. I was amazed they let me go down and see this chaos. I could check a lot by binoculars from my room at the consulate, on the side of a hill. To go down there and see it, I'd find no organized effort being made to move it.

They were complaining that they weren't getting enough locomotives or flatcars. They were getting a shipload of alcohol weekly from which to make vodka and they were getting consumer food. Finally with my one yeoman I said, "Well, let's take a hike, get some vodka together, some chocolate bars, and Russian clothing." We were requested not to go outside the city limits of Vladivostok. We went past the city limits guard, bribing him with some vodka and a chocolate bar. We were dressed like Russians. All of a sudden, within a couple of miles of the city limits, on a railroad spur, we found something like 10 or 12 new locomotives, a lot of flatcars, all new, that had been sent over by Lend-Lease and had not been used. We made a list of the serial numbers on the locomotives and flat cars and went on back to the consulate. I sent a one-time pad message to Admiral King in Washington, information to Ambassador Harriman.[†]

One of the things we were not supposed to do in U.S.S.R. was really collect military intelligence. This was supposedly one of the agreements applying to the U.S. military mission. This was in our own interest. They claimed they weren't getting enough Lend-Lease to move this equipment, when they had new locomotives up there

---

[*] Admiral Ivan Stepanovich Yumashev, Commander of the Soviet Pacific Fleet.
[†] A one-time pad is a means of encrypting messages.

and new flatcars not being used. I sent this message to Washington around Christmas 1944. Within less than a week, I received a call from U.S.S.R. liaison about 3:00 o'clock in the morning. "We have to have a meeting right away," said my liaison captain. Each time we met, it was in a variety of different office buildings or special locations in Vladivostok. There was no uniform procedure or pattern. I got in there, and the liaison officer was all excited.

He said, "You're going to get shot as a spy."

I said, "Why?"

He said, "You're a spy."

I asked, "What to you mean?"

"You sent a message to Washington to say new locomotives here are not being used." So-and-so and so-and-so.

I said, "I don't know what you are talking about."

"Yes, you sent it. You are the only one that would know this. The only way you could find it out is by violating the restriction of the city limits and going up there to see them and collect this kind of information."

He was scared. I said, "Okay, don't worry. I'm sorry. I didn't do it. I will report to Washington I don't know who did it." He was all right after that and never mentioned the subject again. I sent a message to Washington and told them my embarrassment. And, here again, Washington never wanted to believe the trying conditions in U.S.S.R. under which we worked and lived. They considered the Soviets were an ally. My message was automatically sent to the Soviet Lend-Lease Commission on 16th Street in Washington for comment before anybody in the Navy Department intelligence had even started reading it. Wasn't that wonderful? The wrong Soviet official might have shot me as a spy, and no one would have known the true facts.

Paul Stillwell: What was your intent that would happen when you sent that message?

Admiral Knoll: I had previously reported the mass of Lend-Lease cargo not being moved. We had evidence they were not using equipment they already had. This was part of our job. If they needed something badly via Lend-Lease, they were supposed to get it, and Roosevelt ordered we should rush to get it to them. They were telling us lies while they were stockpiling railroad cars and locomotives and not using them. All this military equipment on the dock was deteriorating. I felt I had a responsibility to let Washington know about it. It was because of this and a few other incidents that I was told, when I left U.S.S.R. in December '45, I advised that I would be persona non grata if I tried to revisit.

It took me a long time to get to U.S.S.R. I went back in June 1978 for about six days in Leningrad and Moscow. I never left my wife and others in the tour group. I never risked walking around alone to try to revisit any place or familiar neighborhood. They watched me and might pick me up and embarrass me. I wouldn't take that chance. Others who did revisit were embarrassed. I was about to send a message to Gromyko, the Foreign Minister, because the whole group of 30 people coming and going from Erie all received their visas promptly, 30 days before departure. Mine came through 48 hours before I left. They had had it a month with no action. My wife received hers with the group. You know they had paid attention.

These are phenomena that people just don't understand. They're like an elephant. They don't forget anything. They have a completely fantastic dossier on individuals. They know your plusses and minuses. I was told about items in my dossier, namely, that I was very realistic, that I was intelligent, that I understood fairly good Russian, and that I was a difficult man to deal with if they started telling lies. Now, for example, why didn't the weather exchange work? Very simply. They promised to do something that was physically impossible to carry out. Stalin agreed to it. Whether he knew that what he had agreed to was not feasible could not be proven. No one could risk advising him.

Paul Stillwell: What was physically impossible to do—what part of it?

Admiral Knoll: First, they had no radio communications organization for collecting timely weather reports every six hours from Siberia and outlying areas east of the Volga, except near the population centers of Novosibirsk or Khabarovk and Vladivostok. They did collect good climatological data at a central station about once a week and sometimes once a month. They lacked radio communication systems to collect timely reports every six hours for weather maps. They had no teletype system, they had no airway system.

They had agreed to give information that they didn't have and couldn't collect. So, again, national pride prevented them from making a frank admission that they could not carry out this Tehran agreement. With frustration after frustration, we helped them along and avoided a formal complaint to Stalin.

Contrary to advice from the U.S. military mission in preparation for the Yalta Conference, General Hap Arnold and his staff kept saying, "Well, if U.S.S.R. can't collect it, U.S.A. will send them $10 million of equipment to collect it."* You can't imagine the number of messages I sent to Orville or the embassy and explained to the State Department the U.S.S.R. dilemma. Giving the U.S.S.R. weather equipment without the basic communications infrastructure to collect and transmit information did not achieve capability to get weather reports in time for winning the war.

Finally, at Yalta, Hap Arnold had a chance to talk, and he readily offered weather equipment, and they replied, "We'll take it." Of course, they would take it. Washington was determined to obtain more U.S.S.R. weather reports. Two Navy groups were sent to the Far East via Alaska to collect weather in Khabarovsk and Petropavlovsk just as the U.S.S.R. joined the war against Japan.† We told Washington the problems involved. The groups arrived, but the U.S.S.R. didn't want them in the Far East. They received poor cooperation. They brought in everything that was needed in expendable supplies. U.S.S.R. put them in buildings that were uncomfortable and gave them little liaison or support. It was just a matter of time that they quickly realized, "U.S.S.R. doesn't want us here. The quicker we get out of here, the better." We had told them ahead of time. The U.S.S.R. did not have the daily weather reports they needed. All were very uncomfortable and arranged to get out. The expedition created many problems without achieving any improvement in the volume of weather reports every six hours that was needed.

---

* General Henry H. Arnold, USA, was Commanding General of the Army Air Forces from March 1942 to March 1946. He was promoted to four-star rank in March 1943 and five-star rank in December 1944. Yalta, a resort city on the Crimea in the Black Sea, was the site of a meeting of the Allied Big Three—Roosevelt, Churchill, and Stalin—in February 1945. The conference reaffirmed the principle of seeking unconditional surrender by Japan and plans for the postwar division of territory.
† At the Yalta Conference Stalin had agreed that the Soviet Union would enter the war against Japan three months after the conclusion of the war against Germany, which happened on 8 May 1945. The Soviets declared war on 8 August, two days after the United States dropped an atomic bomb on Nagasaki, Japan. Hostilities ended a week later with the Japanese surrender on 15 August.

Paul Stillwell: Did you have equipment of your own?

Admiral Knoll: No.

Paul Stillwell: What were you using as a basis for these weather reports you were sending for the B-29s?

Admiral Knoll: Vladivostok weather and the highs and lows moving east from Asia during the winter months gave valuable info for planning raids on Japan. Accurate temperature, barometer readings, the passage of cold fronts, and wind shifts provided data not otherwise available.

An interesting thing happened shortly after I arrived in Vladivostok. In the first B-29 raid on Tokyo, one B-29 aborted and diverted to U.S.S.R. It landed at the airport near Vladivostok. I asked my liaison to let me go out and talk to the crew. They said, "No, you can't, because the Japanese would misunderstand it." They were right on that. They said, "We'll give you the names of the crew, which you can send to the United States." When the pilot got out of the B-29, he said, "Don't try to fly this plane. It's very touchy. You'll crash." So he carefully warned the Soviet ground crew. The Americans had got out of the plane and wanted to return for their personal effects. The Soviets refused and told them they were interned. Three days after that plane landed at Vladivostok, it was flown by the Russians to Novosibirsk, where they inspected and produced an exact copy of the B-29.

Within ten days, another B-29 came in and landed at the same place. The pilot got out and asked by name, "Where is Lieutenant So-and-so?" The Soviets told me that the second B-29 didn't have anything wrong with it. The Soviets interned him and obtained a second B-29 plane. They had the advantage of tearing down the first plane to duplicate a Soviet copy. The Soviets like three copies of a military item. They keep one as a model. The second one they disassemble and study every component part. The third one goes for research by the Academy of Sciences to learn new techniques.

I've seen this vividly portrayed in one of their laboratories. They had developed in this laboratory about 35 different radio sondes for taking upper-air weather soundings.* They had collected all different radio sondes from other nations. The U.S.A. had developed some of the first ones, the Germans developed one, the Japs developed one, and the Russians developed their own model. Each one was analyzed as to component parts; the different principles that made it operate were identified as to how they collected the pressure and temperature and humidity. Each sample was carefully portrayed in sequence of basic components. They starred the component in the sample that was unique compared to others.

They would point out that their new model included all the outstanding capabilities of the various samples. The U.S.S.R. used the European approach to scientific discussions. At a seminar they cited the basic science and physical law, such as Boyle's Law and illustrate the building block from each proposition. They make sure the audience is up to date on everything that's going to be applied in their final solution. The review takes time but provides a good education.

I was in U.S.S.R. less than six months when I went to Vladivostok via the Trans-Siberian Railroad, 14 days one way. With a dictionary and no interpreter, I got along pretty well. Right after the liberation of Leningrad, I went there to attend a seminar on hydrology at the University of Leningrad. To get ready for that, I prepared a little statement in Russian, "I'm happy to be here, we're allies, we have many problems to work together." They invited me to sit as a member of the presidium during the seminar. I couldn't understand what they were talking about. One Soviet weather individual told me the highlights. All of a sudden, they nominated people to occupy different chairs in the presidium. They were names of officials of the Soviet Union. I occupied the chair in the presidium that represented Stalin. When it came my time to participate and they asked for my remarks, "I said, "Yes, thank you. I'll do it." I gave the three-minute talk in Russian. They gave me an ovation, not knowing that I would speak in Russian. It wasn't perfect, but they understood. They were impressed that I was trying to work with them.

---

* A sonde (French for "probe") is a device for testing physical conditions—in this case at altitude.

Every place I ever went, I would speak a little Russian. If they knew English, they would say something in English. Time and again, Russians avoid foreigners they know don't speak Russian. When General Eisenhower was there to receive a medal, the marshals were all there.* There was a special reception in Spasso House after General Eisenhower received the U.S.S.R. victory medal. We had attended the ceremony in Red Square prior to the reception. General Eisenhower was accompanied by Marshal Zhukov.† They both had a good relationship. The Cossack Marshall Budeny, and Marshal Yoroshilov were there.

I translated about six or seven times for General Eisenhower as he talked to Soviet marshals. Eisenhower repeated to each one, "Together we have a mission for the world. Our people must never fight each other. You do your part, and I'll do mine." Eisenhower could get this across in a very convincing manner. We had a good time at this reception. Some of the younger marshals were only 35 years old and made a point to argue and not be friendly. There was one young Russian with Red Army communications. He said that the U.S.A. was telling a bunch of lies, since there was no such thing as destructive as an atomic bomb—that the U.S.A. was overemphasizing the A-bomb for propaganda purposes.

Finally, I think General Federov saw there was a slight argument, and he came over to me and said, "He's just too young. He doesn't know what he is talking about." These are the things you get involved in and must never permit yourself to show impatience or anger.

Paul Stillwell: Cooperation was pretty much a one-way street, wasn't it?

Admiral Knoll: Upon arrival in Vladivostok, I kept sending my letter to the diplomatic agent to arrange a meeting with the commander in chief of the U.S.S.R. Asiatic Fleet, Fleet Admiral Yumashev, namely an official visit in keeping with protocol. I guess I had been there about three months, and I advised the diplomatic agent, "It's an old custom in

---

* General of the Army Dwight D. Eisenhower, USA, was the Supreme Allied Commander in Europe in 1944-45.
† Marshal Georgy Konstantinovich Zhukov was one of the Soviets' most accomplished military leaders in World War II.

the Navy, the senior naval officers comes into an area, he makes courtesy calls on the senior officer present and makes his manners."

Of a sudden, I received a call, "You be ready about 3:00 o'clock in the morning at the rear fence of the U.S. consulate general. An official car with side curtains will pick you up and take you to see Admiral Yumashev."

I had to climb over the fence and wait in the dark alley for the car with blue headlights on and side curtains. The door opened, and I got in. At headquarters I passed barriers en route to the building. The halls and stairs had red carpets on the walls and gold decorations up to the admiral's office. I spent some time with his chief of staff, Admiral Frolov, a submariner, a very pleasant gent, and he knew some English. I didn't have an interpreter. I relied on my dictionary. Finally I went and met Admiral Yumashev. I said, "Admiral King sends his warm regards. I'm happy to have this opportunity to say hello to you. I'm getting a lot of support from my liaison, Captain So-and-so, for which I thank you. I have one request."

He said, "Please."

I said, "You know, we're having a lot of difficulty not knowing when our planes have to abort. A Navy plane has landed in Kamchatka, and an Army plane is here in Siberia. Isn't there some way that if after they abort and land in U.S.S.R. that you could quickly collect the names and tell us? You don't have to tell us exactly where they land, but let us know they landed safely and who survived. Their families are interested to know, and we are, too, what became of them. There has to be some kind of procedure that when a plane has to abort, being in this area, that you or some of your people will let the U.S. consul or me know where they are and their condition. Probably the best thing for that is let us know the procedure you want them to follow so if they do have to abort they will know what to do."

He quickly said, "Well, if they're coming to U.S.S.R. and have to abort anyplace, when we see them coming in and know they're picked up by our radar, we will send a fighter plane or some plane to intercept and wiggle their wings, and that means follow that plane where he takes you. Don't try to go to any airfield that they may think they know exists. We'll escort them to the airport and watch them land. As soon as they land, we will send your consul the list of the names and type of aircraft. That worked. From then on, within about 48 hours they would call and give me a list of the names, and I would send it to Washington. The sequel to this was that we had a special procedure so U.S.S.R. would not be involved with any acts to jeopardize the Soviet Union and the Japanese peaceful relations.

We had to be very careful, but as soon as these people were in control of the Russians, they conveniently were allowed to escape from one prison camp to another until they got to Tashkent and the frontier of Iran. They easily "escaped" into Iran and were met by U.S. reps who sent them back to the States without the Japs knowing about it. There were arguments once U.S.S.R. had control of interned aviators. Many got through this way. We had a couple of officers at the embassy who got to the Tashkent area and arranged for them to cross the frontier into Iran. Internees thought they were escaping, and it was to maintain the fiction. Some thought U.S.S.R. was a country from which escape was all too easy.

Paul Stillwell: What do you remember about Kemp Tolley from those years in Russia?

Admiral Knoll: When I arrived there in February 1944, I was a captain, and he was a commander.[*] I thought there was always a little bit of feeling. He hadn't married Vlada yet. We had a good time in Moscow, but I never was in on some of the horseplay and other antics he talks about in his book.[†] Chronologically some are out of line as to the dates. It's very interesting, an interesting story, but I wouldn't call some of it historically accurate.

I've visited Kemp here in Maryland. I've known Vlada. When I first came back from U.S.S.R. and I was with the United Nations we had a couple of meetings with what we called the Moscow alumni association. I visited Vlada and Kemp when they were stationed at Yokosuka, and I was chief of staff with Seventh Fleet.

Paul Stillwell: I must say that he certainly hasn't held any ill will, because he recommended a couple of times that you be included in the oral history program.

---

[*] This despite the fact that Tolley had graduated from the Naval Academy in 1929 and Knoll in 1930.
[†] Kemp Tolley, *Caviar and Commissars: the Experiences of a U.S. Naval Officer in Stalin's Russia* (Annapolis: Naval Institute Press, 1983). See also Tolley's Naval Institute oral history.

Admiral Knoll: No, no, no, no, no, I didn't mean anything in that. I am flattered to know he thought I could add to the archives.

Six months of 1944, I was not with him. I was in Vladivostok. He was in Moscow for VE day 1945, which was a most scary experience. It was a most impressive event. It showed at a certain point that the Soviet police could not control the Russian people.

Let me say this before I go further. By Christmas Day 1944, I had nothing to do in Vladivostok, so I sent a long message to Admiral King and Ambassador Harriman, giving a summation of all the people I'd met on the Trans-Siberian Railroad going from Moscow to Vladivostok. It took 14 days, and there was no shorter way, no air transport. At each meeting, I'd say to an officer or official, "When is the best weather out there? When war is going to happen, what time of the year is the best time to start it?" Things like that.

Over a period of time, they all replied mid-August, only good time, not much rain, no mud, good weather. So I kept picking up this information. No one would ever admit U.S.S.R. was going to war against Japan—no one. Discussion of this was forbidden in every shape and form. I put this all together, and then I noted the number of troop trains with injured people coming out of the Far East and going back empty and the concentration of airplane factories around Novosibirsk. There were many railroad cars loaded with aluminum ingots. Based on everything I observed, the Russians were going to go to war against Japan before the end of 1945. And based on everything that was being built up, similar to some of the buildup I'd seen in Singapore in July of 1941, the whole attitude of the people, I said that the Russians would go to war against Japan on August 15, plus or minus ten days. I sent this on Christmas Day 1944.

The Yalta Conference was shortly after that time, and I had worked on Yalta papers before leaving Moscow. About a month after that, I received some questions from Washington requesting more information and details on what I based my forecast for the Soviets going to war. About the same time, the Russians started giving me a list of Japanese ships in the Sea of Japan, their coordinates, course, and type of ship. I sent this data to Washington twice, and I promptly got a personal message from Admiral King that said, "Please do not accept or send anything like this again. They're building you up as a cause célèbre for their going to war with Japan." They appreciated the warning and acted accordingly. The message said they had this information from better sources.

Paul Stillwell: They had this from U.S. submarines?

Admiral Knoll: I assumed so. This occurred after I saw Yumashev. All of a sudden, in late February 1945 I received orders: "Return to Moscow as soon as you can." I knew 14 days was the quickest time I could get to Moscow from Vladivostok. I obtained a reservation on an international car of the Trans-Siberian Railroad. We always traveled one full compartment so you didn't have to share it with women and children or other undesirable spy. You took your own food and water along so you could cook your food over the open fire in the boiler that gave heat in the car. You couldn't live too well on what the railroad served. The soup in the dining car was very expensive. At the different railroad stations where they stopped, it was possible to pick up cooked fish and fresh bakery products. Part of the reason it took 14 days was that the train stopped at every important station and averaged only about 35 miles an hour when moving.

They spent about two hours in the really important stations. This gave a chance to walk around town and talk to people, and some of the food was not too bad. I said I'd get back to Moscow about the 19th of March, 1945. I was met at the station, and within the hour I was having a meeting with Ambassador Harriman and George Kennan, General Deane, and Captain Maples.* "Let's discuss your message further." They said it was rather intriguing, because we had an earlier agreement that if U.S.S.R. went to war with Japan, there would be a nucleus of the U.S. military mission, in which I was included, that would immediately accompany the Soviet Chiefs of Staff to a joint headquarters in Vladivostok or Khabarovsk. They wanted to know more for planning purposes. No one criticized or challenged what I had evaluated, or how I collected this information. It was about an hour and a half discussion, very pleasant. They were interested in all I had observed, and I had a notebook full of notes.

After the meeting, Ambassador Harriman called me aside. Whether the others knew what he was going to say, I don't know. He secretly said, "For your information,

---

* Captain Houston L. Maples, USN.

your message was rather intriguing, because the last day at Yalta, Stalin told President Roosevelt the U.S.S.R. would go to war against Japan 90 days after the war ends in Europe." Well, in March 1945 the war hadn't ended in Europe. I forecast they were going to war out there on the 15th of August. Ninety days after the war in Europe, the eighth of May 1945, would be 8 August 1945. Harriman had sent further information to Washington that I had not received information from anyone in U.S.S.R. It was only the result of my evaluation of what I had seen and heard. Admiral King was in on this; it didn't do me any harm.

Paul Stillwell: But there were some other intervening events, like the Potsdam agreement and the atomic bombs that could well have contributed to the timing of the Soviet Union going to war against Japan.*

Admiral Knoll: I was in Moscow for the Potsdam Conference because I'll tell you another story. Wait a second. The atomic bomb didn't happen until August 1945, and I had sent this message on December 25, 1944 from Vladivostok. Christmas Day was lonesome; I kept busy drafting the message to Admiral King.

Paul Stillwell: My point is that the Potsdam agreement and the dropping of the bomb may well have had as much influence as the weather on when the Soviets went to war.

Admiral Knoll: I'm not going to argue that. It showed that the Russians were thinking and knew the type of weather that was ideal for a surprise attack—a surprise to the Axis as well as their allies.

This happened when I was one of the senior members at the military mission while the generals and the admiral were at Potsdam with Truman, Churchill, and Stalin. Through our servants and U.S. correspondents, we knew a prince of the Japanese royal family had been in Moscow for a month trying to meet with Stalin to negotiate for peace

---

* The Potsdam Conference involving President Harry Truman, Prime Minister Clement Atlee, and Premier Josef Stalin was held in Potsdam, Germany, between 17 July and 2 August 1945. Discussions covered a number of European political and territorial issues and the prosecution of the war in the Pacific. The Soviets entered the war against Japan on 9 August 1945, the same day the United States dropped the second atomic bomb.

in the Pacific. I finally had confirmed information, plus the name of the prince through the cooks at the Japanese embassy and from my cooks. I sent this information to Ambassador Harriman and Captain Maples at Potsdam. I said, "A-1 intelligence source, Prince So-and-so has been trying to see Stalin for a month to negotiate a peace in the Pacific." This was known before the atomic bomb was dropped on Hiroshima. Stalin had refused to see the Jap. There are certain parts of this that are rather interesting.

Paul Stillwell: Yes. He didn't want to have peace at that point. He wanted to get some of the spoils.

Admiral Knoll: Let's look at this scenario one step further. Stalin, a very devious bastard, had made a treaty with Hitler and Ribbentrop for the future, cutting up the pie in Central Europe.*

Hitler gave recognition to Stalin that the Baltic states were in his sphere of interest, and Hitler gave recognition to Stalin that parts of Poland were in the German sphere. They both did this with malice aforethought. No doubt about it. Each one was interested in outmaneuvering the other bastard at the appropriate future date. Stalin was advised six months before Operation Barbarossa, Hitler's invasion of Poland, and he refused to make an overt move.† I've had this from some Russian officials who were at Rzhev before the German invasion. They were suspicious that they were never alerted to make any preparations or change in operations or security. This was one of the Soviet military airfields closest to the Polish frontier.

Why were they not alerted? Because Stalin wanted his people to be hurt bad enough initially by a German invasion so the Red Army would fight back. No doubt about it. A lot of Russians felt that way. He wanted to be hurt so he could mobilize the nation and appeal to Rodena, their love of Mother Russia. The Germans made a major invasion into White Russia (Belorussia). The people met the German troops with large loaves of bread and salt, a welcome with traditional Russian hospitality. However, Rosenberg, acting for Hitler, ignored the welcome and proceeded to devastate their

---

* Joachim von Ribbentrop was Germany's Foreign Minister from 1938 to 1945. Included in that period was the non-aggression agreement concluded in September 1939 between Germany and the Soviet Union.
† Operation Barbarossa, the German invasion of the Soviet Union, began on Sunday, 22 June 1941.

homes and assembled citizens into camps. He completely destroyed the willingness of the White Russians to welcome the Germans into the Soviet Union. Hitler played right into Stalin's hands. Russians were ready to assist the Germans and escape Stalin. It is possible that half the casualties in the Red Army in World War II were the troops shot in the back of the head by their own officers when they didn't advance and fight the way they were supposed to.

An agreement to help the Soviet Union with Lend-Lease had a very fundamental reason. U.S.A. knew we were not ready to really fight in Europe. We knew it was worth our salt to get as much Lend-Lease to Stalin as we could to help him and to make sure that at no time would he make an independent peace with Hitler. If he had ever made an independent peace or armistice prior to the landings at Normandy, it would have been a move to destroy us. The Allies wouldn't have had capabilities to land at Normandy until 1950, if Britain could have survived Hitler's raids and assaults. This is what people don't realize. Even before I left Washington in 1943, en route to Tehran, we said, "We have to realize that it's to our advantage to keep Stalin from having any idea of an armistice with Hitler." They're both devious bastards. Written treaties were made to be ignored. Stalin undoubtedly reckoned it would be easier to negotiate with Roosevelt and Churchill than a victorious Hitler when the war in Europe ended.

Paul Stillwell: That's what the Russians did in World War I.[*]

Admiral Knoll: Okay. The Russian Army disappeared; Lenin and Stalin were amazed at the easy way they took control of a defunct nation.[†] Before I left Washington, the first statement from any Soviet officer was, "When are you going to open the second front? They were bearing the brunt of war, but we were giving them materials to make sure they didn't falter. A victory in Europe required the Soviet Army to fight until the United States and Britain were armed and ready. They took the brunt of the war and bled a lot; there's no doubt about it. Of course, the Soviets didn't like it when we landed in Africa

---

[*] On 9 February 1918 the new Soviet government in Russia signed the Treaty of Brest-Litovsk with the Central Powers (Germany, Austria-Hungary, Bulgaria, and the Ottoman Empire), thus ending Russia's participation in World War I.
[†] Vladimir Ilyich Lenin (1870-1924) was the first head of the Soviet Union.

in 1942, rather than on the mainland of Europe. They criticized us for this, even though they could see it was to our advantage to prepare slowly for major invasion of Europe.

Leningrad was a major loss to the Soviets for 900 days. Stalin was ready to shoot some of his generals because they couldn't retake Leningrad from the Germans. Leningrad, the cultural center of the Soviet Union, was a major loss for the Red Army. The German Army made many assaults to surround Leningrad and occupy it. They never succeeded. Hitler wanted Leningrad very badly. Their bombing and shelling avoid an area near the old German embassy, Astoria Hotel, and St. Isaac's Cathedral. Hitler had already printed the invitation to celebrate the 25th anniversary of his first rise to power in Leningrad at the Astoria Hotel. Hitler was sure he was going to take it. We found some of the invitations that had been printed at the Germany embassy in Leningrad. So he never quite got there, because the Red Army was determined that Leningrad would survive the siege. Harrison Salisbury points out in *900 Days* that Marshal Zhukov and other generals had a meeting with Stalin and were ordered to take Leningrad.* After a short discussion, Stalin laid a pistol on the table in front of him, saying, "If you don't take it, I'll have to shoot you and put somebody else in charge." This illustrates how tough decisions were made by Stalin. The siege of Leningrad was a major concern of Stalin and the Red Army generals.

The next major campaign was Stalingrad, which I visited en route to Moscow. The wreckage of the war was everywhere. Airplanes, tanks, guns, weapons carriers were scattered within 100 miles of the city. Some new German Fokker planes were at the airport with combat equipment and entrenching tools, partially unloaded. German tanks were beautifully constructed and equipped. The Soviet tanks were effective but poor examples of good engineering. The engines were assembled without bearings for limited use. The armor was rough without machined edges, and interiors were congested and poorly designed. Soviet gear was designed for a short useful life in battle. There was a fantastic difference between the quality and workmanship in the German equipment compared with the poor quality of the Soviet equipment.

---

* Harrison Salisbury, *The 900 Days: the Siege of Leningrad* (New York: Harper & Row, 1969).

At Stalingrad the Soviets lost a lot, and so did the Germans. It was the turning point for the German Army. Stalingrad, together with the tank battles at Kursk—some of the greatest tank battles in history—thoroughly depleted the German reserves of military equipment. The Germans never had the industry or resources to rebuild what they lost in these battles. This helped the Allied cause terrifically and lessened the German threat at Normandy. If the Germans had ever made an armistice with Stalin, the war would have lasted many more years with huge casualties for all.

Paul Stillwell: Because then they would have taken the resources from the eastern front and put them over in France.

Admiral Knoll: Sure. There would have been no further need for German forces on the eastern front. The elements of surprise and deception were indispensable in preparing for Normandy.

Churchill would release accurate information to send Germans through double agents that Hitler and staff did not believe a highlight of close cooperation between U.S.A. and Britain and U.S.S.R. was in cover and deception techniques carried out months before. The British and U.S.A. were very successful with recruitment of double agents. When U.S.A. entered the war, almost 90% of the German agents in the United States had been spotted by FBI and were promptly arrested. Some people said, "Collect them as soon as you spot them." It is better to find the whole cell and how they communicate. When they were arrested, they could be developed as good double agents, and then you can feed them accordingly to report what you want. It's an interesting game. There are two fundamentals, really, before going into action. One is good intelligence. The other is good deception and surprise. If you don't have both, you are exposing your fighting forces to unnecessary hazards.

Paul Stillwell: Did you have a capacity, along with your weather job as being part of the attaché's organization and providing intelligence?

Admiral Knoll: I was a naval attaché in Moscow only after the end of the war. I was designated as a naval attaché until I was relieved in December 1945. It should be remembered that when the Soviet Union approved the establishment of the U.S. military mission to U.S.S.R., they specifically required that members of the mission were not to operate as intelligence agents. Our reports had to be carefully prepared to meet this caveat.

This should be told. While I was in U.S.S.R. at the end of the war, they celebrated the 220th anniversary of the Soviet Academy of Sciences. General Federov, my weather opposite, was a very prestigious member of the Soviet Academy. In talking with him, I think when we were on the Oka River for that weekend, he said, "Make sure you come to the 220th anniversary meeting."

I said, "That's fine. I hope I can. I appreciate it. In addition, I think Dr. Reichelderfer, Chief of the U.S. Weather Bureau, and Dr. Carl Rossby, senior professor of meteorology and earth sciences of MIT, should be invited."

He said, "That's a good idea."

I said, "Well, I'll write and tell them and see if they'd like to have an invitation."

He said, "Do that."

So I wrote Dr. Reichelderfer and Professor Carl Rossby, and I said, "General Federov is prepared to invite you and some U.S. representatives to the 220th anniversary of the Soviet Academy of Sciences in the fall of 1945." It's the oldest academy in the world. I think it's older than the French Academy of Sciences. It was founded by Peter the Great in 1725. So I received a very nice reply from Reichelderfer and Rossby. They received a formal invitation from the Soviet Academy of Sciences to come over to Moscow for a ten-day period for the anniversary.

I was out at Moscow airport to meet them when they came for this meeting. While I was there, I saw this rather interesting-looking gentleman, and I went over and started meeting with him. His English was pretty good. I said, "You've studied in England?"

"Oh, yes, I was at Cambridge University."

I said, "How long have you been back here?"

"Quite a few years, but I was originally Hungarian." We talked back and forth. I told him I was out there to meet Dr. Reichelderfer and Professor Rossby, and Dr. Harlow Shapley, the astronomer from Harvard. They were coming in on the next plane. I forget whom he was ready to meet.

I said, "What's your name?"

He said, "Pioytr Kapitsa." He was the leading Soviet scientist that developed the nuclear bomb.[*]

I said, "O, my God. And so we visited until the plane landed.

He said, "We'll get together again."

I said, "I'd like to."

I met Reichelderfer and Rossby and took them to the National Hotel next door to the U.S. chancery and across the plaza from the Kremlin. Dr. Rossby was a fantastic, forgetful individual. Reichelderfer knew it. He'd forget his wallet; he'd forget everything. He was a terrific scientist. At MIT he was in charge of the aerological curriculum when I was there. He had been considered as a possible assistant or successor to Reichelderfer at the U.S. Weather Bureau. He died recently, was born in Sweden and had returned back there.[†] He's a world-renowned scientist in meteorology. We had some interesting visits.

I was ready to go to the 220th anniversary meeting, and I received a call from General Federov. He wanted me to accompany Reichelderfer and others to the sessions, but because I was a naval officer on active duty, he regretted there was no way the U.S.S.R. would authorize me to come to the meetings. This is how the U.S.S.R. operates. They don't trust foreign military officers. Some of these officials I encountered again when I was U.S. military secretary at the United Nations.

When I first got to London, it was rather interesting. The U.S.S.R. sent all new people we'd never met before. U.S.S.R. members were rather surprised when they found out General Deane and myself had been in U.S.S.R. for two years, and we would represent the United States delegation at the United Nations. Without them saying

---

[*] Pioytr Kapitsa (1894-1984) was a prominent Soviet nuclear scientist. In 1978 he received the Nobel Prize in physics.
[†] Francis W. Reichelderfer was born 6 August 1895 in Indiana and died 26 January 1983 in Washington, D.C. Carl-Gustave Rossby was born in Stockholm on 28 December 1898 and died there 19 August 1957.

anything between the organizing meetings of the United Nations in London and the beginning of the first sessions of the United Nations in New York, U.S.S.R. replaced their people with military officers we had been working with in Moscow, which facilitated the initial work of the United Nations Military Staff Committee of the Security Council.

The Soviets are unpredictable. On V-E Day in May 1945, as soon as the victory was announced, embassy personnel were warned not to leave the building, because Soviet police couldn't control the crowd. If they saw an American, they had a blanket and wanted to keep tossing each American in a blanket. The crowd in front of the chancery was black with people. It was chaos with singing and shouts. They were right over to the Kremlin Wall, across the plaza. The U.S.S.R. Foreign Ministry kept calling on the phone, "Haul down your flags. Pull down your curtains." Soviet citizens were wild. Police had barricades to keep them from the inner courtyard. They sang, cheered, and yelled for over 24 hours. Russian police couldn't chase them away. At no time did any Soviet citizens assemble near the walls of the Kremlin and cheer Stalin and the Soviet hierarchy. Were the Soviet people in front of the British embassy? No. The French embassy? No. They were all in front of the American embassy for two days. Soviet citizens knew the U.S.A. helped win the war. It was astounding to see citizens demonstrate. The police couldn't control them, and the police couldn't move from the vicinity of the U.S. embassy.

Many appeared the second day. They celebrated for two days. At the end of the second day, we could go out a little bit as Soviet citizens relaxed a little. Otherwise, they wanted to toss you around and ride you around pick-a-back. You could get hurt. At this time, Stalin came on the radio in Russian and said, "The people, the great cogs of Communism, have been the machine that won the war." The Russians openly resented the fact that Stalin referred to them as cogs in a machine. They complained: "We're not cogs; we're human beings." It was a common complaint for a couple of days, that he referred to them as cogs in the machine that won the war. Little things like this occurred when the citizens were relaxed in a large group and could say this without the police making prompt arrests.

On the way back from Vladivostok, I rode for four days with the factory manager of the U.S.S.R. fighter plane factory at Novosibirsk. He was a wonderful, friendly chap. He carried a special valise of aluminum cans with knurled knobs, in which he had pure alcohol. About a quart was in each one of them. He had raw smoked, greasy ham and bacon and black bread for refreshment. He invited me to come to his compartment and have drinks and visit with him. With him you had to be careful when you drank any liquor with those people because they actually use straight alcohol. To make damn sure, you put your tongue in before you took a sip of it and add enough water to make it palatable. They drank pretty close to straight alcohol, from which they make their vodka.

In Leningrad the senior meteorologist took the alcohol out of the binnacle of the compass and started drinking. I asked, "How do you know that's not wood alcohol?" I wouldn't touch it. We took American whiskey with us, and the Soviets could have about two drinks of U.S. whiskey and quickly show the effect. Their reaction was prompt, but Soviets drank vodka or the alcohol. Visiting on a train was safe because he knew no one was there to listen. I had traveled a couple of days en route to Vladivostok with the number-two man in charge of the Dalstroi, which is the secret police in charge of prison camps in Siberia. He boasted, "You know, we have every kind of an official, engineer, and technician in my command, and we can build anything or do anything; they're all our prisoners."

He was a decent guy with the insignia of a general. He talked about many operations, what they could do, and how they took care of prisoners. You knew very well in some of those old camps they'd freeze to death, and others were required to work in Siberia after release from prison camps. I forget how many million prisoners were in the Siberian area. He did not try to boast about the system, except he had every type of engineer and professional needed to carry out any assignment.

The people were there that controlled all work in Siberia as punishment for political misdemeanor, as well as some in Dalstroi supervised the building of a new railroad going north of Lake Baikal. They could build it very slowly, partially due to cold weather. They had to make sure there was a source of water for steam locomotives. The first thing, they had to build a water tower with a furnace in the middle to keep the water from freezing in the wintertime. Water towers had to be spaced so water for the locomotives was assured. The water towers had to be built on the banks of fresh-water streams, because wood was readily available for about 400 or 500 miles. All construction was done by slave labor.

The manager of the Novosibirsk fighter plane factory said his mother was born a serf. Tsar Alexander II abolished serfdom in 1856. The manager was born and educated in the Leningrad area. His family was indentured to a more wealthy family. Tsar Nicholas had started the new educational system before the Communists came to power.* The system would screen all students as to aptitude and scholastic achievement. The leading students in each grade would receive the gold, silver, or bronze medals. They were thus identified and helped to advance through the educational system. Only the best were selected to attend university. The manager regularly had been awarded gold or silver medals in technical school and university. He was able to avoid work on a farm and other labor assignments. He was finally able to advance, by winning medals, to the University of Leningrad to study aeronautical engineering.

He pointed out that when you work hard and study hard and mind your own business and stay out of politics, you could get ahead in the Soviet Union. He actually arranged for his mother to go to school and learn to read and write, even though she was getting on in years. He was ordered to take charge of the fighter plane factory in Novosibirsk, where there was a chance to avoid the politics of Leningrad and Moscow. He enjoyed his work, and he was able to move his family out there. His home had the only piano in Novosibirsk.

He boasted, "As long as I know how to play the game, I don't have to get involved in politics. I live pretty well with my family. I talked to him about the Soviet system, and he knew how you had to be very careful and never be caught making a mistake. He had worked hard. Many people in the system don't give a damn about working hard, because there is nothing to be gained. He had the incentive, he had the interest, and he wasn't afraid to work. He said to me that if he had a chance to get away from the U.S.S.R. without getting caught, he'd go immediately. The world does not realize that many intelligent Soviet citizens would be willing to leave the U.S.S.R. if the

---

* Tsar Nicholas II (1868-1918) was the last Emperor of Russia. He ruled from 1 November 1894 until his abdication on 2 March 1917 following the February revolution of that year. Bolsheviks executed him and members of his family on the night of 16-17 July 1918.

police system did not exist to keep them in bondage. They might be Communists, but if they had a chance to get away with their families, without being punished, they would run away.

You take away the secret police and take down the fortified frontier, 50% of them might run away. They're not allowed to ask political questions when they're going to school or talk to people who ask questions or complain about Soviet policy or government decisions. They can't ask questions about historical events they're not supposed to know about. You ask a taboo question twice in school, you're demoted and may not even be allowed to continue in school.

Their Foreign Language Institute trains individuals in keeping U.S.S.R. policy, such as English language and English history, American history, and international events as viewed by U.S.S.R. Not only the language but everything involved, so you can think and act as a Soviet official. Andre Gromyko and Gromyko's son have been educated at this institute. A senior official attempts to have his children educated at the Foreign Language Institute and enjoy privileges. The hardest thing for anyone who's never lived in a police state like U.S.S.R. is to realize how carefully each citizen has to live in order to survive and still be reasonably happy. It's hard to be happy under those conditions. U.S.S.R. officials who have lived abroad are closely observed, because most realize the advantage of living in a free society, but they are forbidden to mention it. A foreigner in U.S.S.R. has to be continually careful not to criticize the system in the presence of a Soviet citizen. They can be promptly punished if they do not defend all aspects of their way of life.

The Russian scientists over the years have made great contributions to mathematics, physics, chemistry, and philosophy. There's a lot of contemporary development with radio communications engineering. Their scientific achievements have received respect in the West. They may claim achievements that they shouldn't, but in many ways they have made real contributions in sciences. Their institutions have many smart people.

Now, this Pioytr Kapitsa, you see, I didn't finish that. When I returned to the embassy, I was talking with Harlow Shapley, Dr. Riechelderfer, and Dr. Rossby. I said, "I met an interesting character, Pioytr Kapitsa."

They said, "What? You met Pioytr Kapitsa? Can you meet him again?"

I said, "No, I doubt it."

"He's their leading nuclear engineering man." He was singularly honored by the U.S.S.R. Government when they named their nuclear laboratory and facility as the Pioytr Kapitsa Laboratory. He was Hungarian, and he studied physics and chemical engineering at Cambridge University. He went to the Soviet Union for a seminar prior to World War II. When he was ready to return to Cambridge, they wouldn't let him leave. He worked closely with the Soviet Academy of Science. For a while we understood he was having difficulties with the government. He was an interesting character. It illustrates how they recapture some of their scientists.

Paul Stillwell: Speaking of this lack of independence and personal freedom they have, there was the case of the Soviet actress who had a baby by Captain Jack Tate and was put in prison for years afterward.

Admiral Knoll: Jackson Tate was my roommate at the time of this affair with Zoya Fyodorova.* The night that it occurred was V-E Day or right after V-E Day. Zoya and her aunt Marusa were at our apartment frequently for dinner. Jackson Tate was a gruff, crude individual. I think he moved in when Don Felt returned to the States.† We were a little concerned because he was a little gruff and discourteous with the Russians. He had picked up many offensive Russian words dealing with motherhood, some of the vilest pornographic terms relating to females, sex, and prostitution—never mentioned in conversation. At a dinner party he attended he had arranged a date with Zoya; he had a few dates with Zoya Fyodorova. During the dinner he started using offensive, dirty language, and Zoya said, "Now, Jack, I told you not to say that. You don't want to use

---

* Captain Jackson R. Tate, USN, was a former enlisted man who was one of the U.S. Navy's early aviators. During World War II, while a deputy naval attache at the U.S. embaassy in Moscow, he had an affair with Russian actress Zoya Fyodorova that resulted in the birth of daughter Victoria on 8 January 1946. Fyodorova, who was imprisoned for eight years as the result of her relationship with Tate, was later shot and killed in her apartment in 1981. Father and daughter met for the first time when she was permitted to visit the United States in 1975. Victoria Fyodorova told her story in the autobiography *The Admiral's Daughter* (New York: Delacorte Press, 1979).

† In 1944-45 Captain Harry Donald Felt, USN, was the first aviator assigned to the U.S. military mission to the Soviet Union. The oral history of Felt, who retired as a four-star admiral, is in the Naval Institute collection.

those words when women are anywhere present. I don't like it." Also present was Marusa, who lived with Zoya in an apartment on Gorky Street. We had visited her place many times. She was a famous movie star during World War II.

Marusa said, "Jack, if you say that once again, I'm going to punish you so you won't talk that way again."

Well, it was less than five minutes later. I was at the table with Zoya, Marusa, Jackson, and I forget who else was present—about ten of us in all. Jackson started to pronounce more of these vile terms. There was a large pitcher of icewater on the table, and Marusa picked up the pitcher and poured it right over Jackson's head. He was mad as hell. Marusa said, "I told you I don't want to hear it again."

Captain Jackson Tate was sent to the military mission as a favor. He had an excellent war record, and Washington gave him some relaxation. He didn't contribute anything tangible to the work of the mission. They wouldn't let him go to any meetings or conduct negotiations with U.S.S.R. I never had any problem with him. He was a big, heavy man, with dark hair, and could be jolly. Some years ago, I found two of his good linen handkerchiefs with his initials embroidered on them. I planned to send them to Zoya. When I heard she had a child, I was not surprised because when I left U.S.S.R. I heard Zoya was pregnant by Jackson Tate. Recently, I obtained the name and address of her daughter, Victoria, who lives in Connecticut, and I sent her the two handkerchiefs. She sent a nice letter back, "Thank you for thinking of me and giving me some memento of my father." I remember the night Jackson stayed all night with Zoya and came back in the morning. It was unusual for anyone to be overnight on a date.

Paul Stillwell: I've heard that Tate was a great storyteller.

Admiral Knoll: He never impressed me as a storyteller. I don't know—when the Russians hear "maternie" language from a captain in the Navy, it is a black mark and ignored. Hobos, burglars, and thugs use it as a gutter of language. Tate picked up these words and used them in fun. His Russian laugage was never good. I recognize the terms when I hear them. I never used them. Russians as a whole resented his using these words in their presence. He enjoyed seeing the Russians annoyed.

Paul Stillwell: It sounds as if he was going out of his way to be obnoxious.

Admiral Knoll: That's my point. He enjoyed making Russians annoyed. That was one reason that he was not used at meetings with Russians. He returned to the U.S.A. after a short tour in U.S.S.R.

Zoya was an attractive girl. They sent her to Vologda for the birth of Victoria and shaved her head. It was amazing that the Soviet Foreign Office let Victoria come over to see Tate. She married a Pan American pilot. It's amazing she let her go. When Soviet girls become too friendly with foreigners, they take them out of circulation, shave their heads, and keep them away from Moscow. Unless they have acess to a wig or other cosmetics, the girls do not look for dates.

Paul Stillwell: She ultimately got shot, didn't she?

Admiral Knoll: Yes.

Paul Stillwell: Curious circumstances.

Admiral Knoll: I would say so. Something happened. She was shot in her apartment, and somebody had made up their mind this had gone far enough. And that's easy to do over there and receives little, if any, publicity.

Paul Stillwell: What do you recall of Don Felt from that time?

Admiral Knoll: Don Felt was my roommate in Moscow, and he wasn't there very long. It was a good diversion for him. He was a captain and naval aviator. He was the only American that I know the Soviet Navy recognized. He was quiet with great ability. Soviet naval officers took him to one of their airfields south of Moscow. They permitted him to fly a Soviet Stormovich fighter plane. I know of no other Americans who were ever allowed to do this by the Soviets. At that time the Stormovich received a lot of attention. It was designed to support ground troops on the front line. U.S.A. had no planes designed for this sole task. Stormovich had a plastic windshield about two inches thick. It was heavily armored around the pilot and also armored around the engine. He was thrilled to have had that experience. He was a good shipmate and congenial roommate. I always remember the first couple of weeks he was in Moscow. I told him, "One diversion, we go to the ballet once in a while."

He looked at me and said, "The ballet? I'm not interested in anything like that."

I said, "Now, don't say that. We'll get some tickets, and you can go see for yourself and make up your own mind."

I arranged for him to see the ballet twice. From then on he was arranging to get his own tickets. It is difficult to describe the perfection of a Russian in drama, in a Russian ballet, and in a Russian opera. Everyone on stage is acting related to the scene. They are dedicated actors and actresses. Without the control of a police state, if the Russians could live, act, and work uninhibited, as they're capable to do with the arts and science, they would set new standards of world excellence. Those are the Russian characteristics when they're uninhibited by a police supervision or fear of supervision.

They provide inspiring and impressive performances. In the drama *Anna Karenina*'s final scene, the train comes towards the audience, and Anna throws herself in front of it. We tried to arrange to get seats in the first row for strangers to Moscow and observe their reactions. The train comes toward the audience, stops at the footlights, and the act ends. We saw friends drop toward the floor, because they were sure the realistic train was not going to stop at the footlights. It was dramatic and very effective. Tolstoy portrayed Russian life very vividly. Russians have a lot of native talent. If they weren't under continuous police control, the U.S.S.R. could be a great nation. With monolithic control everyone must be subdued and never display ingenuity and never utter an open word of criticism.

Paul Stillwell: What are your recollections of Admiral Olsen?

Admiral Knoll: He was a real friend and wonderful individual. We had a good relationship. He was my boss in charge of the weather exchange. I handled all the meetings, and when we went to a meeting together, I conducted the discussions. I wrote all the letters and handled all the dispatches. The terminology of weather matters was complicated; before each meeting I briefed on what would be discussed. So any time there was an important party, General Federov would always ask Admiral Olsen to come along with me. He picked up some Russian, but I picked up and spoke more than he did. I lived with him in his apartmwent for just the first six months until I went to Vladovostolk. Upon return from Vladivostok, I moved into an apartment with three other people.

Paul Stillwell: Did you know Sam Frankel at all?*

Admiral Knoll: I knew him at the Naval Academy. He was in the classs of 1929, and I was 1930. I went up to Murmansk one time to visit weather facilities on Kola Peninsula. I stayed there with Frankel at the different naval bases. I flew up in a PBY. We took off from Moscow River and flew mostly overland with small lakes everywhere. The plane was loaded with Navy wives, chickens, ducks, baggage, and small freight. The plane was really loaded, but they saved a special place for me to sit at the navigastor's desk while I flew to Murmansk on the water of Kola Inlet. It was a rather interesting flight. I came back by train to Moscow. Captain Frankel had excellent relations with U.S.S.R. officials in Murmansk. The Russians respected him. He was one of the outstanding U.S.A. representatives in U.S.S.R. during World War II.

Paul Stillwell: Do you have any impressions of the Russian people other than what you've given, and their gratitude to the Americans for their help?

Admiral Knoll: The greater the distance from Moscw, the more the average Russian is willing to talk with a foreigner without fear of reprisal. From the Urals eastward, the Russian people readily expressed their thanks for the food and "productie" they were receiving from the United States. At more than one railroad station, an older woman

---

* During World War II, Captain Samuel B. Frankel, USN, served as assistant naval attaché in Moscow and Archangel in connection with U.S. Lend-Lease shipments to the Soviet Union. The oral history of Frankel, who retired as a rear admiral, is in the Naval Institute collection.

approached me, knowing I was American. She kissed my hand and said, "Bolshoi Spasseba," which is "big thanks for your food."

Any time that you meet a Russian, and he is willing to meet you again, you must assume that he is a stool pigeon who is going to report everything you do or say, partiuclarly in Moscow or Leningrad. It's a hell of a way to live, because even your own children report you if you criticize the government or say any unkind things about Stalin in their presence.

Most of the time I was in Moscow; our cook was a Volga German who could be sent east to Siberia. As the U.S.S.R prepared for the Battle of Warsaw, she would never leave our apartment. She slept in the kitchen because she had been warned that the Soviets were picking up anybody with any German ancestry and sending them to Siberia. She feared if she was on the street and was picked up by the police, we'd never see her again, so she wouldn't leave. Marusa knew her way around Moscow; we had to assume that she made regular reports to the secret police on everything we did. Can you believe it? We had a fresh egg for breakfast every day for almost a year, because we had regular rations of sugar, flour, and butter from the diplomatic store. It was more than we could use. She bartered the excess on the black market for fresh eggs and meat. For Christmas we each had a turkey or a goose; vodka; and champagne. At the diplomatic store prices were insignificant. We had excess, particularly because we were four people to an apartment. Marusa had no trouble bartering the excess for eggs. We had eggs regularly for breakfast, more often than Ambassador Harriman did. He raised chickens in his front yard while we obtained our fresh eggs from the black market near the city limits of Moscow. It's amazing the things that can be done. Some of it is illegal, but as long as it doesn't get too involved, they will not crack

It is most important for a foreigner to avoid anything involving political subversion or specualtion with rubles and foreign money. Vodka and chocolate bars are readily accepted gifts to someone for a special favor. I always had an extra pair of silk hose or package of needles for the girls I would meet. My mother and sisters sent me bolts of silk cloth for dresses. A *Cosmopolitan* or *Vanity Fair* magazine with all the latest styles was very popular. They were sent to me by diplomatic mail.. I gave them to friends who would sell them to others for as much as 100 rubles. In a few cases they were dog-eared from being passed around. Once in a while I escorted a former ballerina to movies and dances at the Spasso House. She made a few stylish dresses with silk material, and they were the only dresses, other than heavy dark woolens that she had.

About a week after V-E Day in May 1945, Foreign Minister Molotov gave a formal banquet at his home, Spiridonavka House, a former sugar baron's beautiful house. Military mission personnel, colonel/captain and above, were invited. Upon arrival for the big banquets, we were segregated as to rank and were told in what room we were supposed to remain. In the large center room of this house were Harry Hopkins, Ambassador Harriman, British Ambassador Kerr, Molotov, Vishinsky, and many officials of the Foreign Ministry.* In the outer rooms were military people of the colonel and captain rank in the Navy, the diplomatic corps, according to rank, in other rooms, and we weren't supposed to mix. Kemp Tolley was a commander, and therefore was not invited to Molotov's banquet.

At the last minute, Molotov ordered the Russian officials to bring their wives, and they had to attend. The wives had no evening clothes and no way to obtain such. They came in their wartime heavy woolens, with their big felt boots to Molotov's mansion for this victory dinner, a terrific affair, all the excellent food you could wish. All the decorations on the tables were the same we had seen at formal dinners at the National Hotel or other places we had been entertained. There were stuffed crows and papier mache flowers. The same servants were at these affairs no matter where you'd go. They gave me a small party like this the first week I was in Moscow.

The host would try to drink you under the table. He would have a shot glass with a small hole in it, and yours would be a regular one—one and a half ounces. You had to be careful, because they will try to make you drunk while they remain sober. At Molotov's party we did some visiting back and forth, and I violated this code of staying in the room of my rank more than once in Moscow and also in London. I was reprimanded by the Russians, because I was supposed to stay with my rank. I was far enough away in the main reception room at this V-E Day banquet. Harry Hopkins was there, and Harry Hopkins was not well. He wasn't supposed to take a drop of alcoholic

---

* Andrei J. Vishinsky served as the Soviet Union's Deputy Minister of Foreign Affairs from 1940 to 1949 and Minister of Foreign affairs from 1949 to 1953. He was the Soviet representative to the United Nations from 1945 to 1949 and in 1953-54.

drink. Suddenly he picked up a shot glass of vodka and said, "Do pobeda," which means "to victory." All Russians quickly responded, "Do pobeda," while Hopkins set his glass down without drinking. There was a noise and grumbling, and I went running over to Hopkins at the same time as Ambassador Harriman came in and asked, "What happened?"

I said, "Harry proposed a toast 'Do pobeda' with vodka, and instead of drinking he set it down."

Harriman quickly explained that Hopkins was an ill man and drank two toasts with vodka, one for Harry and one for himself.

About that time a Russian came and said, "You're not supposed to be in here."

I said, "I was helping Harry Hopkins."

The same thing happened some months later when I was having a discussion with Deputy Foreign Minister Andrei Vishinsky at the Soviet embassy in London. He was the senior Soviet official at the embassy before Andrei Gromyko became the senior U.S.S.R. rep at the Untied Nations, number two to Molotov. We were organizing the United Nations. Vishinsky spoke some English; he was pretty good. He was the judge at the purge trials in '32. He wore a pair of glasses that were like magnifying glasses. His eyes looked like the heads of matches. He wanted to intimidate, and he looked mean. As a judge, it was a very effective. He wore normal glasses at a party. He could be a pleasant individual. I had a discussion this time, and I said, "Mr. Vishinsky, I understand you studied in the seminary when you were a youngster."

"Yes."

I said, "Stalin also studied at a seminary. You had a lot of religious education before you became involved in politics." He sort of smiled. I said, "You realize there's nothing permitted about religion or God in the Soviet Union, but every day you recognize God."

"Pray to God?"

"Yes. When you say 'thank you,' you take the name of God. Every day, every Russian says 'thank you' many times. When you say 'thank you,' literally it means 'God save us.'"

So he said, "Spaseba. Spaseba." God save us. Semantically "Spaseba" is the idiom for "Spas Bog" or "Save us, O God." He looked at me. I've used that on more than one Russian, reminding that religion was responsible for the Russian language of St. Cyril and St. Methodius.

Paul Stillwell: What else did Tolley miss?

Admiral Knoll: He also missed the great victory parade in Red Square about July 1945. The Soviets collected tons of Nazi banners, symbols, flags, and decorations that were carried into Red Square and raised high in front of us, just below Lenin's tomb. Big steel banners of swastikas, ceremonial flags and banners from all Nazi societies in the big cities in Germany. Russian troops marched in, and a platoon from each group would step forward and throw loot at our feet. Stalin, Molotov, Harriman, and the British ambassador were above us on Lenin's tomb. It was a typical traditionally Russian victory parade. Guns were fired, and cheers came from each group as they passed in review.. The celebration lasted about four hours. You never saw so much loot. Piles were over six feet high for 100 yards either way. I don't know what they did with all of it. Some were gorgeous banners and memorabilia. It was a typical reproduction of the Tchaikovsky opus, "1812 Overture" with the guns, the flares, and noise. It was an event to remember. Americans were particularly recognized for our help in winning the war. They celebrated V-J Day but never with the demonstrating in front of the U.S. chancery.* The U.S. chancery was downtown, next to the National Hotel. The ambassador lived at the Spasso House, away from downtown. The Spasso House on V-E Day was isolated by a barrier leading to the Spasso; the crowds did not assemble there. Russians wanted to be in front of the chancery across from the Kremlin, with a large plaza for crowds to assemble.

Paul Stillwell: They could literally kill you with kindness.

---

* V-J Day – Victory over Japan Day, marked the end of the war in the Pacific on 15 August 1945. Because of the time difference it was 14 August in the United States when combat ended.

Admiral Knoll: It was a spontaneous mob reaction showing they knew and appreciated what the U.S.A. had done and were not afraid to show it. Because you get in that crowd, and you're American. The Foreign Ministry could not control nor prevent it.

A few characteristics of Russian people are worthy of note. Normally Russians carefully avoid large public gatherings or catastrophes. In Moscow or Leningrad a large fire or auto accident will be ignored by the average Russian. They are not inquisitive. I witnessed a large fire in a Moscow apartment house, and there were no Russian spectators. The only Russians present were the firefighters and the police to control traffic. Any Russian who saw the event quickly took steps not to come near or pass by.

Russians, when participants in a ballet, opera, or dramatic presentation, become fully dedicated to their role with outstanding success. If the Russians were not dominated by an autocratic government, their entrepreneurship would be superb and difficult to surpass. Their scientists over the years have made outstanding contributions to world knowledge when they were free to study, research, and develop without close oversight by a suspicious political system.

When dealing with foreigners under the Tsar, and under the Communists, they have been very realistic and difficult in all negotiations. They seek facts, slowly agree piecemeal on small parts that affect the final solution of a major problem. Normally they do not reply to formal letters and requests for information or action, unless there is some assurance that Russia/U.S.S.R. will benefit considerably from such action. They carefully study all long-range implications before negotiating in good faith. It is most frustrating for a Free World representative. The frustration and procrastination must be tolerated if progress in negotiations is desired. Each phase of any progress is closely monitored by a political commissar, who frequently must seek approval on higher levels himself. No initiative is permitted; monolithic control by the Kremlin is guaranteed, to which every official is subordinate.

Publications such as *Pravda*, *Izvestia*, *Red Star*, etc., are newspapers in name only. Over 90% of their mission is to be propaganda vehicles for spreading Communist doctrine and Soviet government policies. There is no truth in *Pravda*, which translates as "truth," and no news in *Izvestia* (news). Any news is restricted to the last page in small paragraphs of two or three sentences. Real news circulates among the people with greater success through rumors in large cities that move abroad via train/air travelers in U.S.S.R.

Soviets are suspicious of all foreign correspondents. Lozovsky, Deputy Foreign Minister to Molotov, met me at a picnic on a Moscow river shore in the summer of 1944.[*] Lozovsky asked me about the political philosophy of the *New Yorker* magazine, because the *New Yorker* wanted to send a correspondent to Moscow. U.S.S.R. refused to give *New Yorker* magazine a permit because the *New Yorker* refused to state its political philosophy, namely, either Democratic or Republican. I explained that the *New Yorker* was a popular magazine that entertained its readers without supporting a single political system.

Losovsky proceeded to give me a long lecture illustrating that no printed periodical or magazine existed solely to make a monetary profit for its owners. Printed media exist to explain a political system and to help readers understand how to live with and carry out government policy. News is selectively released in small amounts, only when space is available, and the political system must always be portrayed as honest and without fault. The press is expected to exploit machiavellian techniques. The Kremlin is loath to concede the smallest failing before its people with a perception that they are being observed by a hostile world. Kremlin reluctance to release any information stems from a deep-seated conviction that a hostile world is willing and ready to use any information to misrepresent and embarrass the Soviet state and Russian people. Soviet leadership in the Kremlin attempts at all times to present themselves to the Soviet people as a benevolent, infallible, omnipotent god. Soviet leaders believe the world at large is watching and waiting for any type of crack to appear in the Kremlin's omniscient leadership.

Tsar Alexander III, in his negotiations with the French in 1890, displayed many similar suspicions and worries. These characteristics are inherent in the Russian-Communist heritage. The Free World would be better prepared to live and work with the Soviet Government if there was world appreciation of the unique characteristics of the Russians. Each nation has different likes and dislikes. We must try to understand and

---

[*] Solomon Lozovsky, Deputy People's Commissar for Foreign Affairs.

work with them. It serves no useful purpose to avoid and dislike those who do not think and live the way we do.

Russian libraries, particularly at colleges and universities, have excellent references and research materials. They have thousands of volumes for research and study. They are very popular and always crowded. The user is normally restricted as to what references he may access. On one visit to the library of Moscow University, adjoining the U.S. chancery, the volumes of the *Encyclopedia Britannica* were examined. Various topics, sections, and pages had been removed so the Russian user could not read about foreign events or history that were inconsistent with Communist doctrine and education policies.

An interpreter mentioned that a Soviet student might ask an embarrassing political question. The teacher refused to answer. The student persisted, so the student was warned by the teacher that the student could be sent to the political overseer at the school if he continued. For answers to some queries, more than one student went to the library, only to find that material pertinent to the query had been eliminated from foreign references. The Foreign Language Institute apparently reviews all foreign documents before they are included in the library; all data not consistent with Communist doctrine are promptly extracted.

Paul Stillwell: Did you have anything to do with the Yalta meetings?

Admiral Knoll: Yes, to some degree. There is a sad part about the Yalta meetings. One of the papers we worked on dealt with careful wording of any agreement, both in English and Russian, saying exactly the same thing. Stalin, Roosevelt, and Churchill would be discussing future provisional governments for Poland, Yugoslavia, Czechoslovakia, etc,. and using the English word "democratic." The English word "democratic" in translation to Russian "democratic" meant "Communism" to Stalin, etc. We had to carefully address what we meant in terms of freedom, a lack of a police state, and the selection of a new provisional government for Rumania, Poland, Bulgaria, or Czechoslovakia, etc. We worked a couple of months as a committee, talking with Ambassador Harriman and others. We knew we had to make sure what we were saying in Russian and English. This was a very preliminary position.

More time was wasted at the actual plenary session drafting the communique issued at the end of the session. Most of the staff work had already been agreed to before arriving at the meeting. I worked on that before I went out to Vladivostok. Upon my return, I asked, "What happened to all the paperwork we did?" It was sent to Washington to help the Joint Chiefs of Staff. They were told about the importance avoiding the word "democratic" for future provisional governments for occupied areas. We would lost our shirt carrying out agreements after Yalta. The sad part is that we were told that Chip Bohlen was with the President, who had position papers prepared with a lot of effort by the Joint Chiefs of Staff, coordinated with Ambassador Harriman and George Kennan in the military mission in Moscow.[*] Without waiting for the plenary session, President Roosevelt arrarnged a private meeting with Stalin and told him about the position paper concerning the word "democratic." Stalin said, ""You see, we know what it means, so why worry about how the communique is used?" Apparently they both agreed. This demonstrates again that Roosevelt was no longer a well man and should never have really been in a position to make a decision of such importance.[†]

From then on, every meeting to anticipate provisional governments that General Deane and Ambassador Harriman had with the Russians addressed potential leaders for the nucleus of a new government. Those in the occupied areas were frustrated, particularly for Poland. As soon as the West suggested the name of a Polish leader, that individual disappeared and was never seen again. In other words, it was genocide of the Polish elite, acceptable to the West. The inability of the West to nominate reliable Poles gave the Soviets an opportunity to proceed with the formation of their "democratic" government, composed of Polish Communists. The U.S.A. and Britain were frustrated and unable to find reliable Polish representatives. The mere mention of a man's name meant he would disappear and never be located. The Yalta agreement to establish "democratic" provisional governments was achieved by the U.S.S.R. The agreement should have avoided the word "democratic." The Soviet Army delayed the capture of

---

[*] Charles E. Bohlen was a long-time State Department diplomat who served in the Soviet Union before and during World War II.
[†] Roosevelt died a few months later, 12 April 1945, of a cerebral hemorrhage.

Warsaw until the U.S.S.R. knew that a provisional government favorable to the U.S.S.R. was ready to function. The Soviet Army had six times as many troops around Warsaw as would be needed to capture the city. All eligible males were recruited in Moscow and sent to the front as reserves. Many never got near the battle; they were in reserve in the event of a surprise requirement when they encircled Warsaw.

We worked with the British Chiefs of Staff. There were certain terms that could not be used at the conference table. For example, "to table an item" means to the British to bring it up for discussion. For us it's a delayed action. We had guidance for terms and knew to be careful as to meaning when working with foreigners. Similarly, working with the French, you know very well in an official session that they're going to speak French, and you demand an English translation, no matter if they are fluent in English. The French are proud of theirs as the diplomatic language over the years. These are some of the interesting things that one learns through experience. We can be the most fantastic people in the world, but we have to realize to work with the rest of the world as it becomes a global village, people live closer togeher, and they must try to get along and understand their neighbors. You don't have to love them, but you have to undersand them and tolerate them. The world is becoming relatively smaller. The challenge is for us, whether they like us or not, to learn how to get together without resorting to the awful waste of war. War starts when talking has ceased. You haven't gained one item. Frequently a nation goes to war to preserve a way of life. The war ends with surprise changes.

The U.S.A. must have confidence in our way of life. We must have a long-range foreign policy that is bipartisan and not altered each time a new administration occupies the White House. There is need for a long-range foreign policy for Central America and Cuba. A Marshall-type plan could improve the economic and social well-being and develop a dynamic middle class.[*] At present, in the event of war, the first military task would be to neutralize Cuba on our doorstep. Improving the well-being of all in the area should frustrate Communist inroads. The U.S.A. successfully established relations with U.S.S.R. and Communist China. A gradual effort through economic and social programs

---

[*] At the Harvard University commencement in 1947, Secretary of State George C. Marshall made an address in which he outlined a plan for the economic rebuilding of war-ravaged Europe. Congress passed the European Recovery Act, and the program of American support came to be known as the Marshall Plan.

could bring about changes in Cuba. Cuba is the focal point of Communist activities in Central America; therefore, it is of high priority for U.S.A. to brin Cuba into our control and neutralize U.S.S.R. influence in Central America.

Paul Stillwell: Did the end of the war effectively mean the end of your tour there? Was there any point in your staying after that?

Admiral Knoll: I stayed until December 1945. We knew the organizing needs of the United Nations that were taking place in San Francisco. Ambassador Harriman had a very interesting exercise to convince Stalin and Molotov to send a representative to San Francisco.* Stalin claimed the U.S.S.R. had no way of getting there. In desperation, with Washington's approval, Ambassador Harriman agreed that the U.S. Army Air Forces would provide the air transportation for Molotov to go to San Francisco and return. During his absence, we said our prayers every night to make sure Molotov got there safely and returned to Moscow without mishap.

The same way occurred with the United Nations charter. It was only when U.S.S.R. pointed out to Stalin that the veto aspect in the Security Council charter was just as important to us as to him. There was no way in the world, with our Constitution and form of government, that U.S.A. agrees for our military to be in control of the Security Council of the United Nations and ordered into battle as a United Nations force without the approval of our U.S. Congress. United Nations was to have a military force equally composed of the five permanent members of the Security Council—China, Britain, France, U.S.S.R., and U.S.A.—who might immediately be ordered to war when the Security Council determined such was necessary to preserve the peace.

The Russians made it much more difficult, and that's one reason I left the United Nations in November 1946 and went back to sea. The agenda of the military staff committee of the Security Council of the United Nations had one item since November 1946, namely, that the contribution of forces from each nation must be the same kind of force and numbers of personnel. If U.S.A. contributes an aircraft carrier, every other

---

* The organizing conference for the United Nations was began in San Francisco on 25 April 1945. The representatives of the assembled nations produced a charter that was signed on 26 June. The charter was ratified by a majority of member nations on 24 October 1945 and the organization began operation.

nation must contribute an aircraft carrier. If U.S.S.R. contributes a tank division, each nation must contribute a tank division. This stymied all further discussions. Each nation couldn't contribute an aircraft carrier because three of the nations did not have carriers. This impasse quickly nullified the idea of having a balanced military force on call by the Security Council. When Gromyko absented himself from the United Nations at the time of the Korean War, he wasn't present to veto.[*] It was the first and only time. The United Nations force in Korea was established because U.S.S.R. was not present to veto.

Paul Stillwell: Do you want to talk about the United Nations tomorrow?

Admiral Knoll: Yes, I think so.

---

[*] The Korean War began on 25 June 1950, when six North Korean infantry division and three border constabulary brigades invaded South Korea. The troops were supported by approximately 100 Russian-made T-34 tanks. In New York that same day the United Nations Security Council adopted a resolution condemning the invasion.

Interview Number 4 with Rear Admiral Denys W. Knoll, U.S. Navy (Retired)
Place: Bel-Aire Hotel, Erie, Pennsylvania
Date: Friday, 29 June 1984

Paul Stillwell: Admiral, yesterday we were talking about your tour in Russia during World War II. I wonder if you could give me some explanation of the difficulties of dealing with the Soviets.

Admiral Knoll: The main thing is that the longer you deal with the Soviets, the more you realize they are not free to talk about any subject unless it's in keeping with the written guidance they've received from Moscow. You're at their mercy. They may want to meet, but any discussion is very limited. To be safe you always go to a meeting with at least one other person to be able to corroborate. The longer you negotiate with them, the more you realize that some knowledge of the Russian language is very important. Your interpreter must promptly interfere and say, "Will you please repeat that, because my interpreter hasn't told me the whole story." It was to my advantage to know the highlights of what the Russians were saying in Russian. In dealing with any foreign interpretation, that's important. You must know your subject and be prepared for any unusual play that gives your direct Soviet opposite an advantage.

One of our difficulties was with items related to Lend-Lease. The Soviets knew that in Washington the policy of President Roosevelt was that anything the Soviets asked for, we were supposed to arrange for them to receive such. We did have one particular affair when they wanted an exorbitant amount of seaplanes, about 60 PBYs. In 1944 it was obvious the Soviet Navy would never need that many seaplanes to win the war. We tried to reduce that number and recommended reductions to Washington. We tried to negotiate with a Soviet naval aviator, but he refused to provide justification. Because we didn't agree with what he wanted, he quickly ended the meeting and refused any discussion. We never saw him again. They finally received approximately that number of PBYs over our embassy objections.*

You must realize that any Soviet who comes to a meeting in Moscow is thoroughly briefed on what he can agree to and what he can discuss. He usually has an accompanist who is a member of the secret police or a political commissar from the office to which he is attached. The assistant makes note of everything said and how it is said. No derogatory remark about the Soviet Union is allowed in the presence of a Soviet individual. He will be reported if he hasn't defended the Soviet Union as he should. A Soviet rep is always at the mercy of this commissar who is listening to him. If the Soviet doesn't behave right, he will be punished, and you'll never see him again. We did develop a good relationship and understanding with a capable group of Soviet officers whom we met regularly over the months. Occasionally, in response to a special request, they were able to provide some reply and quietly arrange a trip, for example, to Leningrad after first replying that such a trip was completely impossible.

We experienced many frustrations dealing with the Soviet Union. We came to realize how realistic they were, how factual they were, how they religiously adhered to Kremlin policy. It was that democratic centralism or the monolithic control that is so different from any other nation. Staff discussions on new subjects are possible with the British, the French, the Chinese, or other Free World nations around the world. Ambassador Harriman, George Kennan, and others determined it was to the advantage of officials in Washington that with our experience we would try to document the frustrations and differences when dealing with the Soviet Union. With a better understanding of this, the United States might have some success in the future.

No one is going to change their way of doing business, but with better understanding the U.S.A. will have a chance of successful negotiation and be able to find the areas where U.S.S.R. wants to negotiate. We came to appreciate more and more, there was only one way to approach a new problem which required a new policy. Any new problem, Harriman had to first talk about it with Stalin. This was done with the concurrence of Winston Churchill and President Roosevelt. If a subject was approached

---

* The Naval Institute oral history of Vice Admiral Herbert D. Riley offers an interesting variation on this story. Riley said the United States provided the Soviet Union with a squadron of 28 PBNs, a variant of the PBY that didn't really fit into the U.S. Navy's desired inventory.

on the Molotov Foreign Minister level, it would never get to Stalin. It was the kiss of death. Everything had to originate with Stalin as if it was his own idea. Stalin was very rigid on this; it was apparent that even from Molotov a new idea from foreigners was due to die. We had extra time after Yalta; Yalta in many ways had not accomplished what it was supposed to in terms of setting up ground rules and procedures for establishing future provisional governments for the nations of Central Europe, that is, Rumania, Bulgaria, Poland, etc. We hoped to develop a document giving experience and ground rules that would help U.S.A. in the future and avoid the frustrations of trying to think and negotiate in Western fashion. Soviets have a Communist way of dealing with foreigners in use from the time of Peter the Great and other Russian officials such as the deception of Potemkin and Catherine the Great.*

A working group analyzed all the communications that had been exchanged with the Soviet Foreign Ministry, starting with Ambassador Bullitt's opening the embassy in U.S.S.R. in 1933 and continuing into 1944.† We recorded what happened after letters got to the Soviet Foreign Office. After evaluating all documents and communications, it was revealed that about 92% were never really answered and never acknowledged. The remaining 8% were analyzed as to why they were answered. In keeping with the realism of the Soviet Union, the Foreign Ministry replied only to communications that were of some importance to U.S.S.R. Soviet actions were dependent upon obtaining an advantage for U.S.S.R. Even where U.S.S.R. would have some benefit, action was very slow, because other bureaus and activities were careful to adhere to party policy. A document was prepared, and different embassy personnel were briefed on the pattern of Soviet actions.

Harry Hopkins came over there about every few months, even though he wasn't well. He'd show up in Moscow and give us a debriefing about what was happening in Washington and what Roosevelt was thinking and other official background. It was very

---

* Peter I (the Great) ruled Russia and the Russian Empire from 1682 to 1725. The city of St. Petersburg, Russia, is named in his honor. From 1924 to 1991, during the Soviet regime, it was called Leningrad.
"Potemkin Villages" is a term used to describe something that is built only to impress, not for any real value. It comes from fake villages constructed on the banks of the Dnieper River by Russian Minister Grigory Potemkin when Empress Catherine II visited the Crimea in 1787.
† William C. Bullitt (1891-1967) had a colorful career. He had previously served as U.S. ambassador to the Soviet Union, 1933-36, and to France, 1936-41. He was a special assistant to the Secretary of the Navy in 1942, and in 1944 he enlisted in the French Army.

educational and illuminating. About ten senior people from the embassy military mission always attended these meetings with Harry Hopkins.

Finally, Ambassador Harriman was impressed with the document and said, "This is ready to be put into the smooth" for forwarding to Washington. It analyzed all the problems we had encountered and what we had learned. Even with the urgency of war, the Soviets did not act promptly. Certain recommendations were made as to how to deal in the future. The document was ready to go to Washington, and Ambassador Harriman had checked with Washington to find when it would be convenient for his visit. U.S. Army planes were not kept in U.S.S.R. When they were ready in Washington, Harriman had to arrange with the Soviet Foreign Office for a Soviet navigator and Soviet radioman to be aboard the U.S. plane before it entered the Soviet Union and stay with the plane until it left the Soviet Union.

Ambassador Harriman was about ready to leave Moscow the same day as word was received that President Roosevelt had died.[*] There was some discussion whether Harriman should wait with this important document, or whether he should go right away and brief President Truman.[†] It was quickly decided that this was the ideal time to get to Washington right away and give President Truman the benefit of this analysis of ten years of experience working with the Soviet Union, particularly during a wartime emergency.

Harriman went, and when he returned about ten days later, he debriefed us as to the reaction of President Truman. The President was very impressed with the whole study, but his comments to Harriman were to the effect, "I've just announced to the nation and the world that I'm going to continue all the policies of President Roosevelt. What I've learned here, I'm going to quickly need to change some policy." As a result of that, I think his naval aide, when the first issues arose in the United Nations in New York at meetings of the General Assembly and the Security Council, subsequent to the organizing meetings in London, about March of 1946, Admiral Robert Dennison called me more than once to ask (1) what I thought the Soviets would do in regards to withdrawing from Iran and (2) what I thought the Soviets would do with regard to the

---

[*] President Franklin D. Roosevelt died at Warm Springs, Georgia, on 12 April 1945.
[†] Harry S. Truman, who had been Vice President, succeeded to the presidency on Roosevelt's death.

Greek problem."* Dennison said that President Truman wanted my reaction because he knew I had worked on this study. It was because of that study that the President took a strong position that the Soviets had to withdraw promptly from Iran and became very emphatic until they agreed to withdraw.[†]

I was at a meeting of the Security Council as one of the U.S. observers with Secretary Stettinius during the discussion in New York.[‡] I think Andrei Gromyko was the Soviet representative, and he finally said yes, they would withdraw, which was a surprising change in their policy.[§] U.S.S.R. was allowed into Iran in 1942 to assist with operation of a railroad carrying Lend-Lease from the Persian Gulf to U.S.S.R. Based on our experience with the provisional governments of Central Europe, we were afraid that they would assert this as an area of influence. The background on working with U.S.S.R. has produced other useful achievements.

I wrote a couple of articles for the U.S. military staff for Admiral Turner and General George Kenney and General Ridgway, analyzing all articles by Alexander Worth and his visit with Stalin.[**] It was an analysis of the answers in terms of what they meant from the Soviet point of view and what they meant from the American point of view, which were considerably different. It was about a 12- or 14-page document, and it was sent to Washington with the idea I might write for publication to make more people aware of how difficult it is to deal with the Russians. We are not going to change them, but let us understand their peculiarities, their realism, and their monolithic control. Then you may have a better chance of having a more beneficial relationship. Not an ideal situation but at least better than confrontation.

Within less than a week, I received a letter from the head of naval intelligence, addressed to me, with copy sent to my record. It told BuPers and others that I was

---

* Admiral Knoll's recollections do not jibe with the chronology of events. Robert Dennison was still a captain in 1946; he did not become Truman's naval aide until February 1948. If Truman actually was influenced by Knoll's views, they must have reached him by some other means.
† The United Nations Security Council passed a resolution on 30 January 1946 calling for the Red Army to withdraw from Iran. The Soviets withdrew their forces in the spring of 1946.
‡ Edward Stettinius Jr. was Secretary of State from 1 December 1944 to 27 June 1945. From December 1945 to June 1946 he was the first U.S. ambassador to the United Nations.
§ Andrei Gromyko was the Soviet ambassador to the United Nations, 1946-48.
** Admiral Richmond Kelly Turner, USN, was the Navy Representative on the United Nations Military Staff Committee in 1945-47. During that period, General George C. Kenney, USAAF, was Army Air Forces representative to the U.N. Military Staff Committee. Lieutenant General Matthew B. Ridgway, USA, was the Army representative on the U.N. committee.

forbidden to write for publication while I was on active duty because of my association with high policy foreign affairs and intelligence matters during World War II. General Deane was about to write about the same thing. He was thinking about writing a book, and I told him that I couldn't. He wrote his book *The Strange Alliance*, which was published by him.* I received a lot of the proofs while he was working on it, because it dealt with the contents of this document. *The Strange Alliance* illustrated the strange way of working with an ally, the Soviet Union, the slow progress and frustrations of which were tolerated rather than achieving nothing at all. When this was published, the date of publication was such that General Deane's date of retirement was a few days afterward. There was some adjustment made so he would not be found releasing unnecessary information while still on active duty. The book never received the attention it should. It is an excellent document.

Many Americans expect our allies are going to kowtow to us. In Washington all during the war, no one realized the problem and frustration under which we lived, working with the Soviet Union. They were our ally in name, and that's why it was a "strange alliance." It's a strange relationship today. There's no other recourse. There's no other solution than to continue to meet and talk, just like you do with your neighbors in the city. You don't have to love them, you don't have to befriend them, but you have to continue to find a way you can live in peace without fighting them. Such is true of the Soviet Union. If it weren't for the police state, they wouldn't exist. Materialistic Communism couldn't exist without a police control. Fifty percent of the Soviet citizenry would run away if the secret police relaxed their vigilance.

After almost two years indoctrination in U.S.S.R., I returned to Washington about December 22, 1945. Within a couple of hours, I was registered at the Mayflower Hotel. A message arrived saying, "Kelly Turner wants to see you at OpNav tomorrow morning." Admiral Turner greeted me with, "We're leaving for London on the *Queen Elizabeth* on December 29."† That didn't make my wife very happy either. We had been separated for 22 months, but I left shortly for the organizing meetings of the United Nations. The U.S.

---

* John R. Deane, *The Strange Alliance: the Story of Our Efforts at Wartime Cooperation with Russia* (New York: the Viking Press, 1947).
† The diary of Eleanor Roosevelt, part of the collection of her papers at the FDR presidential library, reported the *Queen Elizabeth*'s departure date as 31 December 1945.

delegates aboard the *Queen Elizabeth* numbered about 60.* We had the advantage of preliminary conferences every day en route with the U.S. delegation, consisting of the Secretary of State, Mrs. Eleanor Roosevelt, John Foster Dulles, Adlai Stevenson, Alger Hiss; Frank Walker, et al.† We met around a large table for discussion of U.S. position papers for the organizing meetings of the United Nations and becoming acquainted with each other, and the responsibilities we shared.

Paul Stillwell: How did you get assigned to the United Nations delegation from the billet in Russia?

Admiral Knoll: As war came to an end and the U.S. military mission was dissolved, my designation was changed from a naval member of the military mission to assistant naval attaché with the U.S. embassy. Each of us waited to be relieved. An officer was ordered and finally arrived to relieve me in early December 1945. I had about a month's time to brief him on intelligence matters.

I had a chance to go one more time to Leningrad. This is an interesting story. I remarked at one of the meetings with my Russian Navy liaison, "I'd like to visit Leningrad one more time before I return to U.S.A."

The Soviet liaison replied, "You can go any time you want."

So I sent the transportation people to obtain my ticket to Leningrad, via the train on which I traveled about three times before. I didn't have a permit to buy the ticket. Normally when you apply you obtain a permit to buy the ticket. It is issued with the approval of the Foreign Ministry and your liaison agency, the weather bureau of the Navy Department. In talking to Captain Mike Kostrinsky, I said, "They won't sell me a ticket to Leningrad."

He said, "They'll sell you a ticket."

I said, "No, you need a permit or pass."

---

* The passenger ships *Queen Mary* and *Queen Elizabeth* of the British Cunard Line were converted for use during World War II as high-speed troop transports. Each was capable of nearly 30 knots.
† Mrs. Roosevelt was the widow of the recently deceased President; John Foster Dulles was a Republican foreign policy expert, later Secretary of State, 1953-59; Adlai E. Stevenson II was a special assistant to the Secretary of State, later unsuccessful Democratic nominee for President in 1952 and 1956; Alger Hiss was secretary-general of the United Nations organization meeting in San Francisco in 1945. Frank C. Walker.

He said, "You don't need a permit to go to Leningrad now. The war's over."

I said, "That's what you think."

He said, "You go up there tomorrow. They'll sell you the ticket with a permit."

So I obtained a ticket without argument for myself and Lieutenant Hatch, who was one of the naval communicators. I said, "If you'd like to come along, I never like to travel alone in U.S.S.R. except on the Transiberian Railroad going to Vladivostok." So Lieutenant Hatch went with me for a three-day visit. We had tickets, and when we went to board the train, they said, "Where's your permit from the Navy?"

I replied, "The Navy told me I can travel to Leningrad without a permit." There was a smile or some discussion back and forth. I boarded the train because the Navy had taken steps with certain people to fool me and waive the permit. We rode in a double compartment in the international car, an overnight trip from Moscow to Leningrad. Upon arrival at the station in Leningrad, we were met by one of the "intourist" girls that had assisted me on an earlier visit. Before she could ask me for a permit, which is required for registering at the hotel, I said, "I'm up here again with the permission of Navy headquarters who said I didn't need a permit this time, so don't ask for it. Here is my passport."

We went to the Astoria Hotel and at the registration desk I said, "I don't need a permit, but if you have any question, call the Red Navy headquarters here. They know I'm here with Moscow permission." This procedure was used during the entire visit, and I never had a piece of paper that is always required. The Navy had tried to convince me that I could travel in U.S.S.R. without permit and made a real effort to convince me. Everyone at the embassy knew this was contrary to established procedure. Today in U.S.S.R. travel between cities requires a permit, particularly for foreigners.

Paul Stillwell: Evidently you were able to succeed by telling them this story everywhere you went.

Admiral Knoll: I never thought I could succeed, but I was willing to try it. It shows that private arrangements, "You do this for me, and I will do such for you," is a Soviet device that can circumvent official procedures. The unusual sometimes happens. It can be done with the right people having been alerted. I told Mike Kostrinsky later on, "Thank you. You're a sly guy, but it worked."

He said, "Sure it worked. I told you to go without permit."

I said, "Try to do this for an ordinary foreigner or another naval officer who has not been in U.S.S.R. for a year or more." Navy headquarters were trying to fool me, because at the same time I was complaining that NKVD officers were following me at all times, day and night, in their jeep.[*]

I was surprised to learn that Ambassador Harriman and General Deane had recommended that I be one of the U.S. advisors to the organizing meetings of the United Nations. Harriman convinced Stalin to send Molotov to San Francisco for the United Nations meeting. Air transportation was provided by U.S.A.; otherwise, a U.S.S.R. rep would never have gone to San Francisco. At San Francisco it was decided to have the organizing meeting of the United Nations in London.

En route in the *Queen Elizabeth*, we were anxious to see who would be representing the Soviet Union. I was designated because of my U.S.S.R. experiences and my secretarial work with the Joint Chiefs of Staff and Combined Chiefs of Staff. The British delegation had as secretary Captain Richard Lord Coleridge, an officer with whom I'd worked in the British secretariat in Washington. We were designated to work with Sir Gladwyn Jebb, who had been British ambassador to France.[†] He acted as Secretary-General in London for the organizing meetings. The first week we met with Jebb and discussed how we documented the papers of the Joint Chiefs of Staff and the Combined Chiefs of Staff during the war and the procedures we followed for committee work and preparation of agendas. It was essentially the Dewey decimal system. It provided reliable documentation for filing each topic with supporting documents.

Subsequent to our briefing him on this, the procedure for documentation in the United Nations was exactly the same documentation used in the U.S. Joint Chiefs of Staff and Combined Chiefs of Staff during the war. It was due to the fact that Richard Lord

---

[*] NKVD are the initials for Narodnyy Komissariat Venutrennikh Del, a Soviet law-enforcement agency.
[†] Hubert Miles Gladwyn Jebb, Fist Baron Gladwyn, was a British civil servant, diplomat, and politician. He was acting Secretary-General of the United Nations from 24 October 1945 to 2 February 1946.

Coleridge and myself had briefed Sir Gladwyn Jebb, who adopted it. Trygve Lie from Norway became the first Secretary-General of the United Nations in London.*

With us on *Queen Elizabeth* were Admiral Fenard, who was French, and his secretary; Admiral Henry Sir Moore, for the British delegation; and the Chinese had many of their delegation also on board.† There was an opportunity to become acquainted and make preparations to organize the military staff committee or the U.N. Security Council.

Paul Stillwell: Did you keep your captain rank during this time?

Admiral Knoll: I retained the captain rank for 13 years. I was a commander. I did revert to commander for two months two years later while all spot promotions were adjusted. I never had to change my uniform, because BuPers said, "Your date will come up, so keep and wear the uniform." It was a good rank in which to stagnate from 1943 to 1957.

As secretary of the U.S. military delegation, I was authorized to select two of the best civilian secretaries of the Joint Chiefs of Staff to accompany us. A former JCS secretary, General Deane, also recognized that we had to have two good secretaries who had working knowledge of the Joint Chiefs system. One of them had been General Deane's private secretary, and the other girl was one of her assistants. They were with us, so we had a good staff for the delegation. General Ridgway joined us when we arrived in London; Admiral Kelly Turner and General George Kenney traveled with us in *Queen Elizabeth*. George Kenney was a smart officer, very friendly, and a real asset to the delegation. He had been deputy for air to MacArthur in the Southwest Pacific.

About the last night before arrival in Southampton on the *Queen Elizabeth*, we were having a party. Captain Elliott Strauss and myself were at the party when we received word that Admiral Kelly Turner wanted to see us in his stateroom.‡ He hadn't been invited to the party or felt neglected. Being the type of man who has a million things on his mind all the time, about what might be done or what could be done, Kelly

---

* Trygve H. Lie was Secretary-General of the United Nations from 2 February 1946 to 10 November 1952.
† Admiral Sir Henry R. Moore, Royal Navy.
‡ Captain Elliott B. Strauss, USN, eventually retired as a tombstone rear admiral. His oral history is in the Naval Institute collection.

Turner was a fertile individual for good ideas. It was 9:00 or 10:00 o'clock at night, and Elliott Strauss and I visited Kelly Turner. Turner said, "Before we dock in Southampton tomorrow noon, we have to have a preliminary draft of the 'rules of procedure' and the 'terms of reference' of the military staff committee. Have copies ready for me to give out at breakfast tomorrow morning to the British and the French and the Chinese representatives."

This was a continuation of a policy which I have used with Admiral Burke for many years and other bosses. When you have an important problem, have a preliminary discussion with knowledgeable people. The first one that puts the problem in writing with suggested courses of action will find that the final document is normally 90% of your first document. This was Kelly Turner's philosophy, having worked with the 1932 arms conference. He said, "Let's get something in writing, and we'll ultimately have something that we can live with."

Elliott Strauss and I sat down, and to our amazement, before midnight we had a draft of each document ready, because we had enough references in files that we had brought along as a guide. We followed the Joint Chiefs of Staff pattern and kept things simple. We needed equipment to reproduce drafts. I said, "All our typewriters are already crated to take off the ship tomorrow noon when we dock."

The two secretaries typed documents into smooth using the purser's typewriter. We asked, "Doesn't the ship have some reproducing equipment that is used to make the dinner menus?" The purser woke up his people there, and we reproduced these documents. They were ready for breakfast. Admiral Kelly Turner, not having been invited to the party, had decided to give us a task that proved to be helpful. The next morning at breakfast Turner went around to each delegation and gave a copy for study. Today 90% of the rules of procedure of the military staff committee and the terms of reference are exactly what Captain Elliott Strauss and I wrote that night on the *Queen Elizabeth*. This is an example of subordinates helping a supervisor do a good job. It helps promotion, and it is not being a "yes-man."

Paul Stillwell: How did you get back from the Soviet Union in 1945?

Admiral Knoll: When I returned then to Washington from Moscow, I knew I had been nominated to go to the United Nations. From Moscow I flew to Berlin; I was in Berlin for about a week because we were fogged in at Tempelhof airport. I had a chance to go around and visit the ruins of Berlin. Similarly, I'd seen the ruins of Leningrad and some of the ruins of Stalingrad. Later, in 1946, in Tokyo, I had a pretty good idea what war could do to places, how horrible it was, even in those days without a nuclear threat. I made some interesting contacts, and I had a chance to talk in Russian to the Soviet guards at Hitler's Reichschancery and bomb shelter. I had a conducted tour through the bomb shelters and Hitler's vast communications center in the Reichschancery. I didn't enter Hitler's bomb shelter where he died. I was at the entry hatch that went down to it. The Russians didn't want to let me in at first. I was in U.S. Navy uniform. I spoke to them in Russian and said, "I've been your ally in Moscow for two years, and now you mean to say I can't go in and see the things I helped you people capture?" A Soviet Army captain came out and took me around to show me almost everything.

Soon after I had reached Washington and registered with my wife at the Mayflower Hotel, Father Braun called and wanted to come and see me. His story is rather interesting, because he had been a Catholic priest in Moscow from 1934 until '45 and went through all kinds of persecution and discourtesies by the Soviets.* Interestingly enough, why, they finally had agreed for another priest to come in and relieve him. Up until that time, they ignored every appeal to let another priest come in a relieve him. It was part of Roosevelt's recognition agreement with Stalin, that with the U.S. embassy in Moscow, there would be a Catholic priest to take care of any Catholics that were attached to the embassy or other embassies. With U.S. recognition of U.S.S.R., they provided the Church of St. Louis, which was in the shadow of Lubianka, the NKVD chief headquarters in Moscow.

When Father Braun's relief arrived in Moscow, Braun started applying for air transportation from Moscow. The Soviets told him there was no air transportation; he must leave via train. Some elderly women who came to confession told him, "Don't go

---

* Father Marie-Léopold Braun (1903-1964). His memoir, edited by G. M. Hamburg, was published after his death. It is *In Lubianka's Shadow: The Memoirs of an American Priest in Stalin's Moscow* (Notre Dame University Press, 2006).

out by railroad, because Soviet police are going to push you off of the train at night before you get to the Polish border." And he told me about this. I relayed this to Harriman and George Kennan.

They said, "Tell Braun to wait and stay packed. If something comes up, we'll get him out some way via air."

It so happened that Braun was there with his bags packed when I left. I brought some of his memorabilia in my luggage that he wanted to get out of the Soviet Union. I knew that Harriman and Kennan were acquainted that the Navy always took care of Father Braun, because from the time Ambassador Steinhardt was there before Standley, when Germans threatened Moscow and foreigners were evacuated to Kubyshev, Steinhardt tried to force Father Braun to go home, because Steinhardt said Braun was an embarrassment to winning the war.[*] Braun could not live in the American facilities that we had occupied to that time. Braun received permission to live in the janitor's house at the French embassy, where he continued to reside after the people came back from Kubyshev. The embassy and the Navy helped supply him with food from the commissary. He had regular services on Sunday, and many parishioners were elderly Russian women and a good number of foreign diplomats who attended church every Sunday. The interesting thing is that Steinhardt had made every effort to get rid of Braun, and within a few years after Steinhardt had left the Soviet Union to become U.S. ambassador to Canada, he was killed in a plane crash as he was taking off from Dorval Airport in Montreal, Canada.[†]

During Steinhardt's time, Soviets raided Father Braun's church and stole the tabernacle with the sacred vessels. Steinhardt refused to try to recover the items. It was the Kubyshev evacuation, and the Germans were about to take Moscow. Sir Stafford Cripps was the British ambassador, just ahead of Sir Archibald Clarke. Cripps went to the Soviet Foreign Ministry and demanded that Father Braun's tabernacle and the sacred vessels be returned when our own U.S. ambassador refused to help him. The tabernacle and all were back the next day.

---

[*] Laurence A. Steinhardt was U.S. ambassador to the Soviet Union, 23 March 1939 to 12 November 1941.
[†] Steinhardt was killed in a plane crash on 28 March 1950 near Ramsayville, Ontario, while en route to Washington.

When Father Braun joined me at the Mayflower Hotel shortly after I had registered, he came in and he went down on his knees and kissed my hand and said, "Thank God you people got me out."

I asked, "How did you get here so soon after me?"

He indicated that Secretary of State Byrnes was attending meetings in Moscow, and his plane came to retrieve him to Washington.* Harriman sent an embassy car to pick up Braun at the French embassy with his bags. As Secretary Byrne was saying goodbye to Foreign Minister Molotov at the Moscow airport, the embassy car drove up with Father Braun. Secretary Byrnes turned to Molotov and said, "I've invited Father Braun to fly back to the U.S.A. with me." Father Braun was most grateful to his embassy friends. He died some years ago. He avoided all public speaking about U.S.S.R. or how he was treated and how the Russian people treated him. He was determined to do nothing that might make it more difficult for his successors to work in Moscow. You couldn't blame him. In many areas, I know in my work with Cardinal Spellman at the United Nations, Braun did provide a lot of valuable background to the Vatican.†

An interesting item that's well to record involves the idea the Soviets did away with churches and religion—the realism of how they dealt with this helped them close the churches. It was a progressive idea after the new economic policy in the early 1930s in U.S.S.R. About the time of the purge trials, Soviets contacted each rector at each Catholic Church or the Baptist Church in Moscow or Leningrad. The Soviets said, "Okay, we want a list of all your parishioners," and they told the rector, "Your taxes for this year are so-and-so." The rector collected from the parishioners and paid. After less than a year was up, they said, "There's been an increased tax requirement. Your taxes are now so-and-so." Each time Soviets increased the taxes, a large number of parishioners disappeared. Within a matter of two years, the priest was unable to pay the taxes, and most parishioners were gone because they refused to help to pay the taxes. The Soviets arrested priests for not paying taxes. More than once, within the month after

---

* James F. Byrnes served as Secretary of State from 3 July 1945 to 21 January 1947.
† Francis J. Spellman had been Archbishop of New York and military vicar of the armed forces since 1939. He was created a cardinal in 1946 and served in that capacity until his death in 1967. In 1951, during the Korean War, he began the practice of spending Christmas with U.S. troops overseas.

the Soviets arrested rectors, they came through with bulldozers and removed the churches. Some were changed to movie theaters or museums of the godless.

You see how they taxed the churches out of existence. It was a sly deception. It is the hardest thing in the world to convince Americans how devious the Soviets can be. No foreigner freely talks with an official in the Soviet Union unless he has obtained policy guidance for such discussion. We're so gullible we don't realize it. A foreigner can never deal safely with anybody in the Soviet Union unofficially. You can't arrange to meet the person a second time unless you realize an official report will be submitted after they see you. It doesn't matter what it is. Do not think you're getting away with something; you're gullible. They don't work that way.

Communism is not like a flu epidemic. The whole country is not going to be overthrown and conquered. Communism only survives when a police state is in control. People who live and cherish their freedom will not become victimized by materialistic Communism. The underprivileged nations are vulnerable because of the low morale and substandard economic and social conditions of the populace. A Marshall-type plan rather than military equipment will counteract any attraction to Communism.[*] The whole concept that the nation's drift toward Communism is wrong, like the domino theory.

After the U.N. meetings in London, an interesting change was made in the group of Soviet military who came to New York. Except for General Vasiliev, the Soviet military arrived late.[†] They were reluctant to meet and discuss U.N. topics. Their English wasn't very good, and they were outside the U.S.S.R. for the first time. I arranged to meet and make protocol calls. All were new Soviets whom I had never met before. The officer who was supposed to be the Soviet military secretary could hardly understand a single word of English. I invited the senior officials to meet me for lunch at the best hotel in London.

Paul Stillwell: Claridge's?

---

[*] At the Harvard University commencement in 1947, Secretary of State George C. Marshall made an address in which he outlined a plan for the economic rebuilding of war-ravaged Europe. Congress passed the European Recovery Act, and the program of American support came to be known as the Marshall Plan.
[†] Lieutenant General Alexander F. Vasiliev was Soviet representative to the United Nations military staff committee.

Admiral Knoll: The Connaught Hotel, at Carlos Place above Berkeley Square—more exclusive than Claridge's. It was the best hotel available, and I wanted to impress them. I ordered a special luncheon and tried to explain the type of work that confronted him. My Russian language was very useful at this point. They requested, "Can't we meet with you regularly to bring us up to date on what happened before we got there?" This I did, and they appreciated it. They suggested, "Anything like that is not American; rather all part of U.S. propaganda to deceive them. They were very receptive.

They had various parties at the Soviet Embassy, and I was invited. All guests were segregated to rooms according to rank and expected to stay in the room. At one of these parties I asked Vishinsky about praying every day when he said, "Thank you (Spaseega—"God Save us"). In London was the first time that I met and visited Andrei Gromyko. Gromyko doesn't visit easily; you can talk with him. However, like every Soviet official, he was cool and never too friendly. We did have some success. Churchill attended a few large receptions. Various affairs were held at Albert Hall. Meetings with Secretary Gladwyn Jebb were at the Church House, Westminster Abbey. The U.S. delegation had a cocktail part about every third day at Claridge's, first Mrs. Roosevelt one day, Frank Walker another, and John Foster Dulles another. John Foster Dulles had important meetings concerning the Trusteeship Council and UNESCO.[*]

I was designated to be the military representative to accompany John Foster Dulles to the Trusteeship Council. Dulles was a pretty intense man—never friendly. He didn't talk very much or communicate easily. He had his own ideas. He displayed a tough attitude in regards to the Soviets. It was a good indoctrination for getting international things started and ultimately to achieve a successful organization for the United Nations. The U.S. military staff had offices in the Naval Forces Europe headquarters adjoining the U.S. embassy in Grosvenor Square. They were excellent accommodations that adjoined Admiral Hewitt's quarters.[†]

Paul Stillwell: Was your main purpose at that point to establish the ground rules under which the United Nations would operate?

---

[*] UNESCO – United Nations Educational, Scientific and Cultural Organization.
[†] Admiral H. Kent Hewitt, USN, served as Commander U.S. Naval Forces Europe/Commander 12th Fleet from August 1945 to September 1946.

Admiral Knoll: My job was to organize the military staff of the Security Council as U.S. secretary. Sir Gladwyn Jebb established documentation for U.N. papers, and many decisions were made for the move to New York as the official headquarters. It wasn't firm, but it was pretty well understood. Preliminary arrangements had been made to use Hunter College for plenary sessions of the United Nations. No mention was made as to the future headquarters for meetings of the military staff committee of the Security Council. They had no provision for that. It was in the middle of March 1946 when the U.S. delegation was ready to board the *Queen Elizabeth* for the return to New York. As secretary of the delegation, I was designated to help find hotel assignments for all the delegations in New York. I announced, "I should fly back early and help get things organized in New York."

"What do you mean, fly back? Everything is reserved on PanAm through October."

I went to the Pan American office, and I said, "When can I get on a flight to New York? I am entitled to an executive seat from Mrs. Archibald."[*]

They checked with Rice, my friend in Singapore whom I had helped in 1941, and within an hour PanAm called me and asked, "When do you want to go back?"

I departed the following night. Upon arrival in New York, I contacted representatives in Robert Moses's office and other city officials.[†] We were assigned an office on the second floor of the Waldorf Astoria Hotel. There were people like Abe Fortas and some from the State Department.[‡] We proceeded to sit down and call every hotel. We had a list of each delegation that was coming, 53 different foreign delegations. We had the number in each delegation and how many rooms were needed in each hotel. We went through this list and assigned all of each delegation to a specific hotel in New York. No hotel would have more than one foreign delegation. It wasn't easy. We would call each hotel and say, "Effective so-and-so, these people will arrive, and a specific

---

[*] Mrs. Anne M. Archibald, the widow of a Marine Corps aviator, was manager of the Washington office of Pan American World Airways.
[†] Robert Moses (1888-1981) was a planner and construction coordinator for many years for New York City. As such, he wielded enormous power in the construction of bridges, buildings, and roads.
[‡] Abraham Fortas worked in the Interior Department under President Roosevelt and under President Truman was part of the delegation that set up the United Nations. He subsequently was an associate justice of the Supreme Court, 1965-69.

foreign delegation will stay there." By the time all arrived from London, delegations had new requirements, and we had many problems satisfying the needs of each delegation.

Paul Stillwell: What role did Robert Moses have?

Admiral Knoll: He was accommodation coordinator for the mayor and took an interest in seeing that everyone was taken care of. I didn't get involved in the arrangements for Hunter College, where the United Nations had the first meetings.* I did visit the manager of the Henry Hudson Hotel. It had been a Navy WAVE hotel during the war, and he was just closing out the Navy contract. I was able to negotiate and have the contract renewed for the top floor with a big solarium as the offices of the United Nations Military Staff Committee. Regular meetings of the entire committee and of secretaries were held there. Each of the five delegations for the Security Council nations was assigned an office for a secretary and discussions at he time of the meetings.

Paul Stillwell: How early did they get set up out at Lake Success on Long Island?

Admiral Knoll: I attended the first meeting at Lake Success in November 1946 when President Truman spoke to all the delegations. I was with the U.S. delegation for the first meeting in November of '46. I left shortly thereafter to take command of the oiler *Severn*.

Paul Stillwell: Did these delegations have any jealousy about what hotel they got, whether they thought that was suitable?

Admiral Knoll: Yes. The big problem was that members of the various delegations had lady friends. They wanted to be with their delegation, but they also wanted to have a room in another hotel where they could live with their lady friend. They didn't want their

---

* Hunter College, an institution for educating women students, had a campus in the borough of the Bronx. During World War II the Navy leased campus buildings for the training of WAVES - Women Accepted for Voluntary Emergency Service. After the Navy left, the college temporarily housed the U.N. Security Council.

delegations to know about it. Many foreigners live this way, and we tried to accommodate.

The Russians had certain requirements, and it was rather interesting. They couldn't live at different hotels. With the assistance of the Soviet embassy in Washington, they were assigned various cold-water flats in Harlem, in the Bronx, and other areas where they were told they had to live and observe each community. This was true except for General Vasiliev, who had a fantastic suite on the top floor of the Pierre. Others were scattered. Admiral Bogdenko lived in apartment in Harlem, and he said the Harlem girls were terrific.[*] The characteristics of people are amazing. We finally got them all settled.

The most important thing was that the entire Soviet delegation returned to Moscow from London before they came to New York. I kept checking how soon the Soviets would arrive. I planned to arrange to meet them. I had access to an official car for that purpose. I heard that they were coming from London at night at Newark airport. I waited, and the plane finally landed. Walking from the plane were two or three officers with whom I had worked for two years in Moscow. One of them was a full colonel in the Red Army. I had worked with him on various problems. The Soviets had changed their secretariat and staff. Not one officer who was in London showed up again in New York. We ended up continuing to work with the officials with whom we had worked in Moscow.

Their secretary came to me the first week, and I had to brief him and bring him up to date on the work we were doing. It was to my advantage, and they were beholden to me in many ways. I was able to educate them the way I wanted them to work with us in the United Nations. The senior Soviet military officers, Admiral Bogdenko and Colonel Studenov and others rode with me in a limousine to New York. We drove down Fifth Avenue, Broadway, and Park Avenue, showing them the sights about 9:00 P.M. before taking them where they were supposed to join their own group. They just couldn't believe what they were seeing. Not on had ever seen a large city like New York before.

Later on I frequently took Colonel Studenov with me for rides. I lived at 50th and First Avenue in an apartment that was rented to me by the inventor of Xerox. He needed

---

[*] Vice Admiral Valentin L. Bogdenko, Soviet Navy.

money to sell his idea and wanted me to invest in it. Unfortunately, I never did. If I had, I probably wouldn't be sitting here today.

I would take Studenov for rides in the countryside with one of his friends. I drove them to Hyde Park to see Roosevelt's grave.[*] I stopped along the road and made them buy a basket of apples. Studenov said, "I don't have a permit."

I said, "Wait a second. You don't need a permit. You can buy anything you want in this country, anyplace you want." The average Soviet seldom sees a surplus of anything, particularly "five-and-ten items."[†] They will buy six of a kind because they want to buy them while such is available. When they first arrive, they have to be careful when seeing surplus anywhere. They can't understand a place where there's plenty for everybody and one does not have to buy more than is needed. I made them buy things along the road and take them back to their delegation. I didn't have an expense account. I took them out and would stop for lunch at roadside places. Studenov just couldn't believe our freedom and plenty. He said, "You have special permits, or you couldn't travel like this."

Admiral Kelly Turner found out that Beardsley Ruml wanted me to retire and become secretary of the Spelman Rockefeller Foundation.[‡] Admiral Turner said, "You better get back to sea duty and stay in the Navy." That led to my getting orders to go to the *Severn*.

Paul Stillwell: Speaking of Turner, he had the nickname of Terrible Turner. Did you see that side of him?

Dr. Herbig: I never knew the word "Terrible." All I knew was Kelly. I know in the forward combat area, his aide, Jack Lewis, told me it was something when a big

---

[*] Franklin D. Roosevelt's estate at Hyde Park is near Poughkeepsie, New York, north of New York City. It is now a National Park.
[†] The United States used to be populated with what were known as "dime stores," in which items sold for five or ten cents. Inflation has long since made the term obsolete.
[‡] Dr. Beardsley Ruml (1894-1960) was an American statistician, businessman, and philanthropist. The Laura Spelman Rockefeller Memorial Fund supported social and behavioral science. Laura Spelman Rockefeller was the wife of John D. Rockefeller, founder of Standard Oil.

amphibious operation started, everyone saw and felt the character of the man.* He was so damn smart, twice as smart as the average individual, a very versatile man, not conceited in one way, but he could quickly become very mad. He'd frequently say, "Don't be afraid of me." That was hard when you'd see him with his eyes fiery and using demanding language. Yes, I've seen one other admiral who could become almost as mad as he did on short notice. That was Stuart Ingersoll. I was his chief of staff in Seventh Fleet for over a year.

Paul Stillwell: Weren't a lot of the people that served around Turner sort of in awe and fear of him?

Admiral Knoll: No, I would not say that anyone feared him. We didn't have that large a group. He could be very nice and courteous when everything was going slowly. He was a stickler on neatness and wearing the right uniform. If someone was not in correct uniform and failed to salute, he was merciless. If you made a big mistake, you were promptly chastised.

Our biggest problem with him was his drinking. It was embarrassing very often. He had a photographic memory and was probably the most intelligent man I have known. He was very smart and knew facts. With Ambassador Stettinius and others in the U.S. delegation, he could quote verbatim every article in the United Nations Charter from memory. At each meeting Alger Hiss was normally present; he would leave and not return while Admiral Turner was present. Hiss managed the plenary sessions of the whole U.S. delegation, but Hiss would not attend extended meetings we had with Stettinius or similar U.S. officials. He always made some excuse to leave, having made no comments.

Paul Stillwell: Why do you think that was?

---

* Commander John S. Lewis, USN. He had served as assistant air operations officer when Turner commanded amphibious forces in the Pacific.

Admiral Knoll: We don't know. He roomed in London with Adlai Stevenson in Kensington. Adlai Stevenson was very friendly to all. Later, at different naval functions or parties, I'd be in a receiving line. Admiral Ingersoll would start to introduce me to Adlai, and Adlai would say, "There's Denny Knoll. We set up the United Nations together in London." He always remembered me. He was an outgoing character, and we could not understand his close association with Alger Hiss.

Paul Stillwell: You mentioned Turner's drinking. In what way did that interfere with things?

Admiral Knoll: The biggest problem was in London after lunch, particularly when he went home for lunch. His aides kept checking to find and dispose of hidden bottles. We tried to make sure he didn't keep liquor in the drawers of his desk in London. Once in London, after lunch, a British officer came into the office and said, "There's an admiral lying in the snow near the hedge of Grosvenor Square." We quickly sent his aide, who picked him up and took him back to the Grosvenor House Hotel on Park Lane. He could be very pleasant and never showed annoyance with an effort to lessen his one weakness. We knew when he went home alone, he would take a good drink.

He told me one time that the worst days of his life were the awful letdowns right after successful amphibious operations in the Pacific. There was intense excitement and worry for a few days before D-day. Everything was a ten-ring circus with troops on the beach, and then there was nothing for him to do. He said, "The only thing that quieted me was drinking a bottle of red liquor." This was the type of reaction that tormented many people who were in combat in the war zone too long during World War II. Maybe if more attention had been given to that type of strain that men in combat were under, a medical doctor might have given the correct therapy. There is no record that he was an alcoholic before World War II. History records that he was the father of amphibious assaults in World War II. His planning, foresight, and operational genius had no equal.

Paul Stillwell: Some of the top admirals, like Lee and McCain and Mitscher died very shortly thereafter, presumably because of that strain.[*]

Admiral Knoll: That's correct. Admiral Kelly Turner retired shortly after I left the United Nations.[†] We returned to New York and were joined by Admiral John Ballentine.[‡] Ballentine checked Turner's desk every day to remove liquor. General Kibbler was Matt Ridgway's assistant, and Colonel Pierre Cabell was George Kenney's assistant. At that time I was secretary for six flag officers. Finally, I obtained an assistant secretary, a Lieutenant Colonel Van Sickle, and then another Army secretary, Lieutenant Colonel Don Faith, who had been on General George Patton's staff. I had a ten-ring circus preparing certain letters and official documents for each service flag officer.

Paul Stillwell: What do you remember about Ballentine?

Admiral Knoll: He was a fine officer, naval aviator, and gentleman. He and his wife were a good addition to the military delegation. When Admiral Kelly Turner looked under the weather in the afternoons, Ballentine would call Mrs. Turner and tell her we were going to send the admiral home or for her to ask the admiral to come home. The admiral had a chauffeur or aide to take him home. He would quickly respond when she told him, "Come on home, Kelly." It was sad to see a man with such ability, fertile mind, and great war record be in poor health. The Navy didn't take adequate care of him after wartime operations. He had to find something to relax himself; apparently he did it with practically a quart bottle full each day. That's sad. It wasn't his fault then. When he was sober, everything he did met the highest standards of professionalism. He had all the superb abilities that I experienced with Admiral Tommy Hart. Sure, they can be tough at times. Then I acted like I wasn't being perturbed.

---

[*] Vice Admiral Willis A. Lee Jr., USN, died 25 August 1945; Vice Admiral John S. McCain, USN, died 6 September 1945; Admiral Marc A. Mitscher, USN, died 3 February 1947. All three had top combat commands in the Pacific during the war.
[†] Admiral Turner retired from active duty 1 July 1947.
[‡] In 1946-47 Rear Admiral John J. Ballentine, USN, served as chief of staff to the CNO's representative, Turner, on the United Nations Military Staff Committee of the Security Council.

Paul Stillwell: Didn't Turner tell you not to be frightened of him?

Admiral Knoll: Yes, many times. When Turner interviewed me in December 1945 to go to the United Nations, I didn't receive orders until he asked for me. Turner had told the other people he'd find a good secretary to bring with him to work with George Kenney and Matt Ridgway. That's why he interviewed me. As he finished the interview, he said, "Now, if I'm not calling you 'Denny' in ten days, you know I'm looking for a relief. He started to call me "Denny" en route to London. He was just like that.

Upon arrival in New York from London, we moved into offices in the General Motors Building at 57th and Broadway. They were nice quarters for all of the U.S. delegation. One corner was assigned to the military group, with a conference room and equipment. The military group increased in size. The Army group were friends of General Ridgway, paratroopers and Army aviators. They were all outstanding people with impressive, fantastic war records. Admiral Turner told me, "Now, remember, as these new people come in here, particularly enlisted men, I want you to be sure that you brief them that if I start bawling them out or correcting them, they're not supposed to be afraid of me. I don't like it when I'm trying to bawl someone out for doing something wrong and they act like they're afraid of me. That's my intention. I just want them to know if they've done something wrong, I'm going to tell them about it. I want you to brief each one. I want you to check them off as they arrive here."

"Yes, sir, Admiral, I'll take care of it."

After about a month, he came in and sat down on the corner of my desk. I went to stand up. He said, "Sit down. Are you briefing these people as they arrive?"

I said, "Yes, I certainly am."

He said, "I just met a boatswain's mate out near the elevator, a chief boatswain's mate with a lot of hash marks." He was wearing a pair of uniform trousers with cuffs on them. I proceeded to tell him he was out of uniform, and tears started coming into his eyes, like he was afraid of me. I don't like that."

I said, "Admiral, when you get mad and bawl someone out, I start getting afraid of you myself." And he roared laughing. Turner told me more than once, "You're going to be Chief of Naval Operations some day. You're not a 'yes man' and not afraid to do all you can to help him do a better job." They appreciated it. I did this with Arleigh Burke and Slim Ingersoll and others with whom I worked. They are smart and consistent, and you always know where you stand. I'm never criticizing them; I'm trying to help them do a better job, and that's the secret of leadership, to try to help people do a better job, no matter on whatever level you're working on. Far less effective people you never know where you stand, and it is difficult to help them.

Admiral Turner was determined that I stay qualified as a naval officer. Otherwise, I'd probably still be with the United Nations because Trygve Lie, the first Secretary-General, didn't want me to leave because he knew I helped to get the United Nations started. I knew most of the senior reps of all the delegations to a degree. The interesting thing in London, when I went to certain meetings of the General Assembly, I would see Prince Faisal of Saudi Arabia. He'd come over and say, "Captain, what position is the U.S. delegation going to take on these items? I want to be sure Saudi Arabia is going to vote for the same things as the United States."[*]

The same way with Jan Masaryk, Foreign Minister of Czechoslovakia, who was later pushed out of the window in Prague by the Soviets.[†] He'd come up to me and want to know the U.S. position on items. He was quite a character and wanted to know what U.S.A. was going to do so he would vote the same. He was a ladies' man from way back, famous for the stories he'd tell. He was always late at a dinner party or reception. The story was told he was at a very formal lords' and ladies' dinner party in London. He arrived late, and the hostess met him as he came in. His nickname was Hansa, and she said, "Oh, Hansa, you're late, but you'll be on time for dinner. Would you like to go to the lavatory before?"

"Oh, no, thank you, My Lady, I went behind a tree before I came in." He always did memorable things wherever he went, so he received many invitations.

I met and knew different people that wanted to be on the U.S.A. side in all the things the U.S.A. was doing. At that time, we were popular and had many allies. Many smaller nations wanted to be on our side. At military staff meetings, different discussions

---

[*] Faisal bin Abdulaziz Al Saud was Saudi Arabia's foreign minister. He later served as Prime Minister and was King of Saudi Arabia from November 1964 until his assassination in 1975.
[†] Jan Masaryk was Czechoslovakia's Foreign Minister from 1940 until his death in 1948. His death was clouded by mysterious circumstances.

occurred, and there were disagreements—at least once I'll never forget. I usually sat between two of our flag officers, Admiral Turner and General Kenney, or between Admiral Turner and General Ridgway. The Russians would talk in Russian, and I would translate what the Russian was saying, whether he was going to agree or not, what his arguments were, so our delegation had advance information while the official translator translated into English. Our delegation had already decided what we were going to reply. Frequently the British came over before an official interview finished and ask, "What did he say?"

One time, I'll never forget, Kelly Turner said to the U.S. group, "One of these times I'm going to have it come out that the British are on the Soviet side of the vote, and the U.S.A. is on the other side." All of a sudden, opportunity arrived, and Sir Henry Moore was amazed that he found Britain was voting with the Soviets, and on the other side of the issue from the U.S. delegation. It was not serious, but the British were surprised. When Admiral Moore's wife died, he married Admiral Wilkinson's widow after Wilkinson had driven off that ferryboat at Norfolk and was drowned.[*] British officers were good friends all the time we were there; they invited me to many dinner parties. The British delegation stayed at the Ritz Carlton.

I gave a cocktail party at the Henry Hudson Hotel before I left the United Nations. It was for many delegations, including the officials of the United Nations secretariat, including the black man who was an Assistant Secretary-General of the United Nations.

Paul Stillwell: Ralph Bunche.[†]

Admiral Knoll: Yes, Ralph Bunche. When some of the U.S. delegation saw I had Bunche and his wife on my invitation list for the reception and cocktails at the Henry Hudson Hotel, their eyebrows went up. They asked, "Will he show up?"

I said, "Sure, he'll show up." And he did. In those times, things were still ticklish, but he was a terrific individual. He came in, made his manners, talked to my

---

[*] Vice Admiral Theodore S. Wilkinson, USN, drowned in a ferry accident at Hampton Roads on 21 February 1946. He managed to save his wife Catherine but drowned himself.
[†] Dr. Ralph J. Bunche was a political scientist and diplomat. In 1950 he became the first black person to receive the Nobel Prize, which was awarded for his mediation of the late-1940s Arab-Israeli conflict in Palestine.

wife and myself. Admiral Turner met and visited with him. He didn't stay more than about 20 minutes, but he came and made an impression. Bunche was one of the best contributions the U.S.A. made to the United Nations. He died too soon.* It was a terrific loss of a well-educated gentleman who impressed everyone he met.

The biggest weakness of the United Nations was from the beginning, that the senior Assistant Secretary-General of the United Nations, by agreement, had to be a representative of the Soviet Union. The Soviet Union has control of too many personnel in the secretariat by that position, because the Secretary-General himself is too busy with so many other problems. Secondly, Soviets, with their knowledge of control and with seniority in the international group, have too much power. Today they probably have more of the same, Soviets working there that were members of the secretariat when I was there. This is idea for continuity and for control. Can you imagine with Jeane Kirkpatrick at present?† Most delegations have no one who's been up there for more than a year or so. A nucleus of the original delegation should have been retained for continuity. That's a hell of a way to belong to the United Nations.

I visited a couple of times to make presentations as hydrographer and oceanographer at UNESCO in Paris. I ran into some foreigners who were in the United Nations when I was there. The United States hasn't maintained adequate experienced representation. We haven't maintained our influence on various levels of power. The Soviet Union has increased its influence, and the U.S.A. has lost much. If you're going to become a part of an organization, you have to maintain enough of a matrix of people who know how it operates and have prestige to influence others. Eleanor Roosevelt frequently said at U.S. meetings, "Remember, gentlemen, it is not what you accomplish at this conference table; it's what you do with your homework." The homework is meeting and getting to know people.

Many times in Washington I would call people and go to lunch with different people, learn their views, and keep contact. When you have a problem, take interested people for lunch and have an hour or so discussion before a formal meeting or after some meetings. Find out ways and means for solving problems. Plenary sessions are easy

---

* Bunche died in 1971 at age 68.
† Jeane Kirkpatrick (1926-2006) was U.S. ambassador to the United Nations from 1981 to 1985.

after doing your homework. You solve few problems solely at a conference table. Informal discussions without commitments are helpful for planning groups in Washington. Sit down and discuss.

For four years, you see, after I returned to Washington in January of '48, Admiral Freddie Boone was OP-30, head of strategic planning.* After I had been to sea in the *Severn*, which was my first command, while in the Far East in 1947 I spent a couple of hours with General MacArthur in the Dai Ichi Building, and he attempted to have me ordered to his staff.† My orders were officially to the CIA because of the influence of the ONI and Admiral Olsen, who was an advisor with the CIA. Captain Sam Frankel was also with the CIA.‡ I wasn't too enthused about going to the CIA, because I didn't necessarily want to be an intelligence specialist for the rest of my life. I thought it was a dead end, in terms of my naval experience. I received the pressure-cooker treatment when I was with the CIA. They put me in an office, told me to read things. I was not to speak or visit with anyone. I guess they were trying to evaluate me or trying to know where to put me. For about a month, nothing happened, and I was thoroughly frustrated.

Paul Stillwell: Why don't we cover the job offer you had to go into civilian life when you were there in New York?

Admiral Knoll: Secretary Stettinius from time to time invited me for some interesting visits with him about my experience in the Soviet Union. He was Secretary of State for that short time until James Byrnes took over, and Stettinius stayed with us in the United Nations. Through Ambassador Harriman, Beardsley Ruml, who was the author of the idea of pay-as-you-go income tax, called me and said, "Let's have lunch.' So we met. He came right out and said, "We're looking for a new secretary of the Spelman Rockefeller Foundation. Salary will be about $25,000 a year plus expense account. I've

---

* Rear Admiral Walter F. Boone, USN.
† On 29 August 1945 General of the Army Douglas MacArthur, USA, became Supreme Commander Allied Powers and presided over the allied occupation of defeated Japan. He was also a United Nations military commander in the Korean War. He was in Japan from 1945 until fired by President Truman in 1951.
‡ Captain Samuel B. Frankel, USN. The oral history of Frankel, who retired as a rear admiral, is in the Naval Institute collection.

received a lot of recommendations from friends of yours that you'd be an ideal secretary." I discussed this meeting with Admiral Turner. I wasn't too enthused.

Admiral Kelly Turner quickly said, "Listen, you're a naval officer. You've been away from the active Navy too damn long, and you have made a terrific contribution to the nation. We want you in the Navy."

At that same time, when the delegation heard I might leave, I received two offers from Army aviators telling me that the Air Force was looking for good staff officers for the future independent service. They suggested I request a transfer from the Navy to the new Air Force.[*] They said they couldn't promise me a promotion, but they were sure I would have as much promotion or more in the Air Force than in the Navy. I said no, I would never consider it. I prefer not to say who offered them to me, but they were very senior officers. I was a captain, U.S. Navy.

I had a couple more meetings with Beardsley Ruml. I pointed out, "Well, right now this is 1946. I graduated in 1930. I have 16 years of active duty. If I did retire, I shouldn't retire until I have 20 years with 50% retirement. Down the road, a salary of $25,000 is not very much living in New York." He told me what was involved, and it was a rather interesting job. But I lacked experience as an individual in financing and funding. I would not be too happy to sit at that job and have a bunch of people running rings around me without knowing what was involved.

I had meetings about once a month with Cardinal Spellman as well and talked to him, because he was interested in what the United Nations was doing. Finally, I told Ruml, "In terms of what the situation is, I appreciate this offer, but I'm going to stay in the Navy." We ended up very good friends. I had letters from time to time after that for a while, not trying to change my mind, because he agreed with me that the equity I had in the Navy was something he couldn't begin to equal. The offer was a five-year contract with renewals and incentives in pay. I had bought an apartment on 72nd Street between Lexington and Park Avenue at a time when it was hard to find a place to live in New York. I purchased it with the idea that I'd probably stay with the United Nations a little

---

[*] On 20 June 1941 the U.S. Army Air Corps was officially redesignated the U.S. Army Air Forces and retained that title until the establishment of the U.S. Air Force as a separate service on 17 September 1947.

longer than I thought. I think I paid $10,000 for it and sold it about three months later for $14,000 because places to live in New York were so scarce in 1946.

While I was finding accommodations for foreign delegations and certain individuals, more than one approached me, saying, "We're going to buy this apartment house in the Bronx where the WAVES were housed. You can be part of the group for $1,000. We'll then sell it to the United Nations for accommodations for much, much more. There will be a quick real profit."

Every time I had that kind of offer, I said, "I'm not interested in this kind of business." There was great speculation for property to sell to the United Nations. I was gunshy and was not going to get involved in real estate in New York. That's the reason I did not take the job as secretary of the Spelman Rockefeller Foundation and was happy to go to sea.

Paul Stillwell: How did you get command of the *Severn* then?

Admiral Knoll: Admiral Kelly Turner called Admiral Denfeld, Chief of BuPers, and said, "I've got an officer that has been with his wife and family for less than a year in the last nine years. I think that's immoral."[*]

Denfeld said, "Yes, I know who he is. He's at the top of the list of officers who haven't been with their families. I'll give him a ship based at Norfolk so he can be with his wife and family when in port."

The orders came through for the *Severn*, which had carried feed water for the amphibious operations in the Pacific and as a result had never been completely equipped as a fleet oiler.[†] When I arrived on board the *Severn* at Long Beach Naval Shipyard, the ship had just been converted from a water carrier to a fleet oiler. The ship had carried chlorinated fresh water in support of amphibious campaigns in the Pacific War. The first load of black oil was loaded, and the ship left the next day for Yokosuka, Japan. En route

---

[*] Vice Admiral Louis E. Denfeld, USN, served as Chief of the Bureau of Naval Personnel from 15 September 1945 to 21 February 1947.
[†] USS *Severn* (AO-61), an *Ashtabula*-class fleet oiler, was commissioned 19 July 1944. She displaced 7,136 tons unloaded, was 553 feet long, 75 feet in the beam, and had a maximum draft of 32 feet. Her top speed was 18 knots. She was originally armed with one 5-inch gun and four 3-inch guns. Captain Knoll took command in November 1946.

the ship stopped and picked up freight at Pearl Harbor. We were then diverted to refuel the small ships that were returning from Bikini after the A-bomb tests and then continued on to Japan.*

The condition of the ship was a most fantastic revelation. The ship had been in commission about two years as a fresh water transport. The commissioning allowance of boatswain's equipment had never been uncrated. The forward storeroom on the main deck had all the equipment still in the packing crates. It was impossible to enter one door and go out the other door. All gear had to be unpacked and stowed properly. Similar equipment had been requisitioned and stowed helter-skelter about the main deck. Every place on the ship gave little appearance as a part of the Navy; it was a mess. In due time I heard that I was ordered to the ship to organize and make it a real Navy ship.

Paul Stillwell: Why would that mean that you'd be sent to it?

Admiral Knoll: My service reputation was pretty good as a division officer and first lieutenant in battleships. The *Texas*, flagship of the U.S. Fleet, was always the cleanest and the smartest in the fleet. The *Oklahoma* was one of the best ships in the fleet with a damage control organization, and I had been the assistant first lieutenant. The *Severn* was part of the Naval Transportation Service, commanded by Rear Admiral Bill Callaghan.† He knew *Severn* needed attention and had asked BuPers for a career officer with battleship experience. This was relayed to me when the NTS operations officer inspected me after I was in command for six months. He gave me an excellent fitness report for my work. Callaghan knew *Severn* was the worst ship in his command. They were looking for someone to clean house.

The supply officer came to me the first day with tears in his eyes and said that at the end of the war his predecessor failed to apply for special relief funds for the over expenditure of goods and other expendables during the war. Almost every petty officer on the ship had keys to storerooms. At night those with the night watch went to the

---

* In July 1946 a joint Army-Navy task force conducted tests at Bikini Atoll in the Marshall Islands to determine the effects of atomic bombs on moored warships. Along with an array of U.S. ships were captured German and Japanese warships.
† Rear Admiral William M. Callaghan, USN.

storeroom and took a can of fruit or peaches to eat during their watch. Volumes of uneaten food were thrown over the side. There had been no control of supplies of any kind while the ship was in the forward area. Many had keys to all the storerooms, which in many ways was necessary during the war in the event of fire or battle damage. If you had to get into a space on account of fire, somebody in the vicinity had a key.

I said, "We'll correct that." The executive officer, supply officer, and the boatswain were told, "Tomorrow morning at quarters pass the word that when the crew comes to quarters, they will bring all the keys they hold for access to storerooms." I told the supply officer, "When everybody is at quarters, you and your staff go to every storeroom and attach a new lock." We collected more than two white hats full of keys. That was one thing, get control of supplies in the storerooms.

The supply officer still had tears in his eyes that he was overextended more than a million dollars for food and supplies that had disappeared. At the end of the war a period of 90 days was granted for each ship to claim specific amounts needed to bring supply records up to date. With appropriate credit each ship would start off with a correct peacetime procedure. The supply officer's predecessor had been detached from the ship and went to a hospital without a contact relief. It took the new supply officer a month or more to get his books in order and find out where he stood. Doing this he found out no one had applied for relief. He was a young supply officer, an ensign on his first assignment.

He asked, "Am I going to jail?"

I said, "Wait a second. You're not going to jail."

He said, "Well, what can I do?"

I said, "Tell me the facts. Sit down. Tell me what happened."

He said, "It was six months ago the ship should have applied for relief, and it hasn't been done."

I said, "That's all right. The people are not dumb in Washington. Let's tell them the situation as it is. You relieved without a contact, you found the books in bad shape, you've gone through an orderly analysis, and you find the ship should have applied for such monetary relief. Tell them what we've done about the keys. We'll send Washington a dispatch and give them the essential facts. You're not liable, but we're trying to bring the ship back in the Navy the way it should be. We will recognize some of these things that are wrong. In the last month you have essential correct procedures and have control. We will estimate the amount over-expended and request a waiver on the amount, even though it is overdue." Within ten days we had a reply. Washington canceled everything and told the ship it had a clean slate. I said to the supply officer, "Don't worry when you get in trouble. Tell your superior the facts." He was a scared young man for a time.

Soon there was another problem. *Severn* was ready to transfer fuel oil, and the pumps would frequently jam up. We had nothing but black oil and some diesel in the three center tanks. By the time the black oil was transferred, the bottom of all oil tanks, 27 of them—three across and nine of them fore and aft—there were pieces of rust two and three feet deep. The oil entered voids where the chlorinated water had been. The tanks hadn't been painted correctly for water. The oil loosened all the rust, and it covered the bottom of each tank. We had to go down with barrels and shovel this rust out so we could pump the oil. The rust fouled and scoured the pump heads and slowed the discharge of fuel. It was an awful mess.

Severn made four trips back and forth between Japan and the Persian Gulf. At this time the Navy started loading at Ras Tanura, the ARAMCO tank farm on the Persian Gulf.* En route the crew had two days' liberty at Singapore one way and at Colombo, Ceylon, on the return, or vice versa. The round trip was 21 days.

Paul Stillwell: That wasn't exactly Norfolk, was it?

Admiral Knoll: No, it was as far away as I could get. It was a wonderful way to relax. I took many of the classics and novels I'd been waiting to read. Steaming singly we traveled like a yacht with little bad weather.

I was disturbed about the appearance of the ship, so with the first lieutenant, the exec, and a couple of division officers, we assembled the division petty officers, and I said, "Now, this sip is a mess. We are going to start working at the bow and work slowly

---

* Ras Tanura is a cape that projects from Saudi Arabia. ARAMCO – Arabian American Oil Company.

slowly to the stern. Every day there's good weather we can gradually clean this ship and make it look like a yacht."

They immediately said, "My division is so-and-so, and my division is so-and-so.

I said, "Listen. We're going to clean this main deck with a joint working party, and the division boundaries are not important. We're going to work aft as a team and paint the whole ship, cleaned up, painted properly, chip where necessary." I asked, "What do we have for the chipping and wire-brushing?"

They replied, "We've only the old wire brushes and chipping hammers."

I said, "You mean to tell me you have no electrical chipping hammers or powered wire brushes?"

"No, no."

I said, "For God's sake. I'll write a dispatch." I wrote a dispatch to Admiral Callaghan and the Bureau of Ships. I said, "In this modern age it's a disgrace when a ship has a small crew of less than 70 on a large ship like a fleet oiler, and the crew is expected to maintain it with an ordinary wire brush and chipping hammer. I recommend immediately an allowance of 12 wire brushes and 12 mechanical chipping hammers be issued to each fleet oiler so the crew can maintain a smart ship in real Navy fashion." The reply came right on back, approving the recommendation. The crew worked as a team, and finally when we arrived in Yokosuka the next time the *Severn* was issued automatic electric chipping hammers and wire brushes. You can't imagine how much faster the crew could do this work instead of the old way with a hammer and wire brush.

The next time we returned, we anchored at Yokosuka, and another fleet oiler came alongside to consolidate. The other Navy oiler was empty, and they consolidated our load so we could return to the Persian Gulf. While the ship was alongside a sister ship of the *Severn*, our ship was as clean as a whistle. For a tanker that's tough, particularly in a rough sea with a heavy load and the ship showered with seawater. Everything gets rusty. The other oiler was cruddy, it was dirty, it was covered with oil marks on the decks and sides. I was standing on the wing of the bridge, and the crews were conversing while some of the crew on my deck were waiting to pass lines over. A petty officer said to my crew, "Boy, what a nice-looking ship you have."

One of my crew replied, "You're damn right. We're organized over here." The morale of my crew was high, and they were proud to be envied by others. They more than once said it was easier to clean the deck as a team than argue about division boundaries.

Paul Stillwell: That was a completely new type of ship for you. How did you learn the operations?

Admiral Knoll: Handling a fleet oiler is not much different than handling a battleship, which has a draft of 32 feet. The main thing, you have to have a reliable cargo officer to handle pumps, valves, and ballast. Always keep center tanks filled and avoid a torque effect along the keel. You become accustomed to clean tanks as you empty them—butterworth them and collect the sludge.* Once organized with a few good officers, it is not too hard. The principal problem was maneuvering a large ship with a deep draft and single screw. Conning a single screw is good as long as you go forward; backing down it never goes where you want it to go.

Paul Stillwell: Did you have an experienced boatswain and boatswain's mates to handle the deck rigging and so forth.

Admiral Knoll: That was no problem. I had good experience on battleships, handling boats, under way and in port as officer of the deck on the *Texas* and *Oklahoma*. And I had about 30 days on *Sirius*, which was a cargo ship, when I went from Norfolk to San Diego after leaving Pensacola and went through the Panama Canal to join the *Texas* on the West Coast. I had an appreciation of what was involved and how to take care of your booms and boats.

I didn't have to get involved with underway replenishment, because *Severn* didn't have the rig for this. It was a point-to-point cargo carrier than a regular fleet oiler, although it was designated as a fleet oiler. This is where a real problem developed later.

---

* Butterworth is the name of a method for cleaning tanks with seawater under pressure.

They had designated *Severn* as a fleet oiler, but the Navy yard did not install the equipment to do a fleet oiler's job.

I made four 21-day round trips to the Persian Gulf. Normally there was a stop in Singapore going one way and a stop in Colombo in Ceylon. You'd have two days' liberty for the crew in each port. I would vary my route along the coast of India, closer to the shore one time and farther east toward the Laccadive Islands. I became familiar with various coastlines and aids to navigation. I thus had a chance to obtain knowledge of that part of the world and transiting the Hormuz Strait into the Persian Gulf. There was a lot of seaborne traffic in and out of the Persian Gulf. The monster tankers did not exist in those days.

It was an ideal opportunity for me to relax and read the classics. I always invited one of the officers to share the evening meal with me. I would always pick up a lot of Scandinavian food in Singapore; from all the Chinese compradors, such as fresh cheese, fresh butter, sardines, kippered herrings, and eggs. One time I went ashore and brought about $50.00 worth of cheese and condiments for my mess. I gave it to my mess attendant. The next day he said, "Oh, Captain, a lot of that cheese was spoiled."

I said, "What do you mean?"

"It was all spoiled." I had to throw it away."

I said, "My God, that's Roquefort," and he was able to retrieve it in time. Fortunately, it hadn't disappeared, but he wasn't going to serve it to me because it was spoiled. You could pick up excellent kinds of smoked fish. I enjoyed a good store of food. I had to pay my own mess bills and so had items not available from the general mess. I had my own galley and mess attendants.

The amazing occurred when returning to the West Coast. I had reported the unsatisfactory condition of my bulk fuel tanks, the excess corrosion, and the deterioration of the cargo pumps—all of which required correction. It was impossible to load clean oil until we had received a satisfactory inspection. Each inspection reported the excess corrosion in Ras Tanura and the reduced capacity of the pumps due to the accumulation of rust.

There was a ship-handling challenge in Ras Tanura when we went alongside. With a load of oil, the draft was 32 feet or more. The ship burned off about a foot returning to Japan with a load. We always loaded as much as we could. By backing away from the pier with a single screw, we threw up lots of sand. There was a hole below the props from many ships backing out. The pilots would remind you, "Remember, there's a hole underneath the propeller with sand behind. If you give too much power trying to get away, there is a reverse action on your rudder from the water coming back against the other side of the rudder through the hole when the ship is close to the bottom." Things like that you learn by talking to pilots. With less power backing down, there was more reliable rudder action.

Paul Stillwell: The Navy was quite a bit undermanned during that period right after the war. Was that a problem for your ship?

Admiral Knoll: It was no problem as long as replenishment of the fleet was not ordered. We didn't have too many. We could have used a few more. In terms of the work required just transporting oil, the crew was adequate. As a point-to-point fuel transport we could function. We never knew when we would get involved with replenishment. As a fleet oiler many more are needed to handle the lines and the refueling hoses.

En route to the West Coast I received a message from Com 12, San Francisco, upon arrival to load black oil, diesel, and gasoline. The gasoline problem hadn't arisen before. I sent for the cargo officer and the exec, and I said, "Do we have a CO_2 smothering system on here? I've never seen it. There are no toggles here on the bridge, and the CO_2 compartment under the bridge is empty. Can we can load gasoline without a CO_2 system?" We searched the ship and found nothing with a smothering system. Normally on a fleet oiler this is one compartment under the bridge with 60 to 100 CO_2 bottles all connected up for smothering an oil or gasoline fire. We checked the regulations and realized we were on the margin of safety of carrying diesel without smothering systems, but in no way could we risk gasoline.

I immediately sent a message to Com 12, information CNO Washington, that *Severn* would be unable to load gasoline because *Severn* had no repeat no CO_2 smothering systems. Apparently there was a commander WAVE handling the fuel desk in Com 12, San Francisco. She told her boss that *Severn* was refusing to carry out her orders and load gasoline. CNO Washington came through and said CNO records indicated *Severn* was a fleet oiler and to carry out Com 12's orders. CNO said checking with the records, the ship had been converted from a fresh water carrier to a fleet oiler in Long Beach, all changes, including the CO_2 smothering system, had been made and paid for at the Long Beach Naval Shipyard.

I answered with a message and requested that prior to loading the gasoline that a representative of the Bureau of Ships or Long Beach yard or San Francisco should come aboard and confirm that I did not have the CO_2 smothering necessary to carry gasoline in accordance with the regulations of the Bureau of Mines. *Severn* was diverted from San Francisco to San Pedro to be investigated by the Long Beach Naval Shipyard that had converted the ship to fleet oiler. Messages were exchanged in essence calling me a liar and questioning my refusal to carry out orders. CNO and Com 12 were very annoyed and convinced that *Severn* did have CO_2.

I arrived and dropped anchor in San Pedro-Long Beach anchorage. A boat was alongside within the hour with representatives from the Long Beach Naval Shipyard, about four officers. I said, "I'm glad to see you here. I'd like you to show me where my CO_2 is. I haven't been able to find it." They were aboard less than a half hour. They had to report that they had inspected *Severn*. They confirmed that *Severn* could not load gasoline until CO_2 smothering was installed. I loaded black oil and diesel and departed for the naval shipyard for extensive overhaul. I arrived at the yard, I visited the commanding officer of the shipyard, and I said, "The work that has to be done on *Severn* will require more than 60 days. Inspect ship and report work needed to make *Severn* a fleet oiler."

The following year I had the CNO desk in Washington that kept records of overhaul, and I was told the turmoil that my messages had caused. *Severn* really hadn't been a part of the operating Navy. It had just been carrying fresh water, which was indispensable for amphibious operations. If the U.S. Armed Forces ever had to operate in the Middle East, fresh water would be needed to keep the Marines ashore in Saudi Arabia.

It was a good experience. My name was known in CNO for refusal, and then for being correct, to the embarrassment of many. I have had a lot of good seagoing experience in battleships and destroyers with ship handling. Out of the blue I became involved with meteorology, intelligence, political-military affairs, and flag secretary. I had not been an active part of the operating Navy. *Severn* was a chance for me to get back into the feel of the ship. Having been on the fleet flagship with some tough skippers, the exec. particularly, on the *Texas*, I knew how a smart ship had to appear. With such background and having a ship of my own, the *Severn*, I wanted to make it a smart ship and reliable as a can-do ship. Maybe I had more ideas from my past experience that helped make the ship what it should be. That's why I went out of my way to fix it up. When I finally arrived on Puget Sound and was unloaded, I carried out the usual processes of preparing to be relieved. One of the first people that arrived in Bremerton was Admiral Callaghan's operations officer.[*]

As I mentioned, Callaghan was the head of the Naval Transportation Service, the forerunner of MSTS in Washington, and had 60-some ships under his command.[†] It included the bulk carriers of the Navy, other than the fleet oilers and cargo ships. Operational administration was controlled in the Pacific via Com 12. In the Far East another office controlled where you went and what you loaded and where you unloaded, i.e., Korea, Philippines, Sasebo, etc. It was a worldwide organization, particularly during the occupation in the Far East. I unloaded black oil in Manila one time, and another time in Pusan, Korea. I had a chance to see or revisit different parts of the Far East, particularly where I had been before World War II.

As I say, the NTS operations officer arrived and said, "*Severn* was the worst ship in the whole NTS operation when you took over, and today, in one year, this is the cleanest and the prettiest ship that NTS now has." This was my record. It didn't do me any harm for future assignment to command, because this command after absence proved I was still a qualified naval officer. It was a pleasure and never a hard task. The crew finally realized it was easier to keep a clean ship in good condition with teamwork. Piecemeal chipping, painting, and touching up take more time. We restored all the storerooms, and you can't imagine the extra boxes and crates that were disposed of when

---

[*] Puget Sound Naval Shipyard, Bremerton, Washington.
[†] MSTS – Military Sea Transportation Service, a part of the Navy that operated ships for support functions. It was created in 1949 in a merger of the Army and Navy transport services. The first commander of the new organization was Callaghan, by then a vice admiral.

we dealt with the commissioning allowance that that had never been uncrated and properly stowed. The equipment we used, and the packing material and crates were disposed of.

Boarding a ship that's been in commission for over two years and the commissioning allowance of deck gear and boatswain's allowance was still in the storerooms. You could see during the war in the battle area, these were busy days for many people who had never been on a ship and knew how to keep things shipshape. *Severn* was in a transition back into the regular Navy. Many people were leaving. One of the previous skippers was a lieutenant commander who had never commanded a Navy ship, never knew how to organize and take care of ship. He was a good operational skipper and kept it out of trouble, didn't run aground. *Severn* had one radar, and all my prior training had been without radar and modern shipboard equipment. The seaman's eye and good ship handling were acquired by practical experience.

Paul Stillwell: That was a learning experience for you.

Admiral Knoll: The interesting thing on *Severn*, if the weather was bad, the entire watch assembled in the pilothouse, including lookouts, who should stay on the wings of the bridge. Coming on the bridge, I asked, "What's the matter? Where are your lookouts?"

The officer of the deck said, "We've got radar to watch, so we have the lookouts out of the weather."

I said, "The radar will not show you everything. You will never hear a whistle in the pilothouse." It was the hardest thing in the world to convince younger officers that when the weather was foggy, they had to have lookouts out and one in the bow with a headphone, listening. There was no provision for such in *Severn*. It was good training and guidance to bring the crew into the regular Navy.

When I arrived in CNO Washington in January 1948, some of the first officers I met were in fleet maintenance. One captain said, "What a guy you are. We had called you all kinds of names when you said you wouldn't load gasoline. Then Long Beach came back and said you were right, and our records were wrong." In BuShips, as well as in fleet maintenance, all said initially that I was a liar until they changed their records showing I was right.

Paul Stillwell: All you had to do was ask them to show it to you.

Admiral Knoll: It helped to establish my service reputation. The whole thing was that I had the facts and stated the facts, but they didn't want to believe me. But can you imagine if I had loaded gasoline and had a casualty? They would have said how dumb I was with no provision for smothering with CO_2.

Upon arrival in Washington my first orders were to CIA. Carl Espe sort of lined me up because of my background and working with Ambassador Harriman.* With my experience in U.S.S.R., it appeared that I was the ideal individual to go to CIA with Captain Frankel and Admiral C. E. Olson.

Rear Admiral Inglis was head of naval intelligence.† Carl Espe, I think, was his deputy. I went over to CIA for about a month and sat there doing nothing all day. I was just reading reports and was not allowed to talk to anybody. I felt I was in "Coventry." I was frustrated in isolation. Admiral Olsen and I would meet for lunch every day at someplace in town and talk over the old days. He knew I was unhappy, but he couldn't do anything about it. He was assigned to another section, and Captain Frankel was on another level, and I couldn't talk to him. Once in a while, he'd come in and talk to me about other intelligence. You could see they were searching around, "Where are we going to put this guy?" Some further clearance would be required and some indoctrination to refrain from talking to one another on almost any topic while in CIA. The CIA ground rules are austere. You can't tell anybody where you're working. It was still in transition state from OSS to CIA after an argument whether a democracy should

---

* Captain Carl F. Espe, USN.
† Rear Admiral Thomas B. Inglis, USN, served as Director of Naval Intelligence from September 1945 to September 1949.

have an official CIA.* I think General Vandenberg was head and then Rear Admiral Hillenkoetter.†

Paul Stillwell: It was set up as the Central Intelligence Group. Sidney Souers was in on that.‡

Admiral Knoll: Right. It so happened that a good friend of mine from Erie was in strategic planning with Rear Admiral Fred Boone. I hadn't seen the friend for quite a few years. We had lunch together, and he said, "I have to get to sea and get a command."

Paul Stillwell: Who was that?

Admiral Knoll: Karl Poehlmann.§ He had a good war record, but he still had to get command of an amphibious ship or similar ship. He said, "With your U.S.S.R. background, I think Admiral Boone ought to get you in strategic planning. Poehlmann was involved with psychological warfare and indirectly with the planning for cover and deception. My work in U.S.S.R. had been associated with some of this planning.

In a matter of days, Admiral Boone sent for me and said, "With your background I need you in OP-30. We need someone who's worked with the Russians and lived in U.S.S.R. Would you like that?"

I said, "I'd be delighted."

Boone said he'd arrange it. The loose relationship between the CIA and naval intelligence was such that Admiral Boone could call BuPers without checking with CIA and ONI and say, "I need Knoll in OP-30." My orders came through in a few days. I

---

* OSS—Office of Strategic Services, formed in World War II to collect and analyze foreign intelligence and to carry out special operations under the control of the Joint Chiefs of Staff.
† Lieutenant General Hoyt S. Vandenberg, USA, served as Director of Central Intelligence from 10 June 1946 to 1 May 1947.
Rear Admiral Roscoe H. Hillenkoetter, USN, served as Director of Central Intelligence from 30 April 1947 to 7 October 1950. On 18 September 1947, as a result of the new National Security Act, the Central Intelligence Agency replaced the previous Central Intelligence Group.
‡ Rear Admiral Sidney W. Souers, USNR, served as Director of Central Intelligence from 23 January 1946 to 10 June 1946.
§ Captain Karl F. Poehlmann, USN.

was transferred, and then CIA and ONI had an argument. CIA said, "What the heck? We got him over here. You're taking him away from us."

CIA called me, and I said, "I haven't done anything in CIA for about a month. I have to do something, or I'm going nuts." Olsen knew I felt this way. I said, "I can do more good in OP-30 than I can in CIA. I can't work with this kind of idea I can't talk to anybody or that I'm going to be under continuous surveillance."

Espe was a little concerned, because at least once or twice in New York I'd been invited to give lectures about working in the Soviet Union. I did it also in London for various discussion groups in the Mayfair area. The British had evening luncheons with 30-40 people, and I would discuss the highlights of my U.S.S.R. experience, that U.S.S.R. was never a true ally and to show how Soviets did business. There were many questions, and it was pleasant to have this dialogue. It so happened that I got into a similar discussion with a group at Greenwich Village, New York City, about the United Nations the first month I was in New York. I had an excellent discussion with a fine group. The question came up, "The Soviets do not have the atomic bomb now. How soon will the Soviets have the atomic bomb?"

I said, "Recognizing the Soviets, if they want it bad enough, they have the type of scientific and technical specialists, engineers, and physicists, once they give priority to a project they will have it. I don't think we can retain any monopoly on the atomic bomb just because we have it now. The fact we have one, they know it can be done, and they will have one soon. That's part of international contemporary development of science. There's no way we can deny this to them." Within 48 hours, the FBI, ONI, and Army counterintelligence were on top of me. I violated so-and-so. I said, "What did I violate?"

"You're not supposed to talk about the atomic bomb."

I said, "Where is it in writing? No one told me."

That was when Admiral Espe said to me, "Don't talk too much."

I said, "I didn't talk. I answered a question." And I got the headlines. There was some U.S. policy not to talk about the atomic bomb.[*] I have never seen it in writing. Bernard Baruch set up his own office in the Empire State Building, at his own expense, to

---

[*] The Soviets first successfully exploded an atomic bomb on 29 August 1949 at a test site in Kazakhstan.

negotiate a United Nations atomic agreement with the Soviets.* They met occasionally for about two years. Baruch was a great individual and was determined that he was going to work out an understanding between U.S. and U.S.S.R. how to control the atomic matters for the future.

I knew that, if I was at CIA, I wouldn't be able to talk about U.S.S.R. at home or otherwise, because CIA said I'd be having access to what CIA was doing. I didn't feel that I was ready for that kind of work. Getting into psychological warfare and cover and deception planning was wonderful because it was in an area where I had made some contribution working with the plans for the defeat of Germany and Japan. It worked out very nicely for about four years. I was there with Bob Campbell and worked on plans and annexes of the Navy and Joint Chiefs plans. I went to frequent meetings of committees of the Joint Chiefs of Staff planning groups.

A coordinating committee composed of the FBI, CIA, State, Army, Navy, and Air Force was established to discuss various international projects relating at times what should be said on the Voice of America.† We analyzed agencies like ONI (Norden broadcasts) and how it operated during the war.‡ There was general agreement that the Voice of America should be the same as the BBC.§ BBC gives a statement of facts with no coloring and has a reputation for accuracy. The present administration of the Voice of America has changed that. Many people with years of experience have left Voice of America because they don't believe in using it as a propaganda weapon.

Over the years, like the Norden broadcasts during the war, the Voice of America had a reputation for accuracy. Norden told the German submarine crews which of their homes had been damaged by bombing in a city where they lived and identified the sub they were aboard and other accurate data. With that kind of accurate information, the Germans wanted to listen to the Norden broadcast every night. It was an effective and ingenious way in which it was handled. The Voice of America tried to have the same

---
* Bernard M. Baruch (1870-1965) was an American financier, statesman, and presidential adviser.
† Voice of America is a radio broadcast to project U.S. information and viewpoints in dozens of languages. It began in 1942 as part of the Office of War Information, was under the State Department from 1945 to 1953, and since 1953 has been under the auspices of the U.S. Information Agency.
‡ During World War II an individual with the pseudonym "Commander Robert Norden" made propaganda radio broadcasts aimed at German U-boat crews. The actual broadcaster was Lieutenant Commander Ralph G. Albrecht, USNR.
§ BBC – British Broadcasting Corporation.

approach. A couple of committees visited New York and observed how they handled the Voice of America broadcasts in various languages.

Planning manuals and guidance were developed for psychological warfare. There were some successful operations with the broadcast in Europe. I was also Navy advisor with the 10/2 group of CIA and accompanied Vice Admiral Rip Struble to policy meetings of a highly classified nature.* There were discussion and review of U.S. resources worldwide for covert operations.

Paul Stillwell: What are some examples of these things that you were thinking about as possibilities?

Admiral Knoll: An idea that Drew Pearson finally exposed was releasing balloons with propaganda messages that the wind would carry to the Soviet Union and Eastern Europe.†

Arrangements were made to interfere with various Communist speakers that came to Washington and attracted large crowds. Electric power and telephone service were cut off to buildings that were scheduled to have a speaker. At another event a drum and bugle band of Boy Scouts started practicing in the same building at the same time as the speaker was due to talk in an adjoining room. The speaker was unable to be heard, and the audience departed. At another event Adamsite dust from chemical warfare was spread over the aisle. The audience walked on this dust, became nauseated, and could stay to hear the talk. The perpetrators were never revealed.

Cardinal Spellman, with help in New York, developed a colored pamphlet to ridicule Communists and illustrated with cartoons how Communists operate. A few thousand were printed and distributed to various five-and-tens and novelty stores in Washington, D.C., to sell. They sold very well, and suddenly the stores were intimidated and forced to return to the news service. It was about the time of Joe McCarthy's Senate debate.‡ The magazine distributing center in Washington was at a loss. The exposé by

---

* Vice Admiral Arthur D. Struble, USN, served 1948-50 as Deputy Chief of Naval Operations (Operations), OP-03. His oral history is in the Naval Institute collection.
† Andrew Pearson was a muckraking syndicated newspaper columnist.
‡ As a U.S. senator from Wisconsin in the early 1950s, Joseph R. McCarthy went on an anti-Communist witch-hunt that came to be dubbed by the pejorative term "McCarthyism." The Senate eventually censured him.

cartoons ridiculed Communism, it was so factual and convincing. The distributor was visited and asked, "How many booklets do you have that have been returned?" They cost about 25 cents. He had a few thousand. He was asked, "How much are they worth?"

He said, "I'm going to have to throw them in the trash. Everybody is sending them back, 100 here and 100 there. I can't sell them."

He was told, "Okay, we'll give you so much for the lot of them." It was a very small sum.

"That's fine." An organization arranged to distribute them to various churches in Washington the next Sunday and created a favorable reaction.

It was a period when a series of speakers favorable to Communism visited Washington. The group would meet about once a week.

The State-Army-Navy Coordinating Committee consisted of people from the State Department and the services and had experience working in U.S.S.R. A study was developed over a period of weeks—what the United States should do when Stalin died. All the implications were analyses and the reaction to be expected in U.S.A. and U.S.S.R. There was good preliminary thinking what to do when Stalin died. No one retained a copy. The study was left with the State Department. I didn't attempt to keep a copy because it was a closely held document. There was advantage in having such thinking for an event certain to occur.

It was about four or five years later I received a call from the State Department. They said, "You worked on a study of what we should do when Stalin died. Do you have a copy of it?" They couldn't find it.*

Paul Stillwell: All that for naught?

Admiral Knoll: It showed good advanced thinking. It was an ideal way to anticipate psychological warfare themes for Voice of America with a coordinated national approach. I was busy attending a lot of different meetings. I was in strategic planning, OP-30, for about four years. In 1948 I purchased a house in Chevy Chase and had a chance to be with my wife in our home—the first time since our marriage in 1940.

---

* Joseph Stalin died on 5 March 1953.

Paul Stillwell: That was a pretty long tour of duty.

Admiral Knoll: It was longer than normal. I advanced from lesser offices in strategic planning and became OP-301, joint and Navy plans. I was 301G, initially, psycho warfare. And who was deputy? Rear Admiral Don Felt, who had been with me in Moscow for a year. And who was the boss, Rear Admiral Arleigh Burke after Boone. Burke was 30, Don Felt was 30B, and I was 301. I handled all the plans and papers relating to joint planning for Arleigh Burke, who attended regular JCS meetings with Admiral Struble or OP-03. I attended all the preliminary meetings, developing (1) the capabilities plan; (2) the requirements plan; and (3) the long-range strategic estimate. I would always go with Don Felt. We were the only people at JCS planning meetings with the Marines, the Army, and Air Force who had worked in the Soviet Union. Most of the planners possessed an erroneous concept of the Soviet Union when they had never been there. Admiral Felt and I made special efforts to explain the real strengths and weaknesses of the U.S.S.R.

Paul Stillwell: What about Burke? What kind of a fellow was he to work for?

Admiral Knoll: He's a terrific individual, and the most capable officer with whom I've been privileged to work. He had known my reputation and seen Admiral Hart's report on me when Burke was the secretary of the General Board with Admiral Hart. Admiral Hart was in Washington and Burke's boss the first time I met Arleigh. We would frequently meet in the Pentagon parking lot about 7:00 o'clock in the morning and walk in together to his office and mine. Before I worked with him in OP-30, we had a good relationship. At the time Arleigh Burke was coming up for promotion to rear admiral. I think the first time I met Arleigh he was a captain. Of a sudden word came from the White House that President Truman had taken Arleigh's name off the promotion list for rear admiral.* The next morning I met him as usual, and I said, "Captain, this is wrong. Something has to

---

* Admiral Knoll's memory had it backward. Burke's name was taken off the promotion list by Secretary of the Navy Francis Matthews. President Truman restored Burke to the list at the behest of his presidential naval aide, Captain Robert L. Dennison, USN, a Naval Academy classmate of Burke.

happen. It can't be this way." Burke had a superb war record as a combatant in the forward area.

Any time something occurred while he was OP-30 and later when he was CNO, I'd go in for a few seconds and check with him. His aide was my first cousin, Commander Tom Weschler, nine years junior to me. I'd say, "I'd like to see Arleigh for a minute." I'd never waste his time, but I'd go in and tell him what he wanted to hear. I tried to be present when he gave a talk or made a presentation. After the event, I'd go in and say, "Admiral, you'd probably like to know the reaction of the audience. I'm not criticizing. I know you want to know."

He said, "That's the kind of information I need."

Paul Stillwell: When you were in strategic planning, what are your recollections of Admiral Struble?

Admiral Knoll: He was a wonderful and capable officer. Vice Admiral Struble relieved Vice Admiral Gardner as OP-03 about a year after I joined OP-30.[*] I had met Struble off and on. I knew he had an excellent service reputation. He was an understanding planner and had good relations with the service planners. Matt Gardner was again a jewel and managed all conferences impressively. He listened to a whole discussion and guided all the meetings smoothly. Like Admiral Hart or Admiral Turner, he said, "Now we've heard all the words. What is the meat of the coconut? Let's get back to basics." Having worked with these excellent officers, you learn how to solve problems.

CNOs I worked for were Admiral Denfeld and Admiral Bill Fechteler and Admiral Mick Carney.[†] Carney was really one of a kind, the CNO ahead of Arleigh Burke. Mick Carney later told more than one acquaintance that I was qualified to be CNO.

---

[*] Vice Admiral Matthias B. Gardner, USN.
[†] Admiral Louis E. Denfeld, USN, served as Chief of Naval Operations from 15 December 1947 to 2 November 1949. Admiral William M. Fechteler, USN, served as Chief of Naval Operations from 16 August 1951 to 17 August 1953. Admiral Robert B. Carney, USN, served as Chief of Naval Operations from 17 August 1953 to 17 August 1955.

Rip Struble was Commander Seventh Fleet some years before I was there with Vice Admiral Mel Pride as chief of staff.* Pride had a stature like Admiral Hart, but he didn't have all the characteristics of Admiral Hart. He was more friendly. After Admiral Struble retired, I met him around Washington at various alumni parties. His first wife died, and he married the widow of his classmate whose family operated the Tabasco sauce industry in Louisiana. I think Struble died recently.† He was a smart, friendly man to work with. It is good to work with people that are looking for realistic solutions. They know what they want and provide solutions in as few words as possible.

Paul Stillwell: How about Fred Boone?

Admiral Knoll: He was very quiet, very convincing operator, and an effective planner. It was a pleasure to work with him. He never inspired the confidence that I had in working with Arleigh Burke, Bob Dennison, and Slim Ingersoll. I always had the best of relations with him. I never got to know and work with him as I did with those other three. Boone was the one that brought me into the strategic planning business. He said, "We need you," and I apparently satisfied him. Any time I met with him, he was always very friendly and interested in my proposals. I was younger then. I became more involved with other planners. I enjoyed the work, particularly strategic planning with the committees of the Joint Chiefs. The work provided broad experience for my future.

Paul Stillwell: What changes did it bring for you in strategic planning when the Korean War started?‡

Admiral Knoll: There was a general understanding that U.S. policy was not to intervene. The quick change in policy fooled the U.S.S.R. and the United States. The U.S. had announced to the world initially that Korea was not an area of vital interest. General

---
* Vice Admiral Arthur D. Struble, USN, served as Commander Seventh Fleet from 19 May 1950 to 28 March 1951.
† Struble died 1 May 1983.
‡ The Korean War began on 25 June 1950, when six North Korean infantry division and three border constabulary brigades invaded South Korea. The troops were supported by approximately 100 Russian-made T-34 tanks. In New York that same day the United Nations Security Council adopted a resolution condemning the invasion.

MacArthur had to go over and initiate a prompt action without advance planning in Washington and the Far East. Everything moved very fast, and I was not involved. The President really announced that we were not going to intercede in Korea, you see.

Paul Stillwell: I thought it was Acheson, the Secretary of State, who said it was outside the defensive perimeter.*

Admiral Knoll: It was an administration announcement. You're right. I always believed that Gromyko could not believe it, and had assured U.S.S.R. that U.S.A. would not interfere. Gromyko, with long years of experience, was an authority on U.S.A. and its policies. Then, all of a sudden, the United States joined an assembled United Nations military force for Korea. Gromyko never even showed up for the meeting. Being present at the Security Council he could have vetoed the U.N. force. The U.S.S.R. rep will never be absent from a Security Council meeting. Gromyko undoubtedly was at home waiting for guidance from the Kremlin, where things are never resolved rapidly. The Soviets will always remember General MacArthur's success at Inchon and the first and only United Nations force to preserve the peace.† It doesn't matter what we say today. We never know what might happen overnight because the U.S.A. does not have a long-range policy for most of the major critical world problems. As the U.S.A. matures, we will eventually realize that realistic long-range policy provides emergency guidance while new courses of action are determined to meet contingencies.

Paul Stillwell: When you were in that job, was there any relationship between strategic planning, the office, and the CIA under Hillenkoetter?

Admiral Knoll: No, that was all handled through ONI. OpNav received regular morning briefings every day from ONI. Interesting, when I was part of this affair, particularly

---

* On 12 January 1950 Secretary of State Dean Acheson made a speech at the National Press Club in Washington and talked of a U.S. "defense perimeter" that defined national interests. He did not identify Korea as being within that perimeter. When North Korea attacked South Korea in June 1950, Acheson urged President Truman that the United States should go to the defense of South Korea, which it did.
† On 15 September 1950, U.S. troops under the command of General of the Army Douglas MacArthur made an amphibious landing at Inchon, the port for Seoul, South Korea. The surprise landing, 150 miles behind enemy lines, temporarily turned the tide of war in favor of United Nations forces.

when Admiral Fechteler was CNO, and I was special liaison with CIA, when certain questions would arise about an operation, Admiral Fechteler would say, "Captain Knoll, am I supposed to know anything about this?"

I'd say, "No, sir."

"Okay." And Mick Carney would say the same thing. There were certain developments and operations concerning which I was knowledgeable, and the CNO was wise enough to realize that he did not need to know. They had suspicions and were content that someone in OpNav would tell them when CNO should know.

Paul Stillwell: I would think that intelligence would be an important part of their work.

Admiral Knoll: I know, but my work was a special field involved with different clandestine psychological warfare operations, which were really outside of intelligence. The few people who knew, the better. At times intelligence didn't like some of the things that occurred. They didn't know about covert plans and weren't supposed to know about them.

Paul Stillwell: Did you have any dealings with Admiral Hillenkoetter yourself?

Admiral Knoll: No, not with Hillenkoetter. Later on I had a good relationship with Allen Dulles when he headed the CIA, because I attended some meetings with him and Frank Wisner on some special projects.* The scary thing today is that we openly talk about covert operations, which is a national disgrace. A sovereign nation does not conduct covert operations; it doesn't talk about them. The one time that the Free World was stunned was when President Eisenhower admitted the U-2 flight was a covert operation and would not use the cover story. This British, French, and Norwegians almost lost their minds, because in recent years no nation ever admitted that they were conducting a covert

---

* Allen W. Dulles served as Director of Central Intelligence/Director of the Central Intelligence Agency from 26 February 1953 to 29 November 1961. Frank G. Wisner was head of the plans directorate in the CIA in the 1950s; he retired in 1962.

operation. President Eisenhower admitted the truth, and he quickly canceled his scheduled meeting with Khrushchev in Paris.*

Today U.S. political leaders talk about covert operations like it's just another military operation. I was involved in planning certain things during the Korean War. We never did one thing to violate, really, international law like mining territorial waters and assassinations. That's terrorism. We did have planes to do ferret raids over Communist China, and we made sure there wasn't one item in each plane that had been made in the United States. There was no way to attribute operations to U.S.A. The pilot was a foreigner, the plane was foreign, because covert operations must be infrequent and in such a way that the people conducting them cannot be identified. That's a covert operation. When more than two people know about it, it's hard to keep it covert. Today the CIA must brief Congress ahead of time. How can anything be covert if you have to brief Congress ahead of time? I mean, the term is no longer meaningful.

The British are still adhering to it. In Britain no one knows who is MI-5 or MI-6, and covert operations are never mentioned. In the past I've had meetings with both of them when they visited Washington. They'd come to Washington and the only people in Britain who know who they are do so on a need-to-know basis—the Prime Minister and the Secretary of Defense and a few others. That's the way it should be. If part of our CIA would continue to operate that way, we wouldn't get involved in unnecessary compromising of sensitive information. You have to analyze at time all courses of action and reaction, but that doesn't say you're planning to do it.

We knew during the Korean War, when I was in psychological warfare, there were complaints that too much of the official communications from the mainland of China was going via cable to Manchuria, the forces in Northern Korea. There was an old marine cable between Shantung and Manchuria. We had a covert operation to install diesel engines in the old reliable Chinese fishing junks. Some had worked for Mary

---

* On 5 May 1960 Soviet Premier Nikita Khrushchev announced that Soviet forces had shot down a high-flying American U-2 reconnaissance plane on 1 May near the city of Sverdlovsk in the Ural Mountains. The American pilot, Francis Gary Powers, was tried for espionage and sentenced to ten years' confinement. He was later returned to the United States in exchange for a Soviet spy. On 16 May, 1960, because the United States refused to apologize for the overflight of Soviet territory, the Soviets cancelled their planned participation in a multinational summit conference and withdrew a previous invitation for President Eisenhower to visit the Soviet Union. Eisenhower initially denied the flight's intelligence mission but then admitted to it after the Soviets displayed wreckage from the downed plane and the pilot.

Miles during World War II with SACO. Fishing junks would come into the port of Inchon, and U.S.A. installed a diesel engine in the hulls of some Chinese junks so they'd have additional power besides sail to go out and do fishing. They would collect excellent intelligence about happenings in North Korea. I guess about 20 or 25 of these Chinese junks operated in part of the East China Sea and up towards the Shantung Peninsula. They could cruise around at sea but never use the engines in port. Their intelligence work was never detected.

Paul Stillwell: What year was this?

Admiral Knoll: During the Korean War—I guess it was '51-'52. Word was sent there to arrange for a couple of these junks to go out and locate the undersea marine cable that extended from Shantung to the vicinity of Port Arthur in Manchuria. With grapples Chinese junks picked up the cable and cut out six feet of it. NSA people in radio intercept services were waiting, because they knew the traffic they were missing was going in clear by this cable.* All of a sudden in a couple of days there was an increase of traffic by radio, because the junks had apparently cut the cable. They had to have communications over there, and cable was no longer possible.

It was a couple of years later, when I was in OpNav in Washington, someone came to me and said, "We have a funny message from some junks in China. They've got eight feet of undersea cable they saved, and they want to know what to do with it." I was asked, "Do you know anything about it?"

I said, "Well, I don't know how you got my name. Tell them to sell it for junk." These are the little things in which I became involved in. For example, I was working with psychological warfare and the CIA arranging some Voice of America broadcasts. I had arranged with the Coast Guard to place a cutter in the Aegean Sea and so some Voice

---

* NSA--National Security Agency, the primary U.S. organization in the field of communications intelligence.

of America broadcasting that the CIA wanted done. It was very successful.[*] I talked with Admiral Duncan in that period.[†]

Paul Stillwell: What do you remember about Duncan?

Admiral Knoll: I always had a lot of admiration for him. He was a cool, calm, collected but smart individual. He called me one day, when I was in OpNav, and he said, "Knoll, I know what you're doing, but I want to tell you a little secret. You know, the Coast Guard does not have enough operating ships and funds to do all the jobs they're supposed to do. They don't get enough operating funds from Congress. When you help CIA and contact the Commandant of the Coast Guard for a job like this, it gives the impression the Navy condones it. We have to give them additional support to meet contingencies. The next time anything like this happens, come and tell me. I'm not criticizing. I know what you're doing. I'm all for it, but I want you to realize we're the hidden augmentation of the Coast Guard to make sure they do the things that are supposed to be done, whether it's within their appropriation or not." He was that kind of man. He was low key but very intelligent and very effective, terrific man at paperwork, worked hard, and he knew where all the bodies were buried. He's the same kind of a man as Admiral Burke had around him as VCNO, Admiral Jim Russell.[‡]

Then, in 1952, I went to sea for a year in an amphibious transport, APA, the *Menard*, during the Korean War.[§]

Paul Stillwell: That was quite a change from OpNav, wasn't it?

---

[*] On 15 February 1952 the Coast Guard commissioned a former cargo ship as the cutter *Courier* (WAGR-410). In a joint project with the State Department, her role was to serve as a radio relay ship so that Voice of America broadcasts could be heard in Communist countries behind the Iron Curtain.
[†] Admiral Donald B. Duncan, USN, served as Vice Chief of Naval Operations from 10 August 1951 to 1 September 1956. His oral history is in the Columbia University collection.
[‡] Admiral James S. Russell, USN, served as Vice Chief of Naval Operations from 1 August 1958 to 1 November 1961. His oral history is in the Naval Institute collection.
[§] Captain Knoll served from April 1952 to December 1952 as commanding officer of the attack transport *Menard* (APA-201). She was *Haskell*-class attack transport that was commissioned 31 October 1944. She displaced 6,720 tons, was 455 feet long, 62 feet in the beam, had a maximum draft of 28 feet, and a top speed of 17 knots. She was armed with one 5-inch gun, smaller antiaircraft guns, and carried a variety of landing craft for amphibious warfare operations.

Admiral Knoll: Well, they knew I had to have another Navy command on my record. Once I had the command of an amphibious ship for less than a year, I was ordered back to strategic planning in OpNav.

Paul Stillwell: So that was sort of a ticket-punching operation?

Admiral Knoll: They told me, "You have to get command of a big ship, another command on your record." Arleigh Burke and Bob Dennison both said, "Go out to Korea, and you'll be back in OpNav in a year," which I did.[*] I had about six months in the Far East and had a chance to visit various harbors in Japan and Korea. I even visited Hong Kong, and that surprised me. I anchored in Hong Kong for recreation for the crew. Within a half hour, three Chinamen came aboard to see me. One of them was an old friend, T. Y. Lee, who sold me merchandise in Tsingtao that came from Peking. They wanted to know if I had some of the old snuff bottles that were sold to my wife. They were ready to buy them back at a big price. The other two wanted to know if I had any special operations for them to do, and I said, "I don't know what you're talking about."

They said, "You have conducted intelligence in the past. Anything special we can do?" They practically said, "You want anybody assassinated or anything done? Two hundred dollars."

I said, "I don't know what you're talking about."

"You've been in China before. We know your record out here." Some way or other, they'd been tipped off that I'd worked for CIA. At that time, I remember, I was ashore for a cocktail party in one of the high-rise apartments. The new high-rise apartments were built to amortize investment in six years. It was a beautiful party. I forget who gave it. And who came walking in but Allen Dulles, then head of the CIA?[†] He was out there on a trip. We had met before, and we had an interesting exchange on various topics. He was so much different from his brother, John Foster. Allen Dulles was great. He was a real can-do intelligence guy, and he had delivered with a great ob in Europe during World War II. He did a lot for the CIA while he was in charge. He kept

---

[*] Rear Admiral Robert L. Dennison, USN, was then President Truman's naval aide.
[†] Dulles did not become director of the Central Intelligence Agency until the following year.

good control over covert operations, assisted by Frank Wisner. Wisner, with too much worry on his mind, finally shot himself.* I don't know who's heading it up now. Wisner was capable and very dedicated. He needed assistance at times, and I helped him.

Paul Stillwell: Did the *Menard* get to Korea while you were in command?

Admiral Knoll: Yes, I joined *Menard* in San Diego and went to Korea. I had Marines aboard, and we did feint landings on the west coast of Korea, around the offshore northern islands. The North Koreans never knew if the troops were going to actually land. We put all our 25 boats in the water and maneuvered to do a practice landing on one of the islands. When Jocko Clark was there with his flag in the *Iowa*, there were eight amphibious transports, 25 boats each, about 200 boats were in the water, and a feint assault in around Wonsan was conducted.† All the landing craft headed for the beach; when about two miles from shore all craft turned and returned to the ships. On one such operation, shots from shore guns were fired with no damage to the landing craft.

Paul Stillwell: Wonsan is on the east coast of Korea.

Admiral Knoll: Yes. *Menard* also worked out of Inchon and anchored in the river where the tides are 35 feet. It was a scary experience, nothing like it in your life.

At this time extra barges were anchored alongside the hospital ships so helicopters could deliver injured day or night directly from the front lines. Landing platforms were added to all hospital ships, and the prompt evacuation of injured to hospital ships via helo was perfected later in Vietnam.

Later *Menard* went to Hong Kong for recreation. *Menard* operated out of Sasebo a couple of times, and also Yokosuka. I developed contacts in Sasebo that were very helpful later when I was with the Seventh Fleet. I visited old Admiral Togo's private summer home on a mountain above Sasebo. There we'd have luncheons and cocktail parties for the officers of the Seventh Fleet. *Menard* conducted practice landings at Otaru

---

* After spending time in a mental hospital, Wisner retired from the CIA in 1962 and killed himself in 1965.
† Vice Admiral Joseph J. Clark, USN, served as Commander Seventh Fleet from 10 May 1952 to 1 December 1953.

on the west coast of Hokkaido and cruised through the Tsugaru Strait. We visited Pohang-dung north of Pusan and also Pusan itself. *Menard* made various short visits in various ports. For example, we went to Kobe and the Inland Sea through Shimonoseki Strait.

Every time a Navy ship would return from Korea for rest and recreation or overhaul at the Yokosuka Navy Yard, within about 48 hours a task for the Navy would come from MacArthur's staff for special operations.* The Army was obsessed with the idea that if a ship was in port, it was idle and had nothing to do. They completely ignored the need for upkeep of boilers or recreation. I think Admiral Briscoe was with General MacArthur, and Captain Benny Decker was at Yokosuka before Vice Admiral Bill Callaghan.† The Navy finally convinced Army personnel around MacArthur's staff, "Just because a Navy ship is in port doesn't mean it is lacking necessary work.

One time *Menard* got under way and went up to Sendai for a couple of days' recreation during the rice harvest, rather than remain at anchor in Yokosuka. *Menard* transited Tsugaru Strait between Honshu and Hokkaido at night with a ship that couldn't go faster than about 16 knots. With the tidal current, *Menard* went through that strait making 22 knots. You couldn't believe it. It's very deep. The Japs have dug a tunnel under Tsugaru Strait so bullet trains can go to Sapporo, which is not far from Otaru on the west coast of Hokkaido.

Paul Stillwell: In the *Menard* she was underpowered and single screw. What problems did that cause for you?

Admiral Knoll: It didn't have the power, and the main thing is with a single-screw ship you can go almost anywhere you want as long as you keep going ahead. When you start backing down, you better be ready for erratic control. I quickly learned that when going

---

* General of the Army Douglas MacArthur, USA, commanded Allied occupation forces in Japan from 1945 to 1951. He had been relieved from that job by the time Knoll commanded the *Menard*.
† Vice Admiral Robert P. Briscoe, USN, served as Commander U.S. Naval Forces Far East from 4 June 1952 to 2 April 1954. Vice Admiral William M. Callaghan, USN, served as Commander U.S. Naval Forces Far East from 2 April 1954 to 14 September 1956.
Captain Benton W. "Benny" Decker, USN, served as Commander Fleet Activities Yokosuka from April 1946 to June 1950. "Fleet activities" is a euphemism for naval base, to avoid offending the Japanese. The on-base Benny Decker Theater is named in his honor.

alongside a dock, I always made sure I dropped an outboard anchor. The anchor helped the bow of the ship keep clear of the dock as you left. It improved control going in and kept the ship off the dock when leaving. You could spring a ship away from the dock with a line or anchor a lot better than a deep-draft fleet oiler or the cruiser *Roanoke*, which was very long.

Paul Stillwell: Did you get any school or special indoctrination in amphibious warfare before you took command?

Admiral Knoll: Yes, we went through the amphibious school for about a month at Coronado before we left.

Paul Stillwell: So this was new to you.

Admiral Knoll: Well, that part, yes, but it was amazing, once you went through, the most important thing was handling those landing craft and getting them in the water fast enough. Then training the troops so they stayed close to the net when they descended to the boats. If they stayed far away from the net, they couldn't pull themselves back with a heavy backpack. It was an interesting operation and good experience with timing and teamwork. Two heavy LCMs back with the heavy booms were another problem.[*]

I'll never forget the economy of manpower and the cheapness of labor in Japan. I was in Yokosuka and getting ready to go to Korea. I wanted to have my booms checked before going out for the feint operation off Wonsan. I waited for two or three days for the booms to be checked. I finally said to the cargo officer, "Find out when it is going to happen."

He replied, "They'll be out this afternoon."

Of a sudden, I saw a small tug and barge with one man running the tug and the other man on the barge, approaching *Menard*. They came alongside. On the barge were the various heavy weights. They came aboard, rigged the different weights on each

---

[*] LCM – landing craft mechanized, a type of craft equipped with a bow ramp that can be lowered on a beach during an amphibious landing.

boom, lifting them up, carrying out tests, and the one man would take out his stamping equipment and stamp each boom they'd checked on, given a date. They completed all the tests in about two hours, two men. In a Navy yard in the United Sates the same job would take about 18 people. You'd have to have riggers for one thing, crews for the tug and barge, and other laborers. Here two people did the whole job. The Korean War was the best thing that ever happened for Japan. We purchased everything possible that could be made out in Japan, canisters for bombs and other military needs. Labor costs compared to U.S.A. were about 14 to 1.

When I was with Seventh Fleet, the Congress started clamping down because of labor union pressure, because every excuse was used when any ship that was due to deploy to the Far East delayed the scheduled docking in the United States, and the Navy would dock the ship when it arrived in Yokosuka. The dry dock at Yokosuka was ideal. We had to certify that every dry-docking was an emergency docking to convince Congress that we weren't taking advantage of Japanese cheap docking and denying that work to American labor. We had to be very careful on that, in spite of the taxpayers' dollars we could save.

With Korea the Navy wanted the Japs to put the machine shops in Yokosuka and Sasebo in full operation. Many key components of each machine were missing. The word went out for all people that used to work in Navy yard shops to apply for jobs. You know what happened? When foremen arrived there and they went to each piece of machinery with jacks, jacked up the bedplate, reached in, and brought out the key parts of each machine that had been packed at the end of the war in oil, wrapped in cloth, and been stowed under the base plate of the pedestal of each machine. In a few days all the important machines were ready to operate.

Paul Stillwell: I've talked to a number of officers, contemporaries of yours, who said they commanded an oiler or an amphibious ship, and then got, say, a cruiser, and the cruiser was easier because they had a lot more talent to work with.

Admiral Knoll: I was lucky in many ways to have a capable cargo officer and exec on the *Severn*, as well as the type of people I had to help me on the *Menard*. They knew their business. When the Marines would come back aboard after their different training exercises off Inchon on those islands, they might be gone for a couple of days. When they were coming back, the supply officer was ready with two steaks for every one of the Marines, and they had all they could eat. Morale was good, and it was a happy ship. After Marines got on board, they wanted a hot shower. Little things like that make a difference. Heads of department were interested in trying to keep them content and happy. We balanced the budget but not at the expense of individual comfort. It paid dividends.

Paul Stillwell: Did the Marines and sailors get along pretty well?

Admiral Knoll: Very well. When you have 25 landing craft and had to get them in the water as fast as you could, everyone had to do his job correctly. There were certain advantages of the whole affair that worked out to my advantage. Based upon experience with former inspections and operations, heads of department had provided for all kinds of contingencies during an amphibious operation. For example, for other than the regular ship communication systems, they had proceeded to rig sound-powered telephones that you would quickly rely on to reach any part of the ship. When superiors came aboard for an inspection as to readiness, they pulled different electrical circuits, and we'd quickly pick up sound-powered phones and maintain communications to whom we wanted to talk to. Inspectors hadn't anticipated this backup. The same old deal. When I was in destroyers, inspectors pulled electrical circuits to see your reaction. We had sound-powered telephones for emergencies, and they paid dividends at times. You had about eight of them rigged at strategic places that assured effective control and communications in spite of a casualty.

Paul Stillwell: Did you help set up the liberty schedule for the *Menard* in the Far East, or did the fleet take care of that?

Admiral Knoll: *Menard* set up our own, because most moves were independent. I was part of an amphib group command, and the commodore was very cooperative. He sort of let me run the show. He knew that I had past Far East experience. In fact, at least twice he suggested the ship anchor out and not go through the net and enter the inner harbor of Yokosuka. He said the weather was too bad. I said, "What's the matter, Commodore? It's not bad."

"It's blowing and raining and miserable."

I said, "I have been in a lot worse weather. We'll go inside where it's quiet and we can grant liberty for the crew." A couple of times I'd come in after conning a ship to anchorage with wind and the rain. I'd be wet through all clothing down to my waist, even though I had raincoats and foul-weather gear. When you have the feel of a ship, and net controls at the harbor entrance are ready, there is never any justification to avoid going to the scheduled anchorage.

One time the commodore said, "Well, you're going to take it in all right." He told the other ones if they didn't want to come in, they could anchor outside; however, they followed me in. Later on, everyone said, "Thank God, it's so much quieter in here. Why would we roll our guts out there in the open roadstead just because the weather was bad to come in?

Paul Stillwell: Who was this?

Admiral Knoll: I forget. He sort of left the impression he was over-cautious and did not have much ship-handling experience. I said, "Well, I'm the skipper. I'm going to go in," and I did. I forget his name now. I should remember.

Paul Stillwell: He was the amphibious squadron commander?

Admiral Knoll: No, no, he was the amphibious group commander. He just had a group. Within that group we had an APA, which was mine; and an AKA, which was the cargo ship with a smaller group, and made a couple of tractor groups. At times we had a group that composed LMS, two LSTs, one AKA, and *Menard* (APA) was the flagship. APAs rotated from San Diego to the Far East, while smaller craft remained in the Far East.

Sometimes I'd go up on the bridge to check up when the weather was bad with low visibility. I was going into fog in Pusan, and the officer of the deck would have the lookouts inside the pilothouse. I said, "Wait a second. Why aren't the lookouts out there on the wings of the bridge in the weather?"

"We're watching for targets with radar."

I said, "Now, wait a second. There are certain targets which the radar is not going to pick up, and that's why the lookouts must be outside; in poor visibility they're the eyes of the ship." The younger officer thought being inside out of the weather was showing concern for the health of the lookouts. I wasn't trained that way. There's only one place when you're conning. You get out there in the weather and are alert for any eventuality.

Paul Stillwell: Did you have a very large staff in your ship?

Admiral Knoll: No, no. I think it was some kind of a job with seniority, giving him the satisfaction that he had a seagoing job on his record. In other words, it wasn't a big job. It was the last seagoing job he was going to have, or he wasn't going to command a big ship. There were many people out there putting in time. There were a lot of amphibious ships there in the event the Korean War would escalate into North Korea.

Paul Stillwell: Did the ship have any operations off the West Coast of the United States while you were in command?

Admiral Knoll: No, only a couple of drills after I took command in San Diego before we left. Everything was oriented to train new people for deployment, both my crew as well as the officers in ground school at the amphibious base. They were new to amphibious operations, and the Navy was preparing for any future contingency.

Paul Stillwell: Admiral, right after your service in command of the USS *Menard* you moved back into OpNav in early 1953.

Admiral Knoll: Yes, I was in OP-30 for a second tour. I became OP-301, in charge of Navy plans with OP-30, strategic plans.

When President Eisenhower arrived, he made Admiral Arthur Radford Chairman of the JCS.* John Foster Dulles was his Secretary of State, and Admiral Mick Carney was CNO.† President Eisenhower asked Radford to develop a whole new strategy for the Department of Defense. The ad hoc working group was composed of two members from each service, namely Frank Everest, a colonel from the Air Force; Slim Ingersoll and myself from the Navy; and I forget the two Army people.‡ One was a Marine colonel, and Admiral Radford was the Chairman.

The working group met every day, normally until 6:00 or 7:00 o'clock for about three weeks. Our study was used for preparation of the first budget Eisenhower would send to the Congress, called the "New Look" strategy.§ Every sovereign nation should provide manpower and equipment for its own frontier defense. Similarly, each sovereign nation should not be expected to provide and operate a navy. The more affluent and major nations should provide naval forces. One thing that each nation must have—the willingness, the capability, and the manpower to defend themselves.

Approaching strategy this way, decisions could be made concerning military aid to be given. Frank Everest of the Air Force was excellent. I remember telling him, "I don't like the procedure that's been going on in the Air Force for so many years. Each year we can tell how many wings the Air Force is going to request for next year, because it's a straight-line increase that keeps the aviation industry happy." I showed him that for three or four years it was 29 wings the first year, 31 the next, 34 the next; it plotted on a straight line. Today there is talk of a 600-ship Navy, which has little meaning. It's the type of ships—not the number—and the strategy that they will support. It is the most unrealistic thing to tell the world we're going to build 600 ships. Numbers of ships are

---

* Dwight D. Eisenhower served as President of the United States from 20 January 1953 to 20 January 1961. Admiral Arthur W. Radford, USN, served as Chairman of the Joint Chiefs of Staff from 15 August 1953 to 14 August 1957.
† John Foster Dulles served as Secretary of State from 21 January 1953 to 22 April 1959.
‡ Colonel Frank K. Everest Jr., USAF.
§ An important element of the New Look strategy was the containment of Defense Department costs; it emphasized the role of nuclear weapons, rather than conventional military forces, to deter the Soviet Union from making war.

not the criterion, the same way Air Force wings are not. What type of planes do we need, and how are they going to be used to carry out a strategy?

The study group developed the strategy and forces needed for the current capability plan, namely, what we have today and what we can do to meet any contingency. We proposed what the buildup should be for the next four or five years to improve current capabilities. This is called the requirement plan. With these plans, the Congress can be told, "Now, this money in the budget is for continuing current capabilities. Next the requirement plan identifies the budget to improve our capability for the strategy of the future. Each year the next Congress is told, "Now, we've come this far. This is the next phase." The group determined how many divisions the Army should have, the type of bombers and planes and fighter planes the Air Force should have, the types of combatant ships and support ships the Navy should have. We finally ended up with good agreement among the Air Force, the Army, the Navy, and the Marines concerning balanced armed forces.

Towards the end, Slim Ingersoll and I met each night to brief Mick Carney on our progress. He was terrifically impressed by what we had accomplished and what we were finding out. We made suggestions how the Joint Chiefs could act on our study. It was a large document and keeping informed Carney made it much easier when it came time for the Joint Chiefs to act, and certainly make some changes.

I initiated major paperwork for the group's meetings. Slim knew that after every meeting I'd write up all the minutes for records or draft new papers for the next day's meeting. All drafts were approved by Slim the next day before I put them in the smooth. I'd tell him, "Anything special you want me include?" Slim and I, as Navy reps, were making presentations on various topics and reduced it to writing for discussion as we went from one meeting to the other. The Navy did the most work. We did what you call completed staff work.

Of course, Slim always told me that I was the real negotiator and did all the staff work for the new Look strategy, because there were only eight of us, and we were the only ones that talked. It was a congenial group. We could take down our hair and talk frankly about anything. It showed when selection of these people was done. There was a real effort to have officers with experience in planning. Admiral Carney was always grateful for our briefings that prepared him for action by the Joint Chiefs on the New Look strategy.

Paul Stillwell: Why do you speak so favorably of Admiral Carney's term as CNO?

Admiral Knoll: Admiral Carney as CNO set the pattern that was followed by Admiral Burke when he relieved Carney. Prior to that time, I don't mean to make any derogatory remarks, but neither Admiral Denfeld nor Admiral Fechteler really gave the impression of being knowledgeable about strategic planning. They were BuPers specialists. Mick Carney appreciated such work when he was with Admiral Halsey as his chief of staff.[*] Arleigh Burke had similar experience with Admiral Mitscher.[†] They seemed to talk a different language in testifying before Congress. They talked with a different conviction, and the Congress respected their views.

In that job I was working with Bob Dennison, who had relieved Arleigh Burke.[‡] Dennison said that when the right ship came available, he would ask BuPers to release me. He wanted to make sure it was the right ship, because I didn't just want to take any big command that was available. For a while I hoped to get the *Iowa*, which was BB-61, the same number as AO-61, the *Severn*. At first BuPers called and wanted me to take the *Pittsburgh*, a cruiser. Because I was from Pennsylvania, it would be interesting. I mentioned it to Admiral Dennison, and he said, "I'm not going to release you to go to *Pittsburgh*. They have to come up with something better." I don't know what was taking place behind the scenes. He repeated that I wasn't available unless I got the right ship. I was definitely going to a good command.

When I was released from OpNav, I joined the *Roanoke* (CL-145) in Norfolk.

Paul Stillwell: Why was the *Roanoke* considered a better ship than the *Pittsburgh*?

---

[*] In 1944-45, as a rear admiral, Carney was chief of staff to Admiral William F. Halsey, Jr., USN, Commander Third Fleet.
[†] Vice Admiral Marc A. Mitscher, USN, served as Commander Task Force 58, the fast carrier task force, in 1944-45.
[‡] In 1954 Rear Admiral Robert L. Dennison, USN, who had been on the Asiatic Fleet staff with Knoll in 1941, became director of the Strategic Plans Division of OpNav.

Admiral Knoll: *Pittsburgh* was from World War II. The *Roanoke* was one of the new cruisers with the most modern gunnery installation in the fleet.* The *Roanoke* had received the Atlantic Fleet cruiser prize for a couple of years in a row, and it continued to receive it both times I was on board. In gunnery accuracy the *Roanoke* class was the fleet leader. The *Pittsburgh* at the time was in the Pacific. The cruiser division commander flew his flag in the *Roanoke*. That was Butch Parker, a terrific individual to work for, with a lot of personality and a very good friend.† I had an excellent executive officer and very competent gunnery officer. The gunnery officer had been in *Roanoke* more than two years, and he knew his battery from A to Z.

One of the requirements before the ship left to go to the Sixth Fleet was to have a radio-controlled drone come out for target practice off the Virginia Capes. I talked to the gunnery officer, and he said everything was lined up; the battery was in good condition. He said, "And when we fire, we'll shoot a full broadside. We won't do a spotting-in shot; we'll shoot the drone down. Don't worry about it." Normally, in the old days in battleships, we would fire two spotting-in shots to see how close we were to the target before firing all the guns. There were six twin mounts of 6-inch guns. They could rotate through 360 degrees and fire in an arc of 180 degrees, except when near the masts.

The drone came out at an altitude of 12,000 to 14,000 feet. The drone was in control from another surface ship near us. *Roanoke* opened fire, and the drone flew to pieces on the first salvo. We received complaints from the people who had maintained the drone for more than two years. They hadn't been used since the end of the war, and none had been shot down. It was thrilling to hear the crew cheer, and Butch Parker, an old gunner himself, was elated. We went to the Sixth Fleet with a happy crew.

We had a good cruise. In fact, the cruise with the Sixth Fleet passed all too rapidly.‡ While *Roanoke* was there, it was the first time a large ship of the Sixth Fleet had gone for visits to Barcelona. The carrier *Coral Sea* with Dave McDonald visited at

---

* USS *Roanoke* (CL-145), a *Worcester*-class light cruiser, was commissioned 4 April 1949. She had a full-load displacement of 18,400 tons, was 680 feet long, beam of 71 feet, maximum draft of 26 feet, and top speed of 32 knots. She was armed with twelve 6-inch guns and 24 3-inch guns.
† Rear Admiral Edward N. Parker, USN, Commander Cruiser Division Six.
‡ The *Roanoke* departed Norfolk on 23 March 1955 and made the following port visits: Gibraltar, 2-5 April; Toulon, France, 7-14 April; Naples, Italy, 23-30 April; Barcelona, Spain, 7-13 May; Gibraltar, 14-17 May; return to Norfolk, 26 May.

the same time.* It was a new relationship between Spain and the U.S.A. We were very welcome. It looked very familiar to me, because I had been in there in 1929 for ten days on a midshipmen's cruise. It was good to see the changes and to renew some acquaintances. We had a good time there and a lot of interesting receptions. We spent some time in Naples and also went to the French Navy yard at Toulon for a visit.

I had a unique experience with Butch Parker in Toulon. The French welcomed us and gave a formal dinner party. The French admiral refused to attend and sit at the head table. He resented the fact that the U.S. Navy had fired on the French fleet at Casablanca in World War II when he was in command of a French ship in the harbor. When our crew went ashore, it appeared that the French Navy created many incidents. They caused many of the crew to be put on report by the shore patrol. The result was great alarm at breakfast the next morning. Admiral Parker announced that liberty was canceled for the *Roanoke*'s crew the rest of the time in port. The order came through Parker's chief of staff. It didn't make me very happy. I assembled my exec, personnel officer, and chaplain. We talked it over, and I said, "What should we do about it? I refused to get excited. I was very concerned, because *Roanoke* was my ship, not his. I as skipper was responsible for the conduct of my crew.

About an hour later, after the word got around to the crew about no more liberty, I went to Parker and said, "Admiral, I'd like to talk to you about this cancellation. It's my responsibility if my crews get in trouble ashore, and I'm going to make sure it doesn't happen again. I'm also responsible for the morale of my crew. I ask you to reconsider the order not to give liberty. Let those of the crew go ashore that I know are not going to get in trouble. I'd like you to think it over so I can tell those that are qualified that they may go ashore. I'll talk to the division officers and make certain there isn't anybody on the liberty list that's prone to getting in trouble. We'll have extra people ashore with the buddy system. If anyone starts getting in trouble, they will be returned to the ship. The French are trying to create trouble."

An hour later, he sent for me and said, "Okay, you've made a good argument that you're in charge, and I shouldn't give you an order on how to handle your crew." It worked out very well. We may have had a few more incidents but nothing like the first

---

* Captain David L. McDonald, USN, commanded the aircraft carrier *Coral Sea* (CVA-43) in 1954-55.

day. It almost looked like the French ashore were sympathetic with the admiral's attitude toward the U.S. Navy. The French admiral was giving us Coventry treatment and harassed my crew to make *Roanoke* look bad. It worked out all right. The French in general in Paris and elsewhere have never displayed real friendliness for American tourists.

Paul Stillwell: I bet you were popular with the crew after that.

Admiral Knoll: They heard liberty had been canceled; they knew I went to see the admiral and it was restored. It didn't do any harm.

Paul Stillwell: No, indeed.

Admiral Knoll: I forget, but I think Butch Parker told me about two years later, when I met him at a party in Norfolk, "You know, I made a complete report of the incident and sent it to the Chief of Naval Personnel and the Secretary of the Navy and the JAG's office.[*] A full reply finally came through."
    I said, "What did the reply say?"
    Parker said, "It said the captain was right and the admiral was wrong."

Paul Stillwell: It takes a big man to admit that.

Admiral Knoll: Parker said, "You made a lot of good points. I put it all in my report. I wanted to know for the future." I heard it was rather refreshing.

Paul Stillwell: Do you have any other memories of Parker? Was that before he had the problem with his leg?

Admiral Knoll: Yes. He was having some circulation problem, but he had not yet lost the foot. I've seen him many times since this one thing happened.

---

[*] JAG – Judge Advocate General.

One time we were cruising in formation astern of two carriers, and the *Newport News* was astern of me.* We were steaming about 25 knots, about 5:30 in the afternoon. *Roanoke* was probably 1,000 yards astern of the *Coral Sea*, on its starboard quarter. The destroyer plane guards were on station. We saw the helicopters from Naples delivering mail to the carriers. Within a half hour, the signal went up for the destroyers to come alongside in order to pick up their mail on the starboard side. The first plane guard, the *Lawe*, dashed ahead, and I was sitting on the bridge watching.† It is serious business when a formation is moving that fast with big ships. Well, *Lawe*'s skipper—to this day I don't know if he knew what he did or not—picked up the mail and promptly made a 90-degree right turn directly in front of me, less than 500 yards distant.

I jumped off of my chair, and I said, "Hard left rudder. Stop all engines." As soon as I saw I was clearing the destroyer's stern, I said, "Ahead standard. Hard right rudder." I missed *Lawe* by about 100 feet under his stern. If I hadn't been on the bridge, I don't know what would have happened. In a couple of minutes, there was some word in the voice tube from the flag bridge: "Excellent reaction to an emergency, Captain." Butch Parker was down on the flag bridge and observed the incident. No one ever said another word. No one ever suggested reprimanding the *Lawe* people, who were more anxious for mail than safe navigation at 25 knots.

Paul Stillwell: What was the *Roanoke* like to handle?

Admiral Knoll: Beautiful. *Roanoke* was maneuverable like an automobile. It had a lot of power, it was long, and it had a good draft. Eph McLean relieved Butch when we returned from the Sixth Fleet.‡ *Roanoke* went for fleet operations in the Caribbean.§ We spent a long weekend in Havana as the guests of General Batista and the Cuban Navy.**

---

* USS *Newport News* (CA-148) was a heavy cruiser.
† USS *William C. Lawe* (DD-763).
‡ Rear Admiral Ephraim R. McLean Jr., USN, was Commander Cruiser Division Two from June 1955 to August 1956.
§ With midshipmen on board for training, the *Roanoke* had the following itinerary: Panama Canal Zone, 25-29 July 1955; Havana, Cuba, 5-9 August; Guantánamo Bay, Cuba, 9-26 August; return to Norfolk, 31 August.
** Fulgencio Batista was the dictator and military leader who was President of Cuba from 10 October 1940 to 10 October 1944 and from 10 March 1952 to 1 January 1959. His government was overthrown by rebels under the leadership of Fidel Castro.

They gave parties for us at the Tropicana. They scared the daylights out of us when I rode an official Cuban car with Admiral McLean. On the front seat next to the driver was a man with a machine gun, and in the car behind us was another car with three men with machine guns. Cuba was an armed camp shortly before Batista was deported. No one was taking any chances with U.S. Navy visitors.

Paul Stillwell: Who provided these men with the machine guns?

Admiral Knoll: It was all part of the Cuban Navy security for us and the Cuban CNO, Admiral Calderon. We anchored right over the place where the *Maine* had been sunk, and the *Newport News* was beyond. We would just clear each other as we swung with the tide and the wind.*

Right after that, *Roanoke* went out for the annual inspection towing ships, damage control, and all kinds of tests. I was told to prepare to tow the *Newport News*. I had adjusted the scale on the stadimeter instead reading in hundreds of feet into tens of feet, and I rigged all towing gear on the outside of the lifeline.† The whole towing cable was secured with stoppers for quick release. I adjusted *Roanoke*'s speed to about two knots and passed within 50 feet without touching the *Newport News*, passed the towing shackle over and had *Newport News* in tow without a hitch. Everybody in the crew had done their job, handling a lot of heavy gear that was dangerous.

I had a good first lieutenant. We talked about it all in advance, assigned each task. After an exercise of less than an hour Eph McLean said, "I never saw such an easy way of picking up a tow." The sea was quite good. Using this stadimeter, I knew just how many feet there was between *Roanoke* and the *Newport News*. *Roanoke* promptly responded with orders on the bridge. The stadimeter just told me, and I was within less than 100 feet, where it was easy to hand the lines back and forth and take the tow. *Roanoke* maneuvered beautifully.

---

* USS *Maine* was commissioned 17 September 1895. On the evening of 15 February 1898, while the ship was anchored in Havana, Cuba, she was rocked by internal explosions that destroyed her and contributed to the subsequent Spanish-American War.
† The stadimeter is a mechanical device for measuring the range to another ship when the height of her mast is known.

Newport News was air-conditioned, and *Roanoke* was not. I said, "This is sad. Let's run a test. Without anybody knowing what we are doing, we will have general quarters sounded by signal from the flagship for the *Newport News* and *Roanoke*." This was in the morning after everyone had been sleeping, right after breakfast. General quarters was sounded, and then we determined how many minutes it took for *Newport News* to man its guns and how many minutes it took *Roanoke* to man our guns. It was about eight minutes' difference in the tropical waters. I used this later as an argument why the ships with the messing area and the berthing area air-conditioned have greater readiness and relaxed crews for emergency, due to air-conditioning. When I got to OP-43, the first thing I did was obtain funds for air-conditioning in all messing spaces of every active duty destroyer, based on this analysis. A report was made to OpNav, another example of helping the admiral do a good job and improving the habitability of Navy ships.

Paul Stillwell: The *Newport News* and *Roanoke* were beautiful, impressive-looking ships. What was the reaction of foreigners?

Admiral Knoll: The *Roanoke* was really different. I'll never forget when we came into Gibraltar. The *Worcester*, a sister ship, came in to relieve us as the flagship, and we were due to return to U.S.A. The *Iowa* was docked ahead of us. We were just secured, and about that time there had been a mistake on the *Iowa*; they forgot to deactivate their portable conning gear on the upper level. The bridge level was disconnected, and *Iowa* started to move with all lines secured. The OOD caught it quickly enough, but you could see the *Iowa* move and stop.

An hour later, George Wales came in with the *Worcester*.[*] He and an admiral came aboard, and there were comments back and forth. We were sister ships. Why did the *Worcester* look so drab compared to the *Roanoke*? I know Butch Parker was talking. I forget who the other admiral was. I said, "Well, this is a flagship. We keep it so it looks smart and neat and clean. There's something about it, and this is the difference.

---

[*] Captain George H. Wales, USN, commanded the light cruiser *Worcester* (CL-144) from 3 May 1955 to 10 August 1956.

Roanoke looks smarter than the *Iowa* ahead of us." I said to Butch, "Look at the stanchions, the hand rails, and the chains. Through the whole ship the horizontal hand rails and lines are painted white; the stanchions and verticals are painted gray, which makes it look like a yacht fore and after and up each mast." By the time *Roanoke* left Gibraltar the next day, George Wales's crew were painting the *Worcester* to look like *Roanoke*.

Paul Stillwell: How had theirs been painted?

Admiral Knoll: It was all gray. We just added that extra white paint that made it look like a smart, clean warship.

Paul Stillwell: So there was great emphasis on spit and polish, I take it.

Admiral Knoll: It was the pride of the crew. The knew people said, "You look so neat." A little bit was added to the ship's reputation. It was the smartest-looking ship in the fleet, and it was kept that way by each succeeding commanding officer.

I made an unusual observation in relieving Creed Burlingame, a submariner, as commanding officer.[*] After Creed left, I had to re-indoctrinate practically everybody on the bridge to conform with surface operation. A former submarine commander organized a surface ship like a submarine. On the submarine, the skipper makes every decision, and in combat he is at the periscope. On a surface ship with a large bridge spread, with watch personnel and lookouts widely dispersed, you have to have decentralization of control, and each watch officer or petty officer knows what to do.

I had a standing regulation on *Roanoke* and on other ships that a junior officer who was trying to qualify as officer of the deck could conn the ship under observation. He could ask to be officer of the deck while the ship was replenishing alongside a tanker or supply ship while I was on the bridge supervising the operation. When I was on the bridge, they could ask to take the conn. I said, "The quicker you learn how to handle the

---

[*] Captain Creed C. Burlingame, USN, commanded the light cruiser *Roanoke* (CL-145) from 15 September 1953 to 3 March 1955.

ship and have confidence in your ability and know what to do, the better for the Navy. Keeping station at 125 and 150 feet alongside during replenishment was good experience. Quite a few junior officers took advantage of this and became good ship handlers. They would ask, "Captain can I have an hour trying to keep in position?

I'd say, "Sure, get up there and take turns as OOD."

Heads of department were acting commanding officers in port, and some had never conned a ship. A chief engineer should have some training to conn a ship. I tried this on different ships, but most engineers were not interested. My concern was in an emergency, at an anchorage with a storm when I was not aboard, the senior one on board as acting commanding officer should know what to do to get under way. I tried to anticipate this and have it incorporated in training the heads of department who had the duty, particularly on a weekend. There's no use having a chief engineer on duty on a weekend when an order to get under way would come from the senior officer present.

Paul Stillwell: Do you have any particular memories of the Marine detachment on board your ship?

Admiral Knoll: No, I don't. *Roanoke* had a small detachment, but I don't recall any memorable events. It was a refreshing tour of duty, particularly the final month on the West Coast, with liberty in Panama, San Diego, San Francisco, and Seattle. I had friends in each port come aboard for dinner.

Paul Stillwell: Was she going in the yard for a regular overhaul?

Admiral Knoll: *Roanoke* was scheduled for some overhaul; after a short tour of duty in the Far East it returned for inactivation with the reserve fleet at Bremerton. It was sad to see two excellent gunnery ships inactivated. It was better to keep *Roanoke* and *Worcester* than some of the older ones with substandard gunnery capabilities.

Paul Stillwell: They were not very old at that time.

Admiral Knoll: No, they were commissioned a few years after the end of World War II. They were designed and approved for construction in '37 or '38, and because of the R&D of the advanced gunnery installation, they were not commissioned until 1946-49. Some of the gunnery equipment had been incorporated in the *Atlanta*-class cruisers, which the Japs called "bee hives" due to their antiaircraft performance. *Roanoke* and *Worcester*—at one time there were 14 of them scheduled to be constructed. If they had come out early enough for the war, they would have added greatly with their gunnery. They could cruise up to 32 knots, excellent riding in a sea, and handled beautifully. They were like a big destroyer and much more comfortable ships. *Roanoke* with a high bow was a dry ship and in heavy seas rode like a battleship. It was an excellent design.

Paul Stillwell: What was the mission of the ship in the Sixth Fleet, mainly antiaircraft protection?

Admiral Knoll: It was one of the cruisers with the Sixth Fleet. Two cruisers rotated every six months from Norfolk. A third cruiser was permanently in the Med as fleet flagship. At that time, there were two carriers, and cruisers operated in formation with the carriers. There were different fleet exercises and frequent visits to ports in Spain, Italy, and France. I never got to the Eastern Med while I was there. All our work was in the Western Med. The primary base was Naples, and the fleet flagship was based at Villefranche near Nice. There were no antiaircraft gunnery exercises. The primary task was showing the flag.

Paul Stillwell: You spoke of the time you were operating with the carrier and the *Newport News*. Was that a typical kind of operation?

Admiral Knoll: That was a typical operation, yes. The carriers moved off to launch planes and then rejoined the formation. We didn't always work with carriers. The whole Sixth Fleet would operate together for five or six days, and then individual ships would depart for visits in separate ports.

Paul Stillwell: How much time did you spend in port, as opposed to under way?

Admiral Knoll: I would say in port we were about 20%. We were under way more than in port. We didn't get into port too much while we were over there.

Paul Stillwell: Are there any other ports besides those you mentioned that you got into?

Admiral Knoll: Barcelona, Toulon, Gibraltar, and Naples. Naples was the principal place. The ship had to maneuver around and tie the stern to the pier so your bow was at anchor on an offshore heading. To get under way, release your stern lines and take in the anchor. The ship was under way without tug assistance, and heading to the open sea in a few minutes. It was a little bit of maneuvering with a tug to dock the ship. Once docked, the ship was ready to get under way and head to sea without delay. Naples faces the open Mediterranean—no breakwater or channel to navigate.

Paul Stillwell: Med moor, I think that's called.

Admiral Knoll: I think it's a type of Med moor, yes, which is ideal if a storm comes up. There are unusual winds and weather characteristic of parts of the Med. Cruising along and everything is beautiful, stars in the sky, hardly any breeze, and all of a sudden the ship is going through a line squall with strong winds for a matter of about 20 miles. This is particularly seaward of the Rhone River Valley. It will surprise and scare you if you haven't read the sailing directions.

Paul Stillwell: When you got to be the captain of a ship like that and had your own mess, did you miss the camaraderie you used to have as a junior officer?

Admiral Knoll: No. They were an excellent group on the *Roanoke*. At night under way I generally invited someone to eat with me. I found out what was going on from junior officers, heads of department, or others. I always did this on every ship. Relaxing with the officers and learning their likes and dislikes provided ideal background for preparation of fitness reports.

Paul Stillwell: Did you have a good deal of talent in your wardroom?

Paul Stillwell: Oh, yes. I was very happy with everybody. Everybody knew their job. The ship had an excellent reputation, and that inspired everybody to do a better job. We had one problem that involved the executive officer, chaplain, and a division officer. A black boy was determined to get in trouble no matter what we did to help him. He was ready to insult every officer and start a fight with any enlisted man or Marine. He was sent to the brig for three days and started a fight with the Marine guard. The Marines didn't have any sympathy for him. The black boy came to captain's mast, and a report was made that he was surly and disrespectful.* We reported his attitude to BuPers, hoping he could be released from the service. He wasn't worth the effort. I talked with the chaplain about it. I talked to the senior black chief on board, who was head of the chiefs' mess, to see if I couldn't develop a father-son relationship. Nobody seemed to reach him very much. He had been in one division and got in a fight with the division officer, the chief boatswain, and the boatswain's mate in that division.

I sent for him to come to my cabin and talked to him, tried to find out what was behind all the bad behavior. I finally found out that he had promised to send his mother money every payday and promised to write her often, and he wasn't doing either. He was very uncomfortable the first time that I had him to the cabin. I made him sit down and try to tell me what troubled him. I was convinced that he had been oriented by the NAACP to be obnoxious.† Someone in Detroit wanted him to be a problem child and make hell for everybody. He'd been in the brig on bread and water for a couple of days, and he started getting surly again. I again sent him to the brig for another three days on bread and water and warned the Marines. I said, "Now, listen. I don't want you to harass him.

---

* Captain's mast is a sort of court in which the commanding officer of a unit listens to requests, awards non-judicial punishment, or issues commendations. Most often captain's mast is used for punishment of lesser offenses than those that merit courts-martial

† NAACP – National Association for the Advancement of Colored People.

If you're doing anything wrong with the brig, you can be guilty. This guy needs help, and BuPers initially is not going to let me send him home."

Finally, we had another incident, brought him up to captain's mast, and I understood he was going to say that everybody on board was partial, racist, and the Navy did not want blacks. The crew had no use for him. So I arranged to have present the senior black chief, the chaplain, and a senior petty officer from the engine room who was black. I was ready if the black boy made a charge that *Roanoke* was against colored people on their ship. I said, "Now, you can be just like Joe Louis. You've got a job to do. We respect your race, and you have to respect what we want to do, and we have to work together on this. Now, I'm going to give you one more chance here. If you've got any charges to make against anybody aboard here, we've got witnesses for you to make the charge. Here's Chief So-and-so, and here's So-and-so to hear what you say. What have you got to say?"

When he saw they were there, he didn't make any comment about racism. I said, "Okay, I'm going to transfer you to a new division. I'll give you one more chance." After a few weeks, I would send for him and ask, "How are things going?" He relaxed a little bit and was working satisfactorily for weeks to a month. By the time I left the ship, he was getting along all right. It was a mess, but it was a test of what had to be done, particularly when BuPers refused to accept that he was hopeless. Something was behind it; BuPers didn't want to send this man home. I was convinced that he had been specially indoctrinated to make a tough deal for us.

Paul Stillwell: Did you talk to the crew frequently over the 1MC to tell them what was going to be happening?

Admiral Knoll: Yes. When under way with *Menard* and *Roanoke*, we normally had a prayer over the loudspeaker at noon. In the Far East a member of the crew or the chaplain gave a short prayer at noon when eight bells was struck.

Mary Miles did different things to alert the crew. Without telling anybody where he was going, he would disappear into the handling room of a turret and arrange for a casualty drill to happen.* He would not show up for it, and the OOD would start passing the word for the captain. He would observe how the casualty was handled from the periscope in the turret or some other hiding place. The exec and the officer of the deck took charge and took the necessary steps. It was ideal training.

Miles had naval headquarters in the Canal Zone.† Every afternoon about 6:00 o'clock he'd hoist the "What the hell?" pennant, which was an invitation to come around for cocktails. He was a great leader and likable individual. He was a good friend of Arleigh Burke. His wife was equally a superb hostess.

Paul Stillwell: Did you do any shore bombardment with the 6-inch guns?

Admiral Knoll: No. *Roanoke* never had a chance for this. In antiaircraft gunnery, of course, it always did very well. *Roanoke* in gunnery was first among Battleships and Cruisers Atlantic for many years.

We were only out of Norfolk for a two months' cruise to the Med with the Sixth Fleet. Upon return to their families, it was circulated that *Roanoke* was to be transferred from the East Coast to the West Coast. When I heard that was possible, and before anyone made up their mind in Washington, I requested, "When I reach the West Coast, I want to stop at San Diego, Los Angeles, San Francisco, and have a weekend in Seattle before we go to the Bremerton yard." You can't imagine how that paid off. Also, there was a lot of adjustment as to who wanted to remain on the East Coast and who wanted to move to the West Coast. Every wish was granted.

When I was getting ready to leave to take *Roanoke* through the Panama Canal for its first trip into the Pacific, I got a call from the Navy Department that said, "We've got some weather buoys that were developed for you for the Asiatic Fleet to detect the intensity of hurricanes or typhoons in the Far East. They've never been used. When you leave to go through the Caribbean, this being the hurricane season, would you like to take them along and drop them in advance of any hurricane when you pass through the Caribbean?"

---

* Captain Milton E. Miles, USN, commanded the heavy cruiser *Columbus* (CA-74) from January 1947 to December 1947.
† From 1954 to 1956, as a rear admiral, Miles was Commandant Fifteenth Naval District in Panama.

"I'd be happy to." So I received two of them. I never heard the results, except after passing through Windward Passage, I went eastward to be closer to a hurricane that was running westward. I went close until the wind was about 35 or 40 knots, and I dropped one weather buoy. In the western part of the Caribbean, a second buoy was dropped along the hurricane path on my way to the Panama Canal. I was able to place two weather buoys in the path of a hurricane.

Paul Stillwell: Are there any of your officers that you particularly remember from that ship?

Admiral Knoll: No, not offhand. I had the ship for a less than a year. Eph McLean relieved Butch Parker as cruiser division commander. I visited Rip Struble, who was with the United Nations in New York.[*] He knew I was going to *Roanoke*, and he said, "The pity is after working hard all our lives, BuPers cannot allow you to remain for a couple of years and really enjoy it. There are insufficient big commands. They're conditioning you, knowing you will soon be promoted. Enjoy it while you can. Even a little contribution to fleet readiness in that short time aboard, the better it is for the Navy. The Navy is not getting the most out of our good people, because too many of them have to have this qualification to insure promotion."

Paul Stillwell: Then from there you went to the Seventh Fleet staff.

Admiral Knoll: That's right. It expedited my detachment from the *Roanoke*, because while *Roanoke* was en route Seattle, I received a personal message from Slim Ingersoll, asking me to accept assignment as his chief of staff.[†]

Paul Stillwell: Did he pick you because of your previous service together in OpNav?

---

[*] From 1952 to 1955 Vice Admiral Arthur D. Struble, USN, was assigned as a U.S. representative to the United Nations.
[†] Vice Admiral Stuart H. Ingersoll, USN, served as Commander Seventh Fleet from 19 December 1955 to 28 January 1957.

Admiral Knoll: I would say definitely. He knew me and the type of work I could do. Initially Admiral Pride was Commander Seventh Fleet when I arrived.[*] Admiral Pride had requested relief for Donc Donaho, and Slim had cleared my orders with Mel Pride.[†] I flew back from Seattle to see my family for a couple of days and then flew from the West Coast via Honolulu, Wake, Tokyo, Naha, and to Taipei, with a two-hour layover at each stop. I stopped at Pearl Harbor to visit Felix Stump, CinCPac, C. D. Griffin, and Germany Curts.[‡] I went via Pan American plane. I relieved Donaho a couple of days after arrival.

Mel Pride was a good man to work for; they don't come any better. He was not a Naval Academy graduate, rather an MIT graduate.[§] We had something in common there. He was a smart and charming individual to work for. He let me run the show. Slim Ingersoll did also. Vice Admiral Ingersoll spent many hours ashore. I knew where he was. He was always making his manners with Generalissimo Chiang Kai-shek, whom he had to visit every day before he came to the flagship.[**] That was a requirement from Washington. The Navy finally made the Seventh Fleet a special command. An additional three-star admiral was ordered as Commander Taiwan Defense Command, who could stay close to the generalissimo. An annoying problem was the State Department, which continued to criticize Mel Pride because he wasn't spending enough time with the generalissimo. Pride felt that as a fleet commander he should give priority to the fleet.

When Slim arrived, he said, "Now I'll have to bend over backwards and give more attention to the generalissimo. I will live with my wife on the hill, and I will make sure to fulfill the word from Washington to see Chiang every day when the flagship is in

---

[*] Vice Admiral Alfred M. Pride, USN, served as Commander Seventh Fleet from 1 December 1953 to 19 December 1955. The oral history of Pride, who retired as a four-star admiral, is in the Naval Institute collection.
[†] Captain Glynn R. Donaho, USN.
[‡] Admiral Felix B. Stump, USN, served as Commander in Chief Pacific and Commander in Chief U.S. Pacific Fleet, 10 July 1953-14 January 1958. After he was relieved as CinCPacFlt on 14 January, he remained in the joint billet as CinCPac until 31 July of that year. Rear Admiral Charles D. Griffin, USN; Rear Admiral Maurice E. Curts, USN.
[§] MIT – Massachusetts Institute of Technology, Cambridge, Massachusetts.
[**] Originally established in early 1955 as the Formosa Liaison Center, in November 1955 it was renamed the U.S. Taiwan Defense Command and reported to Commander in Chief Pacific. The first commander of the organization was Vice Admiral Alfred M. Pride, USN, who was concurrently Commander Seventh Fleet.

port." Frequently the flagship would get under way, and I went out with the fleet and the carriers. At that time there were four carriers and three cruisers with Seventh Fleet. I was at sea a lot more than Slim. Frequently he'd join the ship by helicopter. When we went to sea and visited Yokosuka, Ingersoll would fly up in his plane and join the flagship there. For many fleet operations in the South China Sea off Subic or near Manila, Ingersoll did not join us. He'd stay up with the generalissimo, so I'd be in charge and participate in seeing many old friends in Manila and attend excellent parties. Ingersoll might come down for a few days. For actual fleet operations the senior officer in carriers acted as officer in tactical command. As chief of staff, I did all the paperwork for Com7thFlt.

Paul Stillwell: You said he lived up on the hill. Where was that?

Admiral Knoll: In Taiwan, the hills above Taipei. The Seventh Fleet command at that time had a nice home assigned. It had a beautiful view overlooking Taipei. The generalissimo lived in a small dwelling the shadow of the main hotel.

Paul Stillwell: The Grand Hotel.

Admiral Knoll: The Grand Hotel, yes, it has recently been enlarged.

I was chief of staff almost a year and a half. I slept aboard the flagship every night except for the two New Year's Eves when I stayed overnight in Taipei with a friend. Every time there was a crisis in the world or in Washington, the priority message arrived about 1:00 in the morning, and the chief of staff had to take prompt action.

The Communist Chinese shot down a Navy ECM plane near Shanghai, and there was great excitement.* As soon as the message came that confirmed that the plane had been shot down, I said, "Give me a message blank," and I was still in my bunk. I said, "Send a message in plain language, priority, all Seventh Fleet ships operationally ready,

---

* ECM – electronic countermeasures. On 22 August 1956 the Navy reported that a P4M Mercator patrol plane based at Iwakuni, Japan, had been shot down with a crew of 16 men on board. The Seventh Fleet recovered the body of one crew member. The plane was about 160 miles north of Taiwan and 32 miles from the Chinese Coast. The People's Republic of China reported that it had shot down a plane, presuming that it was Taiwanese.

get under way immediately, rendezvous 100 miles off Shanghai at first light." Four carriers, three cruisers, and four destroyers got under way. I sent the message for information to CinCPac and CNO.

At that time, I understand Felix Stump, CinCPac, and a couple of other ones, even Vice Admiral Wally Beakley, said, "Knoll's running the Seventh Fleet, because Slim lives ashore."[*] All that came in a message from Admiral Stump in plain language: "Make sure you comply with Article umpty-ump, umpty-ump, which means don't allow any Navy planes to operate within 50 miles of the coastline of Communist China." Not one person canceled or questioned that message.

The Seventh Fleet went out and cruised over the China coast, and Slim came out and remained under way for about two weeks. Every Chinese plane that took off from airfields near the coast never came over the water. We sent in a couple of minesweepers to see if we could find wreckage of the plane in the islands at the entrance of the Yangtze River. We never found anything, but we lost a lot of good classified equipment.

At that time, the Navy flew an ECM flight regularly, and occasionally the plane would get off course, and the Chinese monitor would call and tell them, "You're off course," and the plane would make a change. This time the plane continued on the wrong course, and no one called him. A Chinese plane took off and shot down the ECM plane. The Chinese knew that the Navy was flying these missions 30 years ago. The recent shooting down of the Korean 007 by the Soviets is surprising.[†] If the Korean plane was part of a special mission, it was exposing passengers unnecessarily. The Soviets and U.S.A. have been conducting routine ECM operations for many years. The Korean 007 should not have been used for such a task.

Paul Stillwell: What was the flagship when you were with Seventh Fleet?

Admiral Knoll: There were three heavy cruisers that we changed every six months. Each came to the Seventh Fleet for a six-month tour.

---

[*] Beakley was then serving in the Plans and Policy section of OpNav.
[†] On 1 September 1983 a Soviet SU-15 fighter aircraft shot down a Boeing 747 passenger plane over the Sea of Japan. All 269 people in the plane were killed. The Korean Airlines plane was on flight 007, which was en route from Anchorage, Alaska, to Seoul, South Korea, but strayed off course and violated Soviet airspace over Sakhalin Island.

Paul Stillwell: The *Rochester* was one.

Admiral Knoll: Yes. A classmate of mine, Ken Gentry, had command.* The *St. Paul* was out twice. My classmate Jim Davis was in command, and he relieved me as chief of staff.† The other cruiser was the *Helena*, commanded by Harry Smith, another classmate.‡ Each cruiser had more than adequate space for a fleet staff.

Paul Stillwell: How big a staff did you have?

Admiral Knoll: It was a good-sized staff, about 20 officers and 40 enlisted personnel, plus our radio people. There were two planners, a weather officer, an aviation officer, three or four in intelligence, the admiral's aide, a supply officer, and four communications officers for the code room. When I was chief of staff, no ship ever got near a typhoon. I made sure, with my past knowledge out there, that all ships were advised of any typhoon and how to avoid it. During the typhoon season, Putt Storrs was in tactical command of the carriers and they were operating near Luzon and Taiwan with four carriers and three cruisers.§ A typhoon was developing in the South China Sea, and it looked like it was moving toward the Formosa Strait. Storrs contacted me and said, "We're going to have to fuel. I don't want to fuel in the Taiwan Strait and be surprised with a typhoon."

I said, "You don't have to."

He said, "Where are you going to go?"

I said, "I'll tell you. Taiwan Island is about 400 or 500 miles long. The water is about 1,000 fathoms deep up within a mile of the east coast. There are going to be many heavy waves off the east side of Taiwan, and there's going to be some wind. Any kind of a heavy sea coming against that deep water close to Taiwan will be relatively calm if we stay within ten miles of the coast. We can safely refuel the whole fleet, and we will not

---

* Captain Kenneth M. Gentry, USN, commanded the heavy cruiser *Rochester* (CA-124) from 10 January 1956 to 5 November 1956.
† Captain James W. Davis, USN, commanded the heavy cruiser *St. Paul* (CA-73) from 7 November 1955 to 12 January 1957.
‡ Captain Harry Smith, USN, commanded the heavy cruiser *Helena* (CA-75) from 22 July 1955 to 6 October 1956.
§ Rear Admiral Aaron P. Storrs, USN, Commander Carrier Division Five.

have any problems with the sea and the swell. The backwash of the waves hitting the east coast will calm the seas five to ten miles to the east."

Fueling started at the southern end of Taiwan and the fleet cruised north. The course was reversed, and then the fleet refueled going south. As the typhoon came closer, the fleet had deep water to eastward, and we did not have to worry with getting involved with the typhoon in the Taiwan Strait.

Later Storrs said to me, "You knew what you were talking about." It worked beautifully and surprised many that the seas were small on the weather side of Taiwan.

Paul Stillwell: What do you recall about Admiral Pride as a personality?

Admiral Knoll: He was a gentleman from the beginning to the end. He doesn't give an impression of being overconfident, but you know he's smart in the way he handles things, the way you can discuss any subject with him. He never became excited. He just puts you at ease in dealing with him. I never saw him get mad. With a knowledge of the facts, he calmly made decisions, and it was easy to implement his every wish or command.

Paul Stillwell: I interviewed him, and he struck me as a very reserved, laconic New Englander.[*]

Admiral Knoll: Well, that's part of it. He could have all the responsibility in the world, and it was easy to help him do the job. He was always courteous to the utmost. I know when Pride left he said, "Thank you for helping me so much. You've been a wonderful assistant," or words to that effect. He makes you feel good.

I know Donc Donaho said the same thing about him. You couldn't ask for a nicer, more pleasant guy. You know he knows what's going on, and everybody who ever worked for him admired and respected him. I can name different ones, partially aviation

---

[*] See the Naval Institute oral history of Admiral Alfred M. Pride, USN (Ret.). He was born 10 September 1897 in Somerville, Massachusetts.

people, who thought Pride was the exact opposite of Slim Ingersoll as far as temperament is concerned.

Paul Stillwell: Tell me about Ingersoll then.

Admiral Knoll: I'll tell you, you never knew when he was going "to hit the fan," particularly aboard ship when he wanted to take a shower prior to going ashore. More than once, the water would go off, or he would get steam instead of hot water. One time he was in the shower, and he was soaped up, ready to rinse off. All water stopped, and he came screaming, so I could hear him at my stateroom some distance away. I went to him, and he was in his cabin, soapy and naked. He said, "Where is that chief engineer?" I think it was Jim Davis's ship, and Jim Davis came running. We finally got the water flowing again

I said, "Admiral, relax." I thought he was going to have a heart attack. He was red in the face, and he was wild. It took, I know, 10 to 15 minutes to quiet him. His aide was Aldo Darodda, who was an aviator and a capable guy; he's since died.[*] He married the daughter of the Philippine ambassador to Taiwan, with a big wedding in Taipei. It was at a Catholic church with an apostolic delegate, later a cardinal, performing the ceremony.

The interesting thing was that when Darodda wanted to do something for Ingersoll, instead of coming to me he'd start working with the staff. I sent for him, and I said, "If the admiral wants something done, you're just the aide. You don't go around telling the staff what to do. That's my job. You go in and tell the admiral I told you so."

Every once in a while, referring to Darodda, Ingersoll would say, "You keep that young fellow in line. Whatever has to be done, or how you want it, that's what I want you to do." Ingersoll never once failed to back me up.

I tried to help the flagship skippers that worked with us. I helped them understand the admiral and to do what he wanted without backtalk. One of them, no matter what happened, when the admiral wanted him to do something, he'd talk back, and say, "I have to train my officers so they'll be able to be in command some day." That was the

---

[*] Lieutenant (junior grade) Aldo J. Darodda, USN.

worst thing you could do in command of the flagship, being the first one to go alongside to replenish or refuel and leave to await others. Leave replenishment smartly and proceed to new station, thus giving a good example to other ships. One skipper would slowly move from replenishment and weave around there like he did not know or care where his station was. The admiral would raise hell over the voice talk, and the skipper would come back on the intercom, "I'm training my officer of the deck." There was one incident like this after another.

Paul Stillwell: Who was the skipper?

Admiral Knoll: I prefer not to mention his name. He didn't make flag rank. He blamed me because he didn't make flag rank. I talked to him many times. I said, "For God's sakes, I've worked under similar conditions. You must please the admiral. The flagship is the example. We have to be smart. We have to get out there promptly, and we have to move and show smartness when we change stations." At times he was quite ornery. You can imagine. Slim would jump up and down. The skipper seemed to enjoy teasing him.

Paul Stillwell: I think training your junior officers is a legitimate goal.

Admiral Knoll: Training them to carry out the legitimate wish of the flag, in front of other junior officers. Avoid insubordination in the presence of seniors. I had told the skipper ahead of time, when he first joined Seventh Fleet, "Make every move smartly. I've done it with *Roanoke*, and it pays dividends. Giving good example as the flagship makes other people want to do the same thing. It's the example that counts. It is good Navy doctrine."

This same skipper had dogs, and he brought the dogs aboard—two large French poodles. They messed up the deck. The admiral told the captain he wasn't to bring the dogs aboard. One time when he knew the admiral wasn't going to go to sea, he brought the dogs. (I don't know how he ever thought the admiral wouldn't find out, and I didn't have to tell Slim.) The skipper had a box up near the jackstaff for the dogs to use. A skipper can't do these things and then wonder why he was not promoted.

Paul Stillwell: How would you compare Pride and Ingersoll as far as mental ability and seeing the big picture?

Admiral Knoll: I was with Pride less than two months. I never knew Pride as the Chief of the Bureau of Aeronautics, working as an engineer.* I had worked with Ingersoll in strategic planning. I'd worked with Ingersoll on the New Look strategy for President Eisenhower and Admiral Radford. So I never could quite evaluate Pride the same way. Ingersoll and I were in agreement in terms of what we thought was necessary for long-range planning for fleet requirements. I never was able to compare fleet work with a paperwork job in Washington. My discussions with Pride were fleet matters. I'd be wrong to compare; they were both smart men.

Ingersoll did a great job when he was head of the Naval War College.† He knew his business, and he did a lot to improve the administration of the college. I went up there different times as his guest, and I talked to various seminars with the staff. Pride was without a doubt one of the smartest aeronautical engineers in the Navy. His demeanor reminded me of the smart professors I met at the Massachusetts Institute of Technology. He knew his business and deserved great respect. At that time, not being a Naval Academy graduate, he had to be super to make vice admiral. Unfortunately, Ingersoll's wife had a tragic end at Newport. It was tough on him, but he never complained.

Paul Stillwell: What happened to her?

Admiral Knoll: She fell down the stairs in their home. They had one of these five-gallon green bottles on one landing. She fell and broke the bottle, cut up her face horribly, and died shortly thereafter. It was a tragic end. He then married the widow of the Campbell Soup Company in New York.‡ He and she died recently, in the last year. He had two nice daughters and a son. The son didn't have his father's drive, which Slim thought a

---

* While a rear admiral, Pride served as Chief of the Bureau of Aeronautics, 1947-1951.
† Vice Admiral Stuart H. Ingersoll, USN, served as president of the Naval War College from 13 August 1957 to 30 June 1960.
‡ Ingersoll's first wife, Josephine Springman, died in 1964; His second wife was Elinore Dorrance Hill, daughter of the founder of Campbell's Soup. She died in 1977. Admiral Ingersoll died 2 February 1983.

son should have. He rode him more than he probably should, but his pride was in the oldest daughter. She married a naval officer. He was selected for commander when I was chairman of the selection board. The promotion was made on his own outstanding merits. I had only one vote out of nine

Paul Stillwell: On Ingersoll, you mentioned the shower incident. That reminds me of a story from Jack Coye's oral history. He was CO of the *Rochester* when she was the fleet flagship and Admiral Beakley was the fleet commander.[*] Coye said that only time he ever got in any hassle with Beakley was one time when the admiral's shower got cut off during general quarters.

Admiral Knoll: Beakley came out to Seventh Fleet a few months before I was detached. Of course, I had worked with Beakley in OpNav strategic plans, and I had great admiration for him. He lived with Ruth, a semi-invalid to whom he was devoted. He wrote her a letter every day. After Ruth's death, he remarried, then committed suicide when his second wife died.[†] He had a lot of ability; at times he developed a nervous breakdown that bordered on a mental breakdown. One time, I visited him at the naval hospital in Everett, Massachusetts. He was there for some kind of observation and possible retirement.

Paul Stillwell: Do you think it was a disadvantage to the Seventh Fleet Commander not to be able to operate the Seventh Fleet because he had to pay so much attention to Chiang Kai-shek?

Admiral Knoll: It was wrong trying to give so much attention to Chiang. It certainly flattered him to a great degree. At a certain point I think Chiang felt the Seventh Fleet was his fleet. We had to be very careful when his birthday was celebrated annually. Throughout Taipei were headlines, billboards, banners, and slogans calling it "Operation

---

[*] Captain John S. Coye Jr., USN, commanded the heavy cruiser *Rochester* (CA-124) from 10 January 1958 to 2 January 1959. The oral history of Coye, who retired as a rear admiral, is in the Naval Institute collection. Vice Admiral Wallace M. Beakley, USN, served as Commander Seventh Fleet from 28 January 1957 to 30 September 1958.
[†] Beakley died at Alexandria, Virginia, on 16 January 1975.

Happy Return." We advised Washington and others, "We can't use this term, because an impression was created that this was the happy return to the mainland." U.S. policy did not support such action. The United States babied him too much, to our disadvantage. Today U.S.A. is babying the Israelis too much, to the degradation of good relations with other nations. This is not right for a superpower like U.S. to ignore long-range policy. When the Navy finally divided Commander Seventh Fleet from Commander Taiwan Defense Command, a second vice admiral came to take care of Chiang.[*]

I think it was very poor judgment to use a vice admiral for such duty. I think Beakley felt the same way about it, that it was not fair. Beakley didn't have the same fleet that Slim did. It was changed about the time Ingersoll left and Beakley arrived. Admiral Radford, Chairman of the JCS, told Ingersoll to give special attention to Chiang, more than the previous fleet commander. He carried out his orders. After Chiang received special attention for two years, he complained openly when Beakley was not required to continue the close relationship. I believe Washington and Pearl approved relaxation.

Flag officers were in Taipei; under Ingersoll it was a separate staff from the Seventh Fleet. It was not a prestigious command, just sitting around Taipei to please Chiang. Beakley arrived and became more involved with Seventh Fleet affairs. I knew that my job was going to be a lot easier because Slim Ingersoll took for granted that I was running the fleet. George Anderson was the senior aviator our first year.[†] When he was detached, he said, "You'll be a rear admiral on the next selection list." It did not occur; thus I seemed to stay for the extra year. Done Donaho received promotion to rear admiral just about the time I relieved him.[‡] If it had occurred, I would have been promoted ahead of my class. The selection board proceeded to return to the class of '27 and select four more people, not one of whom ever expected promotion the third time around. I was told by more than one that I would have been one of those four if the

---

[*] Vice Admiral Roland N. Smoot, USN, served as Commander U.S. Taiwan Defense Command from July 1958 to April 1962. Smoot's oral history is in the Naval Institute collection. The job at that point was separate, not concurrent with being Commander Seventh Fleet.
[†] Rear Admiral George W. Anderson Jr., USN, future Chief of Naval Operations, commanded the Taiwan Patrol Force, 1955-56..
[‡] Donaho graduated from the Naval Academy in 1927, Knoll in 1930.

selection board had ignored 1927. I ended up in Washington in OP-43 until I came up for the next time.

Paul Stillwell: So you wound up making it on time but not early.

Admiral Knoll: I made it with my class. I had a good chance of making it one year early. I was told that some of the letters in my record from the Secretary of State and from Admiral Kelly Turner, Admiral Hart, and General Matt Ridgway convinced the selection board that with my record they said, "No doubt you're going to make it sometime, or somebody's crazy."

Paul Stillwell: Do you have any specific memories of Admiral Beakley during the time he was the Seventh Fleet Commander?

Admiral Knoll: When Beakley arrived, the first comment, made in a friendly way, was, "Washington and Pearl know you were operating the Seventh Fleet. Now I will do it."

I didn't stay too much longer. With Beakley I let him indicate how he wanted me to help. I knew Beak wanted a good chief of staff, and I encouraged Jim Davis, commanding officer of the *St. Paul*, to accept the assignment. I hadn't seen my wife in a long time. She was not well, and I was anxious to get home. I was assured of orders to OpNav, because I had a home in Chevy Chase to return to. I had to know in advance so I could tell the Chinese naval attaché, my tenant, that he would have to move. He lived there twice when I was absent from D.C. He later became the Chinese ambassador to Sierra Leone. He had excellent relations with the generalissimo and staff. He's still active with the government in Taiwan, with Chiang Kai-shek's son and successor.*

Paul Stillwell: Was the offshore island crisis heating up during the time you were there?

---

* Chiang Ching-kuo (1910-1988) was the son of Chiang Kai-shek. He succeeded his father, serving as Premier of the Republic of China (Taiwan) from 1972 to 1978 and as President of the Republic of China from 1978 until he died in 1988.

Admiral Knoll: It had been heated up and started quieting at that time. Slim Ingersoll visited Quemoy twice. I wanted to visit there one time, and Slim said he'd prefer not, that I'd better stay with the flagship. Quemoy wasn't my responsibility.

Paul Stillwell: Did the Pacific Fleet Commander in Chief come out at all while you were there?

Admiral Knoll: Yes, Felix Stump came out.

Paul Stillwell: What do you remember of him?

Paul Stillwell: I knew Felix from the time he commanded *Childs*, a tender for patrol planes when the war started in Subic Bay. I knew his reputation, and I had met with him in Pearl. I made an official call on him on my way out to be chief of staff. You have to be awfully good and know your business. Stump was a carbon copy of Admiral Kelly Turner as a stickler for accuracy and performance of duties. He was always quite pleasant to me, but he wasn't about to go around flattering anybody.

Paul Stillwell: He was an excitable individual.

Admiral Knoll: No doubt about that. So was Slim. I know one incident that was very sad. I had no operational control of the fleet. It primarily involved aviators. There was a collision at night between a destroyer and a cruiser.* An investigation was conducted, composed of aviators. The Seventh Fleet flagship was in the formation near Subic when it happened. Slim was not with us, but we had a complete watch on our flag bridge. I knew what had happened, because Putt Storrs, the OTC, put out a tactical signal with darkened ship at night, and the OTC executed the signal to change course before they had

---

* The collision Admiral Knoll recalled occurred shortly before 0400 on 11 March 1956 in the South China Sea. The ships involved were the heavy cruiser *Columbus* (CA-74) and the destroyer *Floyd B. Parks* (DD-884). See David W. Joy, "Collision at Sea," *Naval History*, December 2005, pages 56-61.

acknowledgement from the ships at the end of the line.* The flagship had never received a change of course signal. I was in my bunk, and I quickly went to the flag bridge. The watch officer said, "The OTC executed a change of course without waiting for acknowledgement from all ships." Well, that caused the collision.

Ingersoll conducted the investigation, assisted by three naval aviators.† I said, "There's no use getting me involved in this. It was with the aviators and Ingersoll; they had helped select who should do it. The investigation held the signalman on the carrier at fault rather than the duty officer on the OTC's flag bridge. The signalman carried out the order to execute. The duty officer, a lieutenant commander on the OTC's staff lacked operating experience. It takes a long time for a signal to be acknowledged and then executed.

Paul Stillwell: That verdict was a little strange, wasn't it?

Admiral Knoll: Well, you're damn right. And Felix jumped on that investigation and let everyone know how wrong they were.‡

Paul Stillwell: What did he say?

Admiral Knoll: He promptly said there was no way the signalman could be blamed. Some of those that were on that board never were promoted further nor received bigger responsibilities. A few thought they were going places, but they cut their own throats. Slim never mentioned it to me, and I didn't want to get involved. I was amazed that Slim was not more careful. My initials never showed on the investigation. I didn't read it all the way through. I was dumbfounded they found the enlisted man at fault for executing without acknowledgement. My recollection was that the entire investigation was forwarded without the approval of Felix. The damage was not bad, and there was no further action.

---

* Rear Admiral Aaron P. Storrs, USN, Commander Carrier Division Five, who was embarked in the carrier *Shangri-La* (CVA-38). OTC – officer in tactical command.
† Knoll also told the collision story in a different interview. In that one he said the investigation was conducted by Rear Admiral Thomas B. Williamson, USN, who was a naval aviator.
‡ For Stump's response, see *Naval History*, December 2005, page 61.

Pearl threw out the whole court finding, but it didn't help the skipper of the ship. It didn't help the aviators, because it was the dumbest thing in the world to find an enlisted signalman responsible for a collision. The OTC might have been qualified for greater responsibilities; he retired a few years later.

Paul Stillwell: You could hardly fault the cruiser skipper if he hadn't even gotten the signal.*

Admiral Knoll: We don't know. All I know is that the flagship was at the end of the line, and we had not received the signal. There were three cruisers. The flag bridge knew with darkened ship there hadn't been an acknowledgement with the signal gun. When you start sending a signal like that in darkened ship, you can't get the reply of acknowledgement as fast as you can with a regular open signal. The collision should not have happened. It was no surprise to me when Felix hit the fan.

Paul Stillwell: Anything else on that tour of duty you should include?

Admiral Knoll: Admiral Ingersoll was annoyed about the number of people from the fleet that were shacked up with Japanese girls, particularly around Sasebo. One incident came to our attention. A Navy pharmacist's mate went through a Shinto marriage with a Japanese girl, and the witness at the marriage was a Navy dentist for whom he worked. Senior officers were very mad. A special letter was sent to all the commanding officers of the Seventh Fleet. The chief of police of Sasebo was asked, "What records to you have? How many U.S. sailors are shacked up with Japanese girls here?"

The chief said, "I'll get you a list of all of them in about 24 hours, every sailor, the ship he is attached to, and the house where he is living, and the girl's name." A complete list was obtained, and some names were clever. One name was "Frantic Freddie." It listed the ship he was on, but his real name was missing. The volume and the accuracy were amazing.

---

* Captain George C. Seay, USN, commanded the *Columbus* from 10 February 1956 to 15 March 1957, including at the time of the collision. He was a Naval Academy classmate of Knoll. He was not selected for flag rank on active duty. When he retired in 1959 he received a tombstone promotion to rear admiral.

The letter to all the skippers said it was about time we started acting like Americans. It was a disgrace that many Navy people with families back in the States were living ashore with Japanese girls. Some had Shinto marriages so the girls would not be embarrassed in the eyes of their family back home. We checked with the police, who knew all about the letter. Within a short period of time, you can't imagine the number of girls that went back home as soon as they knew the police had reported their names to the Navy. The word got around, and more of the sailors lived aboard ship.

Before the letter was sent, Admiral Ingersoll and I visited Bill Callaghan, who was the boss at Yokosuka and a classmate of Slim Ingersoll. We discussed the entire situation. Vice Admiral Bill Callaghan was a terrific individual, an honest, religious man. We showed him the proposed letter and mentioned the percentage of people that were shacked up.

There were only two skippers who refused to cooperate. They said that shacking up encouraged reenlistment and made duty in the Far East attractive. Bill Callaghan read the letter, he studied it, and he said to Slim and me, "You make this sound awful bad. It's not that bad, is it?" He really doubted it was a serious problem. He couldn't believe it. He did not object to distribution of the letter by Commander Seventh Fleet.

We said, "You want to come out some night to Sasebo or Yokosuka? We can show you all these places."

He never appreciated that aspect of the sailors getting involved with all these young Japanese girls. Slim said, "You see, that's how good that man is."

Paul Stillwell: He didn't believe people would do something like that.

Admiral Knoll: That's right. We received some encouraging letters from the Chaplain Corps upon return to Washington, saying, "It's about time someone did something like this."

One thing that amazed me as a difference, having been out there with the Asiatic Fleet before the war and then after the war. When I was chief of staff, Seventh Fleet arranged for ships to visit Manila and ports in Japan. There were no visits to the southern islands of the Philippines, to places like Iloilo, Zamboanga, and Cebu. Before the war we visited these cities. Those were interesting to visit, see new places. I talked to the Seventh Fleet destroyer commander. I said, "For our next operation let's see if we can't visit Iloilo or Zamboanga and see other parts of the Philippine Islands. Ships are going to the same ports so the crews can shack up with Japanese girls. Ships should see a little more of the world." They thought it was a good idea. I think we did it with two different divisions of destroyers, and did he get a down check. The crews were complaining there was no USO ashore and nothing to do. The squadron commander recommended that Seventh Fleet not schedule visits to exotic places. I thought that was part of being with the Asiatic Fleet in the old days, to see the area and know the differences of people. Because there wasn't a USO ashore or someone to help them meet the girls, then the current crews were not interested in such.

Paul Stillwell: Times change.

Admiral Knoll: I stopped scheduling visits to new foreign ports.

In many ways, it was a pleasant tour, and the year and a half year passed very rapidly, never an idle moment. I enjoyed it, except I was a long way away from home for too long.

Paul Stillwell: Then you did get back, and you went to OpNav again.

Admiral Knoll: That's correct. When I was OP-43, fleet maintenance officer, with Rear Admiral Irv Duke.[*] I attended hearings in the House of Representatives with Al Mumma on ship construction money.[†] When we were sitting behind him, Arleigh Burke, who was the CNO, would say, "Now, when I start getting excited or angry during testimony with the Congress, pull on my coattail. Remind me when I'm getting mad."[‡]

---

[*] Rear Admiral Irving T. Duke, USN.
[†] Rear Admiral Irving T. Duke, USN. Rear Admiral Albert G. Mumma, USN, served as Chief of the Bureau of Ships from 1955 to 1959. His oral history is in the Naval Institute collection.
[‡] Admiral Arleigh A. Burke, USN, served as Chief of Naval Operations from 17 August 1955 to 1 August 1961. His oral history is in the Naval Institute collection.

One day we had a really heated session in house with Dan Flood and others, and Arleigh became very excited, so we had to pull his coattails.* As we were riding back to the Pentagon in his car, he said, "You know, I have told you people when I get excited, you're supposed to pull my coattail and quiet me down."

I said, "Admiral, we were pulling your coattail till your coat was down around your hips, and you still didn't relax."

There was one hearing with Admiral Burke when I was head of the Ship Characteristics Board.† This involved development of characteristics for the Polaris submarine; the *Enterprise*, first nuclear carrier; and *Long Beach*, first nuclear cruiser. We went to the hearing on ship construction money with the House of Representatives. George Mahon and Jerry Ford were on the committee, also Dan Flood.‡ Dan was unusual; he liked to needle witnesses. They were excited this day because the word came out that the *Enterprise*, when finished, would cost $1 million. Arleigh said, "It's not going to cost $1 million."§

I sat there, and I didn't have a final figure then, but I knew it was getting very high, particularly with the air group. The Air Force was putting out this kind of information, and congressmen were concerned. Here was a ship, the first nuclear-powered ship, going to cost $1 million. At the end of the meeting, to put everybody at ease, Admiral Burke, out of the clear, said to the Appropriations Committee of the House, "The *Enterprise* will not cost more than $434 million."

I looked at Al Mumma and we were stunned. We got in the car to ride back, and Arleigh said, "Denny, I'm giving you a letter today with the characteristics you've called out for *Enterprise*. The ship will not cost more than $434 million."

I said, "Admiral, you have just removed four antiaircraft missile batteries from the four corners of the *Enterprise*." I started checking to find out where some of the money was or where some of the hidden money might be. Within a couple of days, I had a letter

---

* Daniel J. Flood, a Democrat from Pennsylvania, served in the House of Representatives from 1945 to 1947, 1949 to 1953, and 1955 to 1980.
† During the course of this tour of duty, Knoll was promoted to rear admiral.
‡ Gerald R. Ford, Jr., a Republican from Michigan, served in the House of Representatives from 3 January 1949 until his resignation from the House on 6 December 1973, to become the Vice President of the United States. He subsequently served as President from 9 August 1974 to 20 January 1977. George H. Mahon, a Democrat from Texas, served in the House of Representatives from 3 January 1935 to 3 January 1979.
§ Admiral Knoll probably meant $1 billion but misspoke.

from the Bureau of Ships with proposals. I found out that for two or three yeas in a row, Admiral Burke had been testifying the *Enterprise* would be the first ship with electronic scanning radars, both for acquisition of surface targets as well as aircraft. It meant radars would not be rotating on the masts, all rotations accomplished by electronics. I started checking to find out how much money had been spent in R&D for electronic scanning radars. Vice Admiral Chick Hayward, my classmate, was head of Navy R&D. I said, "Chick, find out how much money the Navy spent. Admiral Burke has testified in the Congress a couple of years now that one of the real capabilities in *Enterprise* and *Long Beach* will be the electronic scanning radars, the SPS-33 and SPS-34."*

The reply I received: "We haven't spent any R&D money yet."

I said, "How in the name of God are we going to know how much the ultimate cost will be if we haven't spend the money yet?"

So I went up to Admiral Don Felt, the VCNO.† I said, "Admiral, we've got a problem. Arleigh's been telling Congress the *Enterprise* and *Long Beach* are going to have electronic scanning radar, and Hughes Aircraft doesn't even have money for research and development. There are all kinds of bugs in it, because they've partially tried, and it has failed to work on the *Galveston* for the missile or target acquisition." That wasn't even the electronic scanning. We went in to see Arleigh Burke, and he sent for Chick Hayward.

He said, "Chick, what kind of money are you spending for SPS-33 and –34?"

"Nothing yet."

Arleigh said, "For God's sake, Chick, I've been telling Congress it's going to be. How are we going to have it on time?"

You know where the money came from? Ship Construction (Navy). So that was another charge against the $434 million. The radars were developed and installed. Complete staff work is a constant problem in a large organization.

---

* Vice Admiral John T. Hayward, USN, Deputy Chief of Naval Operations (Development).
† Admiral Harry D. Felt, USN, served as Vice Chief of Naval Operations from 1 September 1956 to 28 July 1958. His oral history is in the Naval Institute collection.

That was a busy time. There was a problem with the first overhaul of the nuclear submarine *Nautilus*.* The first overhaul cost more than the initial cost to build the ship. It was a matter of concern, because it looked like the nuclear reactors would need re-coring every 18 months. Each reactor cost about $125 million. Today nuclear reactors require re-coring after about 18 years. The price hasn't come down much. I was concerned about the price of the reactors and how much stainless steel was put in their design. I tried to get the stainless steel reduced, and that was the one argument I lost with Admiral Rickover.†

At a meeting with the Secretary of the Navy and Admiral Burke, I said we could save some money by reducing the amount of stainless steel. It was included to prevent any kind of contamination. At that time Rickover was correct when he said at that particular stage of development of nuclear power we could not afford to have any type of nuclear casualty, or we'd delay operational acceptance for nuclear power for a generation. I said, with that condition, I withdrew my objection.

Another item I fought hard and won, involving all the new submarine tenders for the nuclear fleet. Rickover wanted to have a nuclear re-coring capability in each new tender, such an addition to cost a few million dollars. I took the position that no captain of a sub tender would ever cut a 6-foot-diameter hole in HY-80 steel two and a half inches thick. It is completely impractical to refuel a nuclear reactor alongside a submarine tender at anchor. A sub tender crew could not reweld that steel to a satisfactory integrity. Putting such a capability in a sub tender, which would never be needed, was a waste of government money. Rickover never forgave me, but he lost, and today there has never arisen a requirement for such work on a reactor other than in a Navy yard.

---

* USS *Nautilus* (SSN-571), the Navy's first nuclear-powered submarine, was commissioned 30 September 1954. She was 324 feet long, 28 feet in the beam, and displaced 3,533 tons. She had a top speed on the surface of 22 knots and undisclosed speed submerged. She was armed with six 21-inch torpedo tubes. Because she did not have to come to the surface frequently to recharge batteries, the *Nautilus* revolutionized submarine warfare.

† Rear Hyman G. Rickover, USN, was considered the father of the nuclear Navy. He ran the U.S. Navy's nuclear-power program for many years, from 1948 until he eventually left active duty in 1982 with the rank of four-star admiral on the retired list. Rickover Hall at the Naval Academy was named in his honor, as was the nuclear-powered attack submarine *Hyman G. Rickover* (SSN-709), which was commissioned 21 July 1984.

Rickover had one characteristic—if he called me, only he talked and said what he wanted me to hear. When I began to reply, he hung up. He never would listen to a reply. He always was annoyed that I did not invite him to meetings of the Ship Characteristics Board, because he was an Assistant Chief of the Bureau of Ships and also a member of the Atomic Energy Commission. I said, "There's no provision in my charter to have a member from the Atomic Energy Commission. If Armand Morgan, the member from the Bureau of Ships, wants to bring you to any meeting, that's his privilege."[*]

Rickover fought tooth and nail because he wanted a prototype of the Polaris submarine.[†] Instead of using an enlarged version of the *Skipjack*, he wanted Polaris subs to have two reactors.[‡] There were two reasons behind this. Rickover knew that he could not be an active member of the Polaris program if we used *Skipjack*. With a new prototype submarine he would have had a voice concerning the whole nuclear reactor. His argument was that for reliability and safety purposes, Polaris needed two reactors. The Polaris program under Red Raborn had a lot of priority projects. Keeping Rickover away was a blessing because he wanted his name as one of the developers of Polaris.[§]

When I was in OP-43, McElroy was Secretary of Defense.[**] We knew that one of the weakest parts of the Navy were our destroyers. They had never been brought up to date with the advanced sonar; they hadn't been brought up to date with the better radar; they lacked an up-to-date antisubmarine capability. So Joe Daniel and Whitey Taylor met with me.[††] Arleigh Burke called a meeting, and we met over the weekend to see what to recommend for bringing the destroyers up to a new standard of fleet readiness in both oceans that would fit with the rest of the Navy.

---

[*] Rear Admiral Armand M. Morgan, USN, Assistant Chief of the Bureau of Ships for Design and Research.
[†] Polaris was the name for the U.S. Navy's first submarine-launched ballistic missile, which became operational in the early 1960s. Its more-capable follow-on was the Poseidon missile, which entered the fleet in 1970.
[‡] USS *Skipjack* (SSN-585), a nuclear-powered attack submarine, was commissioned 15 April 1959, as the first ship of her class.
[§] Rear Admiral William F. Raborn, Jr., USN, was director of the Special Projects Office, which developed the Polaris submarine-launched ballistic missile system. He held the post from 1955 to 1962, being promoted to vice admiral in 1960. His Polaris oral history is in the Naval Institute collection.
[**] Neil H. McElroy served as Secretary of Defense from 9 October 1957 to 1 December 1959.
[††] Rear Admiral John C. Daniel, USN, commanded Destroyer Force Atlantic Fleet from 17 June 1955 to 18 January 1958. Rear Admiral Edmund B. Taylor, USN, commanded Destroyer Force Atlantic Fleet from 18 January 1958 to 21 January 1960.

To evaluate the readiness of the destroyer fleet, it was determined that we have the services of three outstanding civilians, namely, Bill Blewett of Newport News; Dr. Gibson of Hopkins Research Laboratory; and the operating vice president of American Export Lines, a prominent steamship line in New York.* I escorted them on a visit to the fleet in Norfolk and San Diego/Long Beach, with special attention to destroyers. We checked the material condition of various destroyers and determined what should be done. Conditions were not good, and we knew a good deal of money would be needed to build up the fleet destroyers. We had the use of the Secretary of the Navy's plane for all inspections. En route on the plane I prepared a written report based on the views of Blewett and Company and what they wanted to say. I expressed their recommendations literally and put no words in their mouths.

I recorded minutes of every session, then returned to discuss with Arleigh Burke before making it a smooth report. We arranged for Bill Blewett, Gibson, and the third man, whose name escapes me, to see SecDef McElroy alone with no Navy personnel present, civilians talking to civilians. They told McElroy that we had to make a major effort to modernize some of the ships of the fleet, particularly destroyers. We had indicated the radars and antisubmarine defense equipment needed. There was a FRAM-1 and FRAM-2 program, one of them more extensive than the other, depending on the age of the destroyer.† To improve we put helicopters on the stern and ASROC on the FRAM-1s.‡ FRAM-2 was less extensive. Modernization occurred over a three-year period. Secretary McElroy quickly sensed the importance of the project. McElroy saw President Eisenhower at the White House. President Eisenhower said, "Do it. Find the money."

What happened? The Navy found the money; initially about $734 million was taken from aircraft procurement and given to the FRAM program. From then on, my reputation among naval aviators was that Knoll stole the money from aircraft procurement to do the FRAM program on Navy destroyers. It continued for three or four

---

* William E. Blewett, Jr., was president of Newport News Shipbuilding and Dry Dock Company from 1954 to 1961, when he became chairman.
† FRAM is an acronym for the fleet rehabilitation and modernization program. Under this program many U.S. destroyer-type ships of the 1950s and 1960s were substantially modernized by extensive rebuilding that incorporated later technology than that available at the time of original construction.
‡ ASROC – antisubmarine rocket. It entered the fleet in the early 1960s in new-construction ships and in FRAM I destroyer conversions.

years. It was a combination of teamwork with Whitey Taylor and Joe Daniel. We spent a productive weekend working on what was needed and then decided the civilians who should talk to McElroy. McElroy got the money quickly, to the annoyance of naval aviators.

Paul Stillwell: Eli Vinock was involved in that also, wasn't he?*

Admiral Knoll: He worked for me. He had the destroyer desk in OP-43. He certainly helped but did not attend the meetings with Burke, Taylor, Daniel, and myself.

Paul Stillwell: He did a lot of the legwork on that, I think.

Admiral Knoll: I don't say I did it all on the FRAM programs, but it was an effort of the whole office in Washington. It shows how some of the things are accomplished. Someone has to sell the idea with facts, and you must select the right people to sell it. It was Burke's idea to show civilians Navy conditions and then have civilians alone tell the SecDef what they found and what should be done. The civilians never had to write a word; the staff recorded their every wish, so a final report was factual and precise.

Paul Stillwell: How much crossover did you have with BuShips on these things, on what was feasible to put in?

Admiral Knoll: Wait a second. On the Ship Characteristics Board were reps from BuShips, BuAer, BuOrd, Naval Operations, surface and submarine, and from R&D. I was just the chairman. My whole staff worked up the requirements for every program. We'd have regular meetings to bring order out of chaos. It was very interesting. I remember Vice Admiral Bill Rees was the NavAir representative.†

---

* Captain Eli Vinock, USN, headed the destroyer section of the Fleet Maintenance Division. See Vinock's article "FRAM Fixes the Fleet," *U.S. Naval Institute Proceedings*, August 1984, page 70.
† Vice Admiral William L. Rees, USN, served as Commander Naval Air Force Atlantic Fleet from 29 May 1956 to 30 September 1960. Prior to 30 July 1957 the title was Air Force, Atlantic Fleet.

We were getting requirements from the fleet for increasing the accommodations of personnel on aircraft carriers. They were fabulous in what they wanted to increase personnel with the air group on each carrier. There was a 100% increase in about a six-month period. It was about the time the *Forrestal* was commissioned. Fleet air said there was not enough room for personnel.* Bill Rees left and became ComAirLant. At the meetings before he left, he said he didn't think the lack of accommodations on new aircraft carriers was as bad as reported.† We used his testimony to justify no large changes. We knew the air groups were increasing to about six mechanics per plane.

Rees was ComAirLant less than a year when he came through with the most fantastic requirement you can imagine. Each person was a specialist in engines, armament, electronics, and avionics. Accommodations for the air group increased by leaps and bounds. An air group personnel of over 1,000 to 1,500 men was the norm when the old air group on carriers in World War II was 125 planes. Material requirements for modern jet aircraft for radar, avionics, armament, and the personnel to service are tremendous. Each plane instead of one mech per plane now required 14 service personnel for each jet combatant plane. In one year, a vice admiral said accommodations were adequate, and then with new jet aircraft the same vice admiral realized the new carriers needed a quantum increase. There again, you see personnel. Today the crews of nuclear carriers are averaging 5,400 to 6,000. The Navy can't intentionally build an obsolete ship. The ship was initially designed for one type plane.

Another area that embarrassed us was the low overhead on the hangar deck of the *Coral Sea* class.‡ The overhead height was about three feet shorter than in other carriers. We had quite a long argument on how high the Navy was going to continue to make the overhead on the hangar deck. Aviators took one side of the story, that the Navy should build the carriers to match the airplane. We said, "Now, wait a second. You can't build a

---

* USS *Forrestal* (CVA-59) was commissioned 1 October 1955 as the first of the U.S. Navy's big-deck carriers. She had a standard displacement of 56,000 tons, was 1,046 feet long, 129 feet in the beam, and had an extreme width of 252 feet. Her top speed was 33 knots. She was originally armed with eight 5-inch guns and could accommodate approximately 70-90 aircraft. She was in service until finally decommissioned on 11 September 1993. Captain Knoll was in command of the cruiser *Roanoke* when the *Forrestal* was commissioned.
† Rees had already been ComAirLant for a year before Knoll reported as OP-43, the Fleet Maintenance Division.
‡ Known as the *Midway* (CVA-41) class, it also included the *Franklin D. Roosevelt* (CVA-42) and the *Coral Sea* (CVA-43). The first two were commissioned in 1945 and the *Coral Sea* in 1947.

higher and higher tail fin and have the Navy keep raising the deck. We have to live with parameters and standardize plane limitations. The aircraft designer and manufacturer should limit the height of the tail fin to the hangar characteristics. Aviation didn't want to have any limitation on the design of a new airplane.

We had discussions as to where to locate the antennas for the ship and the air group. More than 30 antennas were involved, positioned in every part of the carrier. Each activity wanted the best location. What did they finally have to do? With ONR's cooperation, the Navy developed on the hillside above Ballast Point in San Diego a large leveled space showing a main deck of a ship.* Antennas were located for each activity so as to achieve minimum interference electronically. A topside configuration of each ship was made, and ONR and electronics determined the locations for various frequencies and activities. The Characteristics Board could never have resolved this at a conference table. Today more than 30 frequencies and activities are competing for the best locations on a nuclear carrier. The electronics laboratory continues to select the best place and what height for locating each antenna so there is minimum interference for all the communications. And it's still being done that way.

We had a meeting every week. Rear Admiral Armand Morgan was the BuShips rep for quite a few years. When he retired, he went to work at General Electric, where he was singularly responsible for setting up a research and development group to produce the type of diesel engines that the Navy needed for submarines. The merchant marine was slow in adopting diesel power to replace steam. GE assembled a professional group and in recent years has produced excellent diesel engines. Today there are more merchant ships on the high seas using diesel than there ever were. We had that problem on the Great Lakes when the first bulk carrier was built with diesels controlled from the navigating bridge. Skippers who had relied solely on steam initially opposed, as did the unions. They said, "We don't have enough qualified diesel people to man such ships."

We said, "You'd better start training them."

Paul Stillwell: What kind of an officer was Morgan? Do you have any other recollections about him?

---

* ONR – Office of Naval Research.

Admiral Knoll: He's a very levelheaded ship construction EDO. He had good experience with new construction, and he did a good job keeping operational officers informed of development. There were too many demands, and we had to determine good from bad and develop a ship within limits of tonnage and construction cost. I used to check a lot of things with Arleigh Burke and others to make sure I just wasn't committing CNO and Navy to radical developments. Basically we assembled all the requirements and desired equipment, then a list of what would be nice to have was provided. Methodically we checked each item, to identify what was really needed for the ship's task. Normally only what was really needed became a characteristic. The Navy could not afford more, price-wise and within tonnage. Vice Admiral Bob Pirie was very active in providing carrier needs.[*]

The FRAM program caused an interesting concern. From the end of the war until I became chairman of the Ship Characteristics Board, a major Navy program was to rid ships of all gasoline-operated equipment. For gasoline drums on each stern, there was a trip on the bridge for jettisoning all gasoline over the side. For FRAM we were talking about a new helicopter on the stern platform for all future Navy ships. At one of the SCB meetings, Chick Hayward, Navy R&D, was there. I asked, "Chick, are these helicopters you're designing going to burn gasoline?"

Hayward said, "Of course, they are."

I said, "You mean to tell me with all the effort the Navy has made to get rid of gasoline in the fleet, BuAer is still designing gasoline-burning helicopters?"[†] So in that I advised Arleigh Burke and Don Felt, and they got in touch with Bob Pirie.[‡] The Navy had spent a lot of money with ONR for an antisubmarine helicopter and never once gave attention to the effort the Navy had made to get all the gasoline off ships. Unless you ask tough questions, you wouldn't know what is happening behind your back.

Paul Stillwell: How did that one wind up?

---

[*] Vice Admiral Robert B. Pirie, Jr., USN, served as Deputy Chief of Naval Operations (Air) from 26 May 1958 to 1 November 1962. His oral history is in the Naval Institute collection.
[†] BuAer – Bureau of Aeronautics.
[‡] Admiral Harry D. Felt, USN, served as Vice Chief of Naval Operations from 1 September 1956 to 28 July 1958. His oral history is in the Naval Institute collection.

Admiral Knoll: They investigated the use of jet fuel since it is not as inflammable as gasoline. On a FRAM ship with helicopters more than two aviation people would be needed. Each ship was to have an aviation division. This was another controversy contrary to economic use of personnel.

Paul Stillwell: You mentioned *Enterprise*. There were also a nuclear cruiser and a nuclear destroyer coming out then, the *Long Beach* and the *Bainbridge*.[*] Were you involved in those two?

Admiral Knoll: Our board developed their characteristics, yes. We were partially involved with building *Savannah*, the first nuclear merchant ship.[†] Vice Admiral Rollo Wilson and I went to Camden more than once to see it building.[‡] It was a fiasco. It never proved to be the propaganda ship the U.S.A. wanted. First of all, officials ignored the possibility of going on an around-the-world cruise. It was to visit large ports as a nuclear-powered ship and would need clearance in advance to visit. Ultimately it was going to operate as a cruise ship and advertise American industry and advanced technology. Officials found out the ship couldn't go to any part of the world until advance arrangements were made for a nuclear-powered ship to visit. There was never a chance for such visits, particularly in Japan. Other nations were soon apprehensive about such visits.

Paul Stillwell: Did you have dealings with Rickover on the *Bainbridge* and *Long Beach*?

---

[*] USS *Long Beach* (CGN-9), the Navy's first nuclear-powered cruiser, was the only ship of her class. She was commissioned 9 September 1961. USS *Bainbridge* (DLGN-25), a nuclear-powered frigate, was the only ship of her class. She was commissioned 6 October 1962.

[†] NS *Savannah* was the world's first nuclear-powered passenger-cargo ship as a joint venture of the U.S. Maritime Administration and the Atomic Energy Commission. She was nearly 600 feet long, displaced 22,000 tons, and had a top speed of 24 knots. She was launched 21 July 1959. She carried cargo from 1964 to 1970 after several years of at-sea testing. She was retired in 1971 and later spent several years as a museum at Patriots Point, South Carolina.

[‡] Vice Admiral Ralph E. Wilson, USN, served as Deputy Chief of Naval Operations (Logistics), 1957-60. The construction was at New York Shipbuilding Corporation, Camden, New Jersey.

Admiral Knoll: No, not to any degree. We had some. He fought long and hard against construction of the *Thresher* because of the sound mounting of engine room machinery.* He fought it with all kinds of letters, and when *Thresher* was delivered Rickover went out for sea trials. He wrote personal letters to all members of the Senate and House Appropriations committees, thanking Congress for the foresight and the money to build the *Thresher*, the most modern, quietest submarine ever built.

When the *Thresher* was lost, Rear Admiral Dan Daspit, who was in charge of the board of inquiry, had Rickover as one of the first witnesses.† Rickover brought his letters that were written opposing construction of the *Thresher*. Danny Daspit had all the letters, also copies of the letters that Rickover had written on Electric Boat stationery to all the congressmen, congratulating them on construction of a superb submarine.‡ This was an example of how Rickover had letters pro and con on many subjects. After each successful trial at Electric Boat, it was customary to have a celebration party at the Lighthouse Inn in Groton. All the senior officials would show up, except Rickover. He'd never attend a party. He remained in the office of the president of Electric Boat, writing letters to congressmen.

We did a full-scale mockup of the control room and missile tubes on the Polaris submarine. The missile area was a new addition in the middle of a *Skipjack*-class submarine.§ I crawled through the mockup. The first time we visited, they started pulling cable into the control room until it was completely filled with cabling that would be sorted out and connected. Finally, cabling is incorporated at all phases of construction; cable lengths are known and put in when building the hull, rather than wait to pull cables after the hull is built. I attended the regular meetings for the Polaris project, of which Red Raborn was the chairman. Raborn had brickbat priority and all the

---

* *Thresher* (SSN-593) was commissioned 3 August 1961 as the first ship in her class. She was 278 feet long, 32 feet in the beam, and displaced 3,700 tons surfaced and 4,300 submerged. . She had a top speed on the surface in excess of 20 knots submerged. She was armed with four 21-inch torpedo tubes. She was later lost during trials on 10 April 1963.
† Rear Admiral Lawrence R. Daspit, USN, was a member of the court but not the head. The president of the *Thresher* court of inquiry was Vice Admiral Bernard L. Austin, USN.
‡ The Electric Boat Division of the General Dynamics Corporation is a long-time submarine building yard in Groton, Connecticut.
§ The original hull for the attack submarine *Scorpion* (SSN-589) was laid down on 1 November 1957 by Electric Boat. In December of that year the portion of the hull already built was split, extended, and later renamed *George Washington* (SSBN-598), effective 6 November 1958.

talents and assistance the national could provide to complete Polaris on schedule. You probably have Red Raborn's story on that, don't you?

Paul Stillwell: Yes.*

Admiral Knoll: I was at Electric Boat, checking the development of the *George Washington*, the first Polaris. They were testing how to compensate for the loss of weight of one Polaris missile with a volume of saltwater coming into the voids of the submarine so it would not porpoise when Polaris was launched. That was one of the final big tests of the hull design, to compensate for quantum loss of missile weight and equivalent volume of water. Another item was the design of the jet-a-vators on the base of the Polaris missile. Metal in jet-a-vators cannot melt or warp with the exposure of 22 seconds in 4,000-degree heat. Metallurgists solved this. These were the things you got in on, a little bit of everything.

Paul Stillwell: Did you have any involvement on the characteristics for the old cruisers that were converted to guided missiles at that time?

Admiral Knoll: No. The characteristics board had enough work dealing with new construction. Modernization of cruisers was the responsibility of the type commanders. They had to do what was feasible. We were concerned with the *Galveston* and its control problem with the Talos missile. The acquisition radar didn't work; it was an initial electronic scanner radar developed by Hughes. In the laboratory the radar worked and passed all the tests. Success with the electronic scanning radar in *Galveston* was needed, because the same type radars were called for in *Enterprise* and *Long Beach*.

It might be a simple problem that will exist for all time with computer controls. When the ship was under way, the ambient temperature surrounding radar equipment caused some by the sun on the outside of the hull became too high, much above the design temperature. The solution was to air-condition the space and maintain the ambient

---

* Raborn's Naval Institute oral history is in a special volume on Polaris.

temperature within a range of four degrees. This is a requirement today, even with the avionics of an airplane.

A .50-millimeter bullet through the avionics section of an airplane with all its fancy gear for missile control, and the ambient temperature cannot be maintained within about four degrees. There will be mal performance. This is true for all this tactical data system on present ships. Severe battle damage may quickly destroy modern technology and its exotic capabilities. There is little chance to avoid some battle damage in war. A Mark I eyeball, in a plane flying at Mach 2 will not see the target in time to make a hit.

I visited *Galveston* with BuShips representatives to observe performance. Normally all radio emissions within 100 miles of the ship appeared as small golf balls on the radar scope.

Paul Stillwell: You were experiencing interference.

Admiral Knoll: We were picking them up and unable to make acquisition of an airplane target. Something basically was wrong. After careful analysis and discussion with Al Mumma and Mike Honsinger, Mumma's deputy, I said, "We used help from the design people at Hughes on this ship. We must stop using retired Navy electronics people to tell us what's wrong. This is a design problem. We must tell Hughes the Navy will withhold all payments until Hughes design engineers visit *Galveston* to find out what's wrong."[*] I talked as well to the Inspection and Survey people. I said, "This is not a maintenance problem. This is a design problem, and we're not just going to find it without professional help." They did something about it.

Paul Stillwell: What about the new amphibious warfare ships that were coming out, the LPHs? Were you involved in those?

Admiral Knoll: No. The LPH idea had just seen the light of day. We had just started developing requirements. I think this evolved after study of the New Look strategy. The Navy needed 20-knot amphibious lift. This meant all amphib ships should have 20-knot

---

[*] Rear Admiral Leroy V. Honsinger, USN.

advance speed. There's no doubt about the need, because compared with World War II experience, smaller support ships and little boys couldn't keep up with the amphib force.

Paul Stillwell: Was there a concern during your time of protecting U.S. Navy ships against atomic attack?

Admiral Knoll: Some had started. The topside flushing system and protective clothing were proposed. There were many new ideas. As OP-43 I became involved with a lot of projects. From OP-43 I went as Commander DesFlot 4 and additional duty as recovery commander for NASA's Mercury project. I relieved Claude Ricketts, and subsequently Jack Chew relieved me and continued the work I had started with NASA.[*]

Paul Stillwell: I take it you were selected for rear admiral in the meantime.

Admiral Knoll: I was selected while I was OP-43, yes. I had gotten into the back channel of planning, and I didn't get out of it. I got on the other channel of joint planning, and I couldn't get out of that. The one refreshing thing was when I did get notice that I made flag rank, the number of messages I got from classmates and many friends, a lot of Navy wives and all said, "Congratulations, but my wife wouldn't have put up with many absences you put up with on the way to flag selection." I saw and was with my wife less than a total of 18 months from February 1940 and January 1948. It ruined my first wife's health, and she died in 1963. She couldn't tolerate the idea she was never seeing me. Her mother didn't help any; she never wanted her daughter to marry a Navy officer. We were never divorced. My long absences did ruin her health.

As for becoming a rear admiral, I was frocked the day I was selected, because I had to attend an inter-service meeting at Patuxent Air Station outside Washington.[†]

Paul Stillwell: Frocking was unusual for that era, wasn't it?

---

[*] Rear Admiral Claude V. Ricketts, USN; Rear Admiral John L. Chew, USN. Chew's oral history is in the Naval Institute collection.

[†] "Frocking" a naval officer refers to the practice of allowing him to wear the insignia and assume the title for which he was recently selected. The officer does not receive the pay for the higher rank until a vacancy appears on the lineal list so he can be officially promoted.

Admiral Knoll: It was done occasionally. This was for a closed conference with other services, and they said, "As long as you're going down there, put it on." In other words, the Navy wanted to have as much rank there as it could because of the Army and Air Force. I forget the conference involved.

The Navy had some dealing with Fort Eustis near Newport News involving an Army transport design. The Army conferences provided briefing manuals and helped our knowledge about cargo handling. This was helpful as we improved underway replenishment for the fleet.

As Commander DesFlot 4 at Norfolk, I arranged to plant a long row of trees at the destroyer-submarine base. Each tree had a plaque of the ship that sponsored it. When I relieved Ricketts, I had the sole command of some 90 destroyers in the Atlantic Fleet. By the time Jack Chew arrived, they had broken the flotilla into three groups, one at Charleston and one up at Newport, and a big group remained at Norfolk. The base at Norfolk was for destroyers and submarines. It was a big open expanse with all activity at the docks. The area needed improvement. I talked to different people, including Com Five, Massie Hughes.[*] I said, "I'm going to arrange that each ship is going to contribute a nominal fee from ship service money so we can hire someone to plant trees along the roads. Someday soon it will look a lot better than just having an open dusty lot with nothing being done there." Now, 20 years later, some may complain about the leaves that must be raked up every fall. I haven't seen it recently. Later, when I was ComServLant, I got involved in other projects to make NOB look more like a country club than an industrial complex.[†] That was one of the few things I did there at that time.

Paul Stillwell: Let's talk about the Mercury recovery program.[‡]

Admiral Knoll: I had quite a few meetings. A priority was to find out if there was a reliable continuous communications circuit around the world. There was none. There were blanks in Africa and the Indian Ocean area. This lack developed the requirement to take three Navy fleet oilers or MSTS tankers and use open space for a communication

---

[*] Rear Admiral Francis Massie Hughes, USN.
[†] NOB – naval operating base.
[‡] Project Mercury was the first U.S. manned space program. It ran from 1959 to 1963.

room for television and radio communications.* I visited the first ship when it was completed. It was a huge impressive installation in the cargo space. There were three of these ships. We needed them for the Mercury program, one ship in each ocean—Atlantic, Pacific, and Indian—to make sure that NASA had reliable continuous communications with the Mercury capsule orbiting the earth. There were additional stations on land. I saw one outside of Nairobi, Kenya, in Africa and one in India. It was quicker to have these ships ready for the Mercury communications, even though they weren't used for very long. They were only active for about two years until better land-based communications were built.

Paul Stillwell: As it turned out, you were really just doing the planning for the Mercury recovery at that point.

Admiral Knoll: One of the DesFlot 4 ships had recovered the first monkey that went up into space. The monkey had been trained at Electric Boat, Groton. After the monkey went up into space and came back, NASA was never able to put the special harness on the monkey again. Whatever the monkey experienced in space, he didn't want to do it again. The next one, Shepard, went up without orbiting; then John Glenn made the first orbits.†

Paul Stillwell: According to this bio, you had that job from October 1959 to May 1960. Shepard flew in 1961.

Admiral Knoll: It was in the preliminary. I never stayed for completion. Jack Chew followed me.

Paul Stillwell: Why was your tour so short there?

---

* MSTS – Military Sea Transportation Service.
† On 5 May 1961 Commander Alan B. Shepard, USN, became the first American astronaut to fly into space. He completed a 15-minute sub-orbital flight in a Mercury spacecraft. On 20 February 1962, Lieutenant Colonel John H. Glenn, Jr., USMC, flew the "Friendship 7" spacecraft on the first manned orbital mission by the United States.

Admiral Knoll: OpNav wanted me back in Washington. BuPers wanted a seagoing command on the record again.

Paul Stillwell: As your having had a sea command as a rear admiral.

Admiral Knoll: That's right.

Paul Stillwell: What was your flagship?

Admiral Knoll: The *Sierra*, a destroyer tender. The ship in which I frequently flew my flag was the *Norfolk*, the only ship of this type, a large destroyer.[*] It was a nice ship, and I went to sea in it a couple of times for minor operations. There were too many ships with many schedules.

Zumwalt put his ship in commission at that time as a commander.[†] I warned him that the Navy spent money for automation in the engine room, and I wanted him to operate his engineering department without the regular engine room force of many people. I asked him to operate it using all automatic controls because the Navy had spent money to reduce personnel and improve efficiency. I said, "If you're not going to operate this ship with a reduced number of crew it was designed to do, then the Navy will be unable to spend money for this extra automation. I want you after the first six months to come back and report the success of automation for operations. Talk to your division commander and your squadron commander about this. You're not going to continue to have extra people on the ship and not operate as designed." BuPers was still assigning people to many ships in terms of the old design, without reductions incident to automation.

Zumwalt operated with less people in the engineering spaces. For this I gave him some kind of commendation, but his division commander and his squadron commander

---

[*] USS *Norfolk* (DL-1) was a destroyer leader, also known as a frigate. She was originally projected as a hunter-killer cruiser. The ship was commissioned 4 March 1953.
[†] USS *Dewey* (DLG-14), the U.S. Navy's first guided missile frigate, was a ship of the *Coontz* class. She was commissioned 7 December 1959 with Commander Elmo R. Zumwalt Jr., USN, in command.

were not too happy at first. They talked to me about it. They said, "We have to be careful."

I said, "Wait a second. Future ships must use less personnel. We've gone through this test. We want Zumwalt to prove we can operate and do the job without having all these extra people aboard." And it worked. I know Zumwalt commented on this a couple of times later on. He did very well with the support primarily of SecNav Paul Nitze.*

Paul Stillwell: Did you have any other contact with Zumwalt?

Admiral Knoll: After I retired. They normally had a regular meeting of retired admirals in Washington when we had a chance to talk to each other and be brought up to date on Navy topics. Zumwalt and SecNav Warner appeared with their long hair and amazed the retired admirals.† It was a lively discussion—that their policies were contrary to the long-range interests of the Navy. Zumwalt finally had to moderate. The conference was an ideal opportunity to keep informed and meet old friends at the Marriott Hotel near the airport for two days. We'd have a good briefing with a chance to ask questions. Zumwalt got that reaction and decided never to convene another meeting.

Paul Stillwell: So you came back to Washington in 1960.

Admiral Knoll: Then I became OP-03D.‡ I was in charge of six to eight officers—aviators, submariners, public information, surface war, and legislation. The mission was to see how the Navy might keep the Air Force from achieving a single service. The group wrote various articles analyzing the pros and cons of the present organization and identified the hazards of a single service.

The only service that was an integrated service for each environment was the Navy. The Navy operates under the water, on the water, above the water, and into space.

---

* As a four-star admiral Zumwalt served as Chief of Naval Operations, 1970-74. In the mid-1960s he had been executive assistant to Secretary of the Navy Paul H. Nitze.
† John W. Warner served as Secretary of the Navy from 4 May 1972 to 9 April 1974.
‡ Knoll's title in the OpNav organization was Director, Technical Studies Group.

We're not going to be partial. We're going to be a specialty involving the oceans in what relates to the Navy. In an argument, Colonel Frank Everest said, "I don't have any argument for the need of naval aviation, but I can't understand why the Navy has to spend money for an airplane that can't fly more than about 600 miles inland from a carrier. That's a job for the Air Force. There should be a policy as to what certain planes are needed for the Navy job and the same for Army and Air Force planes."[*]

Our group must have written about 30 or 40 analyses about this and mailed them to naval flag officers about once a month. They conveyed the news circulating in Washington. They were well received. A couple of officers, particularly my own classmates, told me that that was not my job, and I shouldn't do it. Arleigh Burke knew what I was doing and had copies of all of them.

There was one that made the people in Congress quite annoyed, and that's the one that analyzed the checks and balances in a democratic society. We have checks and balances not only on the policy level but on other levels of operations when people are dealing with each other. Well, some way or other, Senator Symington and a few other people, even Senator Lyndon Johnson, got the paper, and they didn't like what it said.[†] Someone talked to Arleigh Burke about what I was trying to say. They inferred that because of the checks and balances the Congress should give attention to Navy views. Congress read something into it that was never meant.

At that time, I obtained a copy of the Air Force black book, telling how they were going to reorganize the whole Department of Defense to be one service and how it was going to use each service.

Paul Stillwell: You got hold of it. Was this a covert thing?

Admiral Knoll: It was a covert job. It was a document for eyes only of the most senior Air Force officers.

---

[*] Colonel Frank K. Everest Jr., USAF, served with Knoll in the mid-1950s in developing the "New Look" strategy..
[†] W. Stuart Symington, a Democrat from Missouri, served in the Senate from 3 January 1953 until 27 December 1976. He had previously been Secretary of the Air Force, 1947-50. Lyndon B. Johnson, a Democrat from Texas, served in the Senate from 3 January 1949 to 3 January 1961. He was Senate majority leader from 1955 to 1961. He was later Vice President from 1961 to 1963 and President from 1963 to 1969.

Paul Stillwell: How did you get one?

Admiral Knoll: Well, I don't remember. Somebody told me such a book existed. I forget the individual who told me. Someone came to me and said, "You know, there's an Air Force book about so thick, tells how the Air Force is going to reorganize all of us and how they're going to run the Department of Defense in the future, and it's all in writing with charts."

I said, "Well, let's go out to dinner and figure out how we can get a copy." This individual was a close friend of an Air Force brigadier general named Richardson.* A copy apparently was on his desk. The general went out of town for a day or so, and the individual gave it to me to read overnight. I had about 12 copies photostatted overnight. I sent one to the Eisenhower staff at the White House, sent one to the Secretary of the Navy, one to Arleigh Burke. All hell broke loose. In a couple of weeks, Drew Pearson was writing about me, that I was operating like OP-23, Arleigh Burke, when he tried to prevent a single service.† Pearson said I was building myself up to be CNO like Arleigh Burke did.‡ I've got a copy of it someplace. The article wasn't written by Drew Pearson; it was written by Jack Anderson, who was a close friend of this Air Force brigadier general, who is working today with the American Security Council. There were two articles like that, and then I saw Drew Pearson in the dining room of the Mayflower Hotel, where he generally ate lunch. I'd go in there from time to time with some friends. I went over to him, and I said, "I don't know why you question my Navy work."

Pearson said, "I know what you're doing, and I know what you've done. I know the effort you've made in psychological warfare. I'm going to correct it." I have one of his corrected columns. Secretary McNamara assumed where there was smoke, there was fire, and that I must be doing something wrong.§

---

* Brigadier General Robert C. Richardson III, USAF, who was involved in long-range planning.
† In 1949 Captain Arleigh A. Burke, USN, headed OP-23, a Navy research group that gathered information critical of the Air Force B-36 bomber and its capabilities. Burke's Naval Institute oral history includes his memories of OP-23 service.
‡ Andrew Pearson was a muckraking syndicated newspaper columnist. Jack Anderson was his assistant. The Pearson column was published in January 1961, shortly after Kennedy became President. It alleged a Navy effort to subvert service reorganization plans.
§ Robert S. McNamara served as Secretary of Defense from 21 January 1961 to 29 February 1968.

At that time there was quite an argument over who was going to have control of space. There were JCS papers on the subject, top secret nature, very limited distribution. To my knowledge, I never saw the sensitive papers. I knew of their existence. All of a sudden, to my amazement, copies of these papers were available to various members of Congress. The provost marshal of Secretary of Defense McNamara determined by some process of elimination that I was the most likely to have sent them. This was a feed in from the Air Force people who were trying to build up a case against me. They had some suspicion that I had their black book and reproduced and distributed it. I was the one responsible, but they couldn't prove it. I thought I had a copy of the book in my files someplace, but I can't find it now.

It was hard to conceive that the Air Force was so naïve as to put something in writing detailing their plans for a single service. At that time I think SecNav John Connally was one with whom I had discussed this.* He told me any time I wanted to come in his office, I was welcome. I was with him and his wife the night President Kennedy was inaugurated, at one of the inauguration banquets.† It was at the Wardman Park Hotel, eight to a table.

Finally I was called for a meeting with the provost marshal of SecDef McNamara, an Army colonel. I was cross-examined about what I knew of the JCS papers. I said I didn't have access. I'd been tipped off by a couple of friends that certain people were sending material to Congress. The courier would leave for the Hill, and en route they would spend time in my office. Then they'd go down to visit George Miller in the strategic survey office of the Joint Chiefs, and finally they'd go to Congress.‡ Someone determined that the JCS material they were taking to Congress was coming from my office.

We had been writing these letters, some of which they didn't approve. There were about eight of us in there working on documents, and Bob Pirie made some suggestion to make sure the naval aviators' position on space was supported. It was an interesting operation. We were very busy. The one paper that we never finished dealt

---

* John B. Connally Jr., served as Secretary of the Navy from 25 January 1961 to 20 December 1961.
† John F. Kennedy served as President of the United States from 20 January 1961 until he was assassinated on 22 November 1963.
‡ Rear Admiral George H. Miller, USN, did strategic planning in OpNav. His oral history is in the Naval Institute collection.

with the military-industrial complex and its relation to the aviation industry that influenced procurement and the national policy, to the degradation of a balanced military program.

I had some contacts in Erie, and around this time I received a call from the Pennsylvania chairman of the Democratic Party. He said, "The articles by Drew Pearson look like you're in trouble. Are you in trouble?"

I said, "I haven't done anything wrong. It looks like a group in the Air Force are annoyed that I'm actually trying to prevent the Air Force from becoming a single service."

He said, "Well, we'll see what we can do. Do you mind if I talk to Jack Kennedy?"

I said, "No."

"Okay, we'll be in touch with you."

About a week later, I received another call. He said, "I've talked to Jack Kennedy, and he says he knows you haven't done anything wrong, and he knows what's behind it. He wants me to tell you that if anything further appears, he wants you to call him at the White House, and he'll talk to you personally. There are two officers who may be fired, one in the Navy and one in the Air Force."

When I heard this, I talked to Arleigh Burke and Jim Russell.[*] I said, "Arleigh, I'm going to Norfolk to see my wife this weekend. I'll go out and brief Bob Dennison."[†]

Burke said, "Fine."

I visited Bob Dennison, whom I had kept advised of events. Normally I would see him on Saturday morning for a half hour at his home. I said, "You'd better have Fitzhugh Lee in here. I think he ought to hear what has happened."[‡] So I told him the whole story and the message from President Kennedy: "A naval officer and an Air Force officer are going to get fired if the adverse comments don't stop. Arleigh told me to do nothing further in OP-03D, just sort of wrap up." I forget what specific jobs I did for

---

[*] Admiral James S. Russell, USN, served as Vice Chief of Naval Operations from 1 August 1958 to 1 November 1961. His oral history is in the Naval Institute collection.

[†] Admiral Robert L. Dennison, USN, served as Supreme Allied Commander Atlantic, Commander in Chief Atlantic, and Commander in Chief Atlantic Fleet from 28 February 1960 to 30 April 1963. His oral history is in the Naval Institute collection.

[‡] Vice Admiral Fitzhugh Lee, USN, Deputy Commander in Chief Atlantic Fleet. Lee's oral history is in the Naval Institute collection.

Arleigh Burke. Fitzhugh Lee just sat there and listened, and I knew Lee knew and Bob Dennison undoubtedly knew who the Navy man was that might be fired. We all had a pretty good idea. I knew pretty well who might be fired in the Air Force. It wasn't hard for the President to know who was behind the bickering between the Navy and the Air Force. The Navy officer was a protégé of Bob Pirie.

Paul Stillwell: Was he an aviator?

Admiral Knoll: Yes.

Paul Stillwell: Can you mention his name?

Admiral Knoll: No, I should not mention names.

I talked to Arleigh Burke about the meeting with McNamara's provost and the message from President Kennedy to call him if the pressure continued. Burke said, "Okay, don't write any more papers." I did various jobs for CNO. He said, "You will be ComServLant soon."[*] I think it was three months later when I received my orders.

Things suddenly quieted down, and I went as ComServLant. I was involved first with Fitzhugh Lee and then Wally Beakley as deputies.

Paul Stillwell: Was ServLant considered a desirable command?

Admiral Knoll: Very much. It had recently been a vice admiral's billet. There were about 100 ships, doing every kind of logistic service. The development of the high-lift transfer and underway replenishment were being tested and developed. The computerized inventories of supply ships were being tested.

---

[*] ComServLant – Commander Service Force Atlantic Fleet. Admiral Knoll held the job from June 1961 to July 1963.

The Cuban Missile Crisis was a busy time.* We had two meetings a day with Admiral Dennison, generally in the morning and then at 6:00 at night. A few times we'd have as many as 60 flag officers of all the services, including reps from Langley Air Force Base. It was a Sunday morning when we were at a meeting when we knew of the agreements between Kennedy and Khrushchev; then the Soviet ships were going to return to the Black Sea. Reports from our carriers and our aircraft were that the Soviet merchant ships were starting to turn around to go back to U.S.S.R. We knew some kind of nuclear material was in the ships. Soviet ships were more than halfway across the Atlantic.

One sad part of the operation was an event that may exist to this day: the Atlantic Fleet had only enough .50-caliber ammunition for two sorties from each carrier. Half of that ammunition was kept on each ammunition ship under my control with the orders it couldn't move without permission of CinCLantFlt or Wally Beakley. Chick Hayward had a carrier group on the south coast of Cuba.† He was checking how much .50-caliber ammunition he had and found out he had only enough for one sortie, so he ordered my ammunition ship alongside to turn over the rest of the .50-caliber ammunition to his carrier. He wanted to be ready. In a matter of about 30 minutes, Hayward had messages from me and CinCLant: "You cannot move any .50 caliber from an ammo ship without the approval of the fleet commander."

Paul Stillwell: What was the purpose of keeping it on the ammo ships instead of the carriers?

Admiral Knoll: In case one carrier or carrier group got in a firefight, we were ready to give where needed. We had allocated equal amounts for all the carriers. McNamara didn't believe that .50-caliber ammunition was in short supply. He kept saying, "You've got all kinds of ammunition; you're hiding it from me." McNamara had a special search

---

* The Cuban Missile Crisis was triggered in mid-October 1962, when a U.S. reconnaissance plane photographed a Soviet nuclear missile site in Cuba and the presence of Soviet bombers. On 22 October President John F. Kennedy went on national television to announce a naval quarantine of Cuba, to be implemented on 24 October. On 28 October Premier Nikita Khrushchev of the Soviet Union notified President Kennedy that he was ordering the withdrawal of Soviet bombers and missiles from Cuba.
† Rear Admiral John T. Hayward, USN, Commander Carrier Division Two on board the *Enterprise*.

team go to all the Navy ammunition dumps to prove there was none in storage. He quickly allowed the production lines to start producing such ammo. McNamara had a policy of disposing of supplies that had been in storage for seven years or more. He assumed huge quantities of ammo were in storage from World War II. With aircraft operations .50-caliber ammo has been used at a high rate.

Paul Stillwell: Let's talk about McNamara and his effect when he came in. You were still in Washington when he started.

Admiral Knoll: Oh, sure, sure.

Paul Stillwell: What changes came about?

Admiral Knoll: It ended up that the services had no control over their destiny. Each service had no control over spending appropriated money or making new contracts. He violated the basic law that the office of the Secretary of Defense should be limited to about 200 people. He ordered the services to send officers and men to augment his staff or civilians to augment the Secretary of Defense's office. Such billets were charged to the services. He circumvented limitation. He sent civilian inspectors to all warehouses without people in Washington knowing about it. They designated vast amounts of spare parts from warehouses to be sold for scrap if in storage for more than seven years.

Paul Stillwell: You discussed that before we turned the tape on, so could you go over that again, please?

Admiral Knoll: An order came out, anything that had been in a warehouse for more than seven years was a waste of time and money. No one ever gave thought how many ships in commission, like T-2 tankers or steam turbine ships that needed turbine blading and spare parts were more than seven years in commission. Turbine blading, even though it's been in the warehouse seven years, would be needed. It was cheaper to have it in storage, ready for an emergency. During the Cuban Missile Crisis, we found there were no tail shafts in storage for T-2 tankers. ComServLant needed to replace my tankers' tail shafts. I had to send a ServLant supply officer and buy Navy tail shafts from a Kearny, New Jersey, junk yard and have them moved to the Navy yard for installation. More tankers would need new tail shafts. Tail shafts for entire ships had been sold without knowledge of the operations of the Navy.

The same way ServLant needed new blading for the first and second stages of some main turbines. Some ships had to operate almost a year at lower speed until new turbine blading was produced to replace quantifies of turbine blading that had been sold, with no attention to how many active fleet ships still had a need for such blading. To produce new blading was very expensive, compared to blading that had been in storage and ready for use for more than seven years.

A new high-lift constant-tension supply ship was under construction for improved underway replenishment. This was the *Sacramento*, built up at the Puget Sound Naval Shipyard.* The officer who had worked for me on the characteristics for this type was the production officer at Puget Sound. I went up there for an inspection visit. He said, "Do you know, this ship will need 64 winches aboard to handle all this highline and booms."

As ComServLant, I briefed Bob Dennison. I said, "We've got an order from SecDef saying that the 64 winches have to be from three different contractors. Only one-third can be from our reliable producer, Hyde Winch. The second third have to be from a contractor the Navy selects, and the last third have to be from a new contractor who has never produced seagoing winches. Can you imagine a new commanding officer or the cargo officer having such a maintenance problem with spare parts for three different makes of winches? Every time the ship goes in for overhaul, the CO is going to have replace the duds with Hydes ultimately to assure good performance with uniform installation supported. by one kind of spare parts."

Bob Dennison was shocked. I helped write a letter on the fiasco, and he sent the letter through CNO to the Secretary of the Navy. Nothing ever happened; SecDef was adamant.

---

* USS *Sacramento* (AOE-1) was the first of a new type known as fast combat support ship. She was commissioned 14 March 1964.

Paul Stillwell: So they got three different kinds?

Admiral Knoll: Started with them. This is the kind of nonsense that was frustrating us in OpNav and in the fleet.

Another situation arose while I was oceanographer-hydrographer. We had to be careful in enforcing a contract that might politically damage someone. I carried out the contract and was told later that I was supported. I had been called by Ted Kennedy and his staff, that I shouldn't cancel the procurement contract, even though a clause with this contractor in Massachusetts had agreed to build a number of current meters for deep-sea analysis for submarine warfare in the Tongue of the Ocean.* The contractor guaranteed to deliver reliable meters on such-and-such a date, and if the meters weren't delivered by then, I was authorized to procure from another contractor and that the original contractor paid the difference in cost. This was all in a valid contract.

There was an indication he was not going to make the delivery date. He hadn't produced one satisfactory current meter. He had all kinds of problems. His meter didn't work the way he promised. I think he was at Maynard, Massachusetts. Oceanography had a project with high priority. We had to start producing research data for the submarine people. I had the contract to obtain the current meters on time. So I called the contractor twice, and I said, "If I don't have delivery of at least one meter within the agreed date, I am giving the contract to a competitor, and you're going to pay the difference."

The phones started ringing—from SecDef, OpNav, and Congress. The meters did not arrive. I put out an official notice that the contract was violated and gave the procurement contract to his competitor. A civilian official from McNamara's office, formerly an Assistant Secretary of the Navy that I knew somewhat, said, "I'm over here to know the whole background on the contract."

I gave him the whole background, showed him the contract, and I said, "I've done nothing wrong. We need material now. I've got a job to carry out for Navy R&D. I

---

* Edward M. Kennedy, brother of President John F. Kennedy, was a Democrat from Massachusetts. He served in the Senate from 3 January 1963 until his death on 25 August 2009.

made the contract. This man hasn't produced. His competitor can deliver, and he pays the different, and I must carry this out."

The McNamara rep spent about a half hour with me, a very nice fellow, and he left without agreeing or disagreeing. I never heard anything more about it until about three months later, at a Navy League affair at the Statler Hotel. The gentleman came over to me, and he said, "Knoll, I went back and made a full report. I told them you were absolutely right." Here again was pressure politically, and you can't imagine the contracts that were given to people to get them started in computer work. The cost of all these spare parts is a part of the basic contracts. The Navy user, who in the past would be able to supervise and have some control, is ignored.

The average individual in SecDef's office today comes from the defense industry. He spends two years there, receives practically a flag officer's pay, and goes back to the defense industry he came from. While in Defense, they make certain their parent industries are kept supplied with contracts. Until the Navy goes back to the competition system that gives the contract to the man best qualified with good past performance, the budget will be high. Single-source contracts must be stopped.

A man in uniform fights this political pressure—cooperate or be sent out of Washington and fail to be promoted. With MSTS I refused to help Sea-Land build 12 or 14 new containerships for the Vietnam War. This would have given them new capability in the Pacific. Sea-Land was owned by Reynolds Aluminum and Malcom McLean.[*]

Paul Stillwell: You just touched on the fringes of the Cuban Missile Crisis. Maybe you cold give a chronological view, just as you remember things—your first notification that this was a problem, let's say.

Admiral Knoll: We had regular meetings every morning with Admiral Dennison, all the type commanders. We met at 8:00 o'clock. There was an intelligence briefing and general discussion of readiness for possible military operations to prevent Soviet merchant units from landing nuclear components for missiles in Cuba.

---

[*] Malcom McLean in 1934 founded McLean Trucking Company, which became one of the largest in the country in its field. In 1955 he introduced containerized shipping of cargo through Sea-Land Service.

Some U.S.S.R. merchant ships from the Black Sea were identified as transporting nuclear weapons to Cuba. Flag officers from the Army and Air Force attended most meetings to prepare for joint operations. The Army wanted the carriers to load jet fuel for helicopter assault. Army jet fuel was more volatile that the aviation jet fuel used by the Navy. According to the Bureau of Mines, the Navy wasn't to load Army jet fuel in Navy tankers and carriers for refueling. The Army wanted to make use of the carrier *Lexington* to carry Army jet fuel and have ServLant fleet oilers transfer this jet fuel to the carrier. I found out that with special precautions, the Navy could probably handle it without violations.

Tests were conducted with Army helicopters and *Lexington*. A high priority was to use as many ships as ServLant had to keep the fleet replenished. Every ServLant logistic ship was under way, particularly to refuel all types of ships, principally destroyers and cruisers. All ServLant ships operated independently, because the cruisers, carriers, and destroyers were widely dispersed, nothing in one central group. There were 13 or 14 fleet oilers under way, and ServLant assigned replenishment as we found need and location. We knew there were some submarines in the area. At least one U.S.S.R. sub fleet was prepared for any event.

It was never clear to us what might be ordered from Washington. More and more preparations were made to invade Cuba in the event Soviets started landing nuclear material. There was one group to land near Havana and another group to land near Camaguey on the south coast. Two groups of two carriers each were ready to support both coasts. Each carrier was supposed to have enough .50-caliber ammunition for one sortie. Additional ammo was ready for the first carrier group that engaged in combat.

One Soviet submarine broke down and had to cruise on the surface. A destroyer was ordered to escort the submarine to the English Channel. The submarine was about 400 miles off the Atlantic coast. The destroyer escort requested fuel. ServLant designated the nearest fleet oiler to overtake the destroyer and submarine for refueling.

The Atlantic Fleet knew where every ship was, and ComServLant maintained a plot of locations of all replenishment ships. CinCLant was advised, "Don't worry. ComServLant has ordered a tanker to join the destroyer for refueling. There was good teamwork for all operations. There were a million and one problems receiving attention.

The tanker gave a wonderful demonstration while trailing the sub. When the tanker arrived, it went alongside the destroyer. About one-third of the submarine crew came topside to watch the refueling. The destroyer escorted the Soviet sub until it was joined by a Soviet tug closer to the English Channel.

Scouting operations were watching with air cover the U.S.S.R. ships that had left the Black Sea and were heading toward Cuba. Some Navy units had provided parachute drops of magazines and candy to the crews of U.S.S.R. cargo ships as a friendly gesture. Some U.S.S.R. ships were identified as carrying some nuclear material. They were watched very closely. Of course, I was involved with supply of food and expendables to all ships.

Before the end of the crisis, ComServLant started loading Christmas trees on all ServLant force ships, to be delivered to units of Atlantic Fleet ships that might remain on patrol over Christmas. The Navy had sent truck convoys to Ohio to obtain extra loads of eggs and butter, because requirements for all ships had pyramided. Ships of the service force operated at wartime tempo, using a lot of operating time. Fortunately, there were no serious casualties, except two tankers needing new tail shafts. With possible combat getting closer and closer, it was a big letdown to hear Kennedy and Khrushchev agree and hear the Soviets had started to turn around for return to the Black Sea.

Paul Stillwell: What about providing nuclear weapons for possible use in Cuba? Did your ships do that?

Admiral Knoll: No, at that time there was no mention of such cargo.

Paul Stillwell: No nuclear rearmament capability?

Admiral Knoll: No, not at that time. There did not appear to be a threat of such a thing. It was an interesting operation, knowing how close we came to confrontation. I think the Soviets knew how ready we were and the many ships that were deployed and ready for any eventuality. The Soviets may have had three or four submarines that were reporting our deployment. Their nuclear submarines were very noisy and easy to detect and identify.

Every ServLant ship was under way during the crisis. Frank O'Beirne and Whitey Taylor suggested that ComServLant should receive some kind of decoration for the reliable service provided.* The only one who received a decoration was Wally Beakley. I was with the group when we visited the Rose Garden at the White House for Admiral Dennison to receive his decoration from President Jack Kennedy. After the decoration, I addressed Kennedy, "Mr. President, I'm Denys Knoll." I reminded him that Drew Pearson had made some critical remarks about me in his column.

Kennedy said, "Anybody still putting out bad word about you?"

I said, "No, everything's fine."

He said, "Remember, if it starts again, you call me personally, because I'm ready to fire a couple of people." A Navy rear admiral and an Air Force brigadier general had circulated rumors that I was making an effort to relieve Admiral Burke.

Paul Stillwell: One of the things you did in that job as ComServLant was have some of your ships serve as a training ground and proving ground for future carrier skippers.

Admiral Knoll: That's correct.

Paul Stillwell: Could you talk about that role?

Admiral Knoll: We had a selection of potential carrier skippers. They were primarily assigned to ammunition ships and supply ships. A big ship like a tanker was good for some work with the fleet. However, a tanker has to operate independently to pick up a load of oil. Tankers provided insufficient experience with the fleet and the handling of ships with fleet formations. There was more opportunity of maneuvering with cargo ships or an ammunition ship, and the ammunition ships were the ones BuPers preferred to

---

* Vice Admiral Frank O'Beirne, USN, was Commander Naval Air Force Atlantic Fleet from 30 September 1960 to 30 September 1963. Vice Admiral Edmund B. Taylor, USN, served from 1960 to 1963 as Commander Antisubmarine Defense Force Atlantic Fleet (later Antisubmarine Warfare Force Atlantic Fleet).

use because it was a good-size command and had good responsibility and permitted supervision to qualification. There was a good check how well each skipper was doing from the reports we received from squadron commanders. BuPers gave them a chance for a year to get a feel handling the ship, but they still had a lot more to learn when they became skipper of the carrier.

Paul Stillwell: How did you get these reports on how well they were doing?

Admiral Knoll: Service Force squadron commanders and my personnel officer kept a check on all operations and ships involved. We did rely a lot on the individual, who knew how well he was doing. We wanted him to admit that he had confidence, and he knew what he was doing. Because some of them had never really handled a ship before. I had some discussion with Ingersoll, Beakley, and even Bob Dennison. From the standpoint of aviation, as an aerologist, association with aviation (except never being on a carrier), my experience in handling a ship was better qualified to be a commanding officer of a carrier than a naval aviator is qualified to command a naval surface ship. Giving in on this would mean the naval aviator would want more big commands and compete with surface officers for command of all surface ships. It might reduce the number of big surface ships available for black-shoe surface officers.

Paul Stillwell: Was it up to you to say whether an individual skipper had passed the test?

Admiral Knoll: Yes. I could say if someone needed a little more time. Normally BuPers would suggest assignments of officers with excellent reputations, and we were ready to cooperate. Normally before taking command a new skipper would call for discussion of his future duties. It was an opportunity to know the individual and his past experience. They were all highly motivated and anxious to obtain experience for handling a carrier in the near future.

Paul Stillwell: Did it ever turn out that somebody didn't get his carrier as a result?

Admiral Knoll: Not to my knowledge. Normally BuPers had carefully screened them; they never sent an officer to me they didn't think would cut the mustard. I had that assurance from Smeddy and others.* On first interview I could have advised BuPers if someone did not impress me as to his aptitude.

Paul Stillwell: In popular lore, the service force and the amphibious force at that time weren't getting as good of officers as went into the cruisers and destroyers. Did you observe that? Is that a fair statement?

Admiral Knoll: Well, I would say this was not necessarily true. Certain individuals show their preference for duty. Some officers gave a preference for duty saying they'd prefer to be on the East Coast in the Norfolk area, with duty with the service force, the amphibious force, or a cruiser, just to be in the Norfolk area, rather than specify a particular type of ship. The cruisers available compared with other ships are limited. Past performance of duties in cruisers, destroyers, and battleships influences BuPers to assist officers with superior performance to be assigned the more desirable billets. Good officers receive attention.

As far as my staff was concerned, I never had a complaint about the caliber of the people assigned, particularly supply officers, the engineers, and the repair officers. They were topnotch. I couldn't ask for anyone better in the Navy. Operation officers were always superior. They knew their business for handling the many variety of ships in the service force. We had many changes in schedule, many things to do, and many operation orders. Many officers knew what they were doing to make sure of the scheduling of all ships to obtain their supplies on time.

Today, with the requisitioning and automatic scheduling by computer, the volume of paperwork by ComServLant should be reduced. Today a ship goes alongside, a pallet is ready, based on normal expenditures. The mean time between failures determines when expendables should be replaced. Experimentation with computers and automatic

---

* Vice Admiral William R. Smedberg III, USN, served as Chief of the Bureau of Naval Personnel from 12 February 1960 to 11 February 1964. His oral history is in the Naval Institute collection.

requisitioning of expendable supplies were in process while I was ComServLant. Control of pay records of carriers was given tests.

Paul Stillwell: So do you think you were getting the best available people in the force?

Admiral Knoll: I never thought I had other than excellent personnel on the ServLant staff. I had people who could do the job, and there was good teamwork. BuPers and the officers in charge of the detail desk made proposals and helped us obtain personnel with good performance records. Assignment to the ServLant staff based in Norfolk was essentially shore duty. There were adequate numbers requesting duty in Norfolk to be with their families. BuPers thus had adequate numbers of good people to meet our needs.

Paul Stillwell: How much time did you spend out aboard ships of your force?

Admiral Knoll: I visited two or three ships in the Norfolk area every week. Twice I inspected ServLant ships with the Sixth Fleet. I visited and inspected the ships when they returned to Norfolk from deployment. The staff visited ships regularly. I knew most of the skippers and knew how well they performed. There was at least one or two changes of command every month. Occasionally a hurricane would move up the coast, and we were ready to get under way and go to sea to avoid damage. Admiral Dennison visited at least once and asked, "Where's the hurricane going to go?" I suggested diversion of ships to avoid the path of a hurricane.

Paul Stillwell: You were the in-house expert.

Admiral Knoll: It was always a friendly visit and an opportunity to discuss other subjects.

Paul Stillwell: Did you work with the Second Fleet Commander on getting your ships ready to deploy?

Admiral Knoll: No, that was his problem. I had many jobs with the fleet salvage force, which was part of ServLant. We had one reserve fleet destroyer under tow that beached on the New Jersey shore high and dry during a spring northeast gale. A salvage force tug dug a trench in the sand and pulled the inactive destroyer back to deep water. It was good training. Navy ships are very tough. It was a reserve fleet ship from Boston with no one aboard. When it finally arrived at Philadelphia after being pulled through the sand and off the beach, there wasn't one leak in the hull, which was unusual for a destroyer with the sonar dome forward. A deep trench surrounded the ship. With assistance of air jets to move sand and four ServLant tugs, the destroyer was refloated.

Paul Stillwell: Do you remember what ship that was?

Admiral Knoll: I think it was the *Monssen*.[*] It had beached with a high wave that carried it over a rock groin and left it high and dry at Ocean Beach, New Jersey. It was possible to walk around the ship in the sand. It took us about six weeks to salvage it. The salvage officer and my operations officer were told, "I want every morning by 6:00 o'clock a status report as to the progress of this salvage operation. The CNO's briefing room would thus have it in time for the morning briefing at 8:00 A.M. Any day a status report is not available, CNO will be asking what we are doing about it."

George Anderson was CNO, and he said, "Denny Knoll is making sure we will not have to ask for a progress report."[†] Experience with Seventh Fleet taught me to keep the admiral informed of progress with any special task."

Paul Stillwell: Any other salvage job during that period that stands out?

Admiral Knoll: We had to search for lost planes that crashed in manmade lakes on the borders of North Carolina and Virginia. Political leaders requested assistance for finding

---

[*] In early 1962, the decommissioned destroyer *Monssen* (DD-798) was being towed down the East Coast to the reserve fleet at Philadelphia. On 6 March the towline to the destroyer parted in high winds and heavy seas. She went aground at Beach Haven Inlet, New Jersey, and remained there for six weeks before being pulled off and completing the original trip. She was sold for scrap in 1963.

[†] Admiral George W. Anderson, Jr., USN, served as Chief of Naval Operations from 1 August 1961 to 1 August 1963. His oral history, including an account of his being relieved of duty as CNO, is in the Naval Institute collection.

the planes and occupants. Salvage had to be careful, because our divers could see only short distances in the brackish waters when below the surface more than about 20 feet. When lakes were made with dams, they failed to clean away the trees and undergrowth. Divers had to use a buddy system and not get fouled up. We had to be very careful when we took these jobs. Fortunately, both times divers went over and found the planes hanging in trees with the individuals in them. Needless to say, we took a lot of precaution not to get fouled up in the former oak trees that had never been cleared before the area was flooded.

Speaking of divers, there was another incident that illustrated why Rickover hated my guts. Bill Blewett, whom I've mentioned in connection with the FRAM program, was president at Newport News Shipbuilding.[*] I received word that they were going to have to dry-dock the carrier *Enterprise* prior to acceptance trials because of some foul-up in the intake through the sea valves to the condenser.[†] I said, "Well, what are you going to have to dock it for?"

He said, "That's the only way we can repair the sea valves."

I said, "My salvage officer with the Service Force Atlantic Fleet with divers would like to do this for practice."

He said, "What do you mean?"

I said, "What's your clearance under the keel at high tide?"

He said, "Three or four feet with the *Enterprise* alongside the dock."

I said, "Well, divers can crawl under there and put a flange on the outer side of your condenser chest so you can open it up from the inside and repair the valve. When you're ready, we remove the flange. Why spend three or four days and thousands of dollars to dry-dock the ship when we can do it over a weekend? Then *Enterprise* can still go out next week and do the trials that Rickover wants to conduct."

He said, "That's a hell of a good idea."

---

[*] William E. Blewett, Jr., was president of Newport News Shipbuilding and Dry Dock Company from 1954 to 1961, when he became chairman.
[†] USS *Enterprise* (CVAN-65) was commissioned 25 November 1961 as the world's first nuclear-powered aircraft carrier.

I said, "Well, I'll call Jimmy James and see if the Bureau of Ships has any objection. I need this training for my salvage force. I'm trying to help out and not waste the money."

I called Jimmy James, who said, "No objection. That's a wonderful idea."

I said, "Fine." I had a good Scotchman who was a terrific diver and a good salvage officer. He said, "That's wonderful. That's different."

I called Bill Blewett, and I said, "My salvage crew will be over there putting the flange on. We'll work over the weekend and put it back on Monday morning so you'll be able to go out on time."

We checked the tides to make sure they had enough time to be under there at high tide with good clearance. About the time the salvage detail left, I received a call from Rickover. He blasted me in a few words and was annoyed because by my helping Bill Blewett Rickover was losing an opportunity for him to make an adverse report on Newport News Shipbuilding.

I said, "What are you talking about?"

"You're doing something to the *Enterprise*."

I said, "No, I'm training my divers for salvage operation. They need some diving for this kind of work."

"That's what you say. So-and-so, so-and-so."

So, sure enough, they did it and completed on time. He knew I was just chuckling. He was trying to say, "See? Newport News couldn't do it on time. There's been so much delay and everything else." And he did things like this, but I always enjoyed it.

Paul Stillwell: What do you remember about the *Thresher* and the search for that wreckage?* She was lost in April 1963.

Admiral Knoll: A couple of ServLant tugs were nearby, and one received the last message from the *Thresher*, with an indication there was an explosion plus an implosion

---

* The nuclear-powered attack submarine *Thresher* (SSN-593) was lost with all hands on 10 April 1963 while operating east of Cape Cod. The presumed cause was a reactor shut-down during a dive.

that was heard. It was later on, when I was oceanographer-hydrographer that the Navy developed, with Professor Edgerton at MIT, the strobe cameras that procured a mosaic of pictures of the entire ocean floor.* They showed pieces of the *Thresher* scattered over an area almost a mile long and half a mile wide. We could identify many important parts. At one time the Navy had talked about salvage of the bow and the new sonar, which was worth $1.5 million. The sonar was a prototype, and there was thought of trying to snag that and pull it up gradually up the slope of the continental shelf from 8,000 feet, where it lay. The pictures revealed a couple of sleeves of petty officers hanging on some of the wreckage but not one sign of a bone or human body. These mosaics were assembled on a floor to show a picture of the whole area. The strobe camera shone back and forth, like a ping-pong ball over on a grid surface. Magnetism of ferrous metal would activate the strobe and camera together. The work was no longer a salvage operation for ComServLant.

Paul Stillwell: One of the type commander's jobs is to go around and inspect the ships of his force. Was that something you enjoyed, a chance to meet the people?

Admiral Knoll: Yes. I had about eight or ten fleet tugs. You met many commanding officers this way, because you were always present at each change of command. Commanding officers, of course, made official calls, and I tried to return each call within a week. I thus had a chance to see all of them in one way or another. It was a good job with an excellent office building on the NOB waterfront. I was the only flag officer ashore on the waterfront where my flag was flown. There was some discussion of moving ComServLant to the CinCLantFlt compound. The many ships of various types were moored nearby, and thus the waterfront was the logical place for ComServLant.

Admiral Dennison, as soon as I was ComServLant, made me the area coordinator for the United Fund. I knew people in Norfolk; they were good friends of mine. I decided to approach United Fund in a new way, namely, tell the people what United Fund services meant to them in terms of saving their money. A small donation now insured the

---

* Harold E. Edgerton (1903-1990) was a professor of electrical engineering at Massachusetts Institute of Technology.

individual, because they were all residents of the Norfolk area as Navy dependents. Getting involved was to their advantage. The first year I was coordinator, I think the Navy doubled the amount that had ever been collected from the Navy in the Hampton Roads area. This made a big affair with Admiral Dennison and the Commandant Fifth Naval District. I know when the Navy delivered the money, a big check was written on white cardboard, 10 feet by 3½ feet. They were thrilled to get it. This happened again the second year I was there and exceeded the previous amount collected. I received a citation from the governor of Virginia for what the Navy had done in the Norfolk area to contribute to community programs. I enjoyed doing things like that. It made Admiral Dennison feel happy, because it was good public relations for the Atlantic Fleet.

Paul Stillwell: How much public speaking did you do to civilian groups during the course of your career?

Admiral Knoll: My citation from the Navy League as oceanographer is in part of my biography.* As oceanographer-hydrographer, I practically spoke at least once in 90% of all of the big cities in the United States. I gave more than 200 speeches, to Rotary, civic groups, etc., concerning the importance of oceanography, the treasures in the oceans, the intelligent use of the ocean depths, such as the farming of the seas. At this time I had a good liaison with Jacques Cousteau.† Cousteau was also on the NATO advisory board in La Spezia, Italy, and I've travel with him and his wife in their hydrofoil *Silverfish*. I've also introduced Cousteau at various seminars. One scientist-oceanographer, Athelstan Spilhaus from South Africa, and Jacques Cousteau attended many scientific sessions with me. Each talk on oceanography was not always the same one. In addition I wrote articles on oceanography for scientific magazines.

Admiral Bob Dennison, with the Secretary of the Navy's support, had the Navy League give me the Admiral Parsons Award at the annual Navy League convention in Dallas for what I had done to awaken the nation and the world to the importance of the

---

* Admiral Knoll served as Oceanographer of the Navy from August 1963 to September 1965.
† Jacques-Yves Cousteau (1910-1997) was a French author, oceanographer, and motion picture producer. He developed many techniques for undersea exploration, including helping to invent the aqualung.

oceans and their potential for the future.* I hold mementos from lectures in St. Louis, Washington, Los Angeles, the Economic Club of Detroit, about 700 people in New York, in Dallas, Texas, and the Rotary Club in Houston, which is Rotary's largest with 700 members. I was a guest at various Navy League affairs.

Traveling around about once a week was refreshing. My wife died as I took over as oceanographer. I was out of Washington almost every week. About every three months I visited London for meetings with my opposite in the Royal Navy. I met a lot of people at Cambridge and Oxford universities who were interested in oceanography. The U.S. Navy and Royal Navy coordinated the collection of ocean depths in the Atlantic for special charts to be used for Polaris submarine operations. Lord Jellicoe, Assistant Secretary of Defence, normally invited me for luncheon at the House of Lords when I was in London. Making speeches was part of my budget for all travel. It was in accordance with BuPers orders. Some few in OpNav thought I made too many speeches and traveled too much.

Paul Stillwell: Who was that?

Admiral Knoll: I prefer not to mention names. James Wakelin was in charge of R&D in the SecNav's office and a good friend.† He welcomed my assignment as oceanographer. If he had stayed there, I probably would have remained longer as oceanographer-hydrographer. I was the first and only oceanographer-hydrographer who also had a degree from MIT in earth sciences. This made some difference when I met with scientists at Woods Hole or Scripps, some of whom I knew at MIT. I had surveyed in the Aleutian Islands and made charts, so I had hydrographic experience.

During my reign, the Navy changed all charts from being printed from copper plates to computer production. The copper plates had to be stored at controlled temperature and removed only to make the charts. Many of these plates are now loaned

---

* The Navy League awards manual says that the Rear Admiral William S. Parsons Award "for scientific and technical progress is awarded to a Navy or Marine Corps officer, enlisted person or civilian who has made an outstanding contribution in any field of science that has furthered the development and progress of he Navy or Marine Corps."
† Dr. James H. Wakelin Jr., served as Assistant Secretary of the Navy (Research and Development) from 5 June 1959 to 30 June 1964. From 1970 to 1973 he was a member of the board of advisers to the president of the Naval War College.

for the tops of cocktail tables at the White House and congressional offices, but they are still in the ownership of the Hydrographic Office. Formally, every time one had to change a sounding or the old sounding was removed, a new one was etched so charts would be correct. Every time a chart was issued, it had to have all corrections up to date in accord with the date of delivery. As a result, there were groups on each coast that made corrections of charts that were ordered. It was a tedious, expensive job.

Today, with a computer, corrections are kept up to date, and as charts are needed they can be printed without involvement of copper plate. Hydro has two of the biggest computers in Washington that are being used about 22 hours a day. Hydro was the only office in Washington that was really getting the maximum use out of computers compared with other activities with computers being used three or four hours a day. I took the IBM executive course at Poughkeepsie, which provided excellent guidance for efficient use of computers. We also went through the manufacturing area; computers had just started using microchips.

While I was the oceanographer-hydrographer, President Kennedy decreed that all government employees could organize a union, including approximately 2,500 people at the Hydrographic Office. The printing of charts made Hydro a target of the printers. Initially, the union treated us royally until all the necessary papers were signed. Now 2,500 additional people belonged to the Printers' Union of the United States. There was a great celebration. The next day, the printers' union called on the phone and said, "Such-and-such is wrong. Take care of it." Then the caller hung up. An apparent union friend for a year started to harass. All kinds of accusations were made. Hydro did not employ enough colored people. I had to prove that a number of colored people had been encouraged to work without success. For the one summer I arranged about 50 black girls from one high school to be hired to correct charts. The average colored person living in the area would not travel by bus to work at Hydro. They came to be interviewed and never would show up for work. They preferred to work in Washington, D.C., rather than Suitland, Maryland. I was held responsible for lacking the right percentage of colored people. The union brought repeated charges, ignoring the fact that blacks did not want to be government printers in Maryland. The union emphasized that Hydro couldn't fire anyone without incriminating yourself in a series of charges and countercharges.

Paul Stillwell: What do you mean by that?

Admiral Knoll: To fire a man with a union of a government organization, one must start giving him unsatisfactory fitness reports, calling him in regularly and telling him he's not doing a good job. One can't without warning tell someone he's going to be fired. The union people, civilian service people in OpNav and the Navy Department, are always ready to cause trouble for an office in charge. Everyone is in the grandstand cheering while you're running around the cinder track trying to protect yourself. It's a thankless job to have a good, organized business with everyone happily working, and then of a sudden have a union harass and create unrest. The more senior you are, the more vulnerable you are. They knew I had never been involved with a union before, but I tried to help my employees. Many did not want to join the union and avoid charges from the organizing union officials.

Paul Stillwell: How did you go about getting that job as oceanographer-hydrographer? Did BuPers give you a shopping list of billets, say, when you were near the end of the term at ComServLant?

Admiral Knoll: Yes. BuPers was very courteous. I wondered what I should do after ComServLant. I had various qualifications. I didn't want to become commandant of a naval district. In looking over available billets, Hydro was attractive with my training at MIT and fleet aerological experience and survey work. My contacts with scientific activities indicated an increased need for oceanographic work and hydrographic work. There was an increased accuracy with weather forecasting because of improved ways of collecting data. I had a few meetings with Si Ramo of Thompson Ramo Wooldridge.[*] These talks involved the quantum increase of data to be collected by computers. I decided Hydro/Oceano was the best place for me to work and make a knowledgeable contribution to efforts with earth sciences. I participated in the worldwide collection data while in U.S.S.R. and with the United Nations.

---

[*] The corporation later became known as TRW Automotive. Simon Ramo was one of the founders in 1958

I mentioned to CNO George Anderson and to Smedberg of BuPers my thoughts. They said, "You're a natural if you want it." I agreed to take it just before my wife died. She wasn't well. I made an agreement with her to move to Washington, and Washington duty was ideal for both of us. Her death a few days before I reported to Hydro changed the picture. It had an effect, and probably over the years I could have done more as oceanographer-hydrographer, or I might have aspired for a more responsible assignment. As long as Wakelin was in SecNav, we had a good relationship and made good progress.

The Navy had to have a quantum improvement of our knowledge of the ocean floor, for two reasons. One, to make sure we knew where all the peaks and deeps were as nuclear submarines went deeper, rather than being surface ships cruising just below the surface. Building a sub that's supposed to be operated like a fish and go below 300 or 400 feet required added knowledge. So one requirement was to locate accurately underwater peaks and shoals with accurate knowledge of the bottom of the ocean and the ability to pick up seamounts. That could enable them to navigate submerged without coming to the surface and breaking radio silence. The plan was to stay submerged for 60 days and know location and stay out of trouble.

Another parameter was an appreciation of the contour and composition of the ocean bottom: locations of sand, rock, gravel, or sludge, each of which had an effect on the performance of the sonar and/or bottom-bouncing sonar. With a bottom bounce from a mushy area, there would be a poor echo back compared to the echo from rock, stone, or sand. Charts were developed to show locations of various regimes for sonar. Such data would be of use to a submarine for submarine detection. An ASW unit taking soundings knows there is better detection with devices such as dipping sonar or sonobuoy. The task is to collect more information so the Navy has a better knowledge of the ocean depths. Charts were good in terms of general depth. Such details as seamounts could have been missed on earlier surveys. Modern techniques, such as explosive sounding, provided a better picture of the whole bottom and the stratification some distance below the ocean bottom.

Paul Stillwell: Please explain what you mean by explosive sounding.

Admiral Knoll: Small charges of dynamite were exploded. Data collected showed the bottom, plus the stratification of the subsurface for 2,000 to 3,000 feet below the ocean bottom. With the knowledge of the earth's crust, new evidence of petroleum and gas were obtained. The British and ourselves and large oil industries collected and exchanged new data for scientific purposes. The Navy gave priority to ocean areas where future submarine operations might occur. A priority for the British and U.S.A. was an area in the North Atlantic around the Iceland and Greenland gap, in the vicinity of the British Isles, along certain maritime trade routes and focal points of traffic in the Atlantic.

The scientific community was making an analysis of the mineral resources of all the earth's area—initiated by DuPont—to determine where future resources of metals and minerals were located in the world and when each resource might be competitive with present sources. The oil companies are doing a lot of research looking for oil. We were able to encourage DuPont or the oil companies who would send us all they received. The Navy recognized the proprietary ownership that controlled release of the data. The British and U.S. Navy checked back and forth to ensure no duplication of work in improving our knowledge of the bottom of the ocean and its contours. In doing this, the Navy had an arrangement to selectively release about 10% of such information annually. Data released would not help the Soviets to detect or give any indication of where the Navy's priority interest lay. This again required good coordination.

It was very rewarding to work with the British, who had the right kind of people with an excellent organization. In the British Admiralty Lord Jellicoe knew about our work. It was started by Eddie Stephan with Admiral Lord Edgerton, British Navy service, and Jim Wakelin.[*] This required many visits back and forth to London. When Wakelin was relieved by Dr. Morse, Morse didn't seem to take an interest in Hydro work.[†] He concentrated on research and development. When I visited him, he sort of listened and didn't comment and never visited Hydro to see what was being done. Wakelin gave this work high priority.

A briefing was available for anyone that came to visit. We had a room and put on a presentation of about 20 minutes, showing what had been done in the past, what was

---

[*] Rear Admiral Edward C. Stephan, USN, was Oceanographer of the Navy, 1960-63.
[†] Robert W. Morse served as Assistant Secretary of the Navy (Research and Development) from 1 July 1964 to 30 June 1966.

being done in the present, and future projects. Without compromising classified information, an important contribution was made concerning the potential future use of the oceans. The Navy had good engineers, scientists, hydrologists, and specialists to work with. I received certain publicity. It appeared that Dr. Morse, who relieved Wakelin, thought I was getting too much publicity about oceanography when Morse thought he should be getting more. Many officers in OpNav weren't having a chance to travel. I enjoyed getting around, meeting scientific groups, talking to them, and becoming involved in question-and-answer seminars. Occasionally I talked at assemblies in different high schools and acquainted students with oceanographic potential.

Paul Stillwell: Was Wakelin your boss then? Was he the guy you reported to?

Admiral Knoll: No, Wakelin was not the boss; he was in the Secretary's office. My boss was the OpNav administrative officer.

Paul Stillwell: Roy Benson?

Admiral Knoll: Roy Benson was annoyed that I was traveling too much.* Have you briefed him?

Paul Stillwell: We have his oral history.

Admiral Knoll: He didn't mention me then?

Paul Stillwell: No.

Admiral Knoll: He was a submariner in the class of 1929. I could see Roy was annoyed. He prepared my fitness reports and probably didn't do me any good.

---

* Rear Admiral Roy S. Benson, USN, whose oral history is in the Naval Institute collection.

Paul Stillwell: Do you remember Captain Ed Snyder, who later became Oceanographer of the Navy?*

Admiral Knoll: Yes, he was Wakelin's number-one man.

Paul Stillwell: What do you remember about him?

Admiral Knoll: He was a typical bureaucrat in many ways. He built himself into the job so no one could replace him, and he ultimately became a hydrographer or oceanographer, I believe. He had some scientific education in oceanography before joining Wakelin. I never had any problems with him. Administratively he picked up experience more from his association with Wakelin and his work in the Secretary's office. He did know what was being done and kept me informed. With his years in R&D for SecNav he had qualifications for ultimately being assigned as oceanographer-hydrographer.

I tried to emphasize to a lot of people that "oceanographer" itself did not inspire too many people, because they'd say you were just another oceanographer. I tried to use oceanographer-hydrographer because the Navy hydrographer in the past was a very important billet in the Navy organization. Eddie Stephan may have lost sight of this traditional aspect. The Navy oceanographer at that time was not definitive to the advantage of the Navy, because hydrographic charts worldwide were produced over the name of the hydrographer.

Paul Stillwell: Could you explain the difference between those two for someone like me who doesn't know all the ins and outs?

Admiral Knoll: Well, the hydrographer essentially was the officer who made the charts for maritime navigation, civilian and government. With these charts he included the knowledge of the ocean, such as currents and temperature. Hydrographer is a production task of importance.

---

* Captain J. Edward Snyder Jr., USN.

Oceanographer is a scientific collector improving knowledge and use of ocean resources. The oceanographer is involved with the three-dimensional water mass and all components relating to the ocean. Benjamin Franklin determined the location and movement of the Gulf Stream, which Maury added to the navigational charts.[*] The oceanographer is a scientific collector of ocean data for further research. With oceanographic research there was a geophysical year with a lot of attention given to the simultaneous worldwide collection in the ocean by all countries participating. It was very productive. The new Law of the Sea interferes with encouragement to people to work together to make the ocean more useful for the future of mankind.

When I was with the United Nations, I helped Captain Orville and Reichelderfer to establish the World Meteorological Organization, the first big international organization as part of UNESCO. It was a sequel to work I had done in the Soviet Union with General Federov and with Reichelderfer, the chief of the U.S. Weather Bureau. The naval officer whom I had relieved as aerologist on the staff of Admiral Hart was the first U.S. representative to the World Meteorological Organization in Paris. The work of the United Nations and the World Health Organization are indispensable for the future well-being of the world. They have done a good job of improving the health and knowledge of the Third World.

Some say the United Nations hasn't done any good. It has helped to prevent a major war for 40-some years. All must learn to live together in the present global village. The United States is not as popular as we used to be. In the next 100 years the United States must be more tolerant and moderate so that people say, "These people are pretty good. We want to follow them again." It is a challenge. The United States, with willing allies, is a power for world good. We should share our views more with our allies.

Dr. Morse, Assistant Secretary of the Navy for R&D, decided I should stay no more than two years. He never talked to me about it. All of a sudden, BuPers said, "You're being relieved by Muddy Waters."[†] It surprised me, and I never could find out

---

[*] Matthew Fontaine Maury (1806-1873) earned the description of "Father of Modern Oceanography and Meteorology." He served as superintendent of the Naval Observatory in Washington, D.C. and was head of the Depot of Charts and Instruments. In 1861, with the onset of the Civil War, he resigned his commission as a commander in the U.S. Navy.

[†] Rear Admiral Odale D. Waters Jr., USN, served as Oceanographer of the Navy from 1965 to 1970. His oral history is in the Naval Institute collection.

who made the decision. Muddy Waters may have wanted it. He did a good job when he was there, as far as I know. He had been in mine warfare. Apparently BuPers said this job was for two years.

Then I was ordered to be the deputy to COMSTS, Donc Donaho.[*]

Paul Stillwell: Did you have operational control of the surveying ships? Who told them where to go?

Admiral Knoll: In the earlier days they were all under the control of the hydrographer. ONI and OpNav determined the part of the ocean for which more information was needed, for example, the North Atlantic. The ships were assigned specific tasks. Hydro supplied the equipment or scientists with which to collect surveying data. Woods Hole and Scripps had operational control of many ships. They were normally under the fleet commander or district commandant.

Paul Stillwell: Did you have input in the decision of what areas would be surveyed?

Admiral Knoll: OpNav determined priority and area. Ships were operated by Woods Hole or Scripps by contract with the Navy. At the time I took over, the Navy oceanographer-hydrographer was one of the directors of the Woods Hole Laboratory at Woods Hole, Massachusetts. This was changed, with justification. Woods Hole, as well as Scripps on the West Coast, was doing work with these ships that had been built by the Navy and turned over to them to collect the data we needed. More than 50% of their work was Navy work. Why should a naval officer be on their board of directors? Letting them run the whole show, more civilian people were trained, and the Navy obtained the data that was needed. The Navy more or less justified the need for survey ships and designated the laboratories that would operate them.

---

[*] Vice Admiral Glynn R. Donaho, USN, served as Commander Military Sea Transportation Service from 1964 to 1967.

Paul Stillwell: What were some of the projects that were done on the oceanographic end, what types of research?

Admiral Knoll: Some of it was done in cooperation with ONR. The Tongue of the Ocean at Andros Island was studied with data relating to sonar performance. A lot of oceanographic work was needed for operation of nuclear submarines and antisubmarine warfare, as well as the tests with Polaris. Some of the original tests found out that a telephone pole with 500 pounds of lead at the base would emerge due to positive buoyancy and break through the surface vertically, similar to a Polaris missile. Many analyses were made of ocean currents and acoustic tests with sonophones. Quite a bit of work was done under contract with Rhode Island Institute, or Narragansett Institute of Oceanography by Dr. Fish and Mrs. Dr. Fish. They recorded undersea noises in the ocean and identified types of fish that made specific noises. They acquired the specific type and frequency of noises by more than 200 fish or marine life. It was valuable for future antisubmarine warfare.

Paul Stillwell: Did you look into this question of harvesting resources from the bottom of the ocean, manganese nodules and that sort of thing?

Admiral Knoll: I have some manganese nodules that were procured from the ocean floor near San Clemente on the West Coast. DuPont studied their value as a resource. The location of the nodules was known, and a contract was made to harvest nodules from the area near San Clemente. The Department of the Interior was paid for that privilege. Of a sudden it was found that the material in the nodules was available in Utah surface resources, and it would be another 50 years before it would be competitive to harvest from the ocean. The contract was canceled, and the agency got their money back. Contracts were issued by the Department of Defense for exploitation of part of the ocean. The new Law of the Sea attempts to limit this. One idea is that the open-ocean resources belong to all the nations outside the 12-mile limit. Other nations want to capitalize on the money the United States spent to know more about the bottom of the ocean. The Navy will continue to acquire knowledge of phenomena that we need to know for our own military purposes.

I can mention a specific thing that improved knowledge of the earth and its environment. I was the oceanographer during the final establishment of a geodetic position in the Pacific that gave data as to the exact shape of the earth. When a geodetic position was established on Nauru Island in the South Pacific—which belongs to Australia—the entire earth was part of the world net of known positions, latitude and longitude. The shape of the whole earth, based upon each geodetic position, was interrelated to show a single sphere with coordinates.

A lot of good work on an east-west coordinate has been done with missiles, which helps with the recovery of satellites from space. The earth is an oblate spheroid. There have never been accurate tests of the north-south coordinates to determine the degradation of that trajectory as missiles pass over the poles. The Soviets might fire missiles at the United States over the pole, and the mean point of impact might be in error because the effect by an oblate spheroid would vary from an east-west trajectory. It's a good problem.

Paul Stillwell: Why was Nauru the last link in the chain?

Admiral Knoll: It was the last area to be geodetically surveyed and was needed for space work. Today every point on the earth can be identified accurately as to latitude and longitude. In the Aleutian Islands in '32-'34, the first geodetic positions were accurately determined on Adak and Attu islands. Modern electronics and star sights helped to accurately locate the large Nauru Island.

Paul Stillwell: It came as a surprise to you when you were told that job would be only two years. Had Admiral Donaho asked for you?

Paul Stillwell: He may have. We were good friends. He had been OP-02, Roy Benson's job, before he went out as chief of staff of the Seventh Fleet. I worked with him in OpNav. He was a tough, capable officer. He had four Navy Crosses for submarine operations in World War II. He had a lot of tough characteristics, and he was thorough and precise. Unless he liked you, you couldn't get along with him. He made an excellent impression on Mel Pride. Mel Pride said I continued the type of job that Donaho did for him. Donaho was a man of few words and a hard worker. He worked harder with every task than any other admiral. He made firm decisions. We had a good relationship at MSTS.

Donaho visited Vietnam three or four times in the two years I was there. COMSTS had problems chartering merchant ships until MSTS had over 250 under charter with a charter rate of $15,000, $18,000, to $23,000 per day in bare boat-charter. There were more charters than necessary. McNamara had determined not to build warehouses ashore in Vietnam. Almost 100 partially unloaded merchant ships were swinging at anchor near Saigon, with a demurrage of $20,000 a day, to be used as warehouses.* This was supposed to be cheaper than building a warehouse ashore. Some ships stayed there for months. With one ship the skipper was tired of sitting at anchor, so he flew back to the United States, took command of another ship, went to Vietnam, and found the first ship he took to Vietnam was still swinging at anchor.

COMSTS wrote numerous letters to SecDef and the Navy, pleading that this was the worst way to use merchant ships and a most expensive waste of taxpayers' money—totally unnecessary. I think we must have written six or seven letters. Caputo was an assistant under McNamara, and he was educated very fast.† SecDef received a fantastic bill from the Army for demurrage charges for one year of over $1 billion. Thereafter Caputo and McNamara became specialists in achieving fast turnaround of merchant ships. This was accomplished by the building of warehouses ashore, using containers that arrived from the States.

Paul Stillwell: Just the opposite.

---

* Demurrage is a charge paid for detaining a ship beyond the time allowed for loading or unloading.
† Vincent F. Caputo headed the Directorate for Transportation and Warehousing Policy in the office of the Assistant Secretary of Defense (Installations and Logistics).

Admiral Knoll: They became authorities on avoiding demurrage. There was never an admission that all our letters had warned them not to use chartered merchant ships as warehouses.

This was about the time Sea-Land wanted a contract to build containerships for the Pacific.* Sea-Land had good contracts in the Atlantic and had successful containership operations with unloading facilities at San Juan, Puerto Rico, and a few ports in Europe on the Atlantic Coast. Seatrain also operated with the containers with nonstandard dimensions, and they came with whalebacks for open cargo that could stack together with containers in a cargo hold.† Sea-Land was the most consistent. Reynolds Aluminum money, McLean Trucking, and Litton shared in the Sea-Land development.

Sea-Land decided a containership capability was needed in the Pacific. They had requirements, Malcom McLean said. Robert Baldwin, the Under Secretary of the Navy and formerly vice president of Morgan Stanley, pressured COMSTS to contract containerships for the Pacific.‡ Baldwin kept telling us, "This is the way we do it at Morgan Stanley," when he was talking to you. He continually put pressure to make a contract for about eight or ten of these ships at $25,000 a day bare-boat charter. Donc Donaho felt we didn't need any more ships if we used the ones that were out there. We did not encourage this Sea-Land contract. I know Donc didn't make the contract. I refused to sign a contract while Donc was out of town.

After Donc was relieved and I was detached, I don't know who signed the contract, whether it was someone in SecDef's or Navy's office, with the help of Bob Baldwin and Captain Bob Carl. The contract was signed, and Sea-Land built these containerships with that contract and arranged with the Army to send loaded containers to Vietnam and not bring containers back. The Army would keep containers there assembled for warehousing. The flying crane helo would lift them inland where they needed them. Every time a new containership went out, it had a new load of containers with cargo and returned empty. Sea-Land developed a container capability in the Pacific, which Donc and I didn't think was necessary while many merchant ships were available under charter to MSTS.

---

* Sea-Land Service Inc., a corporation that emphasized intermodal transportation with containers.
† Seatrain Lines was a corporation that pioneered the use of containers.
‡ Robert H. B. Baldwin served as Under Secretary of the Navy from 2 July 1965 to 31 July 1967.

Paul Stillwell: How do you know that thing is what kept you from relieving him as commander of MSTS?

Admiral Knoll: I don't.

Paul Stillwell: You sort of hinted earlier that that was the one thing.

Admiral Knoll: No, I never quite knew. There were a couple of reasons. About the time I was relieved, Bob Baldwin was being criticized in the newspaper, that he was favoring some of his former accounts with Morgan Stanley. Baldwin resigned and eventually became president of Morgan Stanley. He recently retired from that brokerage house. Red Ramage came and relieved Donaho, and he wanted me to remain.[*] I was originally a year senior to Ramage. I had been told by three or four different vice admirals, including one of my classmates, that I was scheduled to get a third star and was already on the list. Everyone gave the indication that I would relieve Donaho. When I heard Ramage was coming, he called me and said, "I want you to stay with me."

I said, "Thank you very much, but I'm going to request my retirement."

He said, "Stay a month or so," which I did for a couple of months until the first of May 1967.

When I sent my request for retirement to CNO and to BuPers, I received a frantic call from B. J. Semmes, BuPers.[†] He said, "You can't go. We don't want you to go. We'll give you any job you want. Which commandant—do you want to be Com 12?"

I said, "No, I'm going home. I've had it." See, I had two more years to do.[‡] I said, "It's about time that somebody else takes charge."

There is one possibility, which I don't discount. If Kennedy had lived, there's no doubt I would have received a third star. President Lyndon Johnson didn't like some of the letters I wrote about the Air Force's desire for a single service. Lyndon Johnson had some talk with McNamara about this.

---

[*] Vice Admiral Lawson P. Ramage, USN, served as Commander Military Sea Transportation Service from 1967 to 1970.
[†] Vice Admiral Benedict J. Semmes, Jr., USN, served as Chief of Naval Personnel from 1 April 1964 to 31 March 1968. His oral history is in the Naval Institute collection.
[‡] By law Knoll could have remained on active duty until the mandatory retirement age of 62 in 1969.

Paul Stillwell: Lyndon Johnson also had a tie with Drew Pearson.

Admiral Knoll: Jack Anderson did the writing. I'm a Catholic, and President Johnson didn't like Catholics. I knew some of Lyndon Johnson's friends pretty well, particularly one that put in a claim for loss of his household effects at Sangley Point at the beginning of the war. There were a series of little things that built up. A lot of people said that with Kennedy there was no doubt about it. What job I would have received, whether relief of Donc Donaho or something else, was not suggested.

From what I have learned, my name was on the list for new vice admirals when it went from the Navy Department to the White House. Where my name was removed, whether in SecDef's office by McNamara or by Lyndon Johnson, it was definitely never mentioned in Washington. When Lyndon Johnson did anything like that, everyone was warned, "Keep your damn mouth shut, or Johnson will take drastic action." I never tried to question Bob Dennison as to what happened. I never tried to ask George Anderson or Smeddy. I said, "I know something happened, but I know no one can talk." How it happened, I don't know. If anyone knew accurately, it would be Dennison, and he had to maintain secrecy.

When I had talked to President Kennedy a short time before his death, he said, "Remember, I don't like what has happened." He sent me an autographed picture.

Paul Stillwell: If the death of Kennedy was the key event and Johnson didn't like you, then the Sea-Land contract wouldn't really have had anything to do with, would it?

Paul Stillwell: With Kennedy big contracts had prior blessing of the White House. There could have been a report from Bob Baldwin, Paul Nitze, or SecDef McNamara. I hadn't played the game and agreed to sign the contract. There was some interest in the White House for any contact of an amount over $1 million. This was started with Jack Kennedy when I was oceanographer.

Paul Stillwell: But that doesn't necessarily mean that they were going to pay you off with a third star just for signing that.

Admiral Knoll: My record justified a third star; it was no "payoff." If you don't play their game politically, they ask you to retire or retaliate. I wasn't playing their game politically, so they didn't promote me. You know, more and more, this idea, I said to Arleigh Burke a couple of times, "I'm not going to get involved in a lie or deliberate misrepresentation."

He said, "I hope you can live that way."

I said, "I know what you're talking about, Admiral."

I wouldn't give the contract in which Ted Kennedy was interested. The number of people involved was not miniscule. The one interesting thing was for Paul Nitze to tell my golfing partner, his classmate from Harvard, "Knoll will be a vice admiral soon."[*]

One time during my tenure at MSTS, I was with Vice Admiral Callaghan and others.[†] We were playing golf at Chevy Chase Country Club, including the vice president of the Alaska Steamship Company who had been Nitze's classmate. While we were playing golf, this vice president said, "I brought Paul Nitze out from downtown today. I asked him how soon Denys Knoll will be a vice admiral. He said, 'Within a month or so.'"

I said, "What did you say?"

He said, "Paul Nitze said you'll be promoted in a month or so." I didn't say a word. I had been told by good authority that I was about to be a vice admiral. I was practically told so, and I knew that it was a possibility.

So at the end of the golf, when I was sitting at the 19th hole, I said, "Eske, you said I'm going to be a vice admiral in a couple of months. I'll lay you $100.00 bet that I'll never make it if Paul Nitze said so."

About a year went by, and I played some golf on the weekends with the crowd at Chevy Chase or at the Washington Country Club. This same man was there and reminded me, "You know, when you told me that Paul Nitze, a good friend of mine, could not be trusted for accuracy, I could have hit you."

I said, "Well, I'd been warned a long time ago that if Nitze's involved, don't put any money on it."

---

[*] Paul H. Nitze served as Secretary of the Navy from 29 November 1963 to 30 June 1967.
[†] Vice Admiral William M. Callaghan, USN (Ret.), whom Knoll had encountered in previous tours of duty.

Paul Stillwell: Was Nitze by this time Secretary of the Navy?

Admiral Knoll: Yes. I think the one that took my name off the promotion list was President Johnson because of many articles I wrote during my time as OP-03D—"The Danger of a Single Service," and related subjects.[*] I sent these articles to all the flag officers.

Paul Stillwell: Getting back to MSTS, I was interested about the business of reactivating ships from the National Defense Reserve Fleet in order to build up the capabilities to supply Vietnam.

Admiral Knoll: Some of the reserve fleet was reactivated under contract, plus bare-boat charter of ships already in service. Chartering ships is the most complicated task you can imagine. We had to trust our experienced officials in making these contracts with existing shipping lines. From day to day, the charter rates rise and fall, depending on demand. There's a scarcity on tankers, so their charter rates escalate. The same thing happened with cargo ships when more and more were needed. So there were enough ships in service to maintain logistic support of Vietnam. It was cheaper to use ships in commission than to activate ships from the reserve fleet that we didn't need if ships were not detained as floating warehouses. There was no requirement for more ships if existing ships made a quicker turnaround. COMSTS made the charters but had no operational control once they reported to the Army for cargo. The Army paid the charter rates. The Army had the organization for loading cargo and routing all ships under charter. It was their responsibility to load, route, and pay the cost. COMSTS knew the Army wasn't using all of the ships intelligently. COMSTS was complaining about high charter rates and demurrage, but most officials did not understand demurrage.

The charter rates for old Liberty ships was under $10,000 a day.[†] For newer ships and those with greater capability and faster speed, the charter rates increased to 18,000 per day. Owners like Onassis, who had many tankers, knew there was a demand for

---

[*] Lyndon B. Johnson served as President of the United States from 22 November 1963 to 20 January 1969.
[†] The Liberty ship was a mass-produced cargo ship designed by the U.S. Maritime Commission for use by the Allies in World War II. All told, American shipyards built 2,770 Liberties.

tankers, and they obtained charter rates that allowed them to amortize new tankers in a matter or two or three years.[*] Today most of these tankers are idle and a great liability to the owners.

Paul Stillwell: Did you get involved with the ship and company people in the maritime unions?

Admiral Knoll: Yes. Initially MSTS was criticized for not trying to keep involved. Done Donaho and I arranged with the principal shipping representatives in Washington to have a monthly luncheon at the Army-Navy Club in Washington, where we discussed mutual problems. We met with representatives of the union, particularly their lobbyists on the Hill and discussed manning problems of the different shipping lines. Occasionally we visited New York and met with representatives of Seatrain and Sea-Land. They visited our office from time to time. We invited the Assistant Secretary of the Navy to meetings so he would know what was going on. Captain Carl, his staff representative, maintained liaison with us. I understand after Donaho our successors canceled these meetings.

Paul Stillwell: Were you getting pressure from the maritime unions to put more of their people on board the MSTS ships, as opposed to the civil service?

Admiral Knoll: Oh, no, no. The MSTS ships were in the Navy organization, so there was no pressure. All the MSTS ships were civilian manned. MSTS ships were being trained to work with the fleet for underway replenishment.

Paul Stillwell: Were you involved in the phase-out of the passenger ships from MSTS?

---

[*] Aristotle Onassis was a super-rich Greek shipowner. In 1968 he had married the widow of President John F. Kennedy.

Admiral Knoll: Yes, to a degree. There were decreasing requirements for passengers to travel via ship. Some ships went to the Far East for a few trips for Vietnam. Ships were slow and expensive; it became cheaper to transport all personnel via air.

Paul Stillwell: And obviously quicker.

Admiral Knoll: Of course. A lot less headaches. Skippers had to be very careful when children were transported. Many barriers were erected so children could not climb the mast or fall overboard. Parents came aboard and caroused with little attention to the safety of their children. Once they were aboard ship, parents thought ship's officers should worry about the care of the children. Most skippers of those passenger ships were very glad to see the end of those problems.

Paul Stillwell: How did Admiral Donaho divide up the workload with you? What sorts of things did he do? What sorts of things did he have you do?

Admiral Knoll: I was the chief of staff and deputy commander, so nothing went to him unless it had my initials. I knew pretty well what Donaho wanted to sign. I read all the mail. I saw it before he saw it. In fact, if any action had to be started, I started action. Donaho was absent on many trips, and I was always in the office six days a week, so everything came across my desk, which is the best way. He had me present any time he'd call someone to start working on a project. I did the same work with COMSTS as I did as chief of staff and aide to Com7thFlt. Donaho expected me to run the show.

Paul Stillwell: Were you the link also to the area commanders in the Far East and Germany and so forth?

Admiral Knoll: To a degree, with a Navy plane assigned in England when I visited all MSTS representatives in Europe to inspect and find out their problems. There were problems delivering the coal for U.S. forces in Europe. It was for occupation personnel in Europe, was unloaded outside of Rotterdam and moved by barge to various places, namely, England, Netherlands, West Germany, Spain, and Italy. The U.S. Army had bases near the Rhine River. It was cheaper to send good coal from the United States than to buy it in Europe. It was a recurring problem. I think there were six around-the-clock colliers under charter, going back and forth hauling coal to Europe from Norfolk.

Paul Stillwell: I didn't quite understand the one point you made about your wife dying, and you said that changed your outlook somehow.

Admiral Knoll: It was a shock to adjust your way of living. It's not easy to quickly live alone without someone with whom to plan. I always had a guilt complex that my career and my frequent separation from her actually ruined her health. I had a responsibility to her that the war prevented me from fulfilling. I frequently remind friends time and again if they marry into the Navy, their wives must realize they're marrying men with a "mistress that is the United States Navy." I had wanted her to wait until I got back from China, and she said no; she had to go with me. I had never pushed it since she was the one who was determined to accompany me to China. She was sent home after seven months. While I was about a year and a half with the Seventh Fleet, she had serious operations, and her mother resented the fact that I was unable to return and be with her. Flying back from the Far East was not as easy in 1954 as it is 30 years later. Today you can fly back in less than 12 hours nonstop to the West Coast.

Paul Stillwell: When did you remarry?

Admiral Knoll: In 1969, two years after I retired.* I had offers for civilian employment when I retired—from RCA, Raytheon, University of Connecticut, and others. I wasn't going to get involved with a new commitment that might get me married and prevent me from returning to Erie. I preferred, if I got married, to do so and live in Erie. About that time I met my first cousin's wife, whom I'd known slightly. An exchange of visits between Erie and Washington preceded my retirement. It worked out very well.

---

* The admiral's second wife was the former Jean Shaw.

Paul Stillwell: It's fortunate that you were able to find a job that you liked in your old hometown, wasn't it?

Admiral Knoll: Yes. Litton came after me, because they were starting to build a new plant in Erie. I retired in May 1967, and the first of July I started to work public relations for Litton to build this plant, which was a $24 million installation. It hasn't been used for quite a few years now, but that wasn't the fault of local management. It was the fault of the policies of Litton Corporation in Beverly Hills and Pascagoula. That's another story.

Paul Stillwell: What did the plant do, just briefly?

Admiral Knoll: We had contracts for three bulk iron ore taconite carriers with automatic unloading capability. The ship could unload 22,000 tons an hour of taconite pellets from a cargo of 52,000 tons. The ship was 1,000 feet long, 105-foot beam, and we could carry those pellets in nine separate compartments with a belt 10 feet wide going through the keel and out to this automatic unloader. It had two diesel-drive motors, which were controlled from the bridge, like an automobile. We had bow thrusters and stern thrusters, and it was the largest bulk carrier ever built on the Great Lakes, first and largest.[*] It replaced three of the older ore carriers or bulk carriers of the war, each with a crew of 35 and a cargo of no more than 20,000-22,000 tons. The new ship carried practically three times that cargo. It operated with a crew of 14 and at a faster speed with diesel engines instead of being turbine driven steam coal-burners.

In the old days Hewlett unloaders were used to tediously unload the taconite pellets. I had seen the original palletizing pilot plant at Allis-Chalmers. They had built the first palletizing plant in miniature, and the first complete plant was built on Lake Superior, near Mesabi iron ore range, financed by the Ford Motor Company.

Pelletizing accepts every grade of iron ore and passes it through a pulverizer, mixes it with water, and the slurry passes over a large magnetic drum rotating like a washing machine. Ferrous ore adheres to the magnetic drum and is removed on each

---

[*] The tug-barge combination *Presque Isle* made her maiden voyage from Erie in December 1973. The pusher tug was built in New Orleans.

rotation with large windshield wipes. This pure ore is mixed with a catalyst and made into small pellets that are hardened in a kiln at about 2,800 degrees Fahrenheit. The hardened pellets move by belt conveyor to the cargo hold of the ship. The first one built is carrying ore from Lake Superior to the Bethlehem Steel plant at Burns Harbor, Indiana; a trip each way lasts two and a half days. The ship can load or unload 50,000 tons in three or four hours. Five hours later, it's en route back to Lake Superior with the unloading crew remaining at Burns Harbor. The loading crew remains in Lake Superior.

This type ship was the answer to the future. Litton had a contract for three. It was fabricated on an automated production line, robot-controlled, and automatic welding. Sections of this bulk carrier were like slices in a loaf of bread; there were nine sections welded together to form a cargo hold. We did vertical welding for all construction. There was a turning device for rotating the sections for vertical welds. When the ship was being welded together, the cargo hold was connected to the bow and the stern in a dry dock. The prefabricated bow was a single unit that came to Erie from Pascagoula.[*] Litton in Erie did not have engineering capacity for making the bow and stern. Erie made the center body.

Harry Gray came to Erie quite a few times. He was a senior vice president of Litton and is currently the head of United Technology. He said, "We're not going to be able to meet the price we mentioned." Instead of them meeting with Bethlehem and Danny Strohmeyer to discuss the problem, there was an increasing lack of communication. Some Litton reps in Cleveland never built a ship or operated a ship and had poor public relations with U.S. Steel and Bethlehem. Danny Strohmeyer had been building ships his whole life as vice president of shipbuilding for Bethlehem. He flattered Litton when he made a contract for three ships. Litton fought the problem and antagonized Bethlehem, with the result that U.S. Steel, which was ready to give contracts, and others indicated that about 14 were needed for future lake ore carrying ships. And what did they do? The bow and stern were built at Pascagoula without a written contract. Bethlehem wanted to inspect the bow and stern at Pascagoula. They equipped the bridge with secondhand equipment, left at night for Erie without Bethlehem's approval. Erie

---

[*] Litton had a shipyard in Pascagoula, Mississippi. Other sources indicate the bow was from built by Defoe Shipbuilding in Bay City, Michigan.

tried to contact Pascagoula about any problems. Pascagoula said, "We never heard of it. It was a real fiasco.

At Litton's Beverly Hills corporate headquarters Tex Thornton was chairman of the board with his own public relations on one side of the corridor.* His public relations executive was Barney Oldfield, a retired Air Force colonel, a wonderful gent I'd known before. And on the other side of the corridor was President Roy Ash with his public relations.† Everything I sent to Beverly Hills had to be two copies, one for Tex Thornton and one for Roy Ash. At important corporate meetings those who were partial to building up the facility for Navy business at Pascagoula supported Tex Thornton and made decisions accordingly. When Thornton was out of town, Roy Ash would have his meeting to make favorable decisions relating to the improvement of Litton on the Great Lakes. It was awful. The stock of Litton decreased while I took some of my pay in stock. I worked a limited number of hours a day. Litton fell from 121 to about 27 in six months' time.

Observing this, I said, "How can Litton survive when you have two people with different objectives fighting each other?" Harry Gray finally quit and went to United Technology.

Paul Stillwell: So you then retired from Litton after that?

Admiral Knoll: No, Litton started phasing out when Bethlehem changed its contract and built only the one bulk carrier. They told me, "I'm sorry. We won't need you any longer."

I said, "I can understand that."

They said, "You can maintain an office in our facility as long as you want."

I said, "No, I'm getting out of here."

Paul Stillwell: Do you have any overall summary, wrapup thoughts to conclude this story of your life in the Navy?

---

* Charles B. Thornton served in the Army Air Forces in World War II. In 1953 he founded the company that in 1954 became known as Litton Industries.
† Roy L. Ash was co-founder of Litton.

Admiral Knoll: No, maybe I'll put that one when I do the review. That's the best way.

Paul Stillwell: I'm grateful to you for making this suggestion that you be interviewed and for spending this time with me.

Admiral Knoll: I've enjoyed doing it. I've wanted to do it myself in writing, but I knew I'd never get around to it.

Paul Stillwell: This is a much easier way.

Admiral Knoll: I felt, "I've had experiences that are unique to a naval officer. No one will believe it. I think there should be some record of these historical experiences."

Paul Stillwell: Now there will be.

****

The following is an addendum Admiral Knoll submitted after reviewing and making changes to the original verbatim transcript.

The United States of America is a great nation with enormous potential for leading the world on a peaceful course. With our Free World Allies we can and must be the formidable political, diplomatic, economic, and military power the world needs and respects.

The Soviet Union respects this type of power and can never dominate with materialistic Communism that depends upon police control of their citizens.

The future leaders of the United States must recognize that we live in a "Global Village." Education must give greater attention to advanced course in foreign languages, world history, likes and dislikes of ethnic groups, and diplomatic moderation and tolerance. Knowledge of mathematics provides conditioning for realistic, simple, and accurate solutions for world problems. Avoid wishful thinking for solutions to difficult tasks.

In relation with foreigners we must realize that we are in the "People Business." Understand that we are all different, that foreigners like us have inherited traits that they treasure as much as we treasure ours. We must avoid being arrogant and convey the impression that the U.S.A. has the best solutions to all controversies. For every proposal be slow to make or show a reaction.

With foreigners be aware that exact translations, and meaning of idioms, must be true to the English equivalent, to ensure both sides are talking about the same issues. Having worked with foreign languages with United Nations and regular meetings with the British, French, Chinese, and Soviets, I offer observations:

(a) British are easiest and rather friendly with whom to work. (Caveat) – there are British phrases and idioms that do not have meaning in British and American English.)

(b) The Chinese are intelligent, careful, and courteous. Remember: Chinese calligraphy does not permit an exact translation from English into Chinese or vice versa.

(c) The French resort to French language for every official or semi-official discussion. They exude a past pride that French is the accepted diplomatic language.

(d) The Soviets are realistic and will evade discussion or comment on each new subject until they receive guidance from Democratic Central control in the Kremlin. A Soviet representative will be promptly replaced if he dares initiative or innovation. His existence demands he is solely the voice and mind of the Kremlin.

Launched in 1969, the U.S. Naval Institute's award-winning oral history program is among the oldest in the country. Used in combination with documentary sources, oral histories offer a richer understanding of naval history through candid recollections and explanations rarely entered into contemporary records. In addition, they help depict the atmosphere of a particular event or era in a manner not available in official documents.

The nonprofit Naval Institute accomplishes its history projects through contributed funds and gratefully accepts tax-deductible gifts of all sizes for this purpose. This support allows the Institute to preserve the life experiences of today's service men and women so they may enlighten and inspire future generations.

For information about opportunities to underwrite Naval Institute oral history projects, please contact the Naval Institute Foundation at 291 Wood Road, Annapolis, Maryland 21402; by phone at (410) 295-1054; or by e-mail at foundation@usni.org.

Index to the Oral History of
Rear Admiral Denys William Knoll, U.S. Navy (Retired)

Air Force, U.S.
In the early 1950s Colonel Frank Everest was an Air Force representative in the development of the "New Look" military strategy for the Eisenhower administration, 300-301, 351
Navy response in the early 1960s to the perception that the Air Force was trying to take over the other services, 350-355

Alafuzov, Admiral Vladimir Antonovich
Headed the Soviet Navy in World War II, 198-199

Alaska
Navy geographical survey of the Aleutian Islands in 1934, 49-57

Alcohol
Heavy drinking by Soviets in 1945, 219, 228-229
Admiral Richmond Kelly Turner's drinking problem during World War II and shortly afterward, 259-260

Aleutian Islands
Navy geographical survey of the islands in 1934, 49-57

Ammunition
Service Force Atlantic Fleet managed supplies available during the Cuban Missile Crisis in October 1962, 356-357

Amphibious Warfare
The attack transport *Menard* (APA-201) did practice amphibious landings on the coasts of Korea and Japan in 1952, 293-297

Andrews, Rear Admiral Adolphus, USN (USNA, 1901)
Commanded the battleship *Texas* (BB-35), 1929-30, 23, 26-27
Served as Chief of the Bureau of Navigation in the late 1930s when Knoll dated his daughter, 19, 27, 86-89

Antiair Warfare
Use of 3-inch guns on board the battleship *Texas* (BB-35) in the early 1930s, 29
The light cruiser *Roanoke* (CL-145) excelled in antiaircraft gunnery in 1955, 303
Red China shot down a U.S. Navy P4M Mercator electronic surveillance plane in August 1956, 318-319

Army, U.S.
Edgewood Arsenal, Maryland, presented a course on chemical warfare in 1936, 80-82
Involvement in the Philippines in 1941-42 as war came, 130-133, 140-150, 153
Former naval officer Sidney Huff joined General Douglas MacArthur's staff in 1936, received an Army commission, and remained with him for 15 years, 132-133
Role of U.S. Army and Navy nurses in the Philippines in 1941-42, 143, 146, 150-152
During the Cuban Missile Crisis of 1962, Army helicopters were tested with the training carrier *Lexington* (CVS-16), 361

Army Air Forces, U.S.
In September 1941 began ferrying B-17 bombers to the Philippines, 115-116
In early 1942 attempted to install its own weather service in Australia, 163-164
Unsuccessful attempt during World War II to take over all U.S. airport communications, 175-177
Some B-29 bombers were interned in the Soviet Union before that nation entered the war against Japan in August 1945, 198, 204

Arnold, General Henry H., USA (USMA, 1907)
In the early 1930s commanded March Field in California, 25-26
Served as member of the Joint Chiefs of Staff in World War II, 26, 175-177, 203

Ash, Roy L.
In the 1950s was co-founder of the company that became known as Litton Industries, 394

Asiatic Fleet, U.S.
The cruiser *Augusta* (CA-31) was fleet flagship from 1933 to November 1940, 103-105, 119, 123
The cruiser *Houston* (CA-30) was fleet flagship from November 1940 until her sinking in Sunda Strait in early 1942, 123-125
Ship operations in the Far East in 1940-41, 101-107, 117-120, 123-126
In the summer of 1941 the staff moved ashore to the Marsman Building in Manila, 106, 111, 124
Limited capability to oppose Japan in war, 125
Defective U.S. mines were laid around Corregidor in 1941, 126-127
U.S. aid intended for the Philippines in 1941 did not arrive in timely fashion, 127-129

Astronauts
In the late 1950s-1960s Destroyer Flotilla Four was involved in planning for the recovery of NASA astronauts, 347-348

***Augusta*, USS (CA-31)**
Served as Asiatic Fleet flagship until relieved by the *Houston* (CA-30) in November 1940, 103-105, 119, 123-124

Gunnery practice in 1940, 104-105

Australia
U.S. Army and Navy personnel were evacuated to Australia as the Philippines were falling to the Japanese in late 1941-early 1942, 144-163, 166

B-17 Flying Fortress
In September 1941 the Army began ferrying B-17s to the Philippines, 115-116

B-29 Superfortress
Some were interned in the Soviet Union before that nation entered the war against Japan in August 1945, 198, 204

Baldwin, Robert H. B.
Served 1965-67 as Under Secretary of the Navy, 384-386

Ballentine, Rear Admiral John J., USN (USNA, 1918)
Served as part of the U.S. military delegation to United Nations organizing meetings in London in 1946, 260

Barcelona, Spain
The light cruiser *Roanoke* (CL-145) visited Barcelona in 1955, 304

Baruch, Bernard
American businessman who set up an office after World War II to seek an understanding with the Soviet Union on limiting nuclear weapons, 280-281

Beakley, Vice Admiral Wallace M., USN (USNA, 1924)
Commanded the Seventh Fleet, 1957-58, 325-327
Health issues, 325
Served in the early 1960s as Deputy Commander in Chief Atlantic Fleet, 355-356, 363

Benson, Rear Admiral Roy S., USN (USNA, 1929)
In the early 1960s headed administration in the OpNav staff, 377

Berlin, Germany
In December 1945 Knoll toured Chancellor Adolf Hitler's bunker, 249

Bernatitus, Lieutenant (junior grade) Ann A., Nurse Corps, USN
Left the Philippines by submarine in May 1942, 150
In October 1942 received the Legion of Merit for her service in the Philippines at the beginning of World War II, 143

Blewett, William E., Jr.
Served as president of Newport News Shipbuilding and Dry Dock Company from 1954 to 1961, 337, 368-369

Bogdenko, Vice Admiral Valentin L., Soviet Navy
Member of the Soviet delegation to United Nations organizing meetings in 1946, 256

Bolton, Frances P.
Ohio congresswoman who visited the Soviet Union in the spring of 1945, 193-196

Boone, Rear Admiral Walter F., USN (USNA, 1921)
Headed the strategic planning section of OpNav in the late 1940s, 265, 279-280

Bourgeois, Midshipman Aubrey J., USN (USNA, 1930)
Graduated from the Naval Academy in 1930 after being turned back a year, 9, 17

Braun, Father Marie-Léopold
Catholic priest who ministered in Moscow from 1934 to 1945, 249-251

Bridget, Commander Francis J., USN (USNA, 1921)
Served in Patrol Wing Five out of Norfolk in 1940, 154
Captured by the Japanese in 1942 while trying to escape from the Philippines, 154

Brown, Captain Alfred W., USN (USNA, 1907)
In the early 1930s commanded the destroyer tender *Whitney* (AD-4), 47-48

Brown, Lieutenant Charles R., USN (USNA, 1921)
Commanded the minesweeper *Gannet* (AM-41) during the Aleutian survey expedition of 1934, 52-54

Bunche, Ralph J.
U.S. representative to the United Nations in 1946, 263-264

Bureau of Naval Personnel (BuPers)
In the early 1960s identified potential carrier skippers and assigned them to ServLant ships for training, 363-365

Burke, Admiral Arleigh A., USN (USNA, 1923)
Service on the Navy's General Board shortly after World War II, 284
Promotion to flag rank in the late 1940s, 284
In the early 1950s headed the Navy's strategic planning, 284-285
Served 1955-61 as Chief of Naval Operations, 333-337, 341, 351, 354-355, 387

Burlingame, Commander Creed C., USN, (USNA, 1927)
Commanded the light cruiser *Roanoke* (CL-145) in 1953-55, 309

C-47 Skytrain
Cargo/passenger plane in which Knoll flew to the Soviet Union in early 1944, 185-187

Cairo, Egypt
Meeting of Allied leaders in Egypt in November 1943 to discuss war aims, 182-183
Way station for Knoll in his long journey from Washington to Moscow in early 1944, 185-186

California Institute of Technology, Pasadena
One of the schools that the Navy sent officers to in the late 1930s for postgraduate education, 87-91

Callaghan, Vice Admiral William M, USN (Ret.) (USNA, 1919)
In the late 1940s commanded the Naval Transportation Service, 268, 271, 276
From 1954 to 1956 was Commander U.S. Naval Forces Far East, 294, 331
In the mid-1960s played golf in retirement, 387

***Canopus*, USS (AS-9)**
Submarine tender that was scuttled off the Philippines in April 1942 to prevent her capture by the Japanese, 150, 153

Caputo, Vincent F.
In the mid-1960s, during the Vietnam War, was in charge of warehousing policy in the office of the Assistant Secretary of Defense, 383-384

Carney, Admiral Robert B., USN (USNA, 1916)
Served as Chief of Naval Operations, 1953-55, 285, 288, 301-302

Casablanca, French Morocco
In the summer of 1942 the Fleet Weather Central in Washington analyzed years' worth of data to predict weather for the forthcoming invasion of North Africa, 168-172

Cavite Navy Yard, Philippine Islands
Site of an Asiatic Fleet weather center established by Knoll in the early 1940s, 106-107, 111
Suggestion in 1941 to supply machine equipment from Cavite to Singapore, 110-111
Heavily bombed by the Japanese on 10 December 1941, 140

Central Intelligence Agency
Knoll had a brief tour in the CIA in 1947, 265, 278-281

Chase, Admiral Jehu V., USN (USNA, 1890)
Served as Commander in Chief U.S. Fleet (CinCUS) on board the battleship *Texas* (BB-35), 1930-31, 27-29

Chemical Warfare
Edgewood Arsenal, Maryland, presented a course on the subject in 1936, 80-82

Chiang Kai-shek
Chinese generalissimo who in November 1943 attended the Cairo Conference, 182-183
In the mid-1950s a substantial portion of the Seventh Fleet Commander's role was that of attending to Chiang Kai-shek of Taiwan, 317, 324-325

Chicago, **USS (CA-29)**
In October 1933 collided with a merchant ship, 44

China
Operations in the vicinity by the U.S. Asiatic Fleet in the early 1940s, 104-105, 117-122
Liberty in Shanghai in 1940-41 for crew members of Asiatic Fleet ships, 117-122

China, People's Republic of
Covert interruption of Red China's communications during the Korean War by cutting an underwater cable, 289-290
Shot down a U.S. Navy P4M Mercator electronic surveillance plane in August 1956, 318-319

Churchill, Sir Winston S.
Dialogue with American leaders while serving as British Prime Minister in World War II, 173-174, 182-183, 191, 211-212, 215

Civil Service
In the early 1960s employees of the Navy's Hydrographic Office began to unionize, 373-374

Clagett, Brigadier General Henry B., USAAC (USMA, 1906)
Involved in Army air operations in the Philippines in 1941, 115-116

Clark, Midshipman John E., USN (USNA, 1927)
Treatment of plebes while at the Naval Academy in the late 1920s, 10

Clement, Lieutenant Colonel William T., USMC
Senior Marine officer on Corregidor after most of the Asiatic Fleet staff had been evacuated in March 1942, 137

Cluverius, Rear Admiral Wat T., USN (USNA, 1896)
Served in the early 1930s as chief of staff to Commander in Chief U.S. Fleet (CinCUS), 25, 27

Coast Guard, U.S.
In the early 1950s commissioned the cutter *Courier* (WAGR-410) to serve as a relay ship for Voice of America radio broadcasts, 290-291

Codebreaking
Differing U.S. Navy capabilities in Hawaii and the Philippines in 1941-42, 141-142

Collisions
In October 1933 the cruiser *Chicago* (CA-29) collided with a merchant ship, 44
Seventh Fleet collision in 1956 between the heavy cruiser *Columbus* (CA-74) and the destroyer *Floyd B. Parks* (DD-884), 328-330

Columbus (German Commercial Ship)
Scuttled by her crew while trying to steam from Mexico to Germany in December 1939, 95-97

Columbus, USS (CA-74)
Captain Milton Miles commanded the ship in 1947, 314-315
Seventh Fleet collision in 1956 with the destroyer *Floyd B. Parks* (DD-884), 328-330

Combined Chiefs of Staff
Collaboration between British and American officials during World War II, 173-174, 177-180

Commercial Ships
In October 1933 the cruiser *Chicago* (CA-29) collided with a merchant ship, 44
The German liner *Columbus* was scuttled by her crew while trying to steam from Mexico to Germany in December 1939, 95-97
The British passenger liner *Queen Elizabeth* carried the U.S. delegation to United Nations organizing meetings in London in early 1946, 243-244, 246-247
NS *Savannah* was built in the 1950s as a nuclear-powered cargo/passenger ship, 342
Soviet merchant ships, carrying nuclear missile components, were involved in the 1962 Cuban Missile Crisis, 356
Military Sea Transportation Service chartered many ships in the mid-1960s to support the Vietnam War, 383-384, 388-389
In the mid-1960s Sea-Land Service, Inc., got a contract with Military Sea Transportation Service to facilitate establishment of container facilities on the West Coast, 384
The ore-carrying tug-barge combination *Presque Isle* made her maiden voyage from Erie, Pennsylvania, in December 1973, 393-394

Communications
Unsuccessful alleged attempt by the Army Air Forces to take over all U.S. airport communications during World War II, 175-177

Covert interruption of Republic of China communications during the Korean War by cutting an underwater cable, 289-290

In the late 1950s developed communication ships to support NASA's astronaut program, 347-348

Computers
Use of in tracking weather data, 173
In the mid-1960s the Navy's Hydrographic Office began phasing in computers for the printing of navigation charts, 372-373

Congress, U.S.
Role in Knoll's Naval Academy appointment in 1926, 2, 5
A U.S. delegation from Congress visited the Soviet Union in the spring of 1945, 193-196
Concerned in the late 1950s with design aspects of new Navy ships, 332-333
Reacted negatively to a Navy paper in the early 1960s saying that the Air Force was trying to take over the other services, 351-352

Coral Sea, USS (CVA-43)
Deployed to the Sixth Fleet in 1955, 303-304, 306

Corregidor, **Philippine Islands**
Defective U.S. mines were laid around Corregidor in 1941, 126-127
Knoll was evacuated from Manila to Corregidor on Christmas 1941, 136-137
Living conditions on the island in 1941-42, 130-131, 138-154, 159
Captured by the Japanese in May 1942, 112, 151
U.S. Army and Navy personnel were evacuated to Australia as the Philippines were falling to the Japanese in late 1941-early 1942, 144-160

Courier, USCGC (WAGR-410)
Commissioned by the Coast Guard in 1952 to serve as a relay ship for Voice of America radio broadcasts, 290-291

Cousteau, Jacques-Yves
French oceanographer who was involved with the U.S. Oceanographer of the Navy 371

Coye, Captain John S., Jr., USN (USNA, 1933)
Commanded the heavy cruiser *Rochester* (CA-124), 1958-59, 325

Cuba
Visited by the light cruiser *Roanoke* (CL-145) in 1955, 306-307
U.S. plans to invade Cuba during the Missile Crisis of 1962, 361

Cuban Missile Crisis
    Logistic support for Navy ships involved was provided by Service Force Atlantic Fleet, 356-358
    During the Cuban Missile Crisis of 1962, Army helicopters were tested with the training carrier *Lexington* (CVS-16), 361

Daehne, Captain Wilhelm
    Master of the German liner *Columbus* scuttled by her crew in 1939, 96-97

Daniel, Rear Admiral John C., USN (USNA, 1924)
    In the late 1950s provided advice on destroyer modernization, 336-338

Danis, Lieutenant Commander Anthony L, USN (USNA, 1922)
    Took a postgraduate course in meteorology at Massachusetts Institute of Technology in the 1930s, 89
    In the late 1930s monitored postgraduate education while serving in the Bureau of Aeronautics, 94

Darodda, Lieutenant (junior grade) Aldo J., USN
    In the mid-1950s was aide to Commander Seventh Fleet, 322

Daspit, Rear Admiral Lawrence R., USN (USNA, 1927)
    Served as a member of the court of inquiry about the loss of the nuclear submarine *Thresher* (SSN-593) in 1963, 343

Davis, Captain James W., USN (USNA, 1930)
    Commanded the heavy cruiser *St. Paul* (CA-73) from 1955 to 1957, 320, 322, 327
    In 1957 became chief of staff to Commander Seventh Fleet, 327

Deane, Major General John R., USA
    In 1942-43 served as secretary of the Combined Chiefs of Staff, 177-179
    Head of the U.S. military mission to the Soviet Union in 1944-45, 190, 210, 234, 246
    Part of the U.S. military staff committee when the United Nations was organized in 1946, 217
    Wrote a 1946 book, *The Strange Alliance*, about dealing with the Soviets, 243

Dempsey, Lieutenant James C., USN (USNA, 1931)
    Commanded the submarine *Spearfish* (SS-190) that evacuated Army and Navy personnel from Corregidor to Australia in May 1942, 150, 157-162

Denfeld, Admiral Louis E., USN (USNA, 1912)
    Served as Chief of Naval Personnel, 1945-47, 267
    Chief of Naval Operations, 1947-49, 285

Dennison, Admiral Robert L., USN (USNA, 1923)
    Served on the Asiatic Fleet staff, 1940-41, 106, 131, 133, 140
    From 1948 to 1953 was President Harry Truman's naval aide, 284
    In 1954 became head of strategic planning in OpNav, 302
    Served from 1960 through 1963 as Commander in Chief Atlantic Fleet, including the Cuban Missile Crisis in 1962, 354-355, 358, 363, 370-371

Destroyer Flotilla Four (DesFlot 4)
    In the late 1950s-early 1960s was involved in planning for the recovery of NASA astronauts, 347-348
    The guided missile frigate *Dewey* (DLG-14) was commissioned in 1959 with the goal of reducing the number of engineering personnel, 349-350

Dewey Dry Dock
    Used by the U.S. Navy in the Philippines until scuttled in April 1942 to avoid capture, 153

***Dewey*, USS (DLG-14)**
    Guided missile frigate *Dewey* (DLG-14) was commissioned in 1959 with the goal of reducing the number of engineering personnel, 349-350

Dill, Field Marshal Sir John G., British Army
    During World War II was senior British representative on the Combined Chiefs of Staff, 179, 183

Diller, Lieutenant Colonel LeGrande A., USA
    Early in World War II, as General Douglas MacArthur's PR man, issued exaggerated claims on the general's behalf, 145

Disciplinary Problems
    In the early 1930s served as defense counsel in courts-martial involving destroyer sailors, 46-48
    On board the battleship *Oklahoma* (BB-37) in the mid-1930s, 61-62
    On board the light cruiser *Roanoke* (CL-145) in 1955 a misbehaving black enlisted man claimed he was treated unfairly because of his race, 313-414

Divers
    In 1961 ServLant divers put a flange on the hull of the aircraft carrier *Enterprise* (CVAN-65) at Newport News to facilitate valve repair, 368-369

Donaho, Vice Admiral Glynn R., USN (USNA, 1927)
    Personality, 383
    In the mid-1950s served as chief of staff to Commander Seventh Fleet, 321, 326, 382-383
    Served as Commander Military Sea Transportation Service from 1964 to 1967, 380, 382-386, 389-390

Doyle, Commander Thomas J. Jr., USN (USNA, 1914)
Navigator of the battleship *Oklahoma* (BB-37) in the mid-1930s, 70

Dulles, Allen
Intelligence work in World War II and the Cold War, 292-293

Dulles, John Foster
Member of the U.S. delegation to United Nations organizing meetings in London in 1946, 244, 253

Duncan, Admiral Donald B., USN (USNA, 1917)
In the early 1930s was the aviator on the staff of CinCUS on board the battleship *Texas* (BB-35), 33-34
Served 1951-56 as Vice Chief of Naval Operations, 291

Edgewood Arsenal, Maryland
Presented a course in chemical warfare in 1936, 80-82

Egypt
Meeting of Allied leaders at the Cairo Conference in November 1943 to discuss war aims, 182-183

Eisenhower, President Dwight D. (USMA, 1915)
As Supreme Commander in Europe, received an award from the Soviet Union in 1945, 206
Served as President, 1953-61, 288.300-302, 338

Enlisted Personnel
In the early 1930s served as defense counsel in courts-martial involving destroyer sailors, 46-48
On board the battleship *Oklahoma* (BB-37) in the mid-1930s, 61-62, 73-74
Liberty in 1940-41 for crew members of Asiatic Fleet ships, 117-122
On Admiral Richmond Kelly Turner's staff in 1946, 261-262
Crew members of the oiler *Severn* (AO-61), 1946-47, 271-272, 277
In the crew of the light cruiser *Roanoke* (CL-145) in 1955, 304-305, 313-314
Concern in the mid-1950s about Seventh Fleet sailors living with Japanese girls, 330-332

***Enterprise*, USS (CVAN-65)**
Issues in the late 1950s concerning the ship's cost and characteristics, 333-334
In 1961 ServLant divers put a flange on the hull of the *Enterprise* at Newport News to facilitate valve repair, 368-369

Erie, Pennsylvania
Site of Knoll's youth in the 1910s-20s, 2-6

In the 1960s and 1970s Litton Industries had a shipbuilding facility in the city, 392-394

Erie, USS (PG-50)
Gunboat christened in January 1936 by Knoll's mother, 62-63

Espe, Captain Carl F., USN (USNA, 1922)
Deputy Director of Naval Intelligence in the late 1940s, 278, 280

Everest, Colonel Frank K. Jr., USAF
In the early 1950s was an Air Force representative in the development of the "New Look" military strategy for the Eisenhower administration, 300-301, 351

Faisal bin Abdulaziz Al Saud
Saudi Arabia's Foreign Minister at United Nations organizing meetings in 1946, 262

Fechteler, Admiral William M., USN (USNA, 1916)
Served as Chief of Naval Operations, 1951-53, 285, 287-288

Federov, Dr. Yevgeny K.
Served as head of the Soviet Hydrometeorological Service during World War II, 188-189, 198, 206, 216-217

Felt, Admiral Harry D., USN (USNA, 1923)
Served briefly at the U.S. embassy in Moscow during World War II, 222, 224-225
Service on the OpNav staff around 1950, 284
Served 1956-58 as Vice Chief of Naval Operations, 334, 341

Fire Control
During gunnery practice by the battleship _Texas_ (BB-35) in the early 1930s, 24-25, 32-33
During gunnery practice by the battleship _Oklahoma_ (BB-37) in the mid-1930s, 59, 79-80

Fischer, Lieutenant Commander Charles H., USN (Ret.) (USNA, 1899)
Friend who advised Knoll to seek big-ship duty, 59

Fleet Rehabilitation and Modernization (FRAM)
Upgrading of destroyer capabilities in the late 1950s and early 1960s, 337-338, 341-342

Fleet Weather Central, Washington, D.C.
In the summer of 1942 analyzed years' worth of data to predict weather for the forthcoming invasion of North Africa, 168-171

Flight Training
As a new ensign, Knoll took pre-flight training at Norfolk in 1930, 22
Knoll's training at Pensacola in 1931, 23

Florida, USS (BB-30)
Midshipman summer training cruise in the Atlantic and Pacific in 1927, 13

Floyd B. Parks, USS (DD-884)
Seventh Fleet collision in 1956 with the heavy cruiser *Columbus* (CA-74), 328-330

Fort, Commander George H., USN (USNA, 1912)
In the mid-1930s taught leadership at the Navy's Postgraduate School, 84-85

FRAM
See: Fleet Rehabilitation And Modernization (FRAM)

France
The light cruiser *Roanoke* (CL-145) visited Toulon in April 1955, 304-305

Frankel, Captain Samuel B., USN (USNA, 1929)
Member of the U.S. military mission to the Soviet Union in World War II, 226
Served in the Central Intelligence Agency in the late 1940s, 265, 278

Fyodorova, Zoya
Russian actress who, in 1946, bore a daughter fathered by U.S. Navy Captain Jackson R. Tate, 222-224
Murdered in 1981, 224

Galbraith, Rear Admiral William J., USN (Ret. (USNA, 1929)
In the early 1930s served on board ship and participated in the Olympics, 35
During World War II served in the heavy cruise *Houston* (CA-30) and was later a prisoner of the Japanese, 35-36, 124

Galveston, USS (CLG-3)
Radar problems in the converted guided missile cruiser in the late 1950s, 344-345

Gannet, USS (AM-41)
Took part in the Aleutian survey expedition of 1934, 52-54

Gannon, Rear Admiral Sinclair, USN (USNA, 1900)
Served 1925-28 as commandant of midshipmen at the Naval Academy, 55
Commanded a Navy geographical survey of the Aleutian Islands in 1934, 49-51, 54-56

George Washington, USS (SSBN-598)
Mockups of the first Polaris submarine, built in the late 1950s, 343-344

German Navy
During World War II, the U.S. Office of Naval Intelligence sent "Norden" radio broadcasts to German submarines, 281

Germany
The German Commercial Ship *Columbus* was scuttled by her crew while trying to steam from Mexico to Germany in December 1939, 95-97
German forces invaded the Soviet Union in 1941, despite having signed a non-aggression pact in 1939, 212-215
In December 1945 Knoll toured Chancellor Adolf Hitler's bunker in Berlin, 249
In the mid-1960s the Military Sea Transportation Service delivered coal from the United States to Germany to support U.S. forces stationed there, 390-391

Great Britain
London was the site of United Nations organizing meetings in early 1946, 236-237, 242-244, 252-253, 258-260, 262-263

Great Lakes
The ore-carrying tug-barge combination *Presque Isle* made her maiden voyage from Erie, Pennsylvania, in December 1973, 393-394

Griffin, Admiral Charles Donald, USN (USNA, 1927)
Treatment of plebes while at the Naval Academy in the late 1920s, 11-12

Griffin, Commander Virgil C. Jr., USN (USNA, 1912)
In 1939-40 commanded Patrol Wing Five (PatWing 5), based in Norfolk, 95

Gromyko, Andrei A.
Long-time Soviet diplomat who was ambassador to the United States in World War II, 192, 221, 237
Ambassador to the United Nations, 242, 253, 286-287

Gunnery-Naval
Target practice fired by the battleship *Texas* (BB-35) in the early 1930s, 24-25, 29-32
By the destroyers *Southard* (DD-207) and *Preble* (DD-345) in the early 1930s, 42-43
Target practice by the battleship *Oklahoma* (BB-37) in the mid-1930s, 59-60, 70-71, 76-80
The battleship *West Virginia* (BB-48) damaged a turret gun with a star shell in the mid-1930s, 66-67
Practice by the heavy cruiser *Augusta* (CA-31) in 1940, 104-105
The light cruiser *Roanoke* (CL-145) excelled in antiaircraft gunnery in 1955, 303

Haley, Midshipman Thomas B., USN (USNA, 1930)
Roommate of Knoll at the Naval Academy in the late 1920s-30, 7-9, 21
Student at the Postgraduate School in Annapolis, 1936-37, 86

Student at Massachusetts Institute of Technology in the late 1930s, 21
Served on a planning staff in World War II, 37

Harriman, W. Averell
Served as U.S. ambassador to the Soviet Union, October 1943 to January 1946, 183, 186, 189-194, 200, 209-212, 227-230, 234-236, 239-242, 246, 265
Relationship with President Franklin D. Roosevelt, 191

Hart, Admiral Thomas C., USN (USNA, 1897)
Served on the Navy's General Board in the late 1930s and early 1940s, 92, 143, 165-167
Commanded the U.S. Asiatic Fleet, 1939-42, 101-111, 113-115, 123-124, 126, 130, 132-134, 137-138, 141, 143
Evacuated from Corregidor on board the submarine *Shark* (SS-174) on 26 December 1941, 136-137
In July 1942 summoned Knoll for a meeting in Washington to discuss the situation in the Philippines, 165-167
Personality and working style, 101-103, 134, 138
Daughter Isabella, 114-115, 134

Hawaii
The battleship *Oklahoma* (BB-37) made a cruise to Pearl Harbor in the mid-1930s, 74-75

Hayward, Vice Admiral John T., USN (USNA, 1930)
Served in the late 1950s-early 1960s as Deputy CNO Development), 334, 341
During the Cuban Missile Crisis in October 1962, commanded Carrier Division Two, 356

***Helena*, USS (CA-75)**
Served in the mid-1950s as flagship for Commander Seventh Fleet, 319-320

Helicopters
Concerns in the late 1950s for fuel storage on board destroyers that would undergo the FRAM program, 341-342
During the Cuban Missile Crisis of 1962, Army helicopters were tested with the training carrier *Lexington* (CVS-16), 361

Hewitt, Rear Admiral H. Kent, USN (USNA, 1907)
Commanded the invasion task force at Casablanca in November 1943, 169-171

Hiss, Alger
State Department representative at United Nations organization meetings in 1945-46, 244, 258-259

Hitler, Adolf
    Served as chancellor of Germany, 1933-45, 212-214

Hoeffel, Captain Kenneth M., USN (USNA, 1917)
    Became 16th Naval District Commandant when Rear Admiral Francis Rockwell departed on 18 March 1942, 137, 140-141, 146, 149-150, 153, 157-158

Hong Kong, British Crown Colony
    Visited by the attack transport *Menard* (APA-201) in 1952, 292

Honsinger, Rear Admiral Leroy V., USN (USNA, 1927)
    Deputy Chief of the Bureau of Ships in the late 1950s, 345

Hopkins, Harry L.
    American presidential advisor who visited Moscow at time during World War II, 228-229, 240-242

***Houston*, USS (CA-30)**
    In 1940-41 served as Asiatic Fleet flagship, 106, 111, 119-120, 124-125

Howard, Captain Douglas L., USN (USNA, 1906)
    In the 1910s wrote a sassy answer on a promotion exam, 19

Howard, Colonel Samuel L., USMC
    Role in defending against Japanese advances in the Philippines in 1942, 145

Huff, Colonel Sidney L., USA (Ret.)
    In the early 1930s, as a naval officer, served in the battleship *Texas* (BB-35), 131-132
    Joined General Douglas MacArthur's staff in 1936, received an Army commission, and remained with him for 15 years, 132-133
    After World War II tried to recruit Knoll for MacArthur's staff, 133

Hunsaker, Captain Jerome C., USNR (Ret.) (USNA, 1908)
    Taught for many years at the Massachusetts Institute of Technology, 87, 94-95

Hydrographic Office, U.S. Navy
    In the mid-1960s began phasing in computers for the printing of navigation charts, 372-373, 379
    In the early 1960s employees of the Hydrographic Office began to unionize, 373-374

***Hyperion*, HMS**
    British destroyer that operated in the Western Atlantic when the German liner *Columbus* was scuttled in 1939, 97

Ingersoll, Vice Admiral Stuart H., USN (USNA, 1921)
In the early 1950s was a Navy representative in the development of the "New Look" strategy for the Defense Department, 300-301, 316-317
Commanded the Seventh Fleet, 1955-57, 316-331
Personality, 321-322, 328
A substantial portion of his role as Seventh Fleet Commander involved attending to Chiang Kai-shek of Taiwan, 317-318, 324-326
Concern in the mid-1950s about Seventh Fleet sailors living with Japanese girls, 330-331

Intelligence
The Royal Navy received reports from the U.S. Navy while operating in the Western Atlantic in 1939-40, 96-97
Intelligence gathering by the major powers during World War II, 215-216

***Iowa*, USS (BB-61)**
In late 1943 took President Franklin Roosevelt on the first leg of his trip to attend the Tehran Conference, 179-182

Iran
Preparations for the Tehran Conference, which was held in November-December 1943, 179-182
Way station for Knoll in his long journey from Washington to Moscow in early 1944, 185-186
Knoll went to the Soviet Union to help facilitate weather agreements made at the Tehran Conference, 188
The Soviet Union withdrew troops from Iran in the spring of 1946, 241-242

Isbell, Lieutenant Commander Arnold J., USN (USNA, 1921)
In 1939-40 flew PBY patrols as a member of Patrol Wing Five (PatWing 5), 95, 99

Italian Navy
An Italian gunboat was in Shanghai, China, when Italy declared war in June 1940, 118

Italy
Visited by Naval Academy midshipmen on training cruise in 1929, 17

James, Rear Admiral Ralph K., USN (USNA, 1928)
As Chief of the Bureau of Ships in 1961 okayed the use of ServLant divers to facilitate repairs to the aircraft carrier *Enterprise* (CVAN-65), 368-369

Japan
Political situation vis-à-vis the United States as 1941 progressed, 128-130
In late 1941 began sending weather reports from the Mandated Islands in code, 111

Attacks on the Philippines, leading to the capture of Manila in December 1941, Bataan in April 1942, and Corregidor in May 1942, 112, 130-131, 140-159

The Soviet Union was neutral toward Japan until August 1945, 198, 203, 207-210

The oiler *Severn* (AO-61) served in 1946-47 primarily as a point-to-point tanker between Yokosuka, Japan, and Saudi Arabia, 267-273

In 1952 the ship repair facility at Yokosuka did work on the attack transport *Menard* (APA-201), 294-296

Dry-docking of Seventh Fleet ships at Yokosuka in the mid 1950s, 296

Concern in the mid-1950s about Seventh Fleet sailors living with Japanese girls, 330-331

Jebb, Hubert Miles Gladwyn
British diplomat who was acting Secretary-General of the United Nations, 1945-46, 246-247, 253-254

Johnson, President Lyndon B.
As Vice President in the early 1960s, reacted negatively to a Navy paper saying that the Air Force was trying to take over the other services, 351-352
Knoll believes that Johnson was a factor in Knoll not being promoted to vice admiral in the mid-1960s, 385-388

Joint Chiefs of Staff
Work with the British in 1943 as part of the Combined Chiefs of Staff, 173-174

Kanakanui, Lieutenant (junior grade) William A., USN (USNA, 1924)
Commanded the minesweeper *Tanager* (AM-5) during the Aleutian survey expedition of 1934, 52

Kapitsa, Pioytr
Prominent Soviet nuclear physicist who in 1945 attended the celebration of the 220th anniversary of the Soviet Academy of Sciences in Moscow, 216-217, 221-222

Kelley, Captain Frank H. Jr., USN (USNA, 1910)
In June 1942 commanded the troop transport *West Point* (AP-23) during a high-speed run from Australia to New York City, 164-165

Kelly, Captain Colin Jr., USAAF
In 1941 monitored flights of B-17 bombers to the Philippines, later killed soon after war began in December, 115-116

Kempff, Vice Admiral Clarence F., USN (USNA, 1897)
Commanded the battleship *Nevada* (BB-36) in 1926-27, 67-69
In the mid-1930s was type commander for battleships, 26, 67

Kennan, George F.
U.S. Deputy Chief of Mission in the Soviet Union from 1944 to 1946, 190-191, 193, 210, 234, 239

Kennedy, Edward M.
Objected in the early 1960s when Knoll, as Oceanographer of the Navy, cancelled a procurement contract with a supplier in Massachusetts, 359-360, 387

Kennedy, President John F.
Knoll reported that Kennedy was informed in 1961 about heat Knoll was taking over a paper he'd written about the Air Force, 354-355
In 1962, Knoll recalled, he updated the President on the situation, 363
Knoll believes he would have become a vice admiral in the mid-1960s if Kennedy had still been alive, 385-386

Kenney, General George C., USAAF
Part of the U.S. military delegation to organizing meetings of the United Nations in London in 1946, 242, 247, 263

King, Admiral Ernest J., USN (USNA, 1901)
As CNO and CominCh during World War II, was aware of Knoll's activities, 171, 178, 183-184, 200, 209, 211

Kirkpatrick, Lieutenant Commander Charles C., USN (USNA, 1931)
In late 1942, as aide to Admiral Ernest King, called Knoll concerning the invasion of Casablanca, 171, 183

Knoll, Rear Admiral Denys W., USN (Ret.) (USNA, 1930)
Parents, 1-6, 8, 21-23, 40, 166
First wife Genevieve, 19, 98, 101, 114, 165-167, 243, 283, 327, 346, 354, 372, 375, 391
Second wife Jean, 202, 391
Youth in Pennsylvania in the 1910s-20s, 2-6
As a Naval Academy midshipman, 1926-30, 7-22
As a new ensign, took pre-flight training at Norfolk in 1930, 22
Served 1930-32 in the battleship *Texas* (BB-35), 23-35, 39-40
Flight training at Pensacola in 1931, 23, 36-40
In 1932-34 served on board the destroyers *Southard* (DD-207) and *Preble* (DD-345), 40-49
Participated in a Navy geographical survey of the Aleutian Islands in 1934, 49-57
Served in the battleship *Oklahoma* (BB-37), 1934-36, 57-80
Took a three-month course in chemical warfare at Edgewood Arsenal in 1936, 80-82
As a student at the Navy's Postgraduate School, 1936-38, 82-91
As a postgraduate student at the Massachusetts Institute of Technology, 1938-39, 87-95
In 1939-40 served with Patrol Wing Five (PatWing 5), 95-100

Served on the staff of Commander in Chief Asiatic Fleet, 1940-42, 101-160
Transition period from Australia and return to the United States, 160-167
Stationed in Washington, 1942-44 on the CominCh staff, officer in charge of the weather central, and assistant secretary, Joint Chiefs of Staff, 168-184
Long transit in early 1945 from Washington to Moscow, 184-185
In 1944-45 was on the staff of the U.S. ambassador to the Soviet Union, Averell Harriman, to facilitate implementation of Lend-Lease and agreements at the Tehran Conference, 183, 186-246
In 1946 was part of the U.S. military delegation to organizing meetings for the United Nations, 242-267
In 1946 turned down a job offer to be secretary of the Laura Spelman Rockefeller Memorial Fund, 257, 265-266
Commanded the oiler *Severn* (AO-61), 1946-47, 152, 267-278
Brief tour in the Central Intelligence Agency, 1947, 265, 278-281
Service in the strategic planning section of OpNav, 1948-52, 279-291
Commanded the attack transport *Menard* (APA-201) for eight months in 1952, 292-299
Service in the strategic planning section of OpNav, 1953-55, 300-302
In 1955 commanded the light cruiser *Roanoke* (CL-145), 302-316
From 1955 to 1957 served as chief of staff to Commander Seventh Fleet, 316-332
From 1957 to 1959 served in the OpNav fleet maintenance division and as chairman of the Ship Characteristics Board, 332-346
In the late 1950s, Knoll was selected for rear admiral, 327, 346
Served 1959-60 as Commander Destroyer Flotilla Four, 346-350
In 1960-61 was director of the OpNav Technical Studies Group, 350-355
Served 1961-63 as Commander Service Force Atlantic Fleet, 355-371
From 1963 to 1965 was Oceanographer of the Navy, 359-360, 371-382
Last active duty billet, from 1965 to 1967, was as Deputy Commander of the Military Sea Transportation Service, 360, 382-390
Post-retirement activities included employment by Litton Industries, 392-394

Knoll, Mrs. Ida May Illig

Christened the gunboat *Erie* (PG-50), which was launched and commissioned in 1936, 62-63

Knox, William Franklin "Frank"

As Secretary of the Navy during World War II, was involved in medal presentations and discussions with Admiral Ernest J. King, 143, 177

Korean War

In 1950 the United Nations authorized sending combat troops to Korea, 237, 286-287
Covert interruption of Republic of China communications during the Korean War by cutting an underwater cable, 289-290
The attack transport *Menard* (APA-201) practiced amphibious landings on the coast of Korea in 1952, 293-294

Kosco, Commander George F, USN (USNA, 1930)
Weather specialist assigned to the carrier *Ranger* (CV-4) in the early 1940s, 103

Kostrinsky, Captain Third Rank Mikhail Ilyich, Soviet Navy
As Deputy Chief of Foreign Relations (Liaison), conversations with Knoll in 1944-45, 196, 244-245

Land, Rear Admiral Emory S., USN (USNA, 1902)
Served as chairman of the U.S. Maritime Commission in World War II, 173

Leahy, Admiral William D., USN (USNA, 1897)
Served as chief of staff to President Franklin D. Roosevelt in World War II, 181

Leave and Liberty
For the crew of the battleship *Oklahoma* (BB-37) in the mid-1930s, 74-76
Liberty in China in 1940-41 for crew members of Asiatic Fleet ships, 117-122
In Toulon, France, in April 1955 for the crew of the light cruiser *Roanoke* (CL-145), 304-305

Lee, Lieutenant (junior grade) Charles L., USN (USNA, 1924)
Served as a flight instructor at Pensacola in the early 1930s, 37-39

Lee, Vice Admiral Fitzhugh, USN (USNA, 1926)
Served in the early 1960s as Deputy Commander in Chief Atlantic Fleet, 354-355

Lee, Trygve H.
In the late 1940s served as Secretary-General of the United Nations, 247, 262

Legal Matters
In the early 1930s served as defense counsel in courts-martial involving destroyer sailors, 46-48

Lend-Lease
The United States delivered equipment and ammunition to the Soviet Union during World War II, 191, 199-202, 213, 238-239

Leningrad, Soviet Union
Withstood a 900-day siege by German forces in World War II, 214
Knoll visited during the course of his duty in the Soviet Union, 1944-45, 195, 205, 219, 244-246

Lewis, Commander John S., USN (USNA, 1932)
Served with Admiral Richmond K. Turner during the Pacific War and at United Nations organizing meetings in 1946, 257-258

Lewis, Commander Thomas L., USN (USNA, 1921)
Commanded Destroyer Squadron Ten as it escorted the battleship *Iowa* (BB-61) to North Africa in November 1943, 180-182

***Lexington*, USS (CVS-16)**
During the Cuban Missile Crisis of 1962, the carrier did tests with Army helicopters, 361

Litton Industries
In the 1960s and 1970s had a facility in Erie, Pennsylvania, that built the tug-barge ore carrier *Presque Isle*, 392-394

Lockhart, Lieutenant Commander Wilber M., USN (USDA, 1918)
In the late 1930s monitored postgraduate education while serving in the Bureau of Aeronautics, 89, 94

London, England
Site of United Nations meetings in early 1946, 236-237, 242-244, 252-253, 258-260, 262-263

Long Beach, California
Homeport for the big ships of the U.S. Fleet in the mid-1930s, 66-67, 73

Long Beach Naval Shipyard, San Pedro, California
Involvement with the oiler *Severn* (AO-61) in 1946-47, 267, 275-278

***Long Beach*, USS (CGN-9)**
Issues in the late 1950s concerning the ship's cost and characteristics, 333-334

Lozovsky, Solomon
Served as the Soviet Union's Deputy People's Commissar for Foreign Affairs during World War II, 232

MacArthur, General of the Army Douglas, USA (USMA, 1903)
In 1941-42 commanded U.S. Army forces in the Philippines, 108, 130-133, 140, 144-146, 149
Evacuation to Australia in March 1942, 144-145
Wife Jean, 132
Command of United Nations forces during the Korean War, 1950-51, 287

***Macon*, USS (ZRS-5)**
Dirigible that operated with the fleet in the Pacific before crashing off Point Sur, California, in February 1935, 70

Mallison, Commander William T., USN (USNA, 1907)
Commanded the minelayer *Ogala* (CM-4) during the 1934 Aleutian survey expedition, 49-51, 57

Manila, Philippine Islands
In the summer of 1941 the Asiatic Fleet staff moved ashore to the Marsman Building in Manila, 106, 111-112, 124
Anti-Japanese guerrilla activities at the beginning of World War II, 134-136
Knoll was evacuated from Manila to Corregidor on Christmas 1941, 136-137

Maples, Captain Houston L., USN (USNA, 1917)
Stationed at the U.S. embassy in Moscow during World War II, 210, 212

Marine Corps, U.S.
Role in defending against Japanese advances in the Philippines in 1942, 145-146
The attack transport *Menard* (APA-201) did practice amphibious landings on the coasts of Korea and Japan in 1952, 293-297

Martin, Lieutenant Stanley E., USN (USNA, 1920)
Served in the battleship *Oklahoma* (BB-37) in the mid-1930s, 59-60, 67

Masaryk, Jan
Was Czechoslovakia's Foreign Minister during United Nations organizing meetings in 1946, 262

Mason, Rear Admiral Redfield, USN (USNA, 1925)
Served as intelligence officer on the Asiatic Fleet staff in the early 1940s, 103-104, 113-114
Evacuated from the Philippines in December 1941, 134
In the early 1960s was Commander Service Force Pacific Fleet, 115

Massachusetts Institute of Technology (MIT), Cambridge, Massachusetts
Provided courses in meteorology to Navy students in the late 1930s, 86-95

McCoy, Lieutenant Commander Melvyn H., USN (USNA, 1927)
After being captured by the Japanese in 1942, managed to escape from prison camp the following year, 154-155

McCrea, Captain John L., USN (USNA, 1915)
In late 1943 commanded the battleship *Iowa* (BB-61), which took President Franklin Roosevelt on the first leg of his trip to attend the Tehran Conference, 179-182

McElroy, Neil H.
In the late 1950s, as Secretary of Defense, was concerned about the capability of Navy destroyers, 336-338

McGuigan, Captain Joseph L., USN (USNA, 1914)
In April 1942, escaped from the Philippines to Australia in a PBY to avoid being captured by the Japanese, 154-155

McLean, Rear Admiral Ephraim R., Jr., USN (USNA, 1924)
Embarked in the light cruiser *Roanoke* (CL-145) in 1955 while serving as Commander Cruiser Division Two, 306-307

McNamara, Robert S.
In 1961, as Secretary of Defense, had the Defense Department provost marshal investigate Knoll, 352-353
In Knoll's perception was penurious in providing logistic support to the fleet in the early 1960s, 356-358
An investigator from the Department of Defense questioned Knoll in the early 1960s because he had cancelled a contract with a supplier that didn't produce, 359-360
Change in warehousing policy for cargo sent to Vietnam in the mid-1960s, 383-384

Medals and Decorations
Knoll's views on medals he received and those he did not, 143, 146, 363

Medical Problems
Knoll developed a tropical rash while serving in the Philippines shortly before World War II, 159-160

***Menard*, USS (APA-201)**
Deployment to the Far East in 1952, 292-299
Ship handling in 1952, 294-295

***Midway* (CVA-41)-Class Aircraft Carriers**
Discussions in the late 1950s about accommodating aircraft in the hangar deck, 339-340

Miles, Rear Admiral Milton E., USN (USNA, 1922)
During World War II commanded irregular forces in China, 168, 289-290
Commanded the heavy cruiser *Columbus* (CA-74) in 1947, 314-315
Served as Commandant 15th Naval District in Panama, 1954-56, 315

Military Sea Transportation Service (MSTS)
In the late 1950s developed communication ships to support NASA's astronaut program, 347-348
Support in the mid-1960s for the U.S. forces in the Vietnam War, 383-384, 386, 388-389
In the mid-1960s was phasing out passenger ships, 389-390
In the mid-1960s delivered coal from the United States to Germany to support U.S. forces stationed there, 390-391

Mine Warfare
Defective U.S. mines were laid around Corregidor in 1941, 126-127

Missiles
Soviet merchant ships, carrying nuclear missile components, were involved in the 1962 Cuban Missile Crisis, 356

Molotov, Vyacheslav Mikhailovich
Soviet Foreign Minister from 1939 to 1949, 192, 228-230, 236, 239-240, 246
Threw a lavish victory party in 1945 to celebrate the end of war in Europe, 228-229

Monssen, USS (DD-798)
Salvage of the decommissioned destroyer, which ran aground in New Jersey in 1962, 367

Moore, Admiral Sir Henry R., Royal Navy
Part of the British delegation for the United Nations organizing meetings in London in 1946, 247, 263

Morgan, Rear Admiral Armand M., USN (USNA, 1924)
In the late 1950s was a member of the Ship Characteristics Board, 336, 340-341

Morse, Robert W.
Served as Assistant Secretary of the Navy (Research and Development), 1959 to 1964, 376-377, 379

Moscow, Soviet Union
Toured by a group of U.S. congressmen in the spring of 1945, 193-196
Soviets awarded a medal to General of the Army Dwight Eisenhower in 1945, 206
Raucous celebration of VE Day in 1945, 209, 218-219, 228-231
Celebration in 1945 of the 220th anniversary of the Soviet Academy of Sciences, 216-217, 221-222
Father Marie-Léopold Braun was a Catholic priest who ministered in Moscow from 1934 to 1945, 249-251

Moses, Robert
New York City official who coordinated lodging for delegates to United Nations organizing meetings in 1946, 254-257

Mulheron, Lieutenant (junior grade) Edward S., USN (USNA, 1923)
Served as a flight instructor at Pensacola in the early 1930s, 37-39

Mumma, Rear Admiral Alfred G., USN (USNA, 1926)
Served in the late 1950s as Chief of the Bureau of Ships, 333-334, 345

Mundt, Karl E.
South Dakota senator who visited the Soviet Union in the spring of 1945, 193-196

Mussolini, Benito
Dictator who ran Italy when Naval Academy midshipmen visited in 1929, 17

NASA
See: National Aeronautics and Space Administration (NASA)

National Aeronautics and Space Administration (NASA)
In the late 1950s-1960s Destroyer Flotilla Four was involved in planning for the recovery of NASA astronauts, 347-348

Nauru Island
Establishment in the early 1960s of the island's geodetic position, 382

***Nautilus*, USS (SSN-571)**
First refueling in the late 1950s, 335

Naval Academy, Annapolis, Maryland
Indoctrination of midshipmen, physically and mentally, 1926-30, 7-12
Summer training cruises, 1927-29, 9, 13-18
Social life for midshipmen in the late 1920s, 19-20
Ethnic and religious makeup of midshipmen in the late 1920s, 20-21
Academics, 20-21

Naval Postgraduate School, Annapolis, Maryland
In the mid-1930s provided advanced education for officers coming in from sea tours, 82-91
The course in the 1930s included leadership training, 84-85

Naval Transportation Service
The oiler *Severn* (AO-61) served in 1946-47 primarily as a point-to-point tanker between Yokosuka, Japan, and Saudi Arabia, 267-273, 275

Navigation
Training on board a Naval Academy summer cruise in 1929, 18
Navy geographical survey of the Aleutian Islands in 1934, 49-57
In the mid-1960s the Navy's Hydrographic Office began phasing in computers for the printing of navigation charts, 372-373

Neale, Lieutenant Commander Edgar T., USN (USNA, 1924)
As commanding officer of Patrol Squadron 102 (VP-102) in April 1942, escaped from the Philippines in a PBY, 154

Neutrality Patrols
In 1939-40 in the Atlantic by PBYs of Patrol Wing Five (PatWing 5), 95-100

"New Look" Strategy
In 1953-55 officers from the Navy's OP-03 section joined other services for strategic planning for the Defense Department in the Eisenhower administration, 300-303

Newport News, USS (CA-148)
Deployed to the Sixth Fleet in 1955, 306, 311
Operations in the Caribbean in 1955, 307-308

Newport News Shipbuilding and Dry Dock Company
In 1961 ServLant divers put a flange on the hull of the aircraft carrier *Enterprise* (CVAN-65) at Newport News to facilitate valve repair, 368-369

News Media
Soviet publications were not credible, 231-232

New York City
Site of United Nations organizing meetings in 1946, 254-255, 261-267

Nitze, Paul H.
When Nitze was Secretary of the Navy in the mid-1960s, Knoll reported that Nitze said Knoll would soon be promoted to vice admiral, which he wasn't, 387-388

"Norden" Broadcasts
During World War II, the U.S. Office of Naval Intelligence sent "Norden" radio broadcasts to German submarines, 281

Norfolk Naval Base
Homeport for ships of Destroyer Flotilla Four in the late 1950s-early 1960s, 347
In the early 1960s Knoll served as Norfolk area coordinator for raising United Fund donations, 370-371

Norfolk, USS (DL-1)
At times in the late 1950s-early 1960s served as the seagoing flagship for Commander Destroyer Flotilla Four, 349

Normandy, France
Preliminary planning in 1943 by the Combined Chiefs of Staff for the 1944 Allied invasion, 174, 179

North Africa
In the summer of 1942 the Fleet Weather Central in Washington analyzed years' worth of data to predict weather for the forthcoming invasion of Casablanca, 168-172

Nuclear Power Program
   First refueling of the submarine *Nautilus* (SSN-571) in the late 1950s, 335
   In the late 1950s Knoll opposed Admiral Hyman Rickover's desire to build a nuclear re-coring capability into submarine tenders, 335-336
   NS *Savannah* was built in the 1950s as a nuclear-powered cargo/passenger ship, 342

Nuclear Weapons
   The Soviet Union developed atomic bombs in the late 1940s, 280-281
   American businessman Bernard Baruch set up an office after World War II to seek an understanding with the Soviet Union on limiting nuclear weapons, 280-281
   Soviet merchant ships, carrying nuclear missile components, were involved in the 1962 Cuban Missile Crisis, 356, 361
   In 1962 The U.S. Navy did not have the capability for rearming ships at sea with nuclear weapons, 362-363

Nulton, Rear Admiral Louis M., USN (USNA, 1889)
   Served as Naval Academy superintendent, 1925-28, 16

Nurses
   Role of Army and Navy nurses in the Philippines in 1941-42, 143, 150
   Nurses captured by the Japanese were interned in Santo Tomas University in Manila, 151-152
   Some nurses were evacuated from Corregidor by submarine in May 1942, 157-160

Oceanographer of the Navy
   Senator Ted Kennedy objected in the early 1960s when Knoll cancelled a procurement contract by a supplier in Massachusetts, 359-360
   In the early 1960s Knoll made many public speeches to deliver information about the world's oceans, 371-372
   Surveying of the ocean bottom in the early 1960s to facilitate submarine operations, 375-376, 381-382
   Exploration of mineral resources on the ocean bottom in the 1960s, 376-377, 380-381
   Establishment in the early 1960s of the geodetic position of Nauru Island, 382

Office of Naval Intelligence (ONI)
   During World War II, sent "Norden" radio broadcasts to German submarines, 281

***Oglala*, USS (CM-4)**
   Served as headquarters ship for a Navy geographical survey of the Aleutian Islands in 1934, 49-57

***Oklahoma*, USS (BB-37)**
   Gunnery practice in the mid-1930s, 59-60, 70-71, 76-80
   Underway watch standing by officers of the deck, 60-61, 65-66, 69-70
   Enlisted personnel, 61-62, 73-74

Damage control in the mid-1930s, 63
Ship-handling characteristics, 63-64, 78-79
Operations in the Pacific in the mid-1930s, 60-61, 64-67, 69-79
Triple-expansion reciprocating steam propulsion plant, 69-70

Oldendorf, Rear Admiral Jesse B., USN (USNA 1909)
Commanded the heavy cruiser *Houston* (CA-30), 1939-41, later commanded the battle line at Surigao Strait in 1944, 125

Olongapo, Philippine Islands
A Japanese prisoner of war ship sunk there in 1945 was finally removed in the mid-1950s, 156

OP-03
In 1953-55 did strategic planning as part of the development of the "New Look" strategy for the Eisenhower administration, 300-303
Response by the Navy's OP-03D in the early 1960s to the perception that the Air Force was trying to take over the other services, 350-355

Orville, Captain Howard T., USN (USNA, 1925)
In the 1940s was a weather specialist stationed in the Bureau of Aeronautics, 108, 117, 127, 176, 184, 203, 379

PBY Catalina
Flew in neutrality patrols shortly before World War II, 37, 95-10
A Royal Air Force PBY flew Knoll and coding machines to Singapore in 1941, 108-109
In April 1942 PBYs from Patrol Wing Ten escaped from the Philippines ahead of the advancing Japanese, 154-155
Late in World War II, the Soviets asked for a large number of PBYs through the Lend-Lease program, 238-239

P4M Mercator
U.S. Navy electronic surveillance plane shot down by Red China in August 1956, 318-319

Panama Canal
The U.S. Fleet made two rapid transits through the canal in April and October 1934, 57-58
Transit by the battleship *Oklahoma* (BB-37) in the mid-1930s, 63-64

Pan American Airways
Transpacific flights in the early 1940s, 102, 110

Parish, Lieutenant Elliott W. Jr., USN (USNA, 1929)
In 1936-37 was a student at the Navy's Postgraduate School in Annapolis, 84-85

Parsons, Captain William Sterling, USN (USNA, 1922)
    Served in the early 1930s in the gunnery department of the battleship *Texas* (BB-35), 24-25, 29-30
    Married the daughter of Rear Admiral Wat T. Cluverius, 25
    Suggested that Knoll study meteorology to help in gunnery accuracy, 83
    Was on board the B-29 *Enola Gay* for the bombing of Hiroshima in 1945, 30

Patrol Wing Five (PatWing 5)
    In 1939-40 did extensive PBY patrolling from Atlantic Coast bases, 95-100

Pay and Allowances
    In the early 1930s, during the Depression, Navy personnel had to take a pay cut, later restored, 41
    At the beginning of World War II Lieutenant Colonel Sid Huff was drawing pay from both the Army and Navy, 132-133

Olsen, Rear Admiral Clarence E., USN (USNA, 1921)
    Senior naval officer in the U.S. military mission to the Soviet Union in 1944-45, 190, 198, 225-226
    Served with the Central Intelligence Agency in the late 1940s, 278-280

Parker, Rear Admiral Edward N., USN (USNA, 1925)
    Embarked in the light cruiser *Roanoke* (CL-145) in 1955 while serving as Commander Cruiser Division Six, 303-306, 308-309

Pearl Harbor, Hawaii
    The battleship *Oklahoma* (BB-37) made a cruise to Pearl Harbor in the mid-1930s, 74-76

Pearson, Drew
    Newspaper columnist who published articles circa 1950 on U.S. propaganda operations, 282
    In January 1961 published a column that alleged the Navy was trying to subvert service reorganization, 352-354, 386

Pensacola, Florida, Naval Air Station
    Site of flight training for Knoll in 1931, 23, 36-40

Percival, Lieutenant General Arthur E., British Army
    In command at Singapore in 1941 during wartime planning, 109-110

Philippine Islands
    Rear Admiral John Smeallie was relieved as Commandant 16th Naval District in 1940, 101-102
    Asiatic Fleet ship operations in the outlying areas of the Philippines shortly before World War II, 106-107, 120, 123, 126

In the summer of 1941 the Asiatic Fleet staff moved ashore to the Marsman Building in Manila, 106, 111, 124

In September 1941 began ferrying B-17 bombers to the Philippines, 115-116

Defective U.S. mines were laid around Corregidor in 1941, 126-127

U.S. aid intended for the Philippines in 1941 did not arrive in timely fashion, 127-129

Japanese attacks on the Philippines, leading to the capture of Manila in December 1941, Bataan in April 1942, and Corregidor in May 1942, 112, 130-131, 134-137

Anti-Japanese guerrilla activities at the beginning of World War II, 134-136

Knoll was evacuated from Manila to Corregidor on Christmas 1941, 136-137

Living conditions on Corregidor in 1941-42, 130-131, 138-154, 159

U.S. Army and Navy personnel were evacuated to Australia as the Philippines were falling to the Japanese in late 1941-early 1942, 144-151, 154-160

A Japanese prisoner of war ship sunk at Olongapo in 1945 was finally removed in the mid-1950s, 156

In the mid-1950s Knoll scheduled visits to the Philippines by Seventh Fleet destroyers, 331-332

Photography

Photos of the seafloor remains of the nuclear submarine *Thresher* (SSN-593) after she was lost in April 1963, 369-370

Pigeon, USS (AM-47)

Minesweeper that operated out of the Philippines in 1941, 126

Pirie, Vice Admiral Robert B., USN (USNA, 1926)

Served 1958-61 as Deputy Chief of Naval Operations (Air), 341, 353-355

Poland

Soviet control of setting up a new government in the years following World War II, 233-235

Polaris Submarines

Mockups of the first Polaris submarine, *George Washington* (SSBN-598) built in the late 1950s, 343-344

Portugal

Design in the 1980s of a breakwater for the port of Sines, south of Lisbon, 169-170

Potsdam Agreement

Meeting of Allies in Potsdam Germany in the summer of 1945 to make plans to end the war, 211-212

Pratt, Admiral William V., USN (USNA, 1889)

Served as Commander in Chief U.S. Fleet (CinCUS) on board the battleship *Texas* (BB-35), 1929-30, 23, 27-30

Preble, USS (DD-345)
Destroyer that operated out of San Diego in the early 1930s and was part of a rotating reserve, 40-49

Pride, Vice Admiral Alfred Melville, USN
Served as Commander Seventh Fleet, 286, 317, 321-324
Personality, 321-325
As president of the Naval War College, 1957-60, 324-325
Wife injured in the late 1950s and died soon thereafter, 324

Prisoners of War
During World War II Lieutenant William Galbraith served in the heavy cruise *Houston* (CA-30) and was later a prisoner of the Japanese, 35-36, 124
Americans—civilian and military—captured by the Japanese as a result of the fall of the Philippines in 1942, 150-156
After being captured by the Japanese in 1942, Lieutenant Commander Melvyn McCoy managed to escape from prison camp the following year, 154-155
Lieutenant Charles Weschler was captured by the Japanese in the Philippines in 1942 and was later killed in a POW ship in 1945, 6-7, 149-150, 153-156

Promotion of Officers
In late 1943 Knoll received a temporary promotion to captain to facilitate his upcoming duty in the Soviet Union, 183-184
In the late 1950s, Knoll was selected for rear admiral, but not as soon as he expected, 327, 346
Knoll's speculation on why he was not promoted to vice admiral in the mid-1960s, 385

Propulsion Plants
Triple-expansion reciprocating steam plant in the battleship Oklahoma (BB-37) in the mid-1930s, 69-70
First refueling of the submarine *Nautilus* (SSN-571) in the late 1950s, 335
In the late 1950s Knoll opposed Admiral Hyman Rickover's desire to build a nuclear re-coring capability into submarine tenders, 335-336
NS *Savannah* was built in the late 1950s as a nuclear-powered cargo/passenger ship, 342
The guided missile frigate *Dewey* (DLG-14) was commissioned in 1959 with the goal of reducing the number of engineering personnel, 349-350

Prostitution
In 1934 prostitutes did not get advance warning of the U.S. Fleet's rapid transit of the Panama Canal, 58

Pryce, Lieutenant Commander Roland F., USN (USNA, 1927)
Commanded the submarine *Spearfish* (SS-190) during early war patrols, 1941-42, 162

Public Relations
Early in World War II, General Douglas MacArthur's PR man issued exaggerated claims on the general's behalf, 145

Purnell, Rear Admiral William R., USN (USNA, 1908)
Served as Asiatic Fleet chief of staff in the early 1940s, 106, 111, 134, 137-138

Queen Elizabeth, RMS
British passenger liner that carried the U.S. delegation to United Nations organizing meetings in London in early 1946, 243-244, 246-147

Quezón, Manuel L.
Served as President of the Philippines, 1935-44, 107, 111, 148-149

Raborn, Rear Admiral William F., Jr., USN (USNA, 1928)
Headed the Polaris missile/submarine program in the late 1950s, 343-344

Racial Issues
On board the light cruiser *Roanoke* (CL-145) in 1955 a misbehaving black enlisted man claimed he was treated unfairly because of his race, 313-414

Radar
Radar problems in the converted guided missile cruiser *Galveston* (CLG-3) in the late 1950s, 344-345

New radar designed in the late 1950s for the aircraft carrier *Enterprise* (CVAN-65) and cruiser *Long Beach* (CGN-9), 334-335, 344

Radford, Admiral Arthur W., USN (USNA, 1916)
Served as Chairman of the Joint Chiefs of Staff, 1953-57, 300, 324, 326

Ramage, Vice Admiral Lawson P., USN (USNA, 1931)
Served 1967-70 as Commander Military Sea Transportation Service, 385

Rees, Vice Admiral William L., USN (USNA, 1921)
In the late 1950s, as ComNavAirLant, was a member of the Ship Characteristics Board, 338-339

Refueling at Sea
U.S. Navy experiments in the Pacific in the mid-1930s, 64-65

By Seventh Fleet ships near Taiwan during heavy weather in the mid-1950s, 320-321

U.S. warships involved in the Cuban Missile Crisis of 1962 were replenished by ships of Service Force Atlantic Fleet, 361-362

Reichelderfer, Lieutenant Francis W., USN

Officer who served in World War I, stayed on afterward to study meteorology in Norway and at the Massachusetts Institute of Technology, 88
Headed the U.S. Weather Service from 1938 to 1963, 88, 92, 168, 176, 216
In 1945 attended the celebration of the 220th anniversary of the Soviet Academy of Sciences in Moscow, 216-217, 221-222

Religion
In the 1930s the Soviets systematically drove churches out of business, 251-252
Father Marie-Léopold Braun was a Catholic priest who ministered in Moscow from 1934 to 1945, 249-251

Replenishment at Sea
U.S. warships involved in the Cuban Missile Crisis of 1962 were replenished by ships of Service Force Atlantic Fleet, 361-362

Richardson, Brigadier General Robert C. III, USAF (USMA, 1939)
Involved in the early 1960s in long-range planning, 351-352

Rickover, Vice Admiral Hyman G., USN (USNA, 1922)
Involvement with the Ship Characteristics Board in the late 1950s, 335-336
Commissioning of the nuclear submarine *Thresher* (SSN-593) in 1961 and loss in 1963, 342-343
Allegedly unhappy in 1961 when Knoll used ServLant divers to facilitate repairs to the aircraft carrier *Enterprise* (CVAN-65), 368-369

Ridgway, Lieutenant General Matthew B., USA (USMA, 1917)
Part of the U.S. military delegation to organizing meetings of the United Nations in London in 1946, 242, 247, 263

Roanoke, **USS (CL-145)**
Excelled in antiaircraft gunnery in 1955, 303, 311
Two-month cruise to the Mediterranean in 1955, 303-305, 308-309, 311-312
Enlisted crew members, 304-305, 313-314
Operations in the Caribbean in 1955, 306-308
Ship handling, 309-310
Transfer to the Pacific Fleet in late 1955, 310, 315-316

Robinson, Commander Clyde R., USN (USNA, 1907)
Served in the early 1930s as executive officer of the battleship *Texas* (BB-35), 28

Rochester, **USS (CA-124)**
Served in the mid-1950s as flagship for Commander Seventh Fleet, 319-320, 325

Rockwell, Rear Admiral Francis W., USN (USNA, 1908)
Commandant 16th Naval District who was evacuated from Corregidor in March 1942, 137-140, 143

Rome, Italy
   Visited by Naval Academy midshipmen on training cruise in 1929, 17

Roosevelt, Eleanor
   Member of the U.S. delegation to United Nations organizing meetings in London in 1946, 244, 253

Roosevelt, President Franklin D.
   In March 1942 got General Douglas MacArthur to evacuate from Corregidor to Australia, 144-145
   Dialogue with his British counterpart, Prime Minister Winston Churchill, during World War II, 174, 182-183
   Alleged discussion with General Hap Arnold of the Army Air Forces about attempt to take over airport communications in World War II, 175-176
   In November 1943 attended the Cairo Conference, 182-183
   Inclined to give the Soviets whatever they asked for in the Lend-Lease program during World War II, 238-240

Rossby, Dr. Carl Gustav
   Taught meteorology at the Massachusetts Institute of Technology in the late 1930s, 92-94
   In 1945 attended the 220th anniversary of the Soviet Academy of Sciences in Moscow, 216-217, 221-222

Roullard, Commander George D., USN (USNA, 1933)
   Served as assistant naval attaché in the Soviet Union in World War II, 198

Royal, Captain Forrest B., USN (USNA, 1915)
   In World War II served as assistant secretary of the Combined Chiefs of Staff, 177-179, 183

Royal Air Force
   An RAF PBY flew Knoll and coding machines to Singapore in 1941, 108-109

Royal Navy
   Received intelligence reports from the U.S. Navy while operating in the Western Atlantic in 1939-40, 96-97
   In late 1942 sent weather specialists to the Fleet Weather Central in Washington to study methods, 171
   In the early 1960s consulted with the U.S. Oceanographer of the Navy on ocean issues, 372, 376

Sackett, Commander Earl L., USN (USNA, 1920)
   After commanding the submarine tender *Canopus* (AS-9) in the Philippines, he was evacuated to Australia in May 1942, 150, 153

***Sacramento*, USS (AOE-1)**

The Navy was forced to use three different suppliers for winches when the ship was built in the early 1960s, 358-359

St. Paul, USS (CA-73)
Served in the mid-1950s as flagship for Commander Seventh Fleet, 319-320, 322

Salvage
Refloating of the decommissioned destroyer *Monssen* (DD-798), which ran aground in New Jersey in 1962, 367
Salvage of planes that had crashed in the early 1960s, 367-368

Santo Tomas Prison, Manila, Philippines
During World War II, U.S. Army and Navy nurses captured by the Japanese were interned at Santo Tomas, 151

Saudi Arabia
Faisal bin Abdulaziz Al Saud was Saudi Arabia's Foreign Minister at United Nations organizing meetings in 1946, 262
The oiler *Severn* (AO-61) served in 1946-47 primarily as a point-to-point tanker between Yokosuka, Japan, and Saudi Arabia, 267-273

Savannah, NS
Built in the late 1950s as a nuclear-powered cargo/passenger ship, 342

Schofield, Admiral Frank H., USN (USNA, 1890)
Served as Commander in Chief U.S. Fleet (CinCUS) on board the battleship *Texas* (BB-35), 1931-32, 27-28

Sea-Land Service, Inc.
In the mid-1960s got a contract with Military Sea Transportation Service to facilitate establishment of container facilities on the West Coast, 384, 386

Seay, Captain George C., USN (USNA, 1930)
In 1956 was commanding officer of the heavy cruiser *Columbus* (CA-74) when she collided with the destroyer *Floyd B. Parks* (DD-884), 328-330

Semmes, Vice Admiral Benedict, J., Jr., USN (USNA, 1934)
Served 1964-68 as Chief of the Bureau of Naval Personnel, 385

Service Force Atlantic Fleet
Provided logistic support to warships during the Cuban Missile Crisis in October 1962, 356-363
In the early 1960s, aviators selected for carrier commands were given preliminary training by commanding ServLant ships, 363-365
Knoll said that excellent personnel were assigned to ServLant ships and ServLant staffs, 365-366
Knoll's visits to ServLant ships, 1961-63, 366, 370

Refloating of the decommissioned destroyer *Monssen* (DD-798), which ran aground in New Jersey in 1962, 367

Salvage of planes that had crashed in the early 1960s, 367-368

In 1961 ServLant divers put a flange on the hull of the aircraft carrier *Enterprise* (CVAN-65) at Newport News to facilitate valve repair, 368-369

Photos of the seafloor remains of the nuclear submarine *Thresher* (SSN-593) after she was lost in April 1963, 369-370

In the early 1960s Knoll served as Norfolk area coordinator for raising United Fund donations, 370-371

Seventh Fleet, U.S.

Dry-docking of Seventh Fleet ships at Yokosuka in the mid 1950s, 296

In the mid-1950s a substantial portion of the fleet commander's role was that of attending to Chiang Kai-shek of Taiwan, 317-318, 324-325

Fleet operations in the Western Pacific in the mid-1970s, 318-332

Refueling at sea near Taiwan during heavy weather in the mid-1950s, 320-321

Collision in 1956 between the heavy cruiser *Columbus* (CA-74) and the destroyer *Floyd B. Parks* (DD-884), 328-330

Concern in the mid-1950s about fleet sailors living with Japanese girls, 330-331

Severn, **USS (AO-61)**

In World War II was a water carrier in support of amphibious operations in the Pacific, 267

Served in 1946-47 primarily as a point-to-point tanker between Japan and Saudi Arabia, 267-273

Ship handling in 1946-47, 273-274

Operations off the U.S. West Coast in 1946-47, 274-278

Enlisted crew members, 271-272, 277

Shanghai, China

Liberty in 1940-41 for crew members of Asiatic Fleet ships, 117-122

Shark, **USS (SS-174)**

Evacuated Admiral Thomas Hart and other Asiatic Fleet personnel from Corregidor in December 1941, 137

Ship Characteristics Board

Concerned in the late 1950s with design aspects of new Navy ships, 333-340

Ship Handling

On board the battleship *Oklahoma* (BB-37) in the mid-1930s, 63-64, 78-79

On board the oiler Severn (AO-61) in 1946-47, 273-274

In the attack transport *Menard* (APA-201) in 1952, 294

Of the light cruiser *Roanoke* (CL-145) in 1955, 309-310

Shore Patrol
   In Shanghai, China, in 1940-41, 117-119

Singapore
   Knoll visited in the summer of 1941 to confer with British officials, 108-110
   Suggestion in 1941 to supply machine equipment from Cavite Navy Yard to Singapore, 110-111
   Way station and liberty port for the oiler Severn (AO-61) in 1946-47 during trips between Saudi Arabia and Japan, 270

Sixth Fleet, U.S.
   The light cruiser *Roanoke* (CL-145) made a two-month cruise to the Mediterranean in 1955, 303-306, 308-309, 311-312

Smeallie, Rear Admiral John M., USN (USNA, 1905)
   Relieved as Commandant 16th Naval District in 1940 after a suicide attempt, 101-102

Snyder, Rear Admiral J. Edward Jr., USN (USNA, 1945)
   In the mid-1960s served as executive assistant to Assistant Secretary of the Navy James Wakelin, later was Oceanographer of the Navy, 378

***Southard*, USS (DD-207)**
   Destroyer that operated out of San Diego in the early 1930s and was part of a rotating reserve, 22, 40-48

Soviet Navy
   Soviet submarines were active in the Caribbean during the October 1962 Cuban Missile Crisis, 361

Soviet Union
   In the 1930s the Soviets systematically drove churches out of business, 251-252
   Invaded by German forces in 1941, despite having signed a non-aggression pact in 1939, 212-215
   Effects of wartime destruction were evident in 1944-45, 187
   Knoll's mission there in 1944-45 to facilitate the implementation of Lend-Lease and the agreements made at the 1943 Tehran Conference, 166-246
   Bugging of foreign embassies and consulates during World War II, 197
   Prison camps in Siberia for Soviet citizens during World War II, 219-220
   Delegates to the organizing meetings of the United Nations In 1946, 217-218
   Police-state existence for many citizens, 220-221, 227-228, 233, 251-252
   Stormovich fighter plane was used for troop support in World War II, 224-225
   Black market during World War II, 227-228
   Raucous celebration of VE Day in 1945 in Moscow, 209, 218-219, 228-231
   Difficulties for other nations in negotiating with the Soviets, 231-235, 238-240, 264

Father Marie-Léopold Braun was a Catholic priest who ministered in Moscow from 1934 to 1945, 249-250

The Soviets withdrew troops from Iran in the spring of 1946, 241-242

Involvement in the Cuban Missile Crisis in October 1962, 356-361

Soviet Navy
Sent submarines to the Caribbean in October 1962, 361

Spain
The light cruiser *Roanoke* (CL-145) visited Barcelona in 1955, 304

***Spearfish*, USS (SS-190)**
Problems with faulty torpedoes in early war patrols, 1941-42, 162
Submarine that evacuated Army and Navy personnel from Corregidor to Australia in May 1942, 150, 157-162

Spellman, His Eminence, Francis Cardinal
In the late 1940s was consulted about the United Nations, 251, 266
Around 1950 developed an anti-Communist pamphlet that was withdrawn from distribution, 282-283

Stalin, Joseph V.
Dictator who ran the Soviet Union from the late 1920s until his death in 1953, 179, 191-192, 195, 202, 205, 211-214, 219, 229-230, 239-240, 246, 283

Stalingrad, Soviet Union
Effects of wartime destruction were evident in 1944-45, 187, 214-215

Standley, Admiral William H., USN (Ret.) (USNA, 1895)
Served as U.S. ambassador to the Soviet Union, 1942-43, 191

Steere, Lieutenant Commander Richard C., USN (USNA, 1931)
Served as staff meteorologist to Rear Admiral H. Kent Hewitt for the November 1942 invasion of Casablanca, French Morocco, 169-171

Steinhardt, Laurence A.
U.S. ambassador to the Soviet Union, 1939-41, 250

Stephan, Rear Admiral Edward C., USN (USNA, 1929)
From 1960 to 1963 was Oceanographer of the Navy, 376, 378

Stevenson, Adlai E. II
State Department representative at United Nations organization meetings in 1945-46, 244, 259

Stormovich
Soviet fighter plane was used for troop support in World War II, 224-225

Storrs, Rear Admiral Aaron P. III, USN (USNA, 1923)
    Commanded Carrier Division Five in the Seventh Fleet in the mid-1950s, 320-321, 328-330

Strategy
    In 1953-55 officers from the Navy's OP-03 section joined other services to develop the "New Look" for the Defense Department in the Eisenhower administration, 300-303

Strauss, Captain Elliott B., USN (USNA, 1923)
    Part of the U.S. military delegation to the United Nations organizing meetings in London in 1946, 247-248

Struble, Vice Admiral Arthur D., USN (Ret.) (USNA, 1915)
    In the late 1940s was Deputy CNO (Operations), 282
    Served 1952-55 as a U.S. representative to the United Nations, 316

Stump, Admiral Felix B., USN (USNA, 1917)
    Commanded the Pacific Fleet, 1953-58, 319, 328-330

Surveying
    Navy geographical survey of the Aleutian Islands in 1934, 49-57
    Surveying of the ocean bottom in the early 1960s to facilitate submarine operations and investigate resources, 375-376, 380-382
    Establishment in the early 1960s of the geodetic position of Nauru Island, 382

Sutherland, Major General Richard K. USA
    Contacted by Knoll in 1942 to prevent the U.S. Army from duplicating Australian weather services, 163-164

Taiwan
    In the mid-1950s a substantial portion of the Seventh Fleet Commander's role was that of attending to Chiang Kai-shek of Taiwan, 317-318, 324-325
    In the mid-1950s the Seventh Fleet flagship was home-ported at Taipei, 317-318

Tanager, **USS (AM-5)**
    Took part in the Aleutian survey expedition of 1934, 52

Tarnowski, Aerographer's Mate Zemo, USN
    Captured by the Japanese on Corregidor in 1942 and interrogated, 152

Tate, Captain Jackson R., USN
    In 1945 he was stationed briefly in Moscow, where he fathered a baby with actress Zoya Fyodorova, 222-224

Taussig, Rear Admiral Joseph K., USN (USNA, 1899)
Noted for his phenomenal memory, 77
In the early 1940s warned of potential war with Japan, 77

Taylor, Rear Admiral Edmund B., USN (USNA, 1925)
In the late 1950s provided advice on destroyer modernization, 336-338

Tehran, Iran
Preparations for the Tehran Conference, which was held in Tehran, Iran, November-December 1943, 179-182
Way station for Knoll in his long journey from Washington to Moscow in early 1944, 185-186
Knoll went to the Soviet Union to help facilitate weather agreements made at the Tehran Conference, 188

Texas, USS (BB-35)
In the early 1930s served in the Pacific as flagship for Commander in Chief U.S. Fleet (CinCUS), 23-30
Gunnery practice in the early 1930s, 24-25, 29-32
On-board aircraft in the early 1930s, 33-34

Thornton, Charles B. "Tex"
In the 1950s was co-founder of the company that became known as Litton Industries, 394

Thresher, USS (SSN-593)
Commissioned in 1961, later lost on trials in 1963, 343, 369-370

Tibbitts, Lieutenant Frank P., USN (USNA, 1925)
Served in the battleship *Oklahoma* (BB-37) in the mid-1930s, 59-60, 67

Tolley, Commander Kemp, USN (USNA, 1929)
In the early 1930s was on the U.S. Fleet staff on board the battleship *Texas* (BB-35), 34-35
Stationed in China shortly before World War II began, 119
Served in the Soviet Union during World War II, 208-209

Torpedoes
The submarine *Spearfish* (SS-190) had problems with faulty torpedoes in early war patrols, 1941-42, 162

Toulon, France
The light cruiser *Roanoke* (CL-145) visited Toulon in April 1955, 304-305

Trans-Siberian Railroad
Used by Knoll in 1944-45 during his duty in the Soviet Union, 199, 210, 219

Truman, President Harry S.
Succeeded Franklin Roosevelt as President in April 1945, 241
At the Potsdam Conference in the summer of 1945, 211
Action vis-à-vis the Soviet Union in 1946, 241-242
Spoke to United Nations delegates in New York in late 1946, 255

Turner, Admiral Richmond K., USN (USNA, 1908)
Amphibious commander in the Pacific, 1942-45, 259
Part of the U.S. military delegation to organizing meetings of the United Nations in 1946, 242-243, 247, 257-260, 263-264, 266-267
Drinking problem, 259-260
Domineering personality, 261-262

***Tuscaloosa*, USS (CA-37)**
In December 1939 rescued crew members of the scuttled German liner *Columbus*, 96-97

Uniforms-Naval
Knoll had to scramble to find replacement uniforms after being evacuated from Corregidor in 1942, 162-163

United Nations
Organizing meetings in 1945-46 in San Francisco, London, and New York, 217-218, 236-237, 242-244, 252-264
In 1950 authorized sending U.N. forces to the Korean War, 237, 286-287

***Utah*, USS (BB-31)**
Midshipman summer training cruise in the Atlantic in 1928, 13

Van Auken, Captain Wilbur Rice, USN (USNA, 1903)
Commanded the battleship *Oklahoma* (BB-37), 1934-35, 57, 60-64

Vasiliev, Lieutenant General Alexander F.
Soviet representative to the United Nations military staff committee in 1946, 252-253, 256

***Vega*, USS (AK-17)**
Supply ship in which Knoll stood deck watches in 1931, 23-24

Vietnam War
Military Sea Transportation Service support in the mid-1960s for the U.S. forces in Vietnam, 383-384, 388-389

Vishinsky, Andrei J.
In 1945-46 was the Soviet Union's Deputy Foreign Minister, 228-229, 253

Vladivostok, Soviet Union
   Knoll was stationed in the port for six months during the course of his duty in the Soviet Union, 1944-45, 198-201, 206-207

Voice of America
   System of radio broadcasts to inform other countries about the United States, 1940s and 1950s, 281-283, 290-291

Wainwright, Lieutenant General Jonathan M., USA (USMA, 1906)
   Took command on Corregidor after Bataan fell to the Japanese in 1942, 136-137, 140, 143, 146-149, 153-154, 157

Wakelin, Dr. James H. Jr.
   Served as Assistant Secretary of the Navy (Research and Development), 1959 to 1964, 372, 377-378

Wales, Captain George H., USN (USNA, 1929)
   Commanded the light cruiser *Worcester* (CL-144) in 1955-56, 308-309

Warren, Group Captain Herbert Norman
   Headed the Royal Australian Air Force Meteorological Service in World War II, 163-164

Waters, Rear Admiral Odale D., Jr., USN (USNA, 1932)
   Served from 1965 to 1970 as Oceanographer of the Navy, 379-380

Weather
   In the early 1930s an office desk broke loose while the battleship *Texas* (BB-35) was in heavy seas, 29
   During the Aleutian survey expedition of 1934, 56
   The Massachusetts Institute of Technology (MIT) provided courses in meteorology to Navy students in the late 1930s, 86-95
   Establishment of U.S. Weather Service by 1938 by Francis Reichelderfer, 92
   Conditions encountered by PBYs of Patrol Wing Five (PatWing 5) in 1939-40, 96, 99-100
   Knoll's work as aerologist on the Asiatic Fleet staff, 1940-42, 104-109, 111-113, 115-118, 131, 133, 139-141, 152
   Discussions in 1942 with the U.S. Army and Australian officials concerning weather forecasts, 163-164
   In the summer of 1942 the Fleet Weather Central in Washington analyzed years' worth of data to predict weather for the forthcoming invasion of Casablanca, North Africa, 168-172
   In 1944-45 Knoll in the Soviet Union to facilitate implementation of weather agreements made at the 1943 Tehran Conference, 183, 186-190, 202-205
   Use of computers in tracking weather data, 173
   Dealing with adverse weather during operations in 1952 by the attack transport *Menard* (APA-201), 297-299

Sudden bursts of weather in the Mediterranean in 1955, 312

The light cruiser *Roanoke* (CL-145) tested weather buoys during a transfer to the Pacific Fleet in late 1955, 310, 315-316

Refueling at sea near Taiwan during heavy weather in the mid-1950s, 320-321

Weather Service, U.S.
Establishment of by 1938 by Francis Reichelderfer, 92, 100

Wellings, Lieutenant Augustus J., USN (USNA, 1920)
In the early 1930s was gunnery officer of Destroyer Squadron One, 45-46

Weschler, Lieutenant Charles J., USN (USNA, 1932)
Knoll cousin who was captured by the Japanese in the Philippines in 1942 and was later killed in a POW ship in 1945, 6-7, 149-150, 153-156

Weschler, Vice Admiral Thomas R., USN (USNA, 1939)
Knoll cousin who had a successful naval career, including serving as CNO Arleigh Burke's career, 6, 285

Westfall, Lieutenant Commander Theo D., USN (USNA, 1914)
In the early 1930s commanded the destroyer *Preble* (DD-345), 46, 49

***West Point*, USS (AP-23)**
Transport that made a high-speed run from Australia to New York City in June 1942, 164-165

***West Virginia*, USS (BB-48)**
Damaged a turret gun with a star shell in the mid-1930s, 66-67

Willson, Captain James D., USN (USNA, 1903)
In 1934 commanded Destroyer Squadron One, 62

***Worcester*, USS (CL-144)**
Deployed to the Sixth Fleet in 1955, 308-309

Yalta Conference
Meeting of Allied leaders in February 1945 to make plans for the Soviets entering the war and for the postwar period, 209, 211, 233-234

Yarnell, Rear Admiral Harry E., USN (Ret.) (USNA, 1897)
In July 1942 met with Knoll in Washington to discuss the situation in the Philippines, 165

Yokosuka, Japan
The oiler *Severn* (AO-61) served in 1946-47 primarily as a point-to-point tanker between Yokosuka and Saudi Arabia, 267-273

In 1952 the ship repair facility at Yokosuka did work on the attack transport *Menard* (APA-201), 294-296

Dry-docking of Seventh Fleet ships in the mid 1950s, 296

Yumashev, Admiral Ivan Stepanovich
Served as Commander of the Soviet Pacific Fleet in World War II, 200, 206-207, 210

Zumwalt, Admiral Elmo R. Jr., USN (USNA, 1943)
Served as the first commanding officer when the guided missile frigate *Dewey* (DLG-14) was commissioned in 1959, 349-350

As Chief of Naval Operations in the early 1970s met with retired flag officers, 350

www.ingramcontent.com/pod-product-compliance
Lightning Source LLC
Chambersburg PA
CBHW080624170426
43209CB00007B/1507